MESSAGE PRODUCTION:

Advances in Communication Theory

Edited by

JOHN O. GREENE
Purdue University

LEA

LAWRENCE ERLBAUM ASSOCIATES, PUBLISHERS
1997   Mahwah, New Jersey   London

Lawrence Erlbaum Associates, Inc., Publishers
10 Industrial Avenue
Mahwah, New Jersey 07430

Library of Congress Cataloging-in-Publication Data

  Message production : advances in communication theory /
edited by John O. Greene.
        p.   cm.
        Includes bibliographical references and indexes.
        ISBN 0-8058-2323-9 (hardcover : alk. paper). -- ISBN 0-8058-2324-7
  (pbk. : alk. paper)
     1. Interpersonal communication.   I. Greene, John O.,   1954-   .
  BF637.C45M484   1997
     153.6--dc21   97-17200
                                                                            CIP

Books published by Lawrence Erlbaum Associates are printed on acid-free paper,
and their bindings are chosen for strength and durability.

Printed in the United States of America
10 9 8 7 6 5 4 3 2 1

In Memory of
Robert Daniel Greene
1957–1996

CONTENTS

FOREWORD

Glenn G. Sparks
Purdue University

In 1984, John Greene published an article in *Communication Monographs* entitled, "A Cognitive Approach to Human Communication: An Action Assembly Theory." In contrast to most of the cognitive work in communication to that point in time, which addressed issues of input processing, Action Assembly Theory (AAT) addressed issues of behavioral production. There is now a considerable body of work that has arisen from the AAT framework.

As a consequence of the impact of AAT in communication research, I nominated Greene's 1984 article for the Charles H. Woolbert Research Award that is given annually by the Speech Communication Association in recognition of articles that have "stood the test of time and become the stimulus for new conceptualizations of speech communication phenomena." In winning this award, John Greene was invited to coordinate a special panel that was presented at the 1995 meeting of the Speech Communication Association in New Orleans. This book is an outgrowth of that panel presentation.

One of the distinguishing features of the panel presentation is also a feature of the current volume. Instead of focusing on the past literature pertaining to message production processes, the following chapters look to the future and attempt to chart new theoretical ground. Just as I was confident that the original essay on AAT would be recognized in the Woolbert Award competition, I am also confident that this book will be recognized as an important work that helps to move us along in our understanding of the processes of behavioral production that are central to communication behavior. The source of my confidence on this point can be found in perusing the list of contributors and the topics of their chapters. Although it was gratifying to write the nominating letter for the article that won the 1995 Woolbert Award, it is even more gratifying to be associated in this small way with this volume that grew out of that event.

PART

I

THEORIES OF MESSAGE PRODUCTION: HISTORICAL CONTEXT, FUTURE PROSPECTS

1

INTRODUCTION:
ADVANCES IN THEORIES
OF MESSAGE PRODUCTION

John O. Greene
Purdue University

The first decades of the cognitive revolution were marked by considerably less effort devoted to the study of behavioral-production processes than to input processing. Studies of perception, comprehension, and memory for input information multiplied, but with some notable exceptions (e.g., the motor-control literature; see Stelmach, 1976), there was little focus on the nature of the output system. Thus, writing in 1977, Turvey observed that "while theories of perception abound, theories of action are conspicuous by their absence" (p. 211; see also, Clippenger, 1977; Weiner & Goodenough, 1977).

As if in response to Turvey, beginning in the mid-1970s, there was a marked increase in attempts to address problems of behavioral production from a cognitive perspective. Particularly prominent were the various cognitive approaches to *verbal behavior* that were developed by scholars from a variety of academic disciplines and with interests in a wide array of speech-related phenomena. It was at this time that a number of seminal works were published (e.g., Bates, 1979; Butterworth, 1980; Clark & Clark, 1977; Coulmas, 1981; Dechert & Raupach, 1980; Fodor, Bever, & Garrett, 1974; Fromkin, 1980; McNeill, 1979; Rosenberg, 1977; Siegman & Feldstein, 1979) as theorists sought to specify the mechanisms underlying speech errors, syntax, temporal patterns in vocalization, language acquisition, and so on.

Among those scholars interested in verbal message behavior *qua communication*, there were corresponding efforts to develop models of the psychological mechanisms involved in a variety of behavioral phenomena associated with conversational planning (e.g., Cohen & Perrault, 1979; de Beaugrande, 1980; Hobbs & Evans, 1980) and discourse production (see Clippenger, 1977; Freedle, 1977). Further, the rise of cognitive influences in the study of message production was not restricted exclusively to the verbal realm. Increasingly, there were efforts to address behavioral phenomena such as gestural activity (e.g., McNeill, 1979), mutual influence in immediacy behaviors (e.g., Patterson, 1976; Stern, 1974), and the nonverbal correlates of deception (see Zuckerman, DePaulo, & Rosenthal, 1981) via application of the assumptions, constructs, and methods of cognitive science.

In the field of Communication proper, among the earliest programmatic applications of cognitivism to the study of behavioral production was the work of Motley and his associates on verbal slips and prearticulatory editing (e.g., Motley, Camden, & Baars, 1979, 1981). Although in some respects more closely aligned with traditional trait approaches, work on the production of listener-adapted communication by Delia and other "constructivists" (see Bowers, 1979; Delia, 1977) can be seen clearly to reflect elements of cognitivism.

In relatively short order, there emerged a number of models that sought to explicate various message-production phenomena by recourse to intraindividual states and processes (e.g., Andersen, Garrison, & Andersen, 1979; Behnke & Beatty, 1981; Buck, 1980; Cappella & Greene, 1982; Cegala, Alexander, & Sokuvitz, 1979; Greene & Sparks, 1983; Infante, 1980; Planalp & Tracy, 1980). This "first generation" of theories of message production culminated with the development of a number of models and research programs that have proven to be particularly influential. Among these is Berger's work on message planning (Berger, 1988, 1995), O'Keefe's treatment of message design logics (O'Keefe, 1988; O'Keefe & Lambert, 1995), Burgoon's expectancy violations theory (Burgoon & Hale, 1988), action assembly theory (Greene, 1984, 1995a, 1995b), and Kellermann's application of the MOP concept to interpersonal interactions (Kellermann, 1995).

It now appears that we are on the verge of a new wave of theories of verbal and nonverbal message production. In some cases, theorists have refined and extended their original formulations, in other cases, earlier versions of theories have been abandoned in favor new conceptual frameworks, and, finally, a new group of players has come on the scene, bringing with them new theoretical approaches.

The purpose of this volume is to survey this new generation of theories of message production. In approaching the contributors, I asked that, rather than focus on review of previous research and theory, each author look to the future. More specifically, their charge was to pursue either of two ends: (a) presentation of a new theoretical formulation, or (b) development of desiderata for such theories. The various chapters reflect a combination of these objectives and suggest that this area is characterized by a remarkable degree of theoretical vitality.

IN PURSUIT OF COORDINATION AND COHERENCE

We commonly note that one of the primary functions of theory is to reveal and explicate patterns and regularities. In the realm of human message behavior, patterns of behavioral coordination and coherence can be discerned at many levels of analysis; one can explore regularities in syntactic structure, shifts in the topic of conversation, relationships between the verbal content of a message and patterns of eye gaze, the link between one person's immediacy cues and those of his or her interlocutor, regulation of speaker-turn changes, and on and on. The possibilities are both varied and numerous, and moreover, they resist easy systematic classification in terms that hold up under closer scrutiny. Still, at the most general level it is possible to draw a rough distinction between intra- and interindividual message-production phenomena—that is, between patterns of coherence that arise in the message behavior of the individual social actor and those that arise between two or more people.

This distinction is significant in the present context because theories of message production can generally be classified in terms of the relative emphasis they place on these two domains of behavioral phenomena. On one hand, those theorists who have chosen to focus on intraindividual patterns tend to be concerned with the processes by which meaning representations and other internal states arise and are made manifest to others via overt behavior. Thus, a researcher may investigate pauses, or gestures, or eye behavior as cues to the psychological processes involved in formulating and executing a message plan. In contrast, a focus on interindividual coordination tends to raise questions about the processes governing the interdependencies of the interactants' behaviors and meanings and internal states. Researchers might, for example, examine patterns of mutual influence in expressive behaviors, the negotiation of joint definitions of the situation, or coordination of activities in pursuit of some shared task. It is noteworthy that each of these orientations tends to assume what the other problematizes and that the application of theories developed with either intra- or interindividual processes in mind often seem to miss the point, or to be vague (even vacuous) when applied to phenomena of the other sort.

Cutting across the distinction between theories aimed primarily at intra- versus interindividual coherence is the issue of the nature of the constructs invoked in a theory to account for the phenomena of interest. Theories of message production can be seen to make use of three broad types of explanatory constructs: *physiological terms* (e.g., arousal, neurophysiological structures), *psychological terms* (e.g., needs, goals, plans), and *social terms* (e.g., norms, constitutive and regulative rules).[1] Message-production theo-

---

[1]Within each of these broad categories of theoretical terms it is, of course, possible to make finer distinctions. A familiar example would be the case of psychological terms where we can distinguish intentional-stance and functional-stance constructs (see Dennett, 1971).

ries, then, can be distinguished on the basis of the particular *combination* of these three types of terms that they employ (i.e., some theories may make use of just one type of construct, others of two, and still others make invoke terms from all three domains) and on the basis of the *specific nature* of the constructs of each type that the theory posits.

OVERVIEW OF THE CHAPTERS

The chapters comprising this volume reflect a broad spectrum of approaches to problems of interpersonal message production. Among the chapters are some concerned primarily with intraindividual coherence and others focused on questions of interindividual coordination. Within each of these groups, the chapters can be distinguished according to their scope: Some are more narrowly focused on specific communicative phenomena and issues (e.g., McCornack, Kemper and Hummert, and Sanders), while others reflect attempts to develop more general models (e.g., Meyer, Hample, Greene, Burgoon and White, and Buck). As a final point of differentiation, the authors can be seen to invoke various combinations of physiological, psychological, and social constructs in developing their positions.

The book is organized into three major sections; this chapter and the one by Wilson that follows provide some historical context and a point of departure for the subsequent chapters. The second section is comprised of treatments that are focused primarily on various intraindividual phenomena, while the third unit consists of chapters that are more concerned with interindividual processes. I would hasten to add that this distinction is based on the primary focus of each chapter and isn't as clean in its application as its use might imply. Indeed, several of the chapters can be seen to have implications for illuminating both intra- and interindividual coordination.

In chapter 2, Wilson traces the development of theories of message production in the field of Communication, focusing primarily on the work on interpersonal compliance gaining. He shows that the earliest research in this area approached message production in terms of strategy selection. A "second generation" of research and theory involved a shift away from characterizing the production of influence messages in terms of strategy selection and instead emphasized the role of interaction *goals* and *planning* in pursuit of those goals. Finally, Wilson looks toward the future by posing four challenges for theories of message production. He suggests that theories need to become more comprehensive in the sense that they address a wider range of message features, that they should meld global (i.e., cross-contextual) and context-specific forms of analysis, that greater emphasis needs to be given to interindividual processes, and, lastly, that the role of emotion in the production of influence messages needs to be scrutinized.

The continuing centrality of conceptions of interaction goals and planning in theories of message production is evident in the fact that several of the chapters in this book, including those of Berger, Waldron, Meyer, and Dillard are directly concerned with these issues. In chapter 3, Dillard notes that although theories of message production routinely invoke the notion of goals, there is, in fact, little consensus about the nature of the construct itself. In view of this state of affairs, he articulates a set of distinctions and theoretical choice-points that can be used to sharpen conceptual definitions of the goal construct and to clarify points of differentiation between alternative conceptions. Among the issues he examines are the relationship between goals and conscious awareness, notions of goal commitment and goal specificity, and the nature of goal hierarchies. Significantly, he also suggests that attention needs to be given to the dynamics that govern the appearance of goals in, and subsequent decay from, conscious awareness. Finally, Dillard advances a set of recommendations for operationalizing the goal construct in research on message production.

Interaction goals and processes of message planning are the focus of the model developed by Meyer in chapter 4. More specifically, she is concerned with people's ability to determine prior to uttering a message that it may have undesirable social consequences, and, on the basis of this fact, to revise that message. In pursuit of this issue, she develops a general model of message production that explicates processes of goal development, message formulation, anticipation of social outcomes, and message revision. The model addresses these processes by recourse to conceptions of spreading activation in network structures representing goals, situations, behaviors, and social consequences. In the final section of the chapter, Meyer traces the implications of the model for understanding the role of certain individual-difference variables in social behavior.

The predominant focus of models involving conceptions of planning has been on intraindividual coherence; two of the chapters in this volume are noteworthy, however, in that they suggest the potential for bringing aspects of message planning to bear in examining interindividual processes, and for this reason, they are included in the third section of the book. In chapter 9, Waldron identifies three traditions of work on planning in communication. The first of these, the preconversational planning approach, examines relationships between various preinteraction plan attributes (e.g., complexity, specificity) and subsequent message behavior and social outcomes. The second research tradition, the conversational planning approach, attempts to study plans as they emerge, are revised, and discarded during the course of interaction. Finally, Waldron explores a third potential approach, the interactive planning approach, which focuses on the mutual coordination and adaptation of the interactants' action plans.

Like Waldron, Berger (chap. 10) sees a need for models of message production to become more "socialized" by giving explicit attention to the social factors that impact ongoing interaction. His specific concern is with the way that speakers address conditions of ambiguity and uncertainty that inhere in all interchanges. He begins by identifying three sources of uncertainty about our interaction partners and then develops a series of propositions about how these various types of uncertainty will influence message plans. Finally, he examines various hedges that can be used to cope with problems of uncertainty and advances a set of propositions concerning the conditions under which direct and indirect hedges are likely to be employed.

Of the remaining chapters in Section II, those by McCornack and Kemper and Hummert reflect a focus on specific communicative phenomena that not only have attracted the attention of researchers for many years, but that should also continue to energize work on theories of message production for some time to come. In chapter 5, McCornack notes that theories of deception have failed to specify the cognitive mechanisms that underlie the production of deceptive messages, and he challenges a number of pervasive "myths" that characterize the received wisdom in this area. It is particularly noteworthy that McCornack rejects the "cognitive load hypothesis" that formulating lies is more cognitively demanding than telling the truth. He is able to make a convincing case that deception often proceeds with little cognitive effort and that in some instances truth-telling is actually more difficult than lying. With an eye toward developing theories of deceptive-message production, McCornack proposes that the encoding of such messages be viewed in terms of problem solving. One implication of such an approach is that deception may not have its genesis in the formulation of an intention to deceive. In the final section of the chapter, he suggests the potential of local-management models such as that developed by O'Keefe and Lambert (e.g., 1995) for illuminating the processes involved in telling lies.

In chapter 6, Kemper and Hummert address the relationships between aging and various aspects of message production and consider the implications of age-related changes for understanding message-production processes. They begin with a review of research which indicates that some aspects of message behavior (e.g., lexical selection, referential communication) are characterized by declines with advancing age, others (e.g., syntactic processing) remain relatively unaffected in old age, and still others (e.g., narrative skills) appear to improve later in life. In their second section, they consider the sorts of changes in message behavior that accompany progressive age-related dementias, particularly Alzheimer's disease. Finally, they raise two questions about message production by the elderly that future empirical and theoretical work will need to address. The first of these concerns how, despite cognitive and physical declines, the elderly are able to maintain relatively good social interactions. The second issue, driven by the potential of communication problems for identifying Alzheimer's and other dementias, is to identify the changes in message behavior that accompany the onset and course of development of such age-related degenerative conditions.

The final two chapters in Section II are similar in that they propose broad theoretical frameworks intended to apply to a range of communicative phenomena. In chapter 7, I attempt to sketch some of the changes in my own thinking about the nature of the output system that have arisen over the last decade or so. Collectively, these changes comprise the framework of what I call "second generation action assembly theory." Readers familiar with the original theory (Greene, 1984) will find that the new version differs in a number of important respects. Among these are that the conception of a "procedural record" has undergone revision, as has the activation process by which long-term memory information is brought to bear in behavioral production. Additions to the theory include treatments of executive processes and the neurophysiological substrate that underlies the theory's functional architecture. Perhaps the most important developments in second generation action assembly theory, however, concern: (a) the prominence accorded decay in activation level, (b) the notion of "coalitions" of behavioral features, and (c) a reconceptualization of the assembly process that no longer incorporates the serial, top-down, capacity-limited properties of assembly in the original version of the theory.

Hample, in chapter 8, explores the implications of applying field theory (Lewin, 1951) to the realm of message production. He begins with a brief overview of key terms of field theory (e.g., life space, planes of reality and irreality) and then demonstrates how issues of message production can be approached in those terms. Particularly noteworthy in this regard is the conception of goals (positively valenced regions of the life space) and plans (actions projected in the plane of irreality) derived from a Lewinian perspective. Hample contrasts a field-theory approach with the standard goals $\rightarrow$ planning $\rightarrow$ action view and makes a case for the greater comprehensiveness of the former. The author notes that field theory is more correctly identified as a metatheory and that falsification may be difficult or impossible, nevertheless, the view he articulates is characterized by considerable integrative and heuristic power.

As noted earlier, Section III consists of chapters focused primarily on interindividual coordination and begins with the planning-based treatments of Waldron (chapter 9) and Berger (chapter 10). These chapters, with their roots in one of the major conceptual traditions of cognitive science are complemented by the conversational analytic perspective represented by Sanders in chapter 11. Sanders is concerned with specifying the nature of the "cognitive resources" that allow people to act anticipatorily in constructing their messages to others so as to impact the course of the interaction and the interpretations of their interlocutors in particular ways. His project is an extension and revision of his earlier work (Sanders, 1987) on "Principles of Relevance." This revision is based on recognition that verbal and nonverbal behaviors are embedded in ongoing tasks or activities, and, for this reason, are constructed not just in terms of their relevance to the conversation, but with respect to their task implications as well. Sanders concludes by tracing points of commonality and divergence between his perspective and those of Greene (1984, 1995a, 1995b) and O'Keefe (1988; O'Keefe & Lambert, 1995).

Like the second section of the book, Section III concludes with two chapters presenting broad, integrative frameworks. In chapter 12, Burgoon and White address patterns of interpersonal mutual influence from the perspective of Interaction Adaptation Theory. Central to Interaction Adaptation Theory are three classes of influences on a person's behavior: *requirements* (reflecting physical and psychological needs), *expectations* (based on social norms and personal histories), and *desires* (related to preferences, goals, and plans). The particular combination of these three classes of factors define an individual's "Interaction Position," a dynamic disposition to produce certain types of messages. A person's behavior, then, is seen to be a function of his or her Interaction Position, social skills and behavioral repertoire, previous behavior, environmental factors, and the behavior of the other(s) in the interaction. This last source of influence is particularly important in the view of the authors who emphasize that the behavior of one's interlocutor may exert greater influence on his or her behavior than one's own goals, plans, expectations, and so forth. Finally, Burgoon and White address patterns of mutual influence (e.g., compensation, convergence) in terms of the discrepancy between Interaction Position (i.e., needs, expectations, desires) and actual behavior.

The volume concludes with Buck's chapter on the spontaneous communication of emotion. The reader will find a number of themes in this chapter that are reminiscent of points raised by Burgoon and White. At the same time, Buck's approach, emphasizing as it does the physiological basis of the phenomena of interest, provides a unique window on interindividual processes. At the heart of Buck's treatment is the distinction between "symbolic" and "spontaneous" communication systems. In contrast to the symbolic communication system with which it operates in parallel, the spontaneous communication system is seen to be nonsymbolic, nonintentional, and nonpropositional. In Buck's view, the spontaneous communication system is instantiated in biologically based mechanisms that permit the direct expression and reception/processing of the emotional cues of others. In the final sections of the chapter, he applies this "direct readout model" of communication to a consideration of its implications for understanding interindividual processes such as empathy, rapport, charisma, and deception.

CONCLUSION

As I noted before, the aim of this book is to survey a "new generation" of theories of message production. Taken together, the various chapters reflect a number of characteristics and trends worthy of note. Among these are the prominence accorded conceptions of goals and planning, attempts to apply models of intraindividual processes in illuminating interindividual phenomena, treatments which involve hybrid intentional/design-stance approaches, and efforts to incorporate physiological constructs and to meld them with psychological and social terms.

Even a cursory review of the chapters in this volume serves to drive home the point that the processes underlying the production of verbal and nonverbal behaviors are exceedingly complex, so much so that they resist the development of unified explanatory schemes. The alternative is the mosaic of emerging theories such as are represented here—each approach according prominence to certain message-production phenomena (while obscuring others) and providing a window on some portion of the processes that give rise to those phenomena (while remaining mute about other processes). I think it is in the amalgam of disparate treatments, then, that we find the most intellectually compelling characterization of message-production processes. There are points of overlap and consistency in these chapters, but it is also the case that the juxtaposition of various approaches is not always harmonious. Thus, in the end we are confronted on one hand with the wonderful complexities of the system that underlies message production and on the other with a vibrant dialogue engendered by the diverse constellation of theories about the nature of that system.

ACKNOWLEDGMENT

The author wishes to thank Marianne S. Sassi for her helpful comments during the preparation of this chapter.

REFERENCES

Andersen, P. A., Garrison, J. R., & Andersen, J. F. (1979). Implications of a neurophysiological approach for the study of nonverbal communication. *Human Communication Research, 6,* 74–89.

Bates, E. (Ed.). (1979). *The emergence of symbols: Cognition and communication in infancy.* New York: Academic Press.

Behnke, R. R., & Beatty, M. J. (1981). A cognitive-physiological model of speech anxiety. *Communication Monographs, 48,* 158–163.

Berger, C. R. (1988). Planning, affect, and social action generation. In L. Donohew, H. E. Sypher, & E. T. Higgins (Eds.), *Communication, social cognition, and affect* (pp. 93–116). Hillsdale, NJ: Lawrence Erlbaum Associates.

Berger, C. R. (1995). A plan-based approach to strategic communication. In D. E. Hewes (Ed.), *The cognitive bases of interpersonal communication* (pp. 141–179). Hillsdale, NJ: Lawrence Erlbaum Associates.

Bowers, J. W. (Ed.). (1979). A constructivist's olio and other studies. *Communication Monographs, 46*(4).

Buck, R. (1980). Nonverbal behavior and the theory of emotion: The facial feedback hypothesis. *Journal of Personality and Social Psychology, 38,* 811–824.

Burgoon, J. K., & Hale, J. L. (1988). Nonverbal expectancy violations: Model elaboration and application to immediacy behaviors. *Communication Monographs, 55,* 58–79.

Butterworth, B. (Ed.). (1980). *Language production, Vol. 1: Speech and talk.* London: Academic Press.

Cappella, J. N., & Greene, J. O. (1982). A discrepancy-arousal explanation of mutual influence in expressive behavior for adult and infant-adult interaction. *Communication Monographs, 49,* 89–114.

Cegala, D. L., Alexander, A. F., & Sokuvitz, S. (1979). An investigation of eye gaze and its relation to selected verbal behavior. *Human Communication Research, 5,* 99–108.

Clark, H. H., & Clark, E. V. (1977). *Psychology and language: An introduction to psycholinguistics.* New York: Harcourt, Brace, Jovanovich.

Clippenger, J. H., Jr. (1977). *Meaning and discourse: A computer model of psychoanalytic speech and cognition.* Baltimore, MD: Johns Hopkins University Press.

Cohen, P. R., & Perrault, C. R. (1979). Elements of a plan-based theory of speech-acts. *Cognitive Science, 3,* 177–212.

Coulmas, F. (Ed.). (1981). *Conversational routine: Explorations in standardized communication situations and prepatterned speech.* The Hague: Mouton.

de Beaugrande, R.-A. (1980). The pragmatics of discourse planning. *Journal of Pragmatics, 4,* 15–42.

Dechert, H. W., & Raupach, M. (Eds.). (1980). *Temporal variables in speech: Studies in honor of Frieda Goldman-Eisler.* The Hague: Mouton.

Delia, J. G. (1977). Constructivism and the study of human communication. *Quarterly Journal of Speech, 63,* 66–83.

Dennett, D. C. (1971). Intentional systems. *Journal of Philosophy, 68,* 87–106.

Fodor, J. A., Bever, T. G., & Garrett, M. F. (1974). *The psychology of language: An introduction to psycholinguistics and generative grammar.* New York: McGraw-Hill.

Freedle, R. O. (Ed.). (1977). *Discourse production and comprehension.* Norwood, NJ: Ablex.

Fromkin, V. A. (Ed). (1980). *Errors in linguistic performance: Slips of the tongue, ear, pen, and hand.* New York: Academic Press.

Greene, J. O. (1984). A cognitive approach to human communication: An action assembly theory. *Communication Monographs, 51,* 289–306.

Greene, J. O. (1995a). Production of messages in pursuit of multiple social goals: Action assembly theory contributions to the study of cognitive encoding processes. In B. R. Burleson (Ed.), *Communication yearbook 18* (pp. 26–53). Thousand Oaks, CA: Sage.

Greene, J. O. (1995b). An action-assembly perspective on verbal and nonverbal message production: A dancer's message unveiled. In D. E. Hewes (Ed.), *The cognitive bases of interpersonal communication* (pp. 51–85). Hillsdale, NJ: Lawrence Erlbaum Associates.

Greene, J. O., & Sparks, G. G. (1983). The role of outcome expectations in the experience of a state of communication apprehension. *Communication Quarterly, 31,* 212–219.

Hobbs, J. R., & Evans, D. A. (1980). Conversation as planned behavior. *Cognitive Science, 4,* 349–377.

Infante, D. A. (1980). Verbal plans: A conceptualization and investigation. *Communication Quarterly, 28,* 3–10.

Kellermann, K. (1995). The conversation MOP: A model of patterned and pliable behavior. In D. E. Hewes (Ed.), *The cognitive bases of interpersonal communication* (pp. 181–221). Hillsdale, NJ: Lawrence Erlbaum Associates.

Lewin, K. (1951). *Field theory in social science.* New York: Harper & Row.

McNeill, D. (1979). *The conceptual basis of language.* Hillsdale, NJ: Lawrence Erlbaum Associates.

Motley, M. T., Camden, C. T., & Baars, B. J. (1979). Personality and situational influences upon verbal slips: A laboratory test of Freudian and prearticulatory editing hypotheses. *Human Communication Research, 5,* 195–202.

Motley, M. T., Camden, C. T., & Baars, B. J. (1981). Toward verifying the assumptions of laboratory-induced slips of the tongue: The output-error and editing issues. *Human Communication Research, 8,* 3–15.

O'Keefe, B. J. (1988). The logic of message design: Individual differences in reasoning about communication. *Communication Monographs, 55,* 80–103.

O'Keefe, B. J., & Lambert, B. L. (1995). Managing the flow of ideas: A local management approach to message design. In B. R. Burleson (Ed.), *Communication yearbook 18* (pp. 54–82). Thousand Oaks, CA: Sage.

Patterson, M. L. (1976). An arousal model of interpersonal intimacy. *Psychological Review, 83,* 235–245.

Planalp, S., & Tracy, K. (1980). Not to change the topic but . . .: A cognitive approach to the management of conversation. In D. Nimmo (Ed.), *Communication yearbook 4* (pp. 237–260). New Brunswick, NJ: Transaction.

Rosenberg, S. (Ed.). (1977). *Sentence production: Developments in research and theory.* Hillsdale, NJ: Lawrence Erlbaum Associates.

Sanders, R. E. (1987). *Cognitive foundations of calculated speech: Controlling understandings in conversation and persuasion.* Albany, NY: SUNY Press.

Siegman, A. W., & Feldstein, S. (Eds.). (1979). *Of speech and time: Temporal speech patterns in interpersonal contexts.* Hillsdale, NJ: Lawrence Erlbaum Associates.

Stelmach, G. E. (Ed.). (1976). *Motor control: Issues and trends.* New York: Academic Press.

Stern, D. N. (1974). Mother and infant at play: The dyadic interaction involving facial, vocal and gaze behavior. In M. Lewis & L. A. Rosenblum (Eds.), *The effect of the infant on its caregiver* (pp. 187–213). New York: Wiley.

Turvey, M. T. (1977). Preliminaries to a theory of action with reference to vision. In R. Shaw & J. Bransford (Eds.), *Perceiving, acting, and knowing: Toward an ecological psychology* (pp. 211–265). Hillsdale, NJ: Lawrence Erlbaum Associates.

Weiner, S. L., & Goodenough, D. R. (1977). A move toward a psychology of conversation. In R. O. Freedle (Ed.), *Discourse production and comprehension* (pp. 213–225). Norwood, NJ: Ablex.

Zuckerman, M., DePaulo, B. M., & Rosenthal, R. (1981). Verbal and nonverbal communication of deception. In L. Berkowitz (Ed.), *Advances in experimental social psychology* (Vol. 14, pp. 1–59). New York: Academic Press.

2

DEVELOPING THEORIES OF PERSUASIVE MESSAGE PRODUCTION: THE NEXT GENERATION

Steven R. Wilson
Northern Illinois University

"Message production" is a widely recognized area of communication research. This was not the case even 20 years ago. To my knowledge, O'Keefe and Delia (1982) were the first communication scholars to use the term in a chapter that analyzed individual differences in social cognition and multiple-goal messages. By the late 1980s, special issues of journals such as *Journal of Language and Social Psychology* (1985, Vol. *4*, Nos. 3 and 4) and *Human Communication Research* (1989, Vol. *16*, No. 1) were being devoted to the topic. Although absent from the subject index of the first edition of the *Handbook of Interpersonal Communication* (1985), message production appears in the second edition's (1994) index. Littlejohn (1992) also includes a chapter on message production starting with the fourth edition of *Theories of Human Communication*.

Message production scholars are interested in explaining why individuals say what they do during everyday interactions. Scholars have employed numerous schemes to analyze what individuals "say," including: abstract message dimensions such as directness (e.g., Dillard, Segrin, & Harden, 1989) or listener adaptedness (e.g., Clark & Delia, 1977); types of message strategies designed to accomplish a primary goal (e.g., Marwell & Schmitt, 1967) or to coordinate multiple goals (e.g., O'Keefe & Shepherd, 1987); types of content themes (e.g., Saeki & O'Keefe, 1994); specific word choices such as "can you" versus "will you" in requests (e.g., Francik & Clark, 1985); and paraverbal qualities such as onset latencies and filled pauses (e.g., Greene & Lindsey, 1989). Although they have analyzed a wide range of message

features, scholars in this area share a common goal of explicating psychological processes that underlie the production of messages during interaction (Hewes, 1995).

In this chapter, I have chosen to focus on the production of interpersonal
influence messages. In part, this decision reflects the current state of the
message production literature. Although message production scholars have
investigated other communicative functions such as seeking information
(e.g., Waldron, 1990), communicating criticism/rejection (e.g., Greene & Lindsey, 1989), and comforting distressed others (e.g., Burleson, 1985), the largest body of research has investigated how individuals exert/resist influence
(see Dillard, 1990a; Seibold, Cantrill, & Meyers, 1994). Aside from simply
reflecting the current literature, however, the focus on influence reflects my
own belief that adequate explanations of message production must be developed at multiple levels of abstraction. Compelling explanations will integrate general models of psychological processes with specific analyses of
message functions and relational/institutional contexts.

In this chapter, I assess the past, present, and potential future for theories
of persuasive message production. Sections one and two sketch how persuasive message production has emerged as a recognizable area of study.
I argue that relevant work can be divided into two time periods: an initial
period of research (the "first generation") that coalesced around the metaphor of message production as "strategy selection," and a current period
(the "second generation") that coheres around the metaphor of message
production as "goal pursuit." Although research on message production
cuts across disciplines, I focus primarily on work by communication scholars who have helped define this area of study. In the final section, I pose
four challenges that we face in developing the "next generation" of persuasive message production theories.

THE FIRST GENERATION: FOCUS
ON STRATEGY SELECTION

Theories of persuasive message production have their genesis in two research traditions: the "compliance-gaining" literature initiated by the late
Gerald Miller and his colleagues at Michigan State University, and the "constructivist" literature associated with Jesse Delia and his colleagues at the
University of Illinois. Although different in many respects, both traditions
focused primarily on developing typologies of message strategies as well as
on predicting individual/situational variation in their use (B. O'Keefe, 1990).
Both traditions emerged in the mid-1970s and began to wane (or were
redefined) by the mid-1980s. Both traditions also influenced subsequent
theories. Miller and associates did not intend to construct a message pro-

duction theory (Boster, 1990, 1995; Miller, 1990), but questions arising from their work provided strong impetus for such theories. Delia and associates did present a rudimentary theory of message production, the limits of which provided important insights for contemporary theories. For each tradition, I review a seminal study, subsequent research, limitations, and implications for current work.

The "Compliance-Gaining" Tradition

Compliance-gaining involves a message source's attempts to induce a message target to perform a desired action that the target otherwise would not have performed. Miller, Boster, Roloff, and Seibold (1977) set the agenda for this research tradition. Arising from Miller and Steinberg's (1975) developmental view of interpersonal communication, the "MBRS study" posed three research questions: (a) how could compliance-gaining strategies be classified/grouped? (b) how was strategy choice influenced by situational differences? (c) how was strategy choice affected by individual differences? (Miller et al., 1977, p. 38). Participants read four hypothetical compliance-gaining scenarios, designed to manipulate two situational dimensions: whether the message source-target relationship was interpersonal/noninterpersonal, and whether the source's request had short-term/long-term relational consequences. After reading each scenario, participants rated how likely they would be to use each of 16 compliance-gaining strategies in that situation. Compliance-gaining strategies were drawn from Marwell and Schmitt's (1967) nominal-level typology, and a specific example of every strategy was written for each situation. Miller et al. (1977) concluded that message sources rated a larger number of compliance-gaining strategies as likely to be used in noninterpersonal/long-term than in interpersonal/short-term situations, and that the clustering of strategies varied substantially across situations.

Aside from specific findings, the MBRS study was influential because it: (a) expanded the attention of persuasion scholars from a more limited focus on public/mediated contexts to include interpersonal contexts (Miller & Burgoon, 1978); and (b) set a research agenda and provided a methodological exemplar for a large body of subsequent research (see Seibold, Cantrill, & Meyers, 1985; Wheeless, Barraclough, & Stewart, 1983). Following publication of the MBRS study, scholars proposed alternative nominal-level typologies of compliance-gaining strategies and debated the most useful means of developing typologies (Boster, Stiff, & Reynolds, 1985; Cody, McLaughlin, & Jordan, 1980; Schenk-Hamlin, Wiseman, & Georgacarakos, 1982; Wiseman & Schenk-Hamlin, 1981). Aside from compliance-gaining, nominal-level typologies of compliance–resistance strategies also were developed (e.g., McLaughlin, Cody, & Robey, 1980).

Other research attempted to predict compliance-gaining strategy choice. Cody and his colleagues (Cody & McLaughlin, 1980; Cody, Woefel, & Jordan,

1983) identified perceptual dimensions along which message sources discriminated compliance-gaining situations, such as intimacy, dominance, rights to persuade, benefits of compliance for both parties, and anticipated resistance. Several studies investigated how these situational dimensions, individually and in combination, affected selection of compliance-gaining/resisting strategies (e.g., Cody, Greene, Marston, O'Hair, Baaske, & Schneider, 1986; Cody, McLaughlin, & Schneider, 1981; Dillard & Burgoon, 1985; McLaughlin et al., 1980; O'Hair, Cody, & O'Hair, 1991; Sillars, 1980). Scholars also explored how a host of individual differences such as argumentativeness, communication apprehension, communication motives, dogmatism, locus of control, Machiavellianism, negativism, and verbal aggressiveness affected strategy choice (e.g., Boster & Levine, 1988; Javidi, Jordan, & Carlone, 1994; Lamude, Daniels, & White, 1987; Lustig & King, 1980; Roloff & Barnicott, 1978, 1979). Others investigated whether selection of compliance-gaining strategies varied across birth order, gender, and culture (e.g., Burgoon, Dillard, Koper, & Doran, 1984; Burgoon, Dillard, Doran, & Miller, 1982; deTurck, 1985; deTurck & Miller, 1982; Hirokowa & Miyahara, 1986). Finally, scholars developed strategy typologies and examined strategy choice within particular contexts, including romantic (e.g., Edgar & Fitzpatrick, 1988; Falbo & Peplau, 1980; Sillars, 1980), parent/child (e.g., deTurck & Miller, 1983); physician/patient (e.g., Burgoon, Parrott, Burgoon, Coker, Pfau, & Birk, 1990), teacher/student (e.g., Kearney & Plax, 1987; Kearney, Plax, Richmond, & McCroskey, 1985); and managerial/employee relationships (e.g., Hirokowa & Miyahara, 1986; Kipnis, Schmidt, & Wilkinson, 1980; Krone, 1992; Lamude et al., 1987).

Despite the MBRS study's heuristic value, the traditional compliance-gaining literature had come under substantial conceptual and methodological attack by the late 1980s (Miller, Boster, Roloff, & Seibold, 1987; D. O'Keefe, 1990). Typologies of compliance-gaining strategies have been criticized as atheoretical on many grounds. Strategies within the same typology typically: are defined ambiguously; are cast at different levels of abstraction; are differentiated inconsistently on numerous grounds (e.g., form, function, content, source); and fail to clearly instantiate one or a few message dimensions (Kellermann & Cole, 1994). Debate has ensued over whether compliance-gaining behavior is most fruitfully conceptualized at the level of individual strategies, strategy clusters, or dimensions underlying all strategies (Dillard, 1988; Hunter & Boster, 1987). Others advocate abandoning the concept of "strategy" altogether (O'Keefe, 1994). Situational and individual predictors of compliance-gaining strategy choice also have been investigated in ad-hoc fashion, with less regard for developing theory that could account for results across studies (Boster, 1995). Aside from these conceptual challenges, the methodology of traditional compliance-gaining studies (i.e., having participants rate likelihood of use for preformulated strategies in response to hypothetical scenarios) also has been criticized as lacking convergent, divergent and predictive validity (Burleson, Wilson, Waltman, Goering, Ely, & Whaley, 1988; Dillard, 1988; Waltman, 1994, 1995). Scholars have debated the relative merits of having participants select preformulated strategies versus construct written/oral messages (Boster, 1988; Burleson & Wilson, 1988; Hunter, 1988; O'Hair et al., 1991; Seibold, 1988; Sorenson, Plax, & Kearney, 1989). Others advocate investigating the sequential and interdependent nature of compliance-gaining/resisting during interaction (e.g., Boster, Levine, & Kazoleas, 1993; Lim, 1990a; Wilson, Cruz, Marshall, & Rao, 1993).

In sum, the compliance-gaining tradition contributed to theories of persuasive message production by initiating a source-oriented perspective on interpersonal influence and by highlighting important research questions for such theories (e.g., accounting for situational/individual variation in persuasive messages).

The "Constructivist" Tradition

As a theoretical perspective, constructivism offers insights about developmental and individual differences in a broad range of social perception and communicative phenomena (see Burleson, 1987; Gastil, 1995). Clark and Delia (1977) set the research agenda for early constructivist analyses of persuasive message production. These authors examined how children acquire person-perception skills that enable them to generate "listener-adapted" persuasive messages. Listener-adapted messages are those in which the message source adapts requests and supporting arguments to the wants and needs of the message target (e.g., "Mom, if you get me a bike for my birthday, I could run errands to the store when you're busy") rather than simply emphasizing the source's own wants and needs (e.g., "Please Mom, I really, really want a bike"; see Clark & Delia, 1976).

According to Clark and Delia (1977), person-perception skills such as the ability to distinguish different message targets (facilitated by interpersonal construct differentiation) and to take the perspective of particular targets are necessary prerequisites for adapting persuasive appeals. Participants in their study, 29 boys and 29 girls ranging from 2nd to 9th grade, stated aloud exactly what they would say in response to three hypothetical persuasive scenarios (e.g., asking their parents to buy them something they wanted very much). Persuasive appeals were scored using a four-level hierarchical coding scheme, ranging from strategies indicating no awareness that the message target had a perspective distinct from the source to strategies that emphasized the advantages to the target of acceding to the source's request. Participants also completed the two-peer version of the RCQ measure of interpersonal construct differentiation (see Burleson & Waltman, 1988), as well as a social perspective-taking measure. As predicted, both construct differentiation and perspective-taking skill were associated with the degree of listener-adaptation in children's persuasive messages, even after controlling for the effects of chronological age (partial r's = .45 and .51, respectively).

Clark and Delia (1977) were the first to document a relationship between interpersonal construct differentiation and adaptation of persuasive messages. Like the MBRS study, Clark and Delia's investigation also was influential because it set a research agenda and provided a methodological exemplar for a large body of subsequent research (see Burleson, 1989). Several studies, using the same basic procedures, replicated Clark and Delia's basic findings (e.g., Delia & Clark, 1977; Delia, Kline, & Burleson, 1979). In addition, scholars attempted to clarify how person-perception skills facilitate adapting persuasive appeals, by investigating how interpersonal construct differentiation and abstractness affect children's abilities to differentiate message targets, anticipate targets' reasons for refusal, produce relevant responses to refusals, and provide sophisticated rationales for their own message choices (Burke & Clark, 1982; Delia & Clark, 1977; Delia et al., 1979). In a related vein, McQuillen (1986) developed a hierarchical scheme for coding degree of listener adaptation in children's strategies for resisting compliance. With maturation, children are more likely to generate listener-adapted resistance strategies, and to vary their level of and reasons for adaptation depending on the message source's identity and choice of compliance-gaining strategies (McQuillen, 1986; McQuillen & Higginbotham, 1985).

Aside from focusing on children, constructivist scholars also documented that stable individual differences in construct differentiation and abstractness are associated with the ability to produce listener-adapted persuasive and regulative messages in adult samples (e.g., Applegate, 1980a, 1980b, 1982; Applegate, Burke, Burleson, Delia, & Kline, 1985; Kline & Ceropski, 1984; O'Keefe & Delia, 1979). In addition to college students, these studies assessed teachers, nurses, and mothers of young children. Construct differentiation also has been associated with the ability to generate listener-adapted appeals when adults resist compliance (Kline & Floyd, 1990). Although the vast majority of these studies, like Clark and Delia (1977), had participants generate oral/written messages in response to hypothetical scenarios, a few showed that interpersonal construct differentiation is associated with the likelihood that individuals will produce listener-adapted persuasive appeals during actual interaction (Applegate, 1980b, 1982; Kline & Ceropski, 1984).

By developing hierarchical coding schemes that analyzed persuasive messages along a specific dimension (listener-adaptation) and then assessing developmental and individual-difference variables relevant to this dimension, the constructivist tradition avoided many pitfalls (i.e., lack of theoretical grounding for describing messages or selecting predictor variables) that befell the compliance-gaining literature. Despite these strengths, the view of message production arising from Clark and Delia (1977) also was being criticized by the mid-1980s (see Burleson, 1987). Critics argued that individual differences in social perception played a role at all stages of the message production process, and not just in the final stage of adapting an already generated "kernel" message. O'Keefe and Delia (1982) argued that constructivist coding schemes could be reconceptualized as tapping "message multifunctionality" (i.e., the degree to which persuasive messages also addressed other goals such as supporting the target's face) rather than "listener adaptation," and that interpersonal construct differentiation was associated with the likelihood that individuals spontaneously would form and pursue multiple goals. Results from several subsequent studies were consistent with this view (Applegate & Woods, 1991; Leichty & Applegate, 1991; O'Keefe & Shepherd, 1987; Wilson, 1990). Critics also charged that early constructivist accounts failed to specify how construct differentiation affected the procedural knowledge that individuals use to adapt messages and pursue goals (e.g., Berger, 1995; O'Keefe, 1988; Waldron & Applegate, 1994; Wilson, 1990). Finally, early constructivist accounts also had little to say about variation in listener-adaptation across situations. For example, research showed that children were more likely to employ listener-adapted persuasive appeals when asking an adult stranger to comply with an altruistic request rather than when asking their own mother to comply with a request that benefited primarily themselves (Clark & Delia, 1976; Delia et al., 1979), but constructivist scholars paid little attention to these findings. In sum, the constructivist analysis of listener-adapted communication contributed to theories of persuasive message production by illustrating how messages could be analyzed in a theoretically driven manner, and by presenting a rudimentary theory of message production that could be redefined and elaborated in subsequent work.

In this section, I have argued that the "compliance-gaining" and "constructivist" traditions represent the first generation of research on persuasive message production. Both traditions analyzed persuasive messages using strategy typologies, and both examined situational and individual-difference predictors of strategy choice. By the mid-1980s, however, scholars from both traditions had turned their attention to the construct of "interaction goals." Within the compliance-gaining tradition, Cody and his colleagues (Cody, Canary, & Smith, 1994) explored how actors organize their knowledge of compliance-gaining situations around influence goals, and Dillard (1990b) proposed a goal-driven model of interpersonal influence. Within the constructivist tradition, Barbara O'Keefe reframed the listener-adaptation model in terms of multiple goals (O'Keefe & Delia, 1982) and knowledge about means for pursuing goals (O'Keefe, 1988). Interaction goals hold promise for explaining individual, situational, and cultural variations in persuasive message production, as well as for modeling how influence interactions tend to unfold over time (Kim & Wilson, 1994; Sanders, 1991; Wilson & Putnam, 1990).

THE SECOND GENERATION: FOCUS
ON GOAL PURSUIT

Interaction goals are states of affairs that individuals want to attain/maintain through talk. From the mid-1980s onward, the concept of "interaction goal" has become a centerpiece in theorizing about persuasive message production (see Wilson, 1995). Individuals are portrayed as pursuing multiple, competing goals when seeking/resisting compliance, and goals are held to set constraints on how compliance is sought/resisted (e.g., Dillard et al., 1989; Hample & Dallinger, 1987; Kim & Wilson, 1994; Saeki & O'Keefe, 1994; Tracy, Craig, Smith, & Spisak, 1984). Indeed, virtually every author in this volume presumes that message production is a goal-driven process. This section briefly reviews five contemporary lines of research on: influence goals as definitions of situations, multiple goals as constraints, the formation of interaction goals, procedural knowledge for pursuing goals, and rational models of message design. Although quite diverse, these lines of research presume that in order to explain why people try to persuade as they do, we need to analyze their interaction goals and their ideas about pursuing goals.

Influence Goals as Definitions of Situations

Erving Goffman emphasized that whenever we enter into interaction, each participant "knowingly and unwittingly projects a definition of the situation" (Goffman, 1959, p. 242). This definition of the situation is our best guess about the nature of the current reality, or our answer to the question "what is going on here?" People actively define situations because they often contain ambiguity about relevant identities, goals, and actions (see Goffman, 1959; McCall & Simmons, 1978).

With regard to persuasive message production, individuals organize their implicit understandings of compliance-gaining situations around influence goals. As Dillard et al. (1989) remark, "the influence goal brackets the situation. It helps segment the flow of behavior into a meaningful unit; it says what the interaction is about" (p. 21). In response to this thinking, several scholars have developed typologies of influence goals that appear meaningful to everyday actors (Cody et al., 1994; Dillard, 1989; Meyer, 1990; Rule, Bisanz, & Kohn, 1985).

Cody et al. (1994) argue that people associate influence goals with a constellation of situational dimensions. For example, message sources associate "gaining assistance" (favors) with high-self/low-target benefits and at least moderate source-target intimacy, while they associate "enforcing obligations" with high rights to persuade, anticipated target resistance, and low target dominance. To assess this claim, Cody et al. re-analyzed data from an earlier study (Cody et al., 1986), in which participants had rated 29 different compliance-gaining situations along seven situational dimensions. Based on a cluster analysis, Cody et al. (1994) proposed a 12-category typology that includes influence goals such as "gaining assistance," "giving advice," and "escalating a relationship." Similar typologies have emerged from participants' open-ended descriptions of their influence goals (Dillard, 1989; Kipnis et al., 1980; Rule et al., 1985). Influence goals presumably are meaningful both to message sources and to targets, though they may not always agree which goal defines their current interaction.

Aside from situational dimensions, individuals also may associate affective reactions, perceived threats to identities, and behavioral responses with situations defined by particular influence goals. Consistent with this claim, message sources vary the degree to which they provide the target with explicit reasons for complying, rely on negative sanctions, and persist after target resistance depending on the particular influence goal (Cody et al., 1994; Dillard, 1989; Meyer, 1994; Wilson, Aleman, & Leathem, in press). Message sources also anticipate different obstacles as they pursue different influence goals, and tailor the content of their persuasive messages to address relevant obstacles (Roloff & Janiszewsi, 1989). Influence goals also offer a framework for analyzing individual difference variables. Locus of control, self-monitoring, and gender all affect people's willingness to enter situations defined by different influence goals, as well as their expectations about success and willingness to persist (Canary, Cody, & Marston, 1986; Smith, Cody, LoVette, & Canary, 1990).

Multiple Goals as Constraints

Although actors define interactions in terms of influence goals, they often pursue additional objectives when seeking/resisting compliance. Three groups of scholars have explored how goals shape and constrain the way that individuals exert influence. Hample and Dallinger (1990) have explored "cognitive editing standards," or reasons why message sources suppress rather than make specific arguments. Based on people's open-ended rationales for rejecting particular compliance-gaining strategies, these authors have identified four categories of editing standards: (a) effectiveness—the strategy would not work or might backfire; (b) principled objections—the message source objects to the nature of the strategy itself; (c) person-centered issues—the strategy could damage either party's self image or their relationship; and (d) discourse competence—the strategy is false or irrelevant. Hample and Dallinger (1987, 1988, 1990; Dallinger & Hample, 1994) subsequently have developed closed-ended rating scales for these four categories, and shown that the salience of particular editing criteria (e.g., effectiveness versus person-centered issues) varies across both persons and situations. Their research illustrates how people's goals shape what they do not say as well as what they do.

Dillard (1990b; Dillard et al., 1989) draws a conceptual distinction between primary (influence) and secondary goals. Aside from defining the interaction, primary goals exert a "push" or an "approach force" that motivates the message source to seek compliance. In contrast, secondary goals are cross-situational concerns exerting a "pull" or "inhibiting" force that shapes and constrains how the message source seeks compliance. When secondary goals are extremely salient they may overwhelm the primary goal, in which case the message source may refrain from seeking compliance at all. Using a strategy rejection procedure similar to Hample and Dallinger (1987), Dillard et al. (1989) identify five types of secondary goals: (a) identity goals—concerns about acting consistently with internal standards for behavior; (b) interaction goals—concerns about managing both parties' social identities; (c) relational resource goals—concerns about not damaging valued relationships; (d) personal resource goals—concerns about expending too much effort or too many material resources to gain compliance; and (e) arousal goals—concerns about becoming too anxious or nervous. Dillard et al. (1989) have developed closed-ended scales to assess each goal, and have shown that the importance of influence and secondary goals together help predict the degree to which message sources: plan their influence attempt in advance; exert effort to gain compliance; and use compliance-gaining messages that are direct, emphasize positive outcomes, and include explicit reasoning.

Finally, both Kellermann (1992; Kellermann & Shea, 1996) and Kim (1994) have explored "metagoals," or ongoing regulators of behavior that constrain message sources' strategic choices. Kellermann (1992) proposes two overarching metagoals. *Efficiency* means accomplishing the influence goal without wasting time/resources, so that direct/simple requests are more efficient than hints (though not necessarily more effective). *Appropriateness* means accomplishing the influence goal in a matter that is socially acceptable or polite, so that promises are more acceptable than threats. Appropriateness would encompass Hample and Dallinger's (1987) "person-centered" editing criteria as well as Dillard's (1990b) "interaction" and "relational resource" secondary goals. When pursuing task-oriented primary goals such as seeking compliance, tension is likely to exist between these metagoals such that the most efficient strategies are not most appropriate (and vice versa). Individual, situational, and cultural factors all may affect the salience of efficiency and appropriateness, and hence the range of compliance-gaining strategies from which message sources might choose (Kellermann & Kim, 1991; Kim, 1994). As an example, Kim and Wilson (1994) had college students from South Korea (a collectivistic culture) and the United States (an individualistic culture) rate 12 forms of requests for efficiency and appropriateness. Participants also judged whether each form would be effective at gaining the target's compliance and whether they would be likely to use each form. Participants from both cultures rated the relative efficiency and appropriateness of the twelve requests forms similarly, but differed dramatically in their effectiveness ratings. Koreans rated inefficient request forms as most appropriate, effective, and likely to be used. American in contrast rated efficient request forms as most effective, and perceived less tension between the appropriateness and efficiency of request forms.

In sum, these three lines of research have explored how people's compliance-gaining appeals are shaped and constrained by multiple goals. Scholars have paid less attention to how multiple goals shape what people do (and do not) say when resisting compliance, even though individuals are concerned about multiple goals when communicating rejection (Saeki & O'Keefe, 1994).

Forming Interaction Goals

Individuals may organize their knowledge of compliance-gaining situations around influence goals, and their influence messages may be shaped by secondary goals. But how do individuals decide what goals to pursue as they seek/resist compliance? Wilson (1990, 1995) has proposed a cognitive rules (CR) model, which contains one explicit set of assumptions about how interaction goals formed. Briefly, the CR model assumes that individuals possess cognitive rules, or associations, in long-term memory between representations of interaction goals and numerous situational features. For example, a message source might associate the influence goal "enforce an obligation" with features such as "the target made a promise," "the target failed to fulfill the promise," "the target's failure has tangible consequences for me," "the target's failure was intentional," and "the target has equal or lesser status than me" (Canary et al., 1986; Wilson & Kang, 1991).

The CR model assumes that a spreading activation process operates on this associative network, and that a cognitive rule must reach a certain activation threshold before it is triggered and forms a goal. The probability that a rule will be triggered is a function of three criteria: fit, strength, and recency. Based on the fit criterion, the probability of goal formation increases when individuals perceive that a larger rather than a smaller number of conditions represented in the rule are present in the current situation. Yet many influence situations are ambiguous or open to multiple interpretations, and hence may partially match and activate a large number of cognitive rules. For example, message sources may be uncertain whether a target's failure to fulfill an obligation was intentional, or even whether a target's behavior constitutes "failure." Within ambiguous situations, cognitive rules are more likely to be triggered if they have been activated recently (the recency criterion) or frequently in the past (the strength criterion).

The CR model hopes to explain variation in interaction goals across individuals, situations, and cultures. Personality attributes and cultural orientations may be reflected in the content of cognitive rules (i.e., the specific situational features associated with goals), the structure of rules (e.g., the number of situational features associated with goals), and/or the chronic accessibility of rules (i.e., how frequently a rule has been activated in the past). Message sources high in interpersonal construct differentiation, for instance, appear to possess more elaborate and accessible rules for forming secondary goals than do less differentiated sources (Wilson, 1995; Wilson, Cruz, & Kang, 1992). Different influence situations are likely to activate different cognitive rules, and ambiguous situations can magnify the effects of personality and culture on goals (Wilson, 1990).

Procedural Knowledge for Pursuing Goals

Interaction goals may motivate individuals to seek/resist compliance, as well as shape their influence messages, but goals alone are not sufficient to explain how messages are produced (Berger, 1995; O'Keefe, 1988). Individuals also must rely on procedural knowledge about possible means for accomplishing goals. The literatures on plans and planning as well as action assembly theory offer explicit assumptions about cognitive structures/processes that underlie message production.

Plans are knowledge structures representing actions that are necessary for overcoming obstacles and accomplishing goals. Plans contain more general and less rigidly sequenced knowledge than do scripts (Berger, 1995). Plans are mental representations, whereas strategies are abstract descriptions of overt behavior (Greene, 1990). *Planning* is the process of recalling, generating, selecting, adapting, and implementing plans into action (Berger, 1995; Dillard, 1990b; Meyer, 1994). Planning may occur in advance of interaction and/or "online" during interaction. Using a stimulated recall procedure immediately after initial conversations between strangers, Waldron (1990) found that 44% of participants' recalled thoughts pertained to goals and/or plans. To date, scholars have investigated the structure of plans as well as the adjustment of plans following initial failure to accomplish goals.

Plans for accomplishing social goals such as exerting/resisting influence can vary in complexity and specificity (Berger, 1995; Dillard, 1990b; Waldron & Applegate, 1994). Complex plans include a larger number of action units than simple plans. When discussing a controversial issue, for example, an individual who plans to "ask her how she felt about the issue" and to "say that I think it costs too much" has a more complex plan than someone who plans only the latter action. Specific plans are fleshed out in detail, whereas abstract plans provide only vague guides for action. An individual who plans to "defend my opinion if it's attacked" has a less specific plan than someone who also anticipates specific attacks and refutations.

Results from three studies suggest that the ability to develop complex and specific plans facilitates accomplishing social goals. In the first study (Berger

& Bell, 1988), students wrote out preinteraction plans for ingratiating a new roommate and asking for a date, and then completed measures of shyness and loneliness. Raters evaluated the effectiveness of these plans. Complex plans were evaluated as more likely to succeed than simple plans, and both loneliness and shyness were inversely associated with plan effectiveness. In a second study (Cegala & Waldron, 1992), participants attempted to learn three pieces of information about a stranger during an initial interaction, after which they provided undirected thought-lists via stimulated recall. Raters evaluated the competence (appropriateness and effectiveness) of participants' information-seeking behaviors. Participants who where judged highly competent reported significantly more goal/plan relevant thoughts than did less competent participants, whereas less competent participants reported more self-assessment thoughts. In the final study (Waldron & Applegate, 1994) participants argued for eight minutes about a controversial issue with a stranger, after which they provided cued thought-lists about their plans during each minute of the interaction via stimulated recall. Participants also completed the RCQ measure of interpersonal construct differentiation. Individuals who generated complex and specific plans during the first four minutes of interaction also were most likely to use integrative strategies (ones which attempted to reconcile the two parties' competing positions) as opposed to competitive or avoidance strategies during the last four minutes of interaction. Highly differentiated individuals generated more complex and specific online plans than did less differentiated persons.

Although these studies suggest that complex and specific plans are advantageous, two qualifications should be noted. Complex plans may be more difficult to implement fluently than simple plans, especially when individuals are pursuing multiple goals and have little opportunity to rehearse in advance (Berger, Karol, & Jordan, 1989; Greene & Lindsey, 1989; Waldron, 1990). Complex/specific plans also may be valued less in collectivist cultures that prefer abstract, long-term plans than in individualistic cultures such as the United States who value short-term, detailed plans (Cai, 1994).

Aside from the structure of plans, Berger and his colleagues have investigated plan adaptation. Berger, Knowlton, and Abrahams (1996) propose a *hierarchy hypothesis*, which states that individuals are more likely to alter concrete, lower level plan elements rather than abstract, higher level elements after encountering initial goal failure, since the latter type of alterations require more cognitive resources. This hypothesis has been tested in a series of studies in which participants have given another individual (a confederate) directions to a local landmark, after which the confederate states that she or he did not understand the directions and asks the participant to repeat them. During their second attempt, participants might change their initial plan at the highest level of abstraction (e.g., describe an entirely different route to the location), at a moderate level of abstraction (e.g., describe the same route again but add more landmarks along the way), or at the lowest level (e.g., repeat the same instructions nearly verbatim while speaking more loudly/slowly). Consistent with the hierarchy hypothesis, participants are most likely to change lower level plan elements rather than higher level elements, even when the direction seeker (confederate) obviously should be able to comprehend the participant's initial speed and volume (Berger & diBattista, 1993). In addition, participants display more signs of cognitive overload (e.g., pauses) if they specifically are asked to provide a new route (a higher level change) rather than simply to repeat the directions while speaking more slowly (Berger et al., 1996). Although not focused on persuasive message per se, these studies provide one account for why message sources may continue repeating the same influence strategies even after encountering resistance from targets.

Aside from plans/planning, Greene's (1984, 1995a) action-assembly theory (AAT) also provides insights about the procedural knowledge underlying message production. AAT adopts an associative network model of procedural memory, in which the basic unit is the "procedural record." Each record is a modular unit of nodes and associative links that stores representations of an action, outcomes associated with the action, and situational features relevant to the action. Procedural records represent knowledge at varying levels of abstraction, from interaction strategies for accomplishing goals (e.g., threaten, ingratiate), to devices for maintaining/changing topics coherently, semantic/syntactic choices and constraints, and even motor commands for producing sounds.

Two processes operate on this associative network. Procedural records are *activated* when goals/situational features represented in the records match those perceived in the current situation. Activation occurs in parallel across levels of abstraction, and makes few demands on cognitive resources. Once activated, procedural records at various levels must be *assembled* into a coherent representation of action. Assembly occurs in a serial fashion, with records at higher levels of abstraction placing loose constraints on which records are permissible at lower levels. Because of this, assembly places heavy demands on cognitive resources, which in turn is evident in temporal features of speech (e.g., latencies, disfluencies). Two conditions minimize the demands of assembly. If individuals have employed the same action frequently in the past to accomplish a goal, then records from various levels of abstraction may be associated and stored together as a *unitized assembly* that can be implemented immediately in the future. Alternatively, if individuals have an opportunity to plan prior to interaction, they may be able to assemble at least the abstract levels of their actions beforehand.

In a series of studies, Greene and his colleagues have applied AAT to understand the production of multiple-goal messages (e.g., Greene & Lindsey, 1989; Greene & Ravizza, 1995; Lindsey, Greene, Parker, & Sassi, 1995;

see also, Greene, 1995b). In each of these studies, participants have been faced with the task of delivering bad news (e.g., a poor performance review, a rejected application for an internship) to an imaginary target. Participants in the single-goal condition have been instructed to be "as clear and direct" as possible in explaining why the target did not succeed, whereas those in the multiple-goal condition have been instructed to be "clear and direct" but also to show "concern for [the target's] feelings and self-esteem." These studies have produced several results consistent with AAT predictions, including that: (a) people in general are less fluent when producing multiple-goal rather than single-goal messages; (b) people produce longer messages and more sociocentric sequences (e.g., "you know, "well") when pursuing multiple rather than single goals; (c) opportunities for advance planning reduce the demands made by multiple goals; and (d) differences between multiple- and single-goal messages reflect cognitive demands rather than social, strategic uses of pauses. Based on careful analyses of onset-latencies and speech hesitations, Greene (1995b) argues that multiple-goal messages are less fluent for two reasons: They require individuals to assemble actions for pursuing one goal that are incompatible with actions for pursuing the second goal, and to formulate/maintain in memory output representations that contain greater quantities of information. Although these studies have not focused specifically on the production of persuasive messages, they have obvious relevance since individuals also commonly pursue multiple goals as they seek/resist compliance.

Rational Models of Message Design

According to O'Keefe (1992, in press), rational models of message design focus on the relationship between message form (e.g., linguistic forms, content themes) and function (e.g., meanings, effects). Rational models presume that speakers attempt to utilize available linguistic resources to manage situationally relevant objectives. In developing rational models, scholars attempt to explain variations in persuasive messages by identifying and recreating shared systems of means–ends reasoning.

Brown and Levinson's (1978) theory of politeness is one example of a rational model. They argue that individuals in all cultures share two basic wants: the desire to be approved of by significant others (positive face), and the desire to be autonomous from unnecessary constraint (negative face). Given the interdependent nature of social relations, individuals have motives to support their partner's face as well as their own face. In the course of pursuing their own aims, however, individuals inevitably perform acts that threaten face (FTAs). Asking a friend for help with homework constrains the friend's use of time; asking a fellow group member to redo his or her part of a project threatens that person's desires for both approval and autonomy (Wilson, Kim, & Meischke, 1991/1992).

According to politeness theory, individuals can exploit two linguistic forms to minimize threats to face: indirectness and redressive action. Indirectness occurs when a speaker says something that (given the circumstances) implies a different or additional meaning. Rather than asking a friend for help with homework directly, a student might exclaim "I don't think I'll ever understand this calculus assignment." By requesting assistance "off-record," the speaker gives the friend the options of offering to help or of strategically hearing the indirect request as merely an expression of frustration. Although indirectness provides the message target more choices, its drawback is that the target may not even recognize that the speaker is requesting help. Indirectness is hence more polite, but less efficient, than making the request "on-record."

When speakers do perform FTAs on record, they still can minimize face threat with redressive action. Redressive actions include accounts, apologies, compliments, downgrades, in-group markers, and other linguistic forms that minimize or compensate for threats to the hearer's desires for approval and/or autonomy. Rather than simply saying "Hey Chris, help me with my calculus homework," a speaker might say "Hey Chris, buddy, I know that you're busy, but is there any way you could spare a few minutes to help me with my calculus homework? I'd really appreciate it." On-record requests without redress are to the point but less polite, whereas on-record requests that include redress are more polite but less efficient.

In sum, Brown and Levinson (1978) claim that politeness forms reflect a speaker's relative concerns about being clear/efficient versus supportive of face. Although specific assumptions of politeness theory have been criticized (e.g., Craig, Tracy & Spisak, 1986; Kellermann & Shea, 1996; Lim, 1990b; Wilson et al., 1991/1992), the theory offers a plausible account for cross-cultural similarities in a wide range of linguistic forms that occur during influence interactions.

B. O'Keefe's (1988, 1990, 1991) theory of message design logics is a second example of a rational model. Based on message features present within persuasive situations, O'Keefe argues for the existence of three distinct "design logics" or systems of beliefs about the functions and coherence of communication. Individuals using an *expressive* design logic: view "saying what's on one's mind" as the primary function of communication; value clear, open, and honest communication; focus temporally on the past; and often generate persuasive messages with content that is "pragmatically pointless" to the influence goal defining the current context. Individuals using a *conventional* design logic: view communication as a "game" in which interactants coordinate their own and their partner's goals by adhering to predefined rules or expectations; value messages that are socially appropriate; focus temporally on the present; and often mention rights and obligations arising from each party's role within their persuasive messages. Individuals using a *rhetorical* design logic: view communication as the process by which interactants create and negotiate selves and situations; see context as a resource that can be exploited to help coordinate their own and their partner's goals; value psychologically centered and flexible messages; focus temporally on the future; and often clarify identities, suggest plans, and make classically "rational" arguments in their persuasive messages.

O'Keefe (1988, 1991, in press) argues that each design logic provides the message source additional options for managing goal conflict: expressives are limited by two choices (say it or don't say it); conventionals can follow the rules for using redressive action as well as choosing to not say the FTA; and rhetoricals can redefine the current reality as well as using redressive actions within the current situation. Consistent with this reasoning, research has found that persuasive/regulative messages displaying the rhetorical design logic are evaluated at least equally effective at accomplishing the influence goal and more effective at accomplishing secondary goals than are expressive and conventional messages (Bingham & Burleson, 1989; O'Keefe & McCornack, 1987; O'Keefe & Shepherd, 1987). Gender and interpersonal construct differentiation have been associated with likelihood of producing persuasive messages displaying the rhetorical design logic (O'Keefe, 1988; O'Keefe & Shepherd, 1987).

In sum, rational models of message design are systems of means–ends reasoning, constructed by scholars, to explain observed relationships between message forms and functions. Although O'Keefe (1988) originally described a design logic as "a constellation of related beliefs" about communication (p. 84) and stated that they "guided message construction and interpretation" (p. 81), in more recent writings she has clarified that message design logics are not intended literally as psychological descriptions of the message production process (see O'Keefe, 1992, in press). She argues that rational models "can be empirical without being cognitive" (1992, p. 643) because they make claims about variations in persuasive messages and their effects that can be assessed independent of cognitive processes. O'Keefe (1992, p. 643) claims that rational models are better thought of as models of communicative competence, where a competence model "specifies what a system is able (or expected) to do; it describes performance in terms of its relationship to [situationally relevant] goals" (p. 643).

O'Keefe (1992) also recognizes, however, that communicative competence has cognitive foundations. Recently, O'Keefe and Lambert (1995) have offered a psychological model that views message production as "the local management of the flow of thought—both the management of thoughts by the producer and the management of the other's thoughts in the service of communicative goals" (p. 55). Although I do not describe their "local management" approach in detail, its assumptions differ markedly from the work on plans/planning and action assembly theory described earlier. One challenge for O'Keefe and Lambert will be to clarify how individual differences known to affect the production of persuasive messages (e.g., interpersonal construct differentiation) are reflected in their model (see Hewes, 1995).

In this section, I have reviewed five lines of scholarship conducted since the mid-1980s and argued that they constitute a second generation of research on persuasive message production. Although diverse, these five lines of research share a common focus on interaction goals: how individuals define situations and organize knowledge around influence goals; how multiple goals shape and constrain influence attempts; how interaction goals get formed; how individuals utilize procedural knowledge to pursue influence goals; and how the message form-function relationship can be understood in terms of systems of means–ends reasoning for accomplishing goals. In my final section, I look to the future. How will current theories of persuasive message production fare? If "strategy selection" and "goal pursuit" have been defining metaphors for the first two generations of research, what metaphor will define the "next generation"? I do not propose direct answers to these questions, since my ill-fated predictions would be especially apparent to future readers. Rather, I close by posing four challenges for our current theories of persuasive message production.

CHALLENGES FOR THE "NEXT GENERATION"

Theories that cast persuasive message production as goal pursuit are sufficiently mature to identify four general concerns about their utility. I pose each as a question.

Can we develop "comprehensive" theories of persuasive message production? By comprehensive, I mean theories that account for variation in a wide range message features present within influence interactions. Critiques of the "strategy typology" approach to message analysis have made it painfully clear that numerous features of persuasive messages may be of interest (Kellermann & Cole, 1994; D. O'Keefe, 1990, 1994). As noted earlier, researchers have examined whether message sources (and to a lesser extent targets): are direct/indirect, make simple requests or include reasoning, frame reasoning from their own or the other party's perspective, exert strong pressure and use antisocial appeals to gain/resist compliance, and so on. Researchers have explored microlinguistic decisions such as verb choice, and paraverbal features of persuasive messages. Researchers also have moved beyond single turns to examine persistence and sequencing of compliance-gaining/resisting strategies.

This vast array of message features raises two issues. First, which features of persuasive messages merit attention? Boster (1990, 1995) argues that we should determine our focus based on message effects. If particular message features explain whether individuals are appropriate and effective at gaining/resisting compliance within specific contexts, then those features merit attention. Aside from message effects, specific message features might be examined to gain insights about developmental processes or individual/cultural differences. Second, can any single theory of persuasive message production account for variation in all of these message features? I doubt it. Greene's (1984, 1995a) action assembly theory, for example, is among the most comprehensive theories in specifying the role of pragmatic, syntactic, and semantic knowledge during message production, yet it has been criticized for explaining only a narrow range of message features (Hewes, 1995; Waldron, 1995). If multiple theories are needed to explain variation in a wide variety of messages features, then can we integrate insights from multiple (and possibly dissonant) theories to gain a comprehensive understanding of persuasive message production?

Can theories of persuasive message production meld global and context-specific forms of analysis? By global, I mean theories that explain message production across communicative functions and contexts. Berger's (1995) work on plans/planning, Brown and Levinson's (1978) politeness theory, Greene's (1984) action assembly theory, Kellermann's (1992) analysis of metagoals, O'Keefe's (1988) theory of message design logics, and Wilson's (1990) cognitive rules model all are global theories in this sense. Yet people do not produce persuasive messages in a vacuum, but rather within particular task and relational contexts. The work on influence goals reviewed earlier illustrates that people share different expectations about asking favors, giving advice, enforcing obligations, and so forth. People also share expectations about what types of requests are "reasonable" within friendships versus family relationships (Rawlins, 1992), and about how requests should be justified or resisted when directed to close friends versus acquaintances (Ifert & Roloff, 1994; Roloff, Janiszewski, McGrath, Burns, & Manrai, 1988). Detailed analyses of influence episodes within particular task/relational contexts are crucial for global theories, for without such analyses we are left in the dark about how assumptions of global theories apply to particular situations.

Given the importance of context-specific analyses, some scholars have advocated abandoning global theories such as politeness theory altogether (e.g., Tracy & Baratz, 1994). I do not concur. Global and context-specific forms of analysis are complimentary. Global theories highlight similarities across context that otherwise might be missed. Berger's (1995) hierarchy hypothesis, for instance, suggests why parents who are regulating perceived child misbehavior and faculty who are debating academic curriculum both may engage in repetitive argument. Cupach and Metts (1994) offer an interesting melding of global and context-specific forms of analysis. Drawing insights from both politeness theory and typologies of relational disengagement strategies, they analyze why people say what they do to persuade their partner to accept relational redefinition. Although context-specific analyses are vital, persuasive message production will best understood by melding global and specific analyses.

Can we develop theories of persuasive message production that provide insights about interaction? Compliance-gaining/resisting are interactive phenomena; hence, theories of message production must be consistent with known properties of conversation as well as cognition. This point has two implications. First, our descriptions of interpersonal influence episodes should be grounded in interaction. Based on strategy selection models, one might assume that most interpersonal influence episodes display the following pattern: A message source makes a request and possibly supplements it with other compliance-gaining strategies, a target either complies or responds with one or more compliance–resistance strategies, the message source either desists or persists with one or more compliance-gaining strategies, and so forth. In a recent analysis of telephone calls soliciting blood donation, several colleagues and I (Wilson, Levine, Humphreys, & Peters, 1994) found more varied patterns. Participants, who were college students volunteering on behalf of the American Red Cross, telephoned actual prior blood donors and asked them to donate again. After verifying the prior donor's background information, participants initially made a scripted request for repeat donation and then used their own judgment about whether, by what means, and how long to persist in seeking compliance.

After transcribing these calls, we analyzed what prior blood donors (targets) said in the conversational turn immediately following the participant's initial request to donate blood again. Slightly over half of the prior donors (56%) immediately responded "no" to the participant's request, and most (80%) of these donors also provided reasons why they were refusing in the turn immediately after the request. Sixteen percent of prior donors immediately responded with an "unconditional yes" to the participant's request These two sequences fit the pattern implied by strategy selection models. Another 12% of prior donors immediately responded to the participant's request with a "conditional yes," indicating that they would be willing to comply if a stated obstacle (e.g., illness, busy schedule) could be overcome. Rather than choosing either to comply or to use compliance–resistance strategies, targets in this pattern initially responded to requests with elements of both. The final 16% of prior donors did not respond immediately with either "yes" or "no," but instead asked questions such as where and/or when they would donate (i.e., insertion sequences; see Nofsinger, 1991). In some cases, these prior donors used the participant's answers as subsequent grounds for compliance–resistance strategies, but in other cases this last group subsequently agreed to donate again.

In sum, patterns of seeking/resisting compliance are more varied than is implied by strategy selection research. Message targets do not necessarily

choose between "complying" and "using resistance strategies" when responding to requests, and their initial responses may not be either. By
observing compliance gaining/resisting in interaction, we will have a better
understanding of what phenomena our theories of persuasive message production need to explain.

Aside from explaining interaction, theories of persuasive message production also need to work within the constraints of interaction. Message
sources often seek compliance without prior planning, in which case they
have to recall/adapt/implement plans online, within the time constraints of
turn-taking, while producing responses that are relevant to the message
target's reactions (which themselves may be unexpected). Message sources
typically do this while coordinating influence and secondary goals, often
under less than optimal conditions (e.g., fatigue, uncomfortable tempera-
tures). In contrast, participants in the majority of studies reviewed above
have selected preformulated influence strategies or constructed writ-
ten/oral monologues in response to hypothetical scenarios. Waldron (1995;
Waldron & Cegala, 1992) raises legitimate concerns about whether assumptions made by theories of message production tested with strategy selection
or monologue tasks will generalize to naturalistic interaction. At the least,
theories of persuasive message production are most compelling when data
bearing on their claims include studies employing interactive tasks (e.g.,
Berger et al., 1996; O'Keefe & Shepherd, 1987; Wilson et al., 1993).

Because theories of message production need to work within interactive
constraints, Waldron and Cegala (1992) have argued that we should rely
primarily on methods tapping the content of conversational thought online.
I do not agree. Although stimulated recall (e.g., Waldron & Applegate, 1994)
and think-aloud protocols (e.g., Berger, 1995) have provided useful insights,
they provide only a partial picture of persuasive message production. Producing a message involves numerous processes, some which at times are
subject to consciousness and others which almost always occur without
awareness (see Greene, 1984; Kellermann, 1992; Sanders, 1992). Although we
often are aware of (at least some) interaction goals, for instance, processes
that underlie goal formation are affected by stimuli occurring completely
outside of awareness (e.g., "priming" effects, see Wilson, 1990). Given the
complexity of understanding persuasive message production, we need any
method that provides insight about questions of interest.

*Can we account for the role of emotion within persuasive message produc-
tion?* Emotions undoubtedly are an important part of why we say what we
do when we want to influence others. Emotions may be associated with
specific influence goals and hence define situations; emotions may motivate
attempts to seek/resist compliance; emotions may be an activating condition
for procedural knowledge; emotions may affect criteria for using/suppress-
ing arguments; emotions may be aroused by success/failure at gaining/

resisting compliance; and regulating emotions may be a secondary goal during influence interactions (Berger, 1988; Dillard et al., 1989; Dix, 1991). Felt emotions may be expressed verbally/nonverbally during influence interactions; emotional displays may reinforce/compliment compliance-gaining/resisting strategies; norms for displaying emotions may be associated with exerting influence within particular roles; and display rules for emotions during influence episodes may vary across culture/gender (Burgoon, 1994; Sutton, 1991). Despite the sensibility of these claims, we know little about the role of emotion within message production. Dillard and his colleagues (Dillard & Kinney, 1994; Dillard, Palmer, & Kinney, 1995) recently have begun to explore affective reactions to influence attempts, but the task of linking these reactions to what individuals actually say when seeking/resisting compliance still remains. The role of emotion within my own cognitive rules model of interaction goals (Wilson, 1990, 1995) is ill specified.

In posing these four challenges, I do not intend to dampen interest in persuasive message production. Theories of persuasive message production are among the most original developed by communication scholars, focused on a phenomenon with pragmatic implications. These four challenges highlight avenues for future research. Whether these challenges can be addressed by current theories of "goal pursuit" or whether they will lead to a new generation of theories is a question that only time will answer.

REFERENCES

Applegate, J. L. (1980a). Adaptive communication in educational settings: A study of teachers' communicative strategies. *Communication Education, 29,* 158–170.

Applegate, J. L. (1980b). Person- and position-centered communication in a day care center: A case study triangulating interview and naturalistic methods. In N. K. Denzin (Ed.), *Studies in symbolic interaction* (Vol. 3, pp. 59–96). Greenwich, CT: JAI Press.

Applegate, J. L. (1982). The impact of construct system development on communication and impression formation within persuasive contexts. *Communication Monographs, 46,* 231–240.

Applegate, J. L., Burke, J. A., Burleson, B. R., Delia, J. G., & Kline, S. L. (1985). Reflection-enhancing parental communication. In I. E. Sigel (Ed.), *Parental belief systems: The psychological consequences for children* (pp. 107–142). Hillsdale, NJ: Lawrence Erlbaum Associates.

Applegate, J. L., & Woods, E. (1991). Construct system development and attention to face wants in persuasive situations. *Southern Communication Journal, 56,* 194–204.

Berger, C. R. (1988). Planning, affect, and social action generation. In R. L. Donohew, H. Sypher, & E. T. Higgins (Eds.), *Communication, social cognition, and affect* (pp. 93–106). Hillsdale, NJ: Lawrence Erlbaum Associates.

Berger, C. R. (1995). A plan-based approach to strategic communication. In D. E. Hewes (Ed.), *The cognitive bases of interpersonal communication* (pp. 113–140). Hillsdale, NJ: Lawrence Erlbaum Associates.

Berger, C. R., & Bell, R. A. (1988). Plans and the initiation of social relationships. *Human Communication Research, 15,* 217–235.

Berger, C. R., & diBattista, P. (1993). Communication failure and plan adaptation: If at first you don't succeed, say it louder and slower. *Communication Monographs, 60,* 220–238.

Berger, C. R., Karol, S. H., & Jordan, J. M. (1989). When a lot of knowledge is a dangerous thing: The debilitating effects of plan complexity on verbal fluency. *Human Communication Research, 16,* 91–119.

Berger, C. R., Knowlton, S. W., & Abrahams, M. F. (1996). The hierarchy principle in strategic communication. *Communication Theory, 6,* 111–142.

Bingham, S. G., & Burleson, B. R. (1989). Multiple effects of messages with multiple goals: Some perceived outcomes of responses to sexual harassment. *Human Communication Research, 16,* 184–216.

Boster, F. J. (1988). Comments on the utility of compliance gaining message selection tasks. *Human Communication Research, 15,* 166–177.

Boster, F. J. (1990). An examination of the state of compliance-gaining message behavior research. In J. P. Dillard (Ed.), *Seeking compliance: The production of interpersonal influence messages* (pp. 7–17). Scottsdale, AZ: Gorsuch Scarisbrick.

Boster, F. J. (1995). Commentary on compliance-gaining message behavior research. In C. R. Berger & M. Burgoon (Eds.), *Communication and social influence processes* (pp. 91–114). E. Lansing, MI: Michigan State University Press.

Boster, F. J., & Levine, T. (1988). Individual differences and compliance-gaining message selection: The effects of verbal aggressiveness, argumentativeness, dogmatism, and negativism. *Communication Research Reports, 5,* 114–119.

Boster, F. J., Levine, T., & Kazoleas, D. C. (1993). The impact of argumentativeness and verbal aggressiveness on strategic diversity and persistence in compliance gaining behavior. *Communication Quarterly, 41,* 405–414.

Boster, F. J., Stiff, J. B., & Reynolds, R. A. (1985). Do persons respond differently to inductively-derived and deductively-derived lists of compliance-gaining message strategies? A reply to Wiseman and Schenk-Hamlin. *Western Journal of Speech Communication, 19,* 177–187.

Brown, P., & Levinson, S. (1978). Universals in language usage: Politeness phenomena. In E. Goody (Ed.), *Questions and politeness* (pp. 56–311). Cambridge, England: Cambridge University Press.

Burgoon, J. K. (1994). Nonverbal signals. In M. L. Knapp & G. R. Miller (Eds.), *Handbook of interpersonal communication* (Vol. 2, pp. 229–285). Thousand Oaks, CA: Sage.

Burgoon, M., Dillard, J. P., Doran, N., & Miller, M. D. (1982). Cultural and situational influences on the process of persuasive strategy selection. *International Journal of Intercultural Relations, 6,* 85–100.

Burgoon, M., Dillard, J. P., Koper, R., & Doran, N. (1984). The impact of communication context and persuader gender on persuasive message selection. *Women's Studies in Communication, 7,* 1–12.

Burgoon, M., Parrott, R., Burgoon, J. K., Coker, R., Pfau, M., & Birk, T. (1990). Patients' severity of illness, noncompliance, and locus of control and physicians compliance-gaining messages. *Health Communication, 2,* 29–46.

Burke, J. A., & Clark, R. A. (1982). An assessment of methodological options for investigating the development of persuasive communication skills across childhood. *Central States Speech Journal, 33,* 437–445.

Burleson, B. R. (1985). The production of comforting messages: Social-cognitive foundations. *Journal of Language and Social Psychology, 4,* 253–273.

Burleson, B. R. (1987). Cognitive complexity. In J. C. McCroskey & J. A. Daly (Eds.), *Personality and interpersonal communication* (pp. 305–349). Newbury Park, CA: Sage.

Burleson, B. R. (1989). The constructivist approach to person-centered communication: Analysis of a research exemplar. In B. A. Dervin, L. Grossberg, B. J. B. O'Keefe, & E. Wartella (Eds.), *Rethinking communication, Vol. 2: Paradigm exemplars* (pp. 29–46). Newbury Park, CA: Sage.

Burleson, B. R., & Waltman, M. S. (1988). Cognitive complexity: Using the Role Category Questionnaire measure. In C. H. Tardy (Ed.), *A handbook for the study of human communication:*

Methods and instruments for observing, measuring, and assessing communication processes (pp. 1–35). Norwood, NJ: Ablex.

Burleson, B. R., & Wilson, S. R. (1988). On the continued undesirability of item desirability: A reply to Boster, Hunter, and Seibold. *Human Communication Research, 15,* 178–191.

Burleson, B. R., Wilson, S. R., Waltman, M. S., Goering, E. M., Ely, T. K., & Whaley, B. B. (1988). Item desirability effects in compliance-gaining research: Seven studies documenting artifacts in the strategy selection procedure. *Human Communication Research, 14,* 429–486.

Cai, D. (1994). *Planning in negotiation: A comparison of U.S. and Taiwanese cultures.* Unpublished doctoral dissertation, Michigan State University, E. Lansing, MI.

Canary, D. J., Cody, M. J., & Marston, P. (1986). Goal types, compliance-gaining, and locus-of-control. *Journal of Language and Social Psychology, 5,* 249–269.

Cegala, D. J., & Waldron, V. R. (1992). A study of the relationship between communicative performance and conversation participants' thoughts. *Communication Studies, 43,* 105–123.

Clark, R. A., & Delia, J. G. (1976). The development of functional persuasive skills in childhood and early adolescence. *Child Development, 47,* 1008–1014.

Clark, R. A., & Delia, J. G. (1977). Cognitive complexity, social perspective-taking, and functional persuasion skills in second-to-ninth grade children. *Human Communication Research, 3,* 128–134.

Cody, M. J., Canary, D. J., & Smith, S. W. (1994). Compliance-gaining goals: An inductive analysis of actors' goal types, strategies, and success. In J. A. Daly & J. M. Wiemann (Eds.), *Strategic interpersonal communication* (pp. 33–90). Hillsdale, NJ: Lawrence Erlbaum Associates.

Cody, M. J., Greene, J. O., Marston, P. J., O'Hair, H. D., Baaske, K. T., & Schneider, M. J. (1986). Situation perception and strategy selection. In M. L. McLaughlin (Ed.), *Communication yearbook 9* (pp. 391–420). Beverly Hills, CA: Sage.

Cody, M. J., & McLaughlin, M. L. (1980). Perceptions of compliance-gaining situations: A dimensional analysis. *Communication Monographs, 47,* 132–148.

Cody, M. J., McLaughlin, M. L., & Jordan, W. J. (1980). A multidimensional scaling of three sets of compliance-gaining strategies. *Communication Quarterly, 28,* 34–46.

Cody, M. J., McLaughlin, M. L., & Schneider, M. J. (1981). The impact of intimacy and relational consequences on the selection of interpersonal influence messages: A reanalysis. *Communication Quarterly, 29,* 91–106.

Cody, M. J., Woelfel, M. L., & Jordan, W. J. (1983). Dimensions of compliance-gaining situations. *Human Communication Research, 9,* 99–113.

Craig, R. T., Tracy, K., & Spisak, F. (1986). The discourse of requests: Assessment of a politeness approach. *Human Communication Research, 12,* 437–468.

Cupach, W. R., & Metts, S. (1994). *Facework.* Thousand Oaks, CA: Sage.

Dallinger, J. M., & Hample, D. (1994). The effects of gender on compliance gaining strategy endorsement and suppression. *Communication Reports, 7,* 43–49.

Delia, J. G., & Clark, R. A. (1977). Cognitive complexity, social perception, and the development of listener-adapted communication in six-, eight-, ten-, and twelve-year-old boys. *Communication Monographs, 44,* 326–345.

Delia, J. G., Kline, S. L., & Burleson, B. R. (1979). The development of persuasive communication strategies in kindergartners through twelfth-graders. *Communication Monographs, 46,* 241–256.

deTurck, M. A. (1985). A transactional analysis of compliance-gaining behavior: Effects of noncompliance, relational contexts, and actors' gender. *Human Communication Research, 12,* 54–78.

deTurck, M. A., & Miller, G. R. (1982). The effect of birth order on the persuasive impact of messages and the likelihood of persuasive message selection. *Communication, 11,* 78–84.

deTurck, M. A., & Miller, G. R. (1983). Adolescent perceptions of parental persuasive message strategies. *Journal of Marriage and the Family, 45,* 543–552.

Dillard, J. P. (1988). Compliance-gaining message selection: What is our dependent variable? *Communication Monographs, 55,* 162–183.

Dillard, J. P. (1989). Types of influence goals in personal relationships. *Journal of Social and Personal Relationships, 6,* 293–308.

Dillard, J. P. (Ed.). (1990a). *Seeking compliance: The production of interpersonal influence messages.* Scottsdale, AZ: Gorsuch Scarisbrick.

Dillard, J. P. (1990b). A goal-driven model of interpersonal influence. In J. P. Dillard (Ed.), *Seeking compliance: The production of interpersonal influence messages* (pp. 41–57). Scottsdale, AZ: Gorsuch Scarisbrick.

Dillard, J. P., & Burgoon, M. (1985). Situational influences on the selection of compliance-gaining messages: Two tests of the predictive utility of the Cody-McLaughlin typology. *Communication Monographs, 52,* 289–304.

Dillard, J. P., & Kinney, T. A. (1994). Experiential and physiological responses to interpersonal influence. *Human Communication Research, 20,* 502–528.

Dillard, J. P., Palmer, M. T., & Kinney, T. A. (1995). Relational judgments in an influence context. *Human Communication Research, 21,* 331–353.

Dillard, J. P., Segrin, C., & Harden, J. M. (1989). Primary and secondary goals in the production of interpersonal influence messages. *Communication Monographs, 56,* 19–38.

Dix, T. (1991). The affective organization of parenting: Adaptive and maladaptive processes. *Psychological Bulletin, 110,* 3–25.

Edgar, T., & Fitzpatrick, M. A. (1988). Compliance-gaining in relational interaction: When your life depends on it. *Southern Speech Communication Journal, 53,* 385–405.

Falbo, T., & Peplau, L. A. (1980). Power strategies in intimate relationships. *Journal of Personality and Social Psychology, 38,* 618–628.

Francik, E. P., & Clark, H. H. (1985). How to make requests that overcome obstacles to compliance. *Journal of Memory and Language, 25,* 181–196.

Gastil, J. (1995). An appraisal and revision of the constructivist research program. In B. R. Burleson (Ed.), *Communication yearbook 18* (pp. 83–104). Thousand Oaks, CA: Sage.

Goffman, E. (1959). *The presentation of self in everyday life.* New York: Doubleday.

Greene, J. O. (1984). A cognitive approach to human communication: An action assembly theory. *Communication Monographs, 51,* 289–306.

Greene, J. O. (1990). Tactical social action: Towards some strategies for theory. In M. J. Cody & M. L. McLaughlin (Eds.), *The psychology of tactical communication* (pp. 31–47). Clevedon, Avon, England: Multilingual Matters.

Greene, J. O. (1995a). An action-assembly perspective on verbal and nonverbal message production: A dancer's message unveiled. In D. E. Hewes (Ed.), *The cognitive bases of interpersonal communication* (pp. 51–86). Hillsdale, NJ: Lawrence Erlbaum Associates.

Greene, J. O. (1995b). Production of messages in pursuit of multiple social goals: Action assembly theory contributions to the study of cognitive encoding processes. In B. R. Burleson (Ed.), *Communication yearbook 18* (pp. 26–53). Thousand Oaks, CA: Sage.

Greene, J. O., & Lindsey, A. E. (1989). Encoding processes in the production of multiple-goals messages. *Human Communication Research, 16,* 120–140.

Greene, J. O., & Ravizza, S. M. (1995). Complexity effects on the temporal characteristics of speech. *Human Communication Research, 21,* 390–421.

Hample, D., & Dallinger, J. M. (1987). Individual differences in cognitive editing standards. *Human Communication Research, 14,* 123–144.

Hample, D., & Dallinger, J. M. (1988). Self-monitoring and the cognitive editing of arguments. *Central States Speech Journal, 14,* 152–165.

Hample, D., & Dallinger, J. M. (1990). Arguers as editors. *Argumentation, 4,* 153–169.

Hewes, D. E. (1995). Cognitive interpersonal communication research: Some thoughts on criteria. In B. R. Burleson (Ed.), *Communication yearbook 18* (pp. 162–179). Thousand Oaks, CA: Sage.

Hirokowa, R. Y., & Miyahara, A. (1986). A comparison of influence strategies utilized by managers in American and Japanese organizations. *Communication Quarterly, 34,* 250–265.

Hunter, J. E. (1988). Failure of the social desirability response set hypothesis. *Human Communication Research, 15,* 162–168.

Hunter, J. E., & Boster, F. J. (1987). A model of compliance-gaining message selection. *Communication Monographs, 54,* 63–84.

Ifert, D. E., & Roloff, M. E. (1994). Anticipated obstacles to compliance: Predicting their presence and expression. *Communication Studies, 45,* 120–130.

Javidi, M. N., Jordan, W. J., & Carlone, D. (1994). Situational influences on the selection or avoidance of compliance-gaining strategies: A test of motivation to communicate. *Communication Research Reports, 11,* 127–134.

Kearney, P., & Plax, T. (1987). Situational and individual determinants of teachers' reported use of behavior alteration techniques. *Human Communication Research, 14,* 145–166.

Kearney, P., Plax, T., Richmond, V. P., & McCroskey, J. C. (1985). Power in the classroom III: Teacher communication techniques and messages. *Communication Education, 34,* 19–28.

Kellermann, K. (1992). Communication: Inherently strategic and primarily automatic. *Communication Monographs, 59,* 288–300.

Kellermann, K., & Cole, T. (1994). Classifying compliance gaining messages: Taxonomic disorder and strategic confusion. *Communication Theory, 4,* 3–60.

Kellermann, K., & Kim, M. S. (1991, May). *Working within constraints: Tactical choices in the pursuit of social goals.* Paper presented at the annual meeting of the International Communication Association, Miami.

Kellermann, K., & Shea, B. C. (1996). Threats, suggestions, hints, and promises: Gaining compliance efficiently and politely. *Communication Quarterly, 44,* 145–165.

Kipnis, D., Schmidt, S. M., & Wilkinson, I. (1980). Intraorganizational influence tactics: Explorations in getting one's way. *Journal of Applied Psychology, 65,* 440–452.

Kim, M. S. (1994). Cross-cultural comparisons of the perceived importance of conversational constraints. *Human Communication Research, 21,* 128–151.

Kim, M. S., & Wilson, S. R. (1994). A cross-cultural comparison of implicit theories of requesting. *Communication Monographs, 61,* 210–235.

Kline, S. L., & Ceropski, J. M. (1984). Person-centered communication in medical practice. In J. T. Wood & G. M. Phillips (Eds.), *Human decision-making* (pp. 120–141). Carbondale, IL: Southern Illinois University Press.

Kline, S. L., & Floyd, C. H. (1990). On the art of saying no: The influence of social cognitive development on messages of refusal. *Western Journal of Speech Communication, 54,* 454–472.

Krone, K. J. (1992). A comparison of organizational, structural, and relationship effects on subordinates' upward influence choices. *Communication Quarterly, 40,* 1–15.

Lamude, K. G., Daniels, T. D., & White, K. D. (1987). Managing the boss: Locus of control and subordinates' selection of compliance-gaining strategies in upward communication. *Management Communication Quarterly, 1,* 232–259.

Leichty, G., & Applegate, J. L. (1991). Social-cognitive and situational influences on face-saving in persuasive messages. *Human Communication Research, 17,* 451–484.

Lim, T. S. (1990a). The influence of receivers' resistance on persuaders' verbal aggressiveness. *Communication Quarterly, 38,* 170–188.

Lim, T. S. (1990b). Politeness behavior in social influence situations. In J. P. Dillard (Ed.), *Seeking compliance: The production of interpersonal influence messages* (pp. 75–86). Scottsdale, AZ: Gorsuch Scarisbrick.

Lindsey, A. E., Greene, J. O., Parker, R. A., & Sassi, M. (1995). Effects of advance message formulation on message encoding: Evidence of cognitively based hesitation in the production of multiple-goal messages. *Communication Quarterly, 43,* 320–331.

Littlejohn, S. (1992). *Theories of human communication* (4th ed.). Belmont, CA: Wadsworth.

Lustig, M., & King, S. (1980). The effects of communication apprehension and situation on communication strategy choices. *Human Communication Research, 7,* 74–82.

Marwell, G, & Schmitt, D. R. (1967). Dimensions of compliance-gaining behavior: An empirical analysis. *Sociometry, 30,* 350–364.

McCall, G. J., & Simmons, J. L. (1978). *Identities and interactions* (Rev. ed.). New York: Free Press.

McLaughlin, M. L., Cody, M. J., & Robey, C. S. (1980). Situational influences on the selection of strategies to resist compliance-gaining attempts. *Human Communication Research, 7,* 14–36.

McQuillen, J. S. (1986). The development of listener-adapted compliance-resistance strategies. *Human Communication Research, 12,* 359–375.

McQuillen, J. S., & Higginbotham, D. C. (1985). Children's reasoning about compliance-resistance behaviors: The effects of age, agent, and type of requests. In R. N. Bostrom (Ed.), *Communication yearbook 9* (pp. 673–690). Beverly Hills, CA: Sage.

Meyer, J. R. (1990). Cognitive processes underlying the retrieval of compliance-gaining strategies: An implicit rules model. In J. P. Dillard (Ed.), *Seeking compliance: The production of interpersonal influence messages* (pp. 57–74). Scottsdale, AZ: Gorsuch Scarisbrick.

Meyer, J. R. (1994). Formulating plans for requests: An investigation of retrieval processes. *Communication Studies, 45,* 131–144.

Miller, G. R. (1990). Final considerations. In J. P. Dillard (Ed.), *Seeking compliance: The production of interpersonal influence messages* (pp. 189–200). Scottsdale, AZ: Gorsuch Scarisbrick.

Miller, G. R., Boster, F. J., Roloff, M. E., & Seibold, D. (1977). Compliance-gaining message strategies: A typology and some findings concerning effects of situational differences. *Communication Monographs, 44,* 37–51.

Miller, G. R., Boster, F. J., Roloff, M. E., & Seibold, D. (1987). MBRS rekindled: Some thoughts on compliance gaining in interpersonal settings. In M. E. Roloff & G. R. Miller (Eds.), *Interpersonal processes: New directions in communication research* (pp. 89–117). Newbury Park, CA: Sage.

Miller, G. R., & Burgoon, M. (1978). Persuasion research: Review and commentary. In B. Rubin (Ed.), *Communication yearbook 2* (pp. 29–47). New Brunswick, NJ: Transaction.

Miller, G. R., & Steinberg, M. (1975). *Between people: A new analysis of interpersonal communication.* Chicago: Science Research Associates.

Nofsinger, R. E. (1991). *Everyday conversation.* Newbury Park, CA: Sage.

O'Hair, M. J., Cody, M. J., & O'Hair, D. (1991). The impact of situational dimensions on compliance-resistance strategies: A comparison of methods. *Communication Quarterly, 39,* 226–240.

O'Keefe, B. J. (1988). The logic of message design. *Communication Monographs, 55,* 80–103.

O'Keefe, B. J. (1990). The logic of regulative communication: Understanding the rationality of message designs. In J. P. Dillard (Ed.), *Seeking compliance: The production of interpersonal influence messages* (pp. 87–106). Scottsdale, AZ: Gorsuch Scarisbrick.

O'Keefe, B. J. (1991). Message design logic and the management of multiple goals. In K. Tracy (Ed.), *Understanding face-to-face interaction: Issues linking goals and discourse* (pp. 131–150). Hillsdale, NJ: Lawrence Erlbaum Associates.

O'Keefe, B. J. (1992). Developing and testing rational models of message design. *Human Communication Research, 18,* 637–649.

O'Keefe, B. J. (in press). Variation, adaptation, and functional explanation in the study of message design. In G. Philipsen & T. Albrecht (Eds.), *Developing theories of communication.* Albany, NY: SUNY Press.

O'Keefe, B. J., & Delia, J. G. (1979). Construct comprehensiveness and cognitive complexity as predictors of the number and strategic adaptation of arguments and appeals in a persuasive message. *Communication Monographs, 46,* 231–240.

O'Keefe, B. J., & Delia, J. G. (1982). Impression formation and message production. In M. E. Roloff & C. R. Berger (Ed.), *Social cognition and communication* (pp. 33–72). Beverly Hills, CA: Sage.

O'Keefe, B. J., & Lambert, B. L. (1995). Managing the flow of ideas: A local management approach to message design. In B. R. Burleson (Ed.), *Communication yearbook 18* (pp. 54–82). Thousand Oaks, CA: Sage.

O'Keefe, B. J., & McCornack, S. A. (1987). Message design logic and message goal structure: Effects on perceptions of message quality in regulative communication situations. *Human Communication Research, 14*, 68–92.

O'Keefe, B. J., & Shepherd, G. J. (1987). The pursuit of multiple objectives in face-to-face persuasive interaction: Effects of construct differentiation. *Communication Monographs, 54*, 396–419.

O'Keefe, D. J. (1990). *Persuasion: Theory and research*. Newbury Park, CA: Sage.

O'Keefe, D. J. (1994). From strategy-based to feature-based analyses of compliance-gaining message classification and production. *Communication Theory, 4*, 61–68.

Rawlins, W. K. (1992). *Friendship matters: Communication, dialectics, and the life course*. New York: Adline de Gruyter.

Roloff, M. E., & Barnicott, E. (1978). The situational use of pro- and anti-social compliance-gaining strategies by high and low Machiavellians. In B. Ruben (Ed.), *Communication yearbook 2* (pp. 193–208). New Brunswick, NJ: Transaction.

Roloff, M. E., & Barnicott, E. (1979). The influence of dogmatism on the situational use of pro- and anti-social compliance-gaining strategies. *Southern Speech Communication Journal, 45*, 37–54.

Roloff, M. E., & Janiszewski, C. A. (1989). Overcoming obstacles to interpersonal compliance: A principle of message construction. *Human Communication Research, 16*, 33–59.

Roloff, M. E., Janiszewski, C. A., McGrath, M. A., Burns, C. S., & Manrai, L. A. (1988). Acquiring resources from intimates: When obligation substitutes for persuasion. *Human Communication Research, 14*, 364–396.

Rule, B. G., Bisanz, G. L., & Kohn, M. (1985). Anatomy of a persuasion scheme: Targets, goals, and strategies. *Journal of Personality and Social Psychology, 48*, 1127–1140.

Saeki, M., & O'Keefe, B. J. (1994). Refusals and rejections: Designing messages to serve multiple goals. *Human Communication Research, 21*, 67–102.

Sanders, R. E. (1991). The two-way relationship between talk in social interaction and actors' goals and plans. In K. Tracy (Ed.), *Understanding face-to-face interaction: Issues linking goals and discourse* (pp. 167–181). Hillsdale, NJ: Lawrence Erlbaum Associates.

Sanders, R. E. (1992). Conversation, computation, and the human factor. *Human Communication Research, 18*, 623–636.

Schenk-Hamlin, W. J., Wiseman, R. L, & Georgacarakos, G. N. (1982). A model of properties of compliance-gaining strategies. *Communication Quarterly, 32*, 92–100.

Seibold, D. R. (1988). A response to "Item Desirability in Compliance-gaining Research." *Human Communication Research, 15*, 152–161.

Seibold, D. R., Cantrill, J. G., & Meyers, R. A. (1985). Communication and interpersonal influence. In M. L. Knapp & G. R. Miller (Eds.), *Handbook of interpersonal communication* (pp. 551–614). Beverly Hills, CA: Sage.

Seibold, D. R., Cantrill, J. G., & Meyers, R. A. (1994). Communication and interpersonal influence. In M. L. Knapp & G. R. Miller (Eds.), *Handbook of interpersonal communication* (Vol. 2, pp. 542–588). Thousand Oaks, CA: Sage.

Sillars, A. L. (1980). The stranger and spouse as target persons for compliance-gaining strategies: A subjective utility model. *Human Communication Research, 6*, 265–279.

Smith, S. W., Cody, M. J., LoVette, S., & Canary, D. J. (1990). Self-monitoring, gender, and compliance-gaining goals. In M. J. Cody & M. L. McLaughlin (Ed.), *The psychology of tactical communication* (pp. 91–135). Clevedon, Avon, England: Multilingual Matters.

Sorenson, G., Plax, T., & Kearney, P. (1989). The strategy selection-construction controversy: A coding scheme for analyzing teacher compliance-gaining message constructions. *Communication Education, 38*, 102–118.

Sutton, R. I. (1991). Maintaining norms about expressed emotions: The case of bill collectors. *Administrative Science Quarterly, 36*, 245–268.

Tracy, K., & Baratz, S. (1994). The case for case studies of facework. In S. Ting-Toomey (Ed.), *The challenge of facework: Cross-cultural and interpersonal implications* (pp. 287–306). Albany, NY: SUNY Press.

Tracy, K., Craig, R. T., Smith, M., & Spisak, F. (1984). The discourse of requests: Assessment of a compliance-gaining approach. *Human Communication Research, 10,* 513–538.

Waldron, V. R. (1990). Constrained rationality: Situational influences on information acquisition plans and tactics. *Communication Monographs, 57,* 184–201.

Waldron, V. R. (1995). Is the "golden age of cognition" losing its luster? Toward a requirement-centered perspective. In B. R. Burleson (Ed.), *Communication yearbook 18* (pp. 180–200). Thousand Oaks, CA: Sage.

Waldron, V. R., & Applegate, J. L. (1994). Interpersonal construct differentiation and conversational planning: An examination of two cognitive accounts for the production of competent verbal disagreement tactics. *Human Communication Research, 21,* 3–35.

Waldron, V. R., & Cegala, D. J. (1992). Assessing conversational cognition: Levels of cognitive theory and associated methodological requirements. *Human Communication Research, 18,* 599–622.

Waltman, M. S. (1994). An assessment of the convergent validity of the checklist of behavior alteration techniques: The association between teachers' likelihood-of-use ratings and informants' frequency-of-use ratings. *Journal of Applied Communication Research, 22,* 295–308.

Waltman, M. S. (1995). An assessment of the discriminant validity of the checklist of behavior alteration techniques: A test of the item desirability bias in prospective and experienced teachers' likelihood-of-use ratings. *Journal of Applied Communication Research, 23,* 201–211.

Wheeless, L. R., Barraclough, R., & Stewart, R. (1983). Compliance-gaining and power in persuasion. In R. Bostrom (Ed.), *Communication yearbook 7* (pp. 105–145). Beverly Hills, CA: Sage.

Wilson, S. R. (1990). Development and test of a cognitive rules model of interaction goals. *Communication Monographs, 57,* 81–103.

Wilson, S. R. (1995). Elaborating the cognitive rules model of interaction goals: The problem of accounting for individual differences in goal formation. In B. R. Burleson (Ed.), *Communication yearbook 18* (pp. 3–25). Thousand Oaks, CA: Sage.

Wilson, S. R., Aleman, C., & Leathem, G. (in press). Identity implications of influence goals: A revised analysis of face-threatening acts and applications to seeking compliance with same-sex friends. *Human Communication Research.*

Wilson, S. R., Cruz, M. G., & Kang, K. H. (1992). Is it always a matter of perspective? Construct differentiation and variability in attributions about compliance gaining. *Communication Monographs, 59,* 350–367.

Wilson, S. R., Cruz, M. G., Marshall, L. J., & Rao, N. (1993). An attributional analysis of compliance-gaining interactions. *Communication Monographs, 60,* 352–372.

Wilson, S. R., & Kang, K. H. (1991). Communication and unfulfilled obligations: Individual differences in causal judgments. *Communication Research, 18,* 799–824.

Wilson, S. R., Kim, M. S., & Meischke, H. (1991/1992). Evaluating Brown and Levinson's politeness theory: A revised analysis of directives and face. *Research on Language and Social Interaction, 25,* 215–252.

Wilson, S. R., Levine, K., Humphreys, L., & Peters, H. (1994, November). *Seeking and resisting compliance: Strategies and sequences in telephone solicitations for blood donation.* Paper presented to the annual meeting of the Speech Communication Association, New Orleans.

Wilson, S. R., & Putnam, L. L. (1990). Interaction goals in negotiation. In J. A. Anderson (Ed.), *Communication yearbook 13* (pp. 374–406). Newbury Park, CA: Sage.

Wiseman, R. L., & Schenk-Hamlin, W. (1981). A multidimensional scaling validation of an inductively-derived set of compliance-gaining strategies. *Communication Monographs, 48,* 251–270.

II

INTRAINDIVIDUAL COHERENCE AND COORDINATION

3

EXPLICATING THE GOAL CONSTRUCT: TOOLS FOR THEORISTS

James Price Dillard
University of Wisconsin-Madison

Why do people produce messages? Although one can conceive of many possible answers to this question, Berlo (1960) made an especially succinct and compelling reply: "to communicate is to influence with intent" (p. 128). From his perspective, people create messages in order to achieve some end. Communication is strategic, motivated, and purposive. Very much in line with this thinking is the notion that message production is the result of a goal-driven process.

In the past decade, we have witnessed a landslide of work attesting to the importance of the goal construct in theories of communication. Some scholars have oriented their effort toward illuminating the nature (Craig, 1986) or the substance of goals (Cody, Canary, & Smith, 1994). Others have studied the operation of goals in contexts such as bargaining and negotiation (Donohue & Diez, 1985; Wilson & Putnam, 1990), conversational retreat (Kellermann, Reynolds, & Chen, 1991), and interpersonal influence (Dillard, 1990; Wilson, 1990). Questions concerning how goals interact with one another to shape message output has also generated considerable interest (Bingham & Burleson, 1989; Greene & Lindsey, 1989; Tracy, 1984; see also Wilson, chap. 2, this volume).

While this accelerating level of research activity signals consensus on the *utility* of the goal construct, it is increasingly apparent that consensus does not extend to a *definition* of the goal construct. With the appearance of each new article, it is possible to see some tacit twist on the basic idea, some additional assumption, some implicit adaptation to the particulars of a specific area of inquiry. Each of these theoretical mutations has the potential to strengthen our theories and our research. But, as new subspecies of the goal construct proliferate we need to be aware of the similarities and differences among them if we are to make informed choices.

My aim in this chapter is to articulate some of the theoretical issues that must be confronted by anyone working with the goal construct. A genuinely thorough analysis of these issues would require a book-length manuscript. Consequently, I have limited my focus to those concerns that I see as fundamental in the sense that they should be addressed before more sophisticated theorizing can proceed.

I hope that the distinctions I have drawn out might be useful tools for those interested in theorizing about goal-directed communication behavior. Accordingly, the approach I've taken is more analytic than argumentative. Rather than advocate the superiority of any particular position, I have presented a reasonably balanced account of some of the conceptual choice-points associated with the goal construct. Given the biases that accrue from my own choices, this manuscript probably fails to achieve a balance that is satisfactory to all. Nonetheless, some understanding of the choice-points in goal theorizing is important. Those decisions will determine how one's research should proceed while simultaneously delimiting what *can be* found. Making an informed selection from the array of alternatives requires that we be explicit about the consequences of that choice. For the most part, the consequences boil down to one overarching question: Is the definition useful? Although there are many features that a construct should possess before it can be judged useful (e.g., Miller & Nicholson, 1976; Smith, 1988), only a subset of them are needed for the current analysis. A brief exposition of those criteria is given next.

CRITERIA FOR EVALUATING
A CONCEPTUAL DEFINITION

One desirable feature of a constitutive definition is *clarity of delineation*. A useful definition is one that plainly denotes the essential features of the construct. Equally important, it must make clear those features considered *non*essential. Which aspects of a construct are necessary, which are sufficient, should also be specified.

A useful construct should exhibit the proper scope or *range of meaning*. A construct that is defined too broadly will inevitably contain phenomena of different sorts; the contents of the definition will be nonhomogeneous. On the other hand, a construct defined too narrowly runs the risks of triviality. It is desirable to encompass as much conceptual terrain as possible while avoiding the problem of nonhomogeneous elements.

A third requirement for a good conceptual definition is the *specification of subcomponents*. Additionally, the relationships among the subcomponents should be spelled out. For example, in the persuasion literature credibility is usually thought to be composed of expertise and trustworthiness. If either is lacking, the speaker cannot be considered credible. Both are necessary, together they are sufficient.

Finally, for those who take empirical observation as an essential element of our craft, the constructs that we work with must *guide operational definition*. Regardless of whether that operational procedure is one of measurement or one of manipulation, it should show close correspondence to the theoretical construct and it should provide good match between the concept and a numerical scale.

QUESTIONS ABOUT GOALS

Sometimes conceptual definitions are developed in a contemplative and proactive manner. At other times, and for a variety of reasons, construct development proceeds without thorough articulation of the assumptions that undergird the construct. When the second case obtains, two outcomes are virtually certain: (a) that the assumptions will become explicit eventually, and (b) that the research would have benefited had that articulation occurred sooner rather than later. In this section, I present a series of questions that anyone working with the goal construct should consider. The various answers that one might make are considered in light of the criteria for evaluating a conceptual definition.

Must Goals Be Conscious?

To the best of my knowledge, no one has advanced the claim that goals are invariably and necessarily unconscious. However, there is great diversity of opinion regarding whether or not goals can exist outside of conscious awareness. Certainly, many writers have taken the position that motivations of some sort *may* exist outside of conscious awareness (Craig, 1986; Freud, 1949). Some contend that goals remain beyond awareness more often than not (e.g., Read & Miller, 1989). A more restrictive position would claim that goals cannot exist outside of conscious awareness. For purposes of contrast with alternative positions, this can be called the *inside-only* perspective to underscore the claim that goals reside *only* within conscious awareness.

When Oatley (1988) argues that "Goals may be unconscious" (p. 15) he implies another position, one that suggests that goals are *typically* conscious (see also Emmons, 1989, p. 101). Though he admits to the possibilty that goals exist on the other side of awareness, the conditions under which this might occur are not specified. Berger (1995) uses the term *implicit* to describe goals of which we are unaware, while Craig (1986) calls them *functional.*

Some reflection on the origin of goals suggests that a meaningful distinction can be drawn within the category of implicit goals. Two possibilities suggest themselves. For one, Peterson (1989) contends that knowledge of one's own goals "may require a level of insight and integrity that is not easy to attain" (p. 340). He apparently assumes that goals exist outside of awareness and that it is only through some effortful process that they may be made apparent to the person who possesses them. This position might be termed the *outside-in* perspective because it asserts that goals have their origin outside of consciousness and only later are they brought into awareness.

A position that reverses that order is the *inside-out* perspective. In this view, goals originate in consciousness, but eventually drift out of awareness as the behavior becomes automatic. A person attempting to master new word processing software may devote considerable effort to learning the keystrokes necessary to cut and paste, scroll screen by screen, or print with a particular font. Soon, however, these actions become well learned. The goal or goals that initially accounted for the behavior(s) vanish even though the behaviors recur. In this way, actions may remain goal directed (i.e., strategic) even though the goal is no longer the proximal cause of the behavior.

Evaluation. Researchers' preferences concerning the degree of consciousness that should be attached to the goal construct appear to be based on the relative concern for scope and precision. Those who privilege scope over precision tend toward one of the positions that places goals out of consciousness (e.g., Donohue, 1990; O'Keefe, 1990). It is argued that one of the advantages to this approach is the possibility of a more detailed analysis, one that attends to the multifunctional nature of human communication. This position depends heavily on the wholly plausible assumption that people often behave far more strategically than they realize (Kellermann, 1992). From this premise, it is sometimes argued that a careful and insightful analyst should be able to reveal motivations for the talk that are inaccessible to or unnoticed by the message producer.

When concern for precision outweighs the desire for scope, researchers opt for an *inside-only* conceptualization of goals. This choice encourages precision on two fronts. Clarity of delineation is enhanced by narrowing the goal construct and, in the process, making the contents of the conceptual area more homogeneous. Operational precision is also strengthened because goals are, in this view, mental representations that are directly accessible by the subject and indirectly accessible to the researcher by self-report.

The reality of social interaction is not likely to be as neat as I have drawn it here, cleanly separating the conscious from the unconscious, awareness from obliviousness. To claim that human communication is the result of both conscious and unconscious forces is hardly controversial. However, Berger (1995) makes clear the problem that this position poses for analysis of goals: "Given that conscious attention is a relatively scarce resource, it is almost a certainty that, in any social-interaction situation, several goals will be implicit [i.e., unconscious] for the actors involved, and that goals at the focal point of conscious awareness will change during the course of most social-interaction episodes . . ." (p. 144). This observation suggests the naivete of posing the question of goal consciousness in a dichotomous fashion. Instead of the either-or formulation, students of the goal construct need to address when goals exist in consciousness, how they arrive there, how long they stay, and by what mechanisms this movement occurs.

Is Commitment a Necessary Feature of Goals?

It is common to see definitions of the goal construct that include commitment as a constitutive element. Klinger (1985) offers an illustration when he says that "*Goal* as used here refers to any desired state of affairs that the individual *is committed to bringing about or maintaining*" (emphasis added; p. 312). But what is meant by commitment? And, to what extent is it a *necessary* component of the goal construct? The answers to these questions are best considered after a brief examination of theoretical perspectives on the causes and effects of commitment. An early treatment of commitment can be found in Kiesler's (1971) work within the cognitive dissonance tradition. He defines commitment as ". . . the pledging or binding of the individual to behavioral acts" (Kiesler & Sakamura, 1966, p. 349). This is often accomplished by publically announcing one's intentions or position on an issue. The effect of commitment is to render actions and cognitions less changeable.

Other theorists deemphasize the social aspects of commitment, privileging instead explanations more psychological in nature. Locke's (1968) goal-setting theory, designed to explain individual performance in organizations, treats commitment in terms of will or determination. Goal-setting theory is quite explicit in its claim that goal difficulty has a positive influence on job performance, but only if the individual is committed to the goal (Locke, Latham, & Erez, 1988). Commitment itself is explained by an expectancy-valence model. That is, goal commitment is a multiplicative function of the attractiveness of the goal and the subjective probability of goal attainment (Hollenbeck & Klein, 1987; Locke, Shaw, Saari, & Latham, 1981). Thus, from the perspective of goal-setting theory, commitment is a moderator variable. Commitment is a necessary side condition for the difficulty–performance relationship, but its conceptual status is independent of the goal construct.

A more elaborate analysis of the means by which commitment arises can be found in Heckhausen and Kuhl's (1985) model of the precursors to action.

To begin, they distinguish between three concepts: wishes, wants, and intentions. *Wishes* are essentially fantasies, that is, they are desires that have not made contact with empirical reality. If wishes exceed a subjective probability-of-attainment threshold, then they may be transformed into wants. Therefore, *wants* are desirable end-states that are possible, perhaps even likely, at some point in the future. The metamorphosis of want to *intention* requires a check for opportunity, time, importance, urgency, and means (abbreviated as OTIUM). If the individual judges that fulfillment of the want is possible on the OTIUM criteria, then it becomes an intention (i.e., a goal).

In this embellished expectancy-valence model, the likelihood of commitment increases as a function of each of the OTIUM variables. Unlike the typical expectancy-valence model, the precise nature of the relationships among the OTIUM criteria (additive, substitutable, etc.) is not specified. In this perspective, we see commitment used as an essential feature of the construct. A goal is not a goal until the threshold of commitment is crossed.

Evaluation. It is readily apparent that commitment and consciousness share some common conceptual space. When individuals are determined to attain a certain goal, they are surely aware of that determination. This fact is further evidenced in the actions that individuals often take to manage their own levels of commitment. "One of the simplest ways to commit yourself to a course of action is to go around telling all your friends that you are definitely going to do something" (Salancik, 1977, p. 6). All of this suggests that commitment is, at least in one respect, conceptually subordinate to goal awareness. The question of commitment does not become meaningful until after an individual becomes aware of a desire. In this application, commitment is used as a means of clarifying the goal construct. It would appear that increased conceptual precision is gained at the expense of scope. However, the expectancy-value models carry us a considerable distance toward regaining any loss of scope by elaborating the process by which desirable outcomes are tested against the standards of possibility and probability of attainment. Rather than slice the goal construct into smaller and smaller static conceptual units, they provide an account of how motivational forces are shaped, focused, and instantiated. Arguably, the sense of process conveyed by these accounts, especially that of Heckhausen and Kuhl's (1985) model takes us beyond construct explication into substantive theory. Decisions about the role of commitment are valuable, perhaps even essential, to action-oriented theories.

One problem remains. We may prefer a more motion-oriented theoretical perspective that places goals outside of conscious awareness. Alternately, some theories are pointedly noncommittal on the issue. Brown and Levinson's (1987) well-known politeness theory provides an illustration. Those theorists contend that speakers and hearers both act to preserve and enhance their own and others' feelings of affiliation and autonomy. Brown and Levinson are explicit in their decision to leave open the question of whether individuals execute these actions with or without conscious awareness (p. 85). Can we be committed to goals of which we are unaware? Such a claim strikes me as oxymoronic. It appears that commitment has little or no role to play in theories that permit goals to exist outside the boundaries of awareness.

What Kind of Hierarchy?

The goal concept is hardly ever mentioned without being accompanied by the claim that goals exist in a hierarchical relationship to one another (e.g., Foss & Bower, 1986). There are at least two distinctly different conceptions of hierarchy in the goals literature.

One form of hierarchy, which may be referred to as the *levels* perspective, is based on the level of abstraction of the goal. For instance, in his work on personological issues, Emmons (1989) suggests four levels: *motives* (e.g., a desire for intimacy), *strivings* (e.g., get to know new people), *concerns* (e.g., determine how to answer advertisements in the Personals section of the newspaper), and *action units* (e.g., answer one of the Personals). Proponents of the levels perspective routinely create as many or as few levels as they view as pertinent to their analysis.

An alternative to the levels perspective is a simple two-step hierarchy that distinguishes only between the end-goal and all of the goals along the way that contribute to obtaining that end-goal. Benoit (1990) advocates this distinction in her discussion of *consummate* goals, or ultimate objectives, and *contributory* goals, or instrumental aims that advance movement toward the ultimate goal. Following Benoit, this is referred to here as the *consummatory* perspective. An example of the distinction can be seen in Schank and Abelson's (1977) work on scripts, goals, and plans.

Evaluation. Part of the difference between the levels and consummatory perspectives is that the consummatory permits two, and only two, levels in its hierarchy. Once the ultimate aim is established, all other relevant goals are conceptually subordinate to it. The levels perspective places no such restriction upon itself. Although different authors prefer varying numbers of layers in their own theorizing, there is no overarching principle that implies an optimal number. Some scholars lean toward a more detailed analysis than the earlier illustrations that I have provided. For example, Parks (1985) made use of a nine-level hierarchy in his analysis of communication competence (see also Carver & Scheier, 1982).

Another means of differentiating the two conceptions of hierarchy can be achieved by attending to the role played by time in each one. Hacker

(1985) comments eloquently on this issue when she says that goals "are reflections of a reality that does not yet exist, but has to be created, and they connect present with future" (p. 278). In the consummatory view, time exists as a line of variable length bounded on one end by development of the goal and on the other by the end-goal. Contributory goals are arrayed at various places on the line. This one dimension is all that is needed to illustrate the idea of hierarchy for the consummatory perspective.

In contrast, two dimensions are required to flesh out the levels perspective. Increasingly abstract goals not only subsume the goals beneath them in the hierarchy, but as movement up the goal structure takes place goals consume a larger portion of the time line. As the number of levels in the goal hierarchy increases, which is to say that as the generality of the top-level goal increases, the temporal length of the two-dimensional representation also increases. Hence, the length of time that is governed by a goal and its level of abstraction are positively correlated.

This partial confounding of time with abstraction might appear to be a theoretical liability. However, there is evidence from studies of the perception of action that the time/level correlation is not so much a conceptual weakness as an empirically reliable phenomenon. Support comes from a study by Wegner, Vallacher, and Kelly (1983, cited in Vallacher & Wegner, 1985). These researchers first developed a questionnaire composed of statements about getting married. Some of the statements reflected action identifications that were low in abstraction, such as "having pictures made" and "wearing a special outfit" while others represented higher level identities such as "showing love" and "making a mistake." Four groups of persons were asked to make judgments regarding how well each of the statements described the act of getting married. The four groups were differentiated in terms of their temporal distance from the act of marriage. One group made the judgments years before they were to marry, another group a month before they were to marry, a third group only a day before marriage, and a fourth group one month after having tied the knot. The results showed evidence of a curvilinear trend for the low-level act identities such that the closer persons were to marriage, the more likely they were to say that low-level statements such as "having pictures made" described the act of marriage.[1] Such findings are quite in line with the notion that low-level goals describe relatively brief segments of the timeline, whereas higher level goals encompass broader segments.

The decision to favor the consummatory perspective over the levels perspective seems to hinge upon the neatness and simplicity of the two-level

---

[1]There was also a linear trend for low-level act identities which can probably be explained by the fact that the four groups were not equidistant from the act of marriage (i.e., "years before," "a month before," "a day before," and "a month after"). Had there been a "years after" group, it seems likely that the linear trend would not have obtained.

approach. It does provide a straightforward method of assigning goals to categories especially when the consummatory goal is apparent. The levels approach, however, maintains the potential for a finer grained analysis by allowing for multiple layers in the hierarchy. Further, although it may not be as crisp a formulation as the consummatory approach, it has the advantage of reflecting an apparently reliable aspect of goal-driven behavior (i.e., the time-length correlation). Of course, the two approaches need not be seen as mutually exclusive. Hybrid models, that combine elements of both, are surely plausible.

Beyond Hierarchy. Regardless of whether one leans toward the levels perspective or the consummatory perspective, both should be recognized as simplifications. One complication arises from the fact that social actors often possess and attempt to achieve multiple goals more or less simultaneously (e.g., Dillard, Segrin, & Harden, 1989; Tracy & Moran, 1983; Waldinger, 1977). As a means of emphasizing that action is almost invariably the result of multiple goals and, consequently, multiple goal hierarchies, Broadbent (1985) offers the term "heterarchy" (p. 290). In the production of a single utterance, we attempt to satisfy both semantic and syntactic goals (Greene, 1984). In the simple act of ending a conversation, we might act upon concerns of efficiency and social appropriateness (Kellermann, 1989). During the negotiation of an intimate relationship, we attend to the plausibility of lasting affection, the potential for rejection, and the prospect of disharmony. All of these examples suggest that a goal theorist would be unwise to limit him or herself to questions of hierarchy. Rather, one must ask what type of hierarchies are best suited to the research at hand, then locate that research within a context defined by multiple motivations.

Are Approach and Avoidance Goals Essentially Different?

Imagine two persons planning to deliver a public speech. One says to himself "I have to make sure that I don't get overanxious." The other says "I must try to remain calm throughout the speech." Although these two examples of self-talk seem to speak to the same goal, the first is framed as an avoidance goal (avoid anxiety), whereas the other is framed as an approach goal (seek calmness).

At first glance, the distinction may appear to be more of a play on words than a contrast of substance. But, such is not the case. In fact, the idea that motivational systems contain both approach and avoidance components is well established. Gray (1991) offers one convincing exposition of the position. Following his review of research, he concludes that separate approach and avoidance systems evolved in organisms ranging from fish to primates. These systems are phylogenetically old and stable. Thus, far from being mere wordplay, there is a physiological basis for distinguishing approach and avoidance goals. Moreover, there are data that document social differences in the operation of approach and avoidance goals. Consider three examples:

1. People whose high-level goals are primarily avoidant have more memories of failed avoidance attempts and more distress about those events than do people whose high-level goals are mostly approach oriented (Singer & Salovey, 1993).
2. Individuals whose high-level goals are predominantly avoidant report lower levels of positive mood, less life satisfaction, and more anxiety when compared to persons whose motivations are primarily appetitive (Emmons & Kaiser, 1994).
3. Husbands' level of avoidant goals is positively associated with marital distress in their wives (King & Emmons, 1991).

Evaluation.   The range-of-meaning criterion that I discussed earlier in this chapter calls for constructs to be delineated such that their contents are homogeneous. Yet, in principle, an infinite number of subdivisions are possible within any construct. So, we must ask which ones matter? The evidence suggests that the approach–avoidance distinction is worthy of thought. The fact that avoidance goals show different effects than approach goals is sufficient to demonstrate that this is a distinction that matters. Theorists need to analyze how the distinction is to be incorporated in their position. And, researchers must take care not to intermingle the two types unwittingly.

Do Goals Have Subcomponents?

Would it be advantageous to conceive of goals as having subcomponents? At least one writer thinks so. Pervin (1986) contends that goals possess cognitive, affective, and behavioral elements. He also allows as to how these components may themselves vary in strength and the degree to which they contribute to any given goal. This provision for variability in the importance of the subcomponents produces some surprising conceptual outcomes. A goal with a strong affective component and a weak cognitive component is experienced as a wish or desire. In contrast, a goal whose cognitive component predominates ". . . has the quality of a belief" (Pervin, 1986, p. 98). Thus, variations in the strength of the subcomponents alters the phenomenological experience of the goal.

Evaluation.   The scope of the goal construct is certainly broadened by the decision to constitute goals out of cognitions, affects, and behaviors. However, this approach is not without certain problems. For one, it becomes difficult to distinguish the goal construct from concepts such as attitude (Eagly & Chaiken, 1993) that have been defined as the combination of three components: cognitive, affective, and behavioral (but see Zanna & Rempel, 1988, for a revision). Thus, the clarity-of-delineation criterion is not met.

Problems of scope also plague this tricomponential treatment of goal. Defined in this way, the scope of the goal construct becomes so vast as to encircle all motivational concepts. The question of what is not a goal becomes difficult to answer. As a result, the range of meaning is so great as to cloud interpretation of the construct.

Should We Distinguish Between Process and Outcome Goals?

When we speak of goals, the term routinely refers to some desired outcome. This use of the word can be seen in the research on affinity seeking (Bell & Daly, 1984). People often have the aim of making others like them. Of course, individuals have other types of goals too, such as gaining information (Berger, 1995), acquiring physical objects (Rule, Bisanz, & Kohn, 1985; Schank & Abelson, 1977), improving work performance (Erez & Rim 1982; Kipnis, Schmidt, & Wilkinson, 1980), checking social reality (McCann & Higgins, 1988), and so on. All of these examples, and in fact a great deal of research, focus on the content goals, that is, *what* social actors are trying to accomplish. They are concerned with *outcome*.

An equally important question, but one that has received relatively less attention is that of *how* individuals seek to achieve the ends they desire. Here I am not concerned with substantive issues of strategy or tactics, but rather with the manner in which the *process* itself is instantiated. Possibly the clearest illustration of a process goal in found in the claim that individuals possess, to varying degrees, a desire for efficiency (Brown & Levinson, 1987; Blum-Kulka, Danet, & Gherson, 1985; Kellermann, 1989). The notion that individuals may decide to pursue outcome goals with varying degrees of vigor or tenacity also helps to convey some of the flavor of process concerns (Wiemann & Daly, 1994).

Evaluation. The distinction between process and outcome goals is intuitively appealing and probably one that deserves further analysis. However, application of the process–outcome distinction requires some appreciation of the context in which the distinction is to be drawn. My point here is that some content goals, such as impression management, may assume either process or outcome status depending on the context in which they occur. The salesperson bent on unloading his merchandise attempts to create liking for instrumental reasons. In this instance, impression management is process. However, it is often the case that people try to engender liking for its own sake. Thus, impression management is an outcome goal. As always, context matters.

In both of the previous examples, outcome refers to the end-goal while process refers to those things that happen in the service of obtaining the end-goal. It might appear that the process–outcome distinction is redundant with the consummatory perspective on goal hierarchy: Process goals are contributory and outcome goals are consummatory. But, the redundancy is only superficial. The process goals of efficiency and vigor reside at a loftier tier in the goal hierarchy than any particular outcome goal that they might influence. Contributory goals, in contrast, must be located below consummatory goals. So, the two distinctions, outcome/process and contributory/consummatory, are not wholly redundant. However, their apparent similarity suggests that clarity of delineation might be enhanced by considering the distinctions jointly.

To What Extent Should Goals Exhibit Specificity?

Goal specificity may be defined as ". . . the degree of quantitative precision with which the aim [goal] is specified" (Locke et al., 1981, p. 126). Accordingly, a goal of increasing production by 10 units is more specific than a goal of increasing production by between 8 and 12 units. And, the 8–12 goal is more specific than "Do your best."

At first glance it might seem that specific goals are simply those that reside near the base of a goal hierarchy. This impression is inaccurate. Specificity is distinct from hierarchy. Proof of the difference can be seen by comparing the intentions of two hypothetical students. Whereas one might seek simply to raise her GPA, another could have the goal of increasing her GPA to a 3.5. Because these goals will require much time (at least one semester) and a myriad of actions, they are necessarily close to the top of a goal hierarchy. Thus, while they differ in specificity, they are similar in level of abstraction. The conceptual distinctiveness of specificity provides part of the grounds for the attention that it receives here. Its empirical effects supply the remaining justification.

Virtually all of the work on goal specificity resides within the organizational behavior literature. From that body of work, one especially robust finding has emerged: Specific goals produce better task performance than ambiguous goals (Mento, Steel, & Karren, 1987). There are several reasons that this should be the case. First, because goals direct attention, as they become more specific, the resulting actions should also become more focused (Beehr & Love, 1983). Second, because goals stimulate the development of planning, specific goals should give rise to task strategies that are closely aligned with those goals (Earley & Perry, 1987). Third, goal specificity reduces ambiguity in evaluating goal attainment (Campion & Lord, 1982). Finally, when goals are made public, specific goals make it a simple matter for onlookers to evaluate an individual's level of success with regard to the goal (Naylor & Ilgen, 1984). To varying degrees, all four of these processes may be mediated by a construct that is the focus of an earlier section of this chapter: goal commitment (Wright & Kacmar, 1994).

Organizational behavior scholars value goal specificity because of its implications for productivity enhancement. People who commit to specific goals work harder than those who possess diffuse goals. Why, then, do people resist formulating precise goals (Reither & Staudel, 1985)? Probably for the same reasons that specific goals prompt effort. First, because goals direct attention and stimulate planning, they instigate the expenditure of effort. To the extent that people prefer to conserve energic resources, they should resist goal specificity. Second, because specific goals channel thought and action, they reduce flexibility. Commitment to one course of action creates opportunity costs in terms of foregoing the alternative courses of action. Third, because goal specificity clarifies progress toward the goal, one's failures become more salient and more resistant to retro-spective reinterpretation (e.g., "Oh, that wasn't all that important anyway. I didn't really care about it"). Moreover, clear failure produces negative affect to a much greater degree than uncertain failure (Segrin & Dillard, 1991). Finally, when specific goals are made public, they allow others to evaluate our progress and to demand that we behave consistently with our stated aims. Ambiguous goal statements have the often desirable property of plausible deniability (Eisenberg, 1984).

Evaluation. The notion of specificity surfaced and matured within the confines of the organizational behavior literature. The emphasis on task achievement inherent in that literature made organizational behavior a nur-turing environment for the analysis of specificity effects. In contrast, com-munication researchers have not shown much interest in questions con-cerning goal specificity. Does this apparent indifference result from design or from oversight? It may stem from the fact that many goals that are relevant to social interaction seem to resist quantification. We rarely encounter in-dividuals who hold goals such as "I plan to increase my partner's liking for me by 2 units on a 7-point scale." Instead, we are more likely to see studies in which one participant tries to make the other like him more (e.g., Palmer & Simmons, 1995) or gather as much information as possible (e.g., Keller-mann & Berger, 1984). This apparent predilection for nonspecific goals may reflect an appreciation for the phenomenology of the social actor. Perhaps we study nonspecific goals because that is the natural form of communica-tive goals.

Apart from current practice, *should* we study goal specificity? The em-pirical findings regarding the influence of specificity on task behavior imply a durable effect. The effect may also be sufficiently general as to encompass a variety of communication phenomena. Can we train individuals to form specific communication goals within skill domains such as public speaking, small group discussion, and conflict management? And, if so, will specific goals produce effects similar to those documented by students of organizational behavior? These questions all suggest the potential benefit of granting greater attention to goal specificity.

Summary

Thus far I have presented seven questions about goals and discussed their implications in terms of clarity of delineation, range of meaning, and specification of subcomponents. The questions vary considerably in importance and some of them overlap with others. Nonetheless, they are all useful questions in that they encourage careful construct development. In the next section, I take up some of the issues concerned with operationalization.

OPERATIONALIZING "GOALS"

The plausibility of any test of theory is constrained by the validity with which the constructs are operationalized. However, there is great diversity of opinion on what passes for "plausible." In what follows, I describe two general approaches to operationalizing goals, then attempt to enumerate some of the threats to inference associated with each of them. Additionally, I try to make clear how earlier-drawn distinctions might nudge a researcher toward one or the other type of operationalization.

Inference From Self-Report

If we are willing to assume that goals are accessible to consciousness or can be made accessible, then it is possible to assess goals in a fairly direct manner; that is, by self-report. This method has been used to assess goals prior to action (Greene & Lindsey, 1989) and after the action has occurred (Dillard et al., 1989). It has been applied to naturally occurring goals and to experimentally induced goals (e.g., Palmer & Simmons, 1995). Thus, one virtue of the self-report approach is its generality.

Of course, self-reports of goals are not immune to problems of inference. It is often noted that one of the potential threats to validity is prevarication. For fear of appearing undesirable, individuals may shade descriptions of their true intentions or fabricate them altogether (Craig, 1986). In my estimation, this is a problem that is fairly well addressed through assurances of confidentiality or guarantees of anonymity. Perhaps a more likely threat is that individuals will deceive *themselves* concerning the real motives for their behavior. They will deny to themselves that their motivations might be aggressive, deceitful, or unethical. However, if we accept self-duplicity about one's goals as a real possibility, then we have shifted our perspective on goal awareness from the inside-only position to the outside-in or inside-out positions. These latter two positions allow as to how goals might exist outside of consciousness, thereby allowing action to be motivated by a goal of which the actor was unaware.

It is surely the case that as distance between time and action increases, individuals' conceptions of their own goals change. Multiple processes are in operation. Intentions regarding future behavior may be influenced by hopes and dreams. Circumstances may change such that unforeseen obstacles to goal completion become apparent. And, as noted in the discussion of hierarchy, as the temporal distance between motive and behavior grows larger, the goal that governs the action becomes more abstract (within the phenomenology of the actor; Vallacher & Wegner, 1985). In addition, recollections of one's goals are colored by the degree of success one had in attaining the goal. All of these concerns argue for assessing goals as close in time to the action under study as is possible.

Waldron and Cegala (1992) offer a thoughtful analysis of three methods of assessing goals as they occur in conversation. The three methods are concurrent verbalization, thought checklists, and videotaped stimulated recall. It is worth noting that the procedures they consider require only that goals *can be* made accessible to consciousness. Methods such as stimulated recall, that is, viewing a videotape of an interaction in which the subject provides data on his or her cognitions at various points in the interaction, allow subjects to voice thoughts that might *not* have been clear, well-formed intentions at the time of action. Thus, the methods are not limited to an inside-only perspective, but might be used by researchers who adopt one of the less stringent positions on awareness relative to the goal construct.

Inference From Circumstance

Theorists who take the position that goals are, or may be, unconscious often infer backwards from the action to the goal (e.g., Brown & Levinson, 1987). Such inference from behavior to goal can be risky business. In fact, some would call it just plain *bad* business. "Intention cannot be inferred from actions: otherwise, it would provide a circular explanation in which the same event is taken as evidence of both cause and effect" (Bandura, 1986, p. 468). In the next section, I explore some of the challenges to action-to-goal inferences.

Canonical Problems of Action-Goal Inferences. Every researcher who would desire to infer goals from behavior is faced with problems of two sorts. For one, different goals might generate the same action. Borrowing from the language of systems theory, we might term this the *problem of equifinality.*[2] As an example, consider that individuals make use of metaphor to achieve five distinct ends: to give the appearance of eloquence, to compare similarities between two ideas, to make their talk more interesting, to provoke thought, and to clarify their intended meaning (Roberts & Kreuz, 1994). So, upon observation of a person uttering a metaphor which of the alternative motivations should we infer? In the absence of any other information, the problem of inference is intractable. And that is the simple case! This predicament looms even larger if one is willing to make the now commonplace assumption that individuals possess and act on multiple goals. It is no longer of a question of inferring *one* goal from a behavior, but a combination of goals.

Another problem is that different actions might be generated by the same goal. Persons who aim to clarify the meaning of an utterance indicate that they achieve that end through a variety of linguistic means: hyperbole, irony, metaphor, simile, idiom, and rhetorical questions (Roberts & Kreuz, 1994). Borrowing again from systems theory, this is the *problem of equipotentiality.*

Clearly, the challenge faced by the researcher is that there are simply too many possibilities to make any kind of claim with certainty. But, how might one go about enhancing the plausibility of an action-to-goal inference? There are several possibilities.

Solution I: Eliminate Alternatives. The application of this strategy takes several forms, one of which is apparent in politeness theory (Brown & Levinson, 1987). The theory proposes that everyone possesses a desire for affiliation/inclusion (i.e., roughly positive face) and a desire for autonomy (i.e., roughly negative face). When an individual attempts to change the behavior of another, one or both of these desires may be threatened. Consequently, speakers create utterances to save their own and other's face. A phrase such as, "I'm sorry to bother you, but . . ." apparently attempts to mitigate the hearer's desire for autonomy by recognizing the intrusion. The researcher might then infer that it arises from the goal of saving negative face. The inference process is simplified by the fact that the theory proposes the existence of only two, mutually exclusive goals. In this instance, alternative goals are eliminated by theoretical decree.

Another application of the Eliminate Alternatives strategy is achieved by selecting or controlling the context in which the communication occurs. This is a common approach among discourse analysts who attempt to interpret the implicit functions of speech within highly specific contexts such as the

---

[2]I've taken some liberty with shades of meaning in my use of these terms. Within systems theory, equifinality and equipotentiality are not seen as properties of problems, but as properties of systems. The concepts are used here to highlight the difficulties of inference that are faced by an observer (the researcher) attempting to understand the workings of the system.

courtroom (Nofsinger, 1983). Whereas discourse analysts typically favor naturally occurring contexts, it is possible to *create* contexts that effectively limit the number of goals that might be in operation. Charlesworth and La Freniere (1983) utilized this approach in their work on resource acquisition. The paradigm places children in a playroom in groups of four. A movie apparatus is present that allows the children to operate in 1 of 3 positions. Through a peephole, one child can view a cartoon movie. This can be accomplished only in cooperation with two other persons. One of the two must turn the crank that causes the filmstrip to move, while the other is needed to press a button that activates the light needed to illuminate the film. The remaining child becomes a bystander. This laboratory setting simplifies the inference problem in two ways. By creating a relatively sterile environment, it eliminates many potential goals. By making certain resources salient, it enhances the likelihood that particular goals will be activated.

Solution 2: Look for Patterns of Behavior. Social actors are often inexplicit about their wants: they beat around the bush, they deny the apparent meaning of their utterance, they say that they did not anticipate the implications of an action. One way in which we solve the attributional dilemma of why-they-did-what-they-did is to look for patterns in the behavior of others. But what kind of patterns?

Some reflection on the meaning of motive (i.e., goal, broadly construed) helps to frame an answer to that question. It is widely accepted that motives influence behavior in three ways. First, motives encourage individuals to choose one course of action over the alternatives. Second, motives energize behavior. This effect can be seen in the intensity or frequency with which actions are performed. Third, when obstacles are present, motives are thought to underlie the persistence with which the individual executes the action. As a general rule, an action-to-goal inference should be stronger to the extent that a pattern can be observed over more, rather than fewer, of these dimensions of behavior. The implications for research design are straightforward:

1. Patterns cannot be seen in isolated utterances. Collect enough message data so that it is possible for patterns to emerge.

2. To the extent that individuals have a range of behavioral options, the act of selecting one becomes more meaningful. Provide individuals with a range of communicative choices.

3. The frequency or intensity of an action can only be judged if one is clear about the unit of behavior. Investigations of message tactics focus on smaller units than studies of message strategies. Construct the sample of behavior such that the largest unit under study has room to vary in frequency or intensity (whichever aspect of behavior is of interest).

4. Often motives do not manifest themselves until they are endangered. One reason that request behavior has been the locus of so much politeness research is that threats to both positive and negative face are likely in that communicative locale. Find or construct situations in which the goals of the social actor are likely to encounter obstacles.

Solution 3: Settle for Weaker Inference. Although most scientific research on message production aspires to empirically valid accounts of how and why messages are formed, this is not the aim of all inquiry. Rather, some writers seek only to demonstrate that their interpretation of a phenomenon is plausible, that a body of discourse *could be* given a particular reading (Stubbs, 1983). Though many would disagree with me, I see this as a much weaker form of explanation than the social scientific standard. Still, such research is not without value. Work conducted from this perspective is often insightful and can provide the basis for generating rigorously testable explanations. Moreover, such research is often a rich source of example and can be used to vivify the account of a message production process. Finally, such research might be used fruitfully in conjunction with more rigorous methods and in this way provide an excellent complement to standard procedures. In communication in general, and in message production in particular, we have no tools of inference so strong that we can afford wholesale dismissal of complementary methods.

A PROPOSAL

Current theories of message production make heavy use of the goal concept. And, the empirical findings suggest that this heavy use is justified; the results of a great many studies indicate strong and reliable relationships between goals and the messages that follow from them (e.g., Dillard, 1989). But, the goal concept could be harnessed in such a way as to pull even greater theoretical weight than it does currently. In addition to serving as an explanatory mechanism *within* theories, goals might be used define research domains. Rather than discuss compliance-seeking as if it were a single, homogeneous social sphere, it would be valuable to, distinguish, for example, between gaining assistance and giving, two different influence goals. The virtues of such an approach are numerous.

One such virtue is that goals are the proximal causes of communication behavior. Early studies of message production, especially studies of influence messages, couched their questions in terms of situational and individual difference variables. Many judged these efforts as unsatisfactory because the results they produced failed to coalesce into a coherent body knowledge (Berger, 1985; Boster, 1995). The shortcomings of these variable-analytic approaches were twofold. Whereas individual differences might assess what persons typically do or want, they measured features of individuals in the abstract, apart from the needs of the moment. And, although situations provided both opportunities and constraints, they gave no hint as to what the individual sought to achieve within the structure provided by those opportunities and constraints. The addition of the goal construct to theories of message production solved these problems by moving the explanatory mechanism closer to the phenomenon of interest.

Moreover, goals provide a parsimonious means for summarizing social reality. This is true in several senses. Consider that interactants typically possess a primary goal (i.e., the goal that defines and motivates the interaction sequence) and one or more secondary goals (i.e., goals that arise from an attempt to achieve the primary goal). For instance, the professor attempting to steer a student gently toward a valuable research project must balance her desire for effectiveness against the student's right to choose. And, in general, primary goals tend to be accompanied by specific configurations of secondary goals (Schrader & Dillard, 1996). Thus, knowledge of the primary goal provides knowledge of the secondary goals that are likely to be activated. Furthermore, certain types of goals tend to cooccur with specific individuals (Miller, Cody, & McLaughlin, 1994). People seek assistance from siblings and peers. They seek permission from persons in positions of power. In sum, knowledge of the actor's primary goal has strong implications for the other concerns that an actor is likely to possess as well as his or her relationship with other interactant.

Using goals to organize inquiry has the additional virtue of encouraging a dynamic approach to the study of communication. Whereas traditional definitions implicitly assume that the situation is static for the duration of the interaction, a goal-based approach recognizes that what an individual is trying to achieve may vary from moment to moment as opportunities and constraints unfold during social discourse. An interaction originally motivated by one party's desire to change the opinion of the other may change course when the message target reacts with disbelief to the audacity of the source. In this instance, the source's primary goal may shift from one of influence to one of relational repair. Though brief, these three arguments make a compelling case for a goal-based approach to inquiry.

CONCLUSION

Constructs, like theories and people, have life cycles. It is often the case that a construct in born is response to the perceived inadequacies of existing constructs. It may then "live" until its own faults become apparent, at which time it is replaced by a new, and one hopes, improved construct. My aim in this chapter is not to rush the goal construct toward its grave. Rather, I hope that making clear the choice points associated with the construct, it will help to ensure a long and productive life for the notion of goal.

REFERENCES

Bandura, A. (1986). *Social foundations of thought and action: A social cognitive theory*. Englewood Cliffs, NJ: Prentice-Hall.

Beehr, T. A., & Love, K. G. (1983). A meta-model of the effects of goal characteristics, feedback, and role characteristics in human organizations. *Human Relations, 36,* 151–166.

Bell, R. A., & Daly, J. A. (1984). The affinity-seeking function of communication. *Communication Monographs, 51,* 91–115.

Berger, C. R. (1985). Social power and interpersonal communication. In M. L. Knapp & G. R. Miller (Eds.), *Handbook of interpersonal communication* (pp. 439–499). Newbury Park, CA: Sage.

Berger, C. R., (1995). A plan-based approach to strategic communication. In D. E. Hewes (Ed.), *The cognitive bases of interpersonal communication* (pp. 141–180). Hillsdale, NJ: Lawrence Erlbaum Associates.

Berlo, D. K. (1960). *The process of communication*. New York: Holt, Rinehart & Winston.

Benoit, P. (1990). The structure of interaction goals. In J. Anderson (Ed.), *Communication yearbook 13* (pp. 407–416). Newbury Park, CA: Sage.

Bingham, S. G., & Burleson, B. R. (1989). Multiple effects of messages with multiple goals: Some perceived outcomes of responses to sexual harassment. *Human Communication Research, 16,* 184–216.

Blum-Kulka, S., Danet, B., & Gherson, R. (1985). The language of requesting in Israeli society. In J. P. Forgas (Ed.), *Language and social situations* (pp. 113–140). New York: Springer-Verlag.

Boster, F. J. (1995). Commentary on compliance-gaining message behavior research. In C. R. Berger & M. Burgoon (Eds.), *Communication and social influence* (pp. 91–114). East Lansing, MI: Michigan State University Press.

Broadbent, D. E. (1985). Multiple goals and flexible procedures in the design of work. In M. Frese & J. Sabini (Eds.), *Goal directed behavior: The concept of action in psychology* (pp. 285–295). Hillsdale, NJ: Lawrence Erlbaum Associates.

Brown, P., & Levinson, S. (1987). *Politeness: Some universals in language usage*. Cambridge, England: Cambridge University Press.

Campion, M. A., & Lord, R. G. (1982). A control systems conceptualization of the goal setting and changing process. *Organizational Behavior and Human Performance, 30,* 265–287.

Carver, C. S., & Scheier, M. F. (1982). Control theory: A useful conceptual framework for personality-social, clinical, and health psychology. *Psychological Bulletin, 92,* 111–135.

Charlesworth, W., & La Freniere, P. (1983). Dominance, friendship and resource utilization in preschool children's groups. *Ethology and Sociobiology, 4,* 175–186.

Cody, M. J., Canary, D. J., & Smith, S. W. (1994). Compliance-gaining goals: An inductive analysis of actors' goal types, strategies, and successes. In J. Daly & J. M. Wiemann (Eds.), *Strategic interpersonal communication* (pp. 33–90). Hillsdale, NJ: Lawrence Erlbaum Associates.

Craig, R. T. (1986). Goals in discourse. In D. G. Ellis & W. A. Donohue (Eds.), *Contemporary issues in language and discourse processes* (pp. 257–273). Hillsdale, NJ: Lawrence Erlbaum Associates.

Dillard, J. P. (1989). Types of influence goals in close relationships. *Journal of Social and Personal Relationships, 6,* 293–308.

Dillard, J. P. (Ed.). (1990). *Seeking compliance: The production of interpersonal influence messages*. Scottsdale, AZ: Gorsuch-Scarisbrick.

Dillard, J. P., Segrin, C., & Harden, J. M. (1989). Primary and secondary goals in the production of interpersonal influence messages. *Communication Monographs, 56,* 19–38.

Donohue, W. A. (1990). Interaction goals in negotiation: A critique. In J. Anderson (Ed.), *Communication yearbook 13* (pp. 374–406). Newbury Park, CA: Sage.

Donohue, W. A., & Diez, M. (1985). Directive use in negotiation interaction. *Communication Monographs, 52,* 305–318.

Eagly, A. H., & Chaiken, S. (1993). *The psychology of attitudes.* Fort Worth, TX: Harcourt Brace Janovich.

Early, P. C., & Perry, B. C. (1987). Work plan availability and performance: As assessment of task strategy priming on subsequent task completion. *Organizational Behavior and Human Decision Processes, 39,* 279–302.

Eisenberg, E. M. (1984). Ambiguity as strategy in organizational communication. *Communication Monographs, 51,* 227–242.

Emmons, R. A. (1989). The personal strivings approach to personality. In L.A. Pervin (Ed.), *Goal concepts in personality and social psychology,* (pp. 327–361). Hillsdale, NJ: Lawrence Erlbaum Associates.

Emmons, R. A., & Kaiser, H. (1994, August). *Approach and avoidance strivings and subjective well-being.* Paper presented at the annual meeting of the American Psychological Association, Los Angeles, CA.

Erez, M., & Rim, Y. (1982). The relationship between goals, influence tactics, and personal organizational variables. *Human Relations, 35,* 871–878.

Foss, C. L., & Bower, G. H. (1986). Understanding actions in relation to goals. In N. E. Sharkey (Ed.), *Advances in cognitive science* (pp. 94–124). Chichester, England: Robert Horwood.

Freud, S. (1949). *An outline of psychoanalysis.* New York: Norton.

Gray, J. A. (1991). *The psychology of fear and stress.* Cambridge, England: Cambridge University Press.

Greene, J. O. (1984). A cognitive approach to human communication: An action assembly theory. *Communication Monographs, 51,* 289–306.

Greene, J. O., & Lindsey, A. E. (1989). Encoding processes in the production of multiple-goal messages. *Human Communication Research, 16,* 120–140.

Hacker, W. (1985). Activity: A fruitful concept in industrial psychology. In M. Frese & J. Sabini (Eds.), *Goal directed behavior: The concept of action in psychology* (pp. 262–284). Hillsdale, NJ: Lawrence Erlbaum Associates.

Heckhausen, H., & Kuhl, J. (1985). From wishes to action: The dead ends and short cuts on the long way to action. In M. Frese & J. Sabini (Eds.) *Goal directed behavior: The concept of action in psychology* (pp. 134–160). Hillsdale, NJ: Lawrence Erlbaum Associates.

Hollenbeck, J. R., & Klein, H. J. (1987). Goal commitment and the goal-setting process: Problems, prospects, and proposals for future research. *Journal of Applied Psychology, 72,* 212–220.

Kellermann, K. (1989, March). *Understanding tactical choice: Metagoals in conversation.* Paper presented at the Temple University conference on goals in discourse, Philadelphia, PA.

Kellermann, K. (1992). Communication: Inherently strategic and primarily automatic. *Communication Monographs, 59,* 288–300.

Kellermann, K., & Berger, C. R. (1984). Affect and the acquisition of social information: Sit back, relax, and tell me about yourself. In R. Bostrom (Ed.), *Communication yearbook 8* (pp. 412–445). Newbury Park, CA: Sage.

Kellermann, K., Reynolds, R., & Chen, J. B.-S. (1991). Strategies for conversational retreat: When parting is not such sweet sorrow. *Communication Monographs, 58,* 362–383.

Kiesler, C. A. (1971). *The psychology of commitment: Experiments linking behavior to belief.* New York: Academic Press.

Kiesler, C. A., & Sakamura, J. (1966). A test of a model for commitment. *Journal of Personality and Social Psychology, 3,* 349–353.

King, L. A., & Emmons, R. A. (1991). Psychological, physical, and interpersonal correlates of emotional expressiveness, conflict, and control. *European Journal of Personality, 5,* 131–150.

Kipnis, D., Schmidt, S. M., & Wilkinson, I. (1980). Intraorganizational influence tactics: Explorations in getting one's way. *Journal of Applied Psychology, 65,* 440–452.

Klinger, E. (1985). Missing links in action theory. In M. Frese, & J. Sabini (Eds.), *Goal directed behavior: The concept of action in psychology* (pp. 262–284). Hillsdale, NJ: Lawrence Erlbaum Associates.

Locke, E. A. (1968). Toward a theory of task motivation and incentives. *Organizational Behavior and Human Performance, 3,* 157–189.

Locke, E. A., Latham, G. P., & Erez, M. (1988). The determinants of goal commitment. *Academy of Management Review, 13,* 23–39.

Locke, E. A., Shaw, K. N., Saari, L. M., & Latham, G. P. (1981). Goal setting and task performance: 1968–1980. *Psychological Bulletin, 90,* 125–152.

McCann, C. D., & Higgins, E. T. (1988). Motivation and affect in interpersonal relations: The role of personal orientations and discrepancies. In L. Donohew, H. E. Sypher, & E. T. Higgins (Eds.), *Communication, social cognition, and affect* (pp. 53–80). Hillsdale, NJ: Lawrence Erlbaum Associates.

Mento, A. J., Steel, R. P., & Karren, R. J. (1987). A meta-analytic study of the effects of goal setting on task performance: 1966–1984. *Organizational Behavior and Human Decision Processes, 39,* 52–83.

Miller, G. R., & Nicholson, H. E. (1976). *Communication inquiry: A perspective on a process.* Reading, MA: Addison-Wesley.

Miller, L. C., Cody, M., & McLaughlin, M. L. (1994). Situations and goals as fundamental constructs in interpersonal communication research. In M. L. Knapp & G. R. Miller (Eds.), *Handbook of interpersonal communication* (pp. 162–198). Thousand Oaks, CA: Sage.

Naylor, J. D., & Ilgen, D. R. (1984). Goal setting: A theoretical analysis of a motivational technology. *Research in Organizational Behavior, 6,* 95–140.

Nofsinger, R. E. (1983). Tactical coherence in courtroom conversation. In R. T. Craig & K. Tracy (Eds.), *Conversational coherence: Form, structure, and strategy* (pp. 243–258). Beverly Hills, CA: Sage.

Oatley, K. (1988). Gaps in consciousness: Emotions and memory in psychoanalysis. *Cognition and Emotion, 2,* 3–18.

O'Keefe, B. (1990). The logic of regulative communication: Understanding the rationality of message designs. In J. P. Dillard (Ed.), *Seeking compliance: The production of interpersonal influence messages* (pp. 87–104). Scottsdale, AZ: Gorsuch-Scarisbrick.

Palmer, M. T., & Simmons, K. B. (1995). Communicating intentions through nonverbal behaviors: Conscious and unconscious encoding of liking. *Human Communication Research, 22,* 128–160.

Parks, M. R. (1985). Interpersonal communication and the quest for personal competence. In M. L. Knapp & G. R. Miller (Eds.), *Handbook of interpersonal communication* (pp. 171–201). Beverly Hills, CA: Sage.

Pervin, L. A. (1986). Personal and social determinants of behavior in situations. In A. Furnham (Ed.), *Social behavior in context* (pp. 83–102). Boston, MA: Allyn & Bacon.

Peterson, D. R. (1989). Interpersonal goal conflict. In L. A. Pervin (Ed.), *Goal concepts in personality and social psychology,* (pp. 327–361). Hillsdale, NJ: Lawrence Erlbaum.

Read, S. J., & Miller, L. C. (1989). Inter-personalism: Toward a goal-based theory of persons in relationships. In L. A. Pervin (Ed.), *Goal concepts in personality and social psychology* (pp. 413–472). Hillsdale, NJ: Lawrence Erlbaum Associates.

Reither, F., & Staudel, T. (1985). Thinking and action. In M. Frese & J. Sabini (Eds.), *Goal-directed behavior: The concept of action in psychology* (pp. 110–122). Hillsdale, NJ: Lawrence Erlbaum Associates.

Roberts, R. M., & Kreuz, R. J. (1994). Why do people use figurative language? *Psychological Science, 5,* 159–163.

Rule, B. G., Bisanz, G. L., & Kohn, M. (1985). Anatomy of a persuasion schema: Targets, goals, and strategies. *Journal of Personality and Social Psychology, 48*, 1127–1140.

Salancik, G. (1977). Commitment and the control of organizational behavior and belief. In B. M. Staw & G. R. Salancik (Eds.), *New directions in organizational behavior* (pp. 1–54). Chicago: St. Claire Press.

Schank, R. C., & Abelson, R. P. (1977). *Scripts, plans, goals, and understanding: An inquiry into human knowledge structures.* Hillsdale, NJ: Lawrence Erlbaum Associates.

Schrader, D. C., & Dillard, J. P. (1996). *Goal structures and interpersonal influence.* Manuscript in preparation.

Segrin, C., & Dillard, J. P. (1991). (Non)depressed persons' cognitive and affective reactions to (un)successful interpersonal influence. *Communication Monographs, 58*, 115–134.

Singer, J. A., & Salovey, P. (1993). *The remembered self.* New York: The Free Press.

Smith, M. J. (1988). *Contemporary communication research methods.* Belmont, CA: Wadsworth.

Stubbs, M. (1983). *Discourse analysis.* Oxford, England: Blackwell.

Tracy, K. (1984). The effect of multiple goals on conversational relevance and topic shift. *Communication Monographs, 51*, 274–287.

Tracy, K., & Moran, J. P. (1983). Conversational relevance in multiple-goal settings. In R. T. Craig & K. Tracy (Eds.), *Conversational coherence: Form, structure, and strategy* (pp. 116–135). Beverly Hills, CA: Sage.

Vallacher, R. R., & Wegner, D. M. (1985). *A theory of action identification.* Hillsdale, NJ: Lawrence Erlbaum Associates.

Waldinger, R. (1977). Achieving several goals simultaneously. *Machine Intelligence, 8*, 94–136.

Waldron, V. R., & Cegala, D. J. (1992). Assessing conversational cognition: Levels of cognitive theory and associated methodological requirements. *Human Communication Research, 18*, 599–622.

Wiemann, J. M., & Daly, J. A. (1994). Introduction: Getting your own way. In J. A. Daly & J. M. Wiemann (Eds.), *Strategic interpersonal communication* (pp. vii–xiv). Hillsdale, NJ: Lawrence Erlbaum Associates.

Wilson, S. R. (1990). Development and test of a cognitive rules model of interaction goals. *Communication Monographs, 57*, 81–103.

Wilson, S. R., & Putnam, L. L. (1990). Interaction goals in negotiation. In J. Anderson (Ed.), *Communication yearbook 13* (pp. 374–406). Newbury Park, CA: Sage.

Wright, P. M., & Kacmar, K. M. (1994). Goal specificity as a determinant of goal commitment and goal change. *Organizational Behavior and Human Decision Processes, 59*, 242–260.

Zanna, M. P., & Rempel, J. K. (1988). Attitudes: A new look at an old concept. In D. Bar-Tal & A. W. Kruglanski (Eds.), *The social psychology of knowledge* (pp. 315–334). Cambridge, England: Cambridge University Press.

4

COGNITIVE INFLUENCES ON THE ABILITY TO ADDRESS INTERACTION GOALS

Janet R. Meyer
University of Miami

The outcomes of a conversation include renewed perceptions of self, other, and the relationship. Efforts to control these outcomes have come to be viewed as relational or secondary goals (Dillard, Segrin, & Harden, 1989). Existing theory suggests that these goals include managing an impression, acting in a manner consistent with one's identity and principles, protecting the hearer's self-esteem, and maintaining a positive relationship (Dillard et al., 1989; Hample & Dallinger, 1987a). In cognitive approaches to the study of communication, it is often assumed that speakers control outcomes related to these goals by making a conscious effort to address the goal at the time a message plan is initially formulated (Greene & Lindsey, 1989; Meyer, 1992; O'Keefe & Shepherd, 1987). It is sometimes the case, however, that individuals become aware of the need to address a relational goal only after a message has been constructed. At that point, a rehearsal of the message may lead the speaker to anticipate an unwanted relational outcome. The speaker might then edit the message to pursue a relational goal not previously addressed. The ability to detect such problems in advance of message production is an importance component of conversational competence. The focus of this chapter is on the cognitive processes underlying this ability.

RESEARCH ON COGNITIVE EDITING

The question of how speakers determine in advance that a message might be better put a different way has been addressed most directly in research on cognitive editing. Existing knowledge in this area has been advanced substantially by research on verbal slips (Motley, Baars, & Camden, 1981, 1983) and the editing of compliance-gaining messages (Hample & Dallinger, 1987a).

Numerous experiments employing the SLIP technique (*Spoonerisms of Laboratory-Induced Predisposition*), have indicated that the production of words is subject to the influence of contextual factors (Motley, Camden, & Baars, 1979). For instance, if a word pair to be read aloud (mad bug) is preceded by a phonologically similar word pair (back mud), participants produce a spoonerized version of the target words (bad mug) on a large number of trials (Dell & Reich, 1981; Motley et al., 1981, 1983). When such errors are made, lexically legitimate errors are more common than lexically anomalous ones (Motley et al., 1983). The latter effect has been labeled the *lexical bias effect.* Motley et al. (1983) proposed that this effect is attributable to spreading activation processes that influence a prearticulatory editing mechanism. According to this model, lexical items in an output plan are compared against the activation levels of corresponding nodes in the lexicon. Lexical items in the output formulation are "approved" for output only if the activation level of the node in the lexicon exceeds a threshold. Because the activation level of nodes in the lexicon can be increased by contextual factors and nodes do not exist for nonwords, the model can account for the lexical bias effect. More recent efforts to explain the lexical bias effect suggest, however, that it may be attributable, not to prearticulatory editing, but rather to spreading-activation processes that influence the initial selection of words (Dell, 1985, 1986; Dell & Reich, 1981; Motley, 1986). According to the latter explanation, activation from phoneme nodes (from an interfering word pair) spreads in a bottom-up manner to raise the accessibility of word nodes representing lexically legitimate errors, making it more likely that these words will be selected for the initial output plan (Dell, 1985).

The manner in which individuals edit plans for an entire message has been investigated most directly by Hample and Dallinger (1987a, 1987b, 1992, 1994). Their research program has focused on the editing criteria underlying individuals' reasons for not endorsing instances of the compliance-gaining strategies in the Marwell and Schmidt (1967) typology. Hample and Dallinger (1987a) note four types of cognitive editing criteria identified in their own past research. These include *effectiveness* (the argument won't work), *discourse competence* (the argument is false, irrelevant, etc.), *principled objection* (the argument is too negative or too high pressure) and *person-centered issues* (the argument would harm the self-image, harm the other, or harm the relationship). Hample and Dallinger (1987a) found that the principled objection and harm to other criteria were more likely to be used by females, persons low in verbal aggressiveness, and persons high in interpersonal orientation. The same individuals were less likely to rely on an effectiveness criterion and rejected a greater number of arguments. A more recent study by Hample and Dallinger (1994) suggested that persons may revise their editing criteria to make less use of harm to other and principled objection criteria and greater use of an effectiveness criterion following a rebuff of their initial argument.

Although Hample and Dallinger's work has focused primarily on compliance-gaining messages, their findings raise the possibility that individuals differ in the criteria they employ to edit messages in a broad range of situations. As Hample and Dallinger have noted, such differences would seem to reflect personality-related differences in the priority assigned to various relational goals. The present chapter is concerned with the nature of the cognitive processes that allow such goals to produce revisions in a preliminary message plan. Although the cognitive processes involved in addressing relational goals have received attention from a number of communication theorists (Berger 1988, 1995; Greene, 1984; Meyer, 1990; O'Keefe & Shepherd, 1987; Wilson, 1990, 1995) the processes underlying the anticipation of relational outcomes and revision of an output plan are not well understood. This chapter outlines a preliminary model of these processes.

The following section describes the general processing assumptions adopted by the model. The next section describes three types of cognitive structures assumed to play an important role in cognitive editing. The model's assumptions about message formulation, anticipating relational outcomes, and revising a message plan are detailed as well. A subsequent section considers the implications of the model for individual differences in the ability to realize relational goals.

GENERAL PROCESSING ASSUMPTIONS

The model distinguishes between long-term memory and working memory. Long-term memory is unconscious and has infinite capacity. It consists of cognitive structures that include goals, schemas, behaviors, consequences of past behaviors, and systems of interconnected beliefs. Working memory includes all cognitive structures in long-term memory that are activated. Knowledge activated in working memory includes knowledge activated to a conscious level (i.e., knowledge in short-term memory) as well as knowledge activated preconsciously (i.e., outside of the individual's awareness). In contrast with the amount of information that can be maintained consciously, which is subject to strict capacity limitations, a very large amount of knowledge can be activated preconsciously. While information can enter conscious awareness in the absence of an effort to retrieve it, it cannot be maintained for long without attentional effort. In contrast, knowledge activated preconsciously may remain activated for a considerable duration of time. It is assumed that conscious awareness is preceded by considerable preconscious processing. Similar assumptions have been made by theorists in the areas of selective attention, emotion, and social information processing (Bargh, 1994; Lazarus, 1991; Mandler, 1984; Marcel, 1983; Neisser, 1967).

The model adopts the general processing assumptions of parallel distributed processing models (McClelland & Rumelhart, 1985). A cognitive structure in long-term memory consists of a network of highly interconnected elements. The same element can form part of many cognitive structures. Structures in long-term memory possess an accessibility (strength) which depends on the strength of the interconnections among elements. The accessibility of a cognitive structure is a positive function of the frequency and recency of its activation (Anderson, 1983; Greene, 1984). Cognitive structures can be activated by external stimuli or by activation spreading from other activated structures. A cognitive structure that is activated (at either a preconscious or conscious level) consists of a pattern of activation distributed across the interconnected elements that compose the structure. The level of activation of a structure is a positive function of the amount of activation converging on it.

COGNITIVE STRUCTURES

The model postulates that three types of cognitive structures play an important role in the formulation and editing of messages. These include situation-action associations, action-consequence associations, and cognitive representations of goals.

Situation-Action Associations

Situation-action associations take the form of an association from a situation schema containing a goal and contextual features to behaviors appropriate to achieving the goal in that context. Their function is to allow a speaker to locate behaviors appropriate to realizing a goal. The goal contained in the schematic situational component of such associations may be a primary communication goal, a relational goal, or a metagoal (e.g., social appropriateness; Berger, 1995). The situational component of these associations is abstracted from past experiences of situations with similar goals and features (Cody, Canary, & Smith, 1994; Meyer, 1996). Situation-action associations may also be viewed as implicit "rules" of behavior (Meyer, 1990).

Primary goals contained in the schematic situational component of situation-action associations exist at different levels of specificity. For instance, a situation schema might contain a goal to ask for a favor. The behaviors activated by such a schema may include speech acts such as a request for action, explanation, or apology (Meyer, 1994). A schema may also contain a goal to perform a specific speech act. The behaviors connected to a schema containing a goal to make a request for action might include words ("could"), mood (the interrogative), conventional phrases ("I was wondering . . ."), syntactical structures, or nonverbal behaviors.

Activating Conditions

Situation-action associations become activated once a speaker has decided to pursue a goal. At that point, speakers tend to become aware of contextual features relevant to realizing the goal. Activation spreading from the goal and features leads to the automatic activation of a situation schema. Once activated, the schema organizes the speaker's perception of the situation and raises the preconscious level of activation of behaviors appropriate in that situation. Whether a behavior will be activated highly enough to have an impact on message design depends on the accessibility of the behavior in long-term memory and the amount of activation converging on it from the situation schema. The same situation schema may activate numerous behaviors in parallel and the same behavior may be activated by numerous schemas.

Action-Consequence Associations

Action-consequence associations take the form of an association from a linguistic behavior and contextual features to beliefs about the consequences of the behavior. Their function is to allow a speaker to anticipate the outcomes of linguistic behaviors. Although action-consequence associations may be acquired as the result of articulating a rule ("Whenever I ask Lou to do something, he acts defensive"), it is assumed that they are, for the most part, acquired implicitly as the result of perceiving and storing the consequences of behaviors. Actions may also become associated to consequences that have been only imagined or acquired from observing others.

The linguistic behaviors forming the action part of action-consequence associations exist at different levels of specificity. For example, the action component of such associations might involve overall *plans* (promising the hearer a reward will increase the likelihood of compliance), *speech acts* (complaining will cause Todd to act aggressively), *mood* (using the imperative will make me look decisive), *nonverbal cues* (raising my voice will prevent others from interrupting), or *words* (saying "mankind" will insult the hearer). As noted earlier, the action component of these associations specifies not only an action, but contextual conditions. Contextual conditions in action-consequence associations may involve not only situational features but other components of a planned message. The ability to store context-sensitive outcomes is essential given that the consequences of a message component often depend on the context.

The consequences activated by action-consequence associations often consist of expectations abstracted from multiple past outcomes of a similar nature. The latter might include hearer reactions such as confirmation, rejection, aggressiveness, submissiveness, or dominance. Consequences may also involve abstract trait-related perceptions of self or other (kind, cultured, ill-informed). If a particular consequence has occurred frequently across contexts, it might be activated by many action-consequence associations.

Activating Conditions

Action-consequence associations become activated when a speaker entertains a plan to produce a message. A single message plan may cause a very large number of consequences to become activated. These consequences are initially activated preconsciously. The preconscious level of activation of a consequence is an additive function of its accessibility in long-term memory and the amount of activation it receives from the speaker's representation of the message plan. The long-term memory accessibility of a consequence is a positive function of the frequency and recency of its activation. The accessibility of a consequence experienced only once may be greater if it received more elaborate processing at the time it was stored (Craik & Lockhart, 1972).

Once a belief about a consequence is activated at a preconscious level, activation spreads to associated beliefs. This spread of activation may initiate a preconscious inferencing process which arrives at consequences only distantly associated to the action. For instance, a woman considering the disclosure "I always vote Republican" to a new acquaintance may activate an action-consequence association that links a disclosure about her party preference to the consequence of being seen as conservative. Further inferencing may activate the beliefs that academics are often not conservative, the hearer is an academic, the hearer is probably not conservative, and persons who are not conservative often see conservatives negatively.

Knowledge of the type embodied in action-consequence associations has parallels in many theories of human behavior. The notion that individuals store and retrieve beliefs about the outcomes of a behavior is a central assumption of the Theory of Reasoned Action (Ajzen & Fishbein, 1980). The assumption that behavioral production is guided by knowledge equivalent to both situation-action associations and action-consequence associations (along with other types of rules) is also assumed in the theory of inductive learning developed by Holland, Holyoak, Nisbett, and Thagard (1986).

Cognitive Representations of Goals

Goals are viewed as cognitive representations stored in long-term memory. Goals pertinent to conversation include primary communicative goals, relational goals, and highly general metagoals such as social appropriateness and efficiency (Berger, 1995). Dillard (1990) has argued that the most general goals correspond to basic motives. Thus, metagoals might include motives that stem from needs for self-esteem, power, achievement or affiliation. The model assumes that most individuals possess cognitive representations of relational goals related to presenting a positive self-image, protecting the other's ego, acting in a manner consistent with one's identity, and maintaining a positive relationship (Dillard et al., 1989; Hample & Dallinger, 1987a), though the tactics available for addressing these goals may vary considerably. Speakers may also store relational goals to dominate, protect the other's need for autonomy, appear superior, or put down the hearer.

Like other structures in long-term memory, goals have an accessibility that is a positive function of frequency and recency of activation. The accessibility of relational goals and metagoals is assumed to vary across individuals. Such differences result from differences in values, social experience, and personality disposition.

Activating Conditions

Cognitive representations of goals become consciously activated when their level of activation exceeds a threshold. The activating conditions for a goal can take a number of forms. Primary goals often become conscious after being retrieved as actions for achieving a larger goal. For example, an individual might possess a situation-action association that associates the goal of getting home (and current features) to the action of asking someone for a ride. If the latter action is consciously retrieved, it may become a primary goal and act as the retrieval cue for a situation schema containing a goal to ask for a favor. Relational goals may sometimes become activated in a similar manner. For example, one might possess a situation-action association linking a goal to keep a client to the action of maintaining a positive relationship. A decision to carry out the latter action would necessitate the conscious maintenance of a relationship management goal.

Relational goals more often become activated as the result of activation spreading from situation schemas containing metagoals. The present model holds that schemas containing metagoals become activated upon entering a conversational situation. The retrieval cues leading to the activation of such a schema are a metagoal that remains activated much of the time plus an immediate social episode.[1] For instance, such a schema might contain a social-appropriateness metagoal and the contextual information that the episode is a conversation. A schema containing a social appropriateness metagoal might also contain the contextual information that the episode is

---

[1]The activating conditions for situation-action associations containing metagoals might include general goals or needs that remain activated at some level at all times. The latter could include needs for self-preservation, happiness, or contentment.

a specific type of conversational situation (e.g., small talk, a job interview, an argument, and so on).

Once a situation schema containing a metagoal is activated, it sends activation to multiple relational goals in parallel. The level of action of a relational goal activated as such is a positive function of the amount of activation it receives from the situation schema and its accessibility in long-term memory. If a relational goal is activated highly enough, it will be consciously retrieved as a possible action (e.g., make a good impression). If a decision is made to carry out the action, the speaker will make an attentional effort to maintain the relational goal in conscious memory. The goal will then act as a retrieval cue for a situation-action association linking the relational goal and current features to behaviors.

The preconscious level of activation of most relational goals activated by a situation schema with a metagoal will be insufficient for the goal to reach conscious awareness. However, such goals will remain activated at a preconscious level during the conversation. The preconscious level of activation of a relational goal depends on the activation it receives from the metagoal and episode activating it and its accessibility for the individual. A relational goal that is consciously activated may become preconscious when the speaker's attention shifts to a different goal (Berger, 1995).

When a relational goal is activated preconsciously, activation spreads from the goal to prime behaviors associated to it. As these behaviors receive less activation than those activated by a conscious goal, they remain activated at a relatively low level. As described in more detail shortly, a relational goal activated preconsciously may become conscious if a speaker realizes that a planned message would conflict with or realize the goal.

COGNITIVE PROCESSES

A complete description of the cognitive processes underlying cognitive editing would need to account for the processing involved in message formulation, the anticipation of consequences, and message revision. The following section provides a brief description of the model's assumptions about the formulation and revision of messages. The primary focus is on the processing that underlies the anticipation of relational outcomes.

Message Formulation

The formulation of a message begins when a speaker activates a primary goal such as expressing an opinion or asking for a favor. If the speaker is consciously maintaining a goal to ask for a favor, activation will spread from that goal and current situational features to activate a situation schema.

Activation spreading from this schema might lead to the preconscious activation of speech acts appropriate to asking for a favor (e.g., an explanation, request for action, promise, and apology). Cognitive representations of these acts will interact with thoughts already activated in working memory to produce a tentative conceptual plan for the message. The latter plan consists of a specification of some number of speech acts plus a vague conceptual representation of the content of each act. For instance, the speaker might activate a plan to make a request for a ride home and then explain that his or her car is in the garage.

As a first step to carrying out this plan, the speaker will activate a goal to carry out the first speech act (i.e., the request for action). At this point, the speaker is representing a goal to produce a request for action, situational features, and a vague conceptual representation of the propositional content of the act. Activation spreading from this representation will raise the preconscious level of activation of syntactic structures and phonological representations of words corresponding to the preliminary propositional content (Bock, 1982; Motley et al., 1983).

At the same time this processing is taking place, the speaker's representation of a goal to make a request for action and current features will activate a schema containing matched (or partially matched) cognitive elements. Activation spreading from the latter schema raises the preconscious level of activation of linguistic behaviors (words, phrases, syntactical formulations, nonverbal cues, etc.) that have been employed in the past to make a request in similar situational contexts.

At this point, it is assumed that top-down processing from the preliminary conceptual representation of propositional content and bottom-up activation from the cues activated by the schema interact to transform the preliminary conceptual plan for the message into an initial output plan that is specified syntactically and phonologically. Decisions among competing plans at this stage are assumed to be resolved partly on the basis of level of activation (Dell, 1986). At various points in the formation of a tentative message plan, bottom-up activation from words or other linguistic representations may lead to revisions in the immediate plan. This processing is assumed to be parallel and highly interactive (Bock, 1987; Dell, 1986; Greene, 1984; Motley et al., 1983).

Anticipating Relational Consequences

Once a speaker has formulated a tentative output plan, the conscious representation of this plan leads automatically to the preconscious activation of action-consequence associations. Because any message plan will contain a large number of action components at different levels of specificity, the number of consequences that could be activated preconsciously by action-consequence associations is potentially very large. Clearly, speakers do not become aware of all possible message outcomes. Before a speaker can consciously anticipate a relational outcome, two conditions must be met. First, knowledge about the *relevance* of a consequence to a relational goal must be activated preconsciously. Second, the speaker must become consciously aware of the same knowledge.

Determining the Relevance of a Consequence to a Goal

Consequences directly activated by some message components will already contain information about how the message is relevant to a relational goal. For example an action-consequence association might link a compliment to the consequence of protecting the other's ego. For many message components, however, the relevance of a directly activated consequence to a relational goal may be arrived at only after some degree of preconscious inferencing. Even when a directly activated consequence contains the relevance of an action to one relational goal, further processing may lead to the knowledge that it could conflict with another goal. For instance, a plan to make a compliment may directly activate the consequence that it would enhance the other's ego. Additional processing may activate the knowledge that assertions enhancing another's ego can be seen as insincere and that insincere behavior is perceived negatively.

The cognitive processes involved in arriving at consequences not directly activated by action-consequence associations are assumed to proceed in the following way. Once a speaker is representing a message plan, consequences associated to different components of the plan are activated preconsciously. Activation spreads automatically from each consequence to beliefs associated to it. At the time the latter knowledge is activated, other knowledge will also be activated preconsciously. The latter knowledge includes relational goals that remain activated at a preconscious level throughout a conversation. When knowledge is activated in working memory, the potential is always present for activation from one source to intersect with activation from another. For instance, it is by such processes that speakers detect the relevance of the other's comments to their own goals. When a consequence and relational goal are activated preconsciously, activation spreading from the consequence and knowledge primed by the relational goal may intersect. Once this occurs, it may be said that the relevance of the consequence to the relational goal is activated. An intersection of this sort is a necessary, though not sufficient, condition for the speaker to become aware that a consequence will conflict with a relational goal.

Whether activation from a consequence will intersect with activation from a relational goal depends on the level of activation of the consequence and the level of activation of the relational goal. When a consequence or a goal is activated to a higher level, more activation will be sent to associated knowledge and the likelihood of activating beliefs about the relevance of the consequence to the goal will be greater. Given the activation assumptions noted earlier, this implies that the likelihood of arriving at the relevance of a consequence to a goal will generally be greater if the consequence is receiving more activation from a message component, the consequence is accessible due to frequency or recency of activation, or the relational goal is an accessible one for the individual.

The foregoing discussion has focused on the processing that occurs when a relational goal is activated at a preconscious level. Because the level of activation of a goal will be highest if it is consciously activated, the likelihood of activating preconscious knowledge about the relevance of a consequence to a goal should generally be greatest for consciously activated primary and relational goals. Given the limited constraints on capacity in preconscious memory, however, it is assumed that individuals often activate preconscious knowledge about the relevance of consequences to numerous relational goals as well as noncommunicative goals.

Becoming Aware of the Relevance of a Consequence to a Goal

Although the preconscious activation of knowledge about the relevance of a consequence to a relational goal is a necessary condition for becoming aware of such knowledge, the fact that the knowledge is activated preconsciously does not guarantee that the speaker will become conscious of it. The fact that individuals often fail to perceive the relevance of a behavior to important beliefs has been offered as one explanation of attitude–behavior inconsistency (O'Keefe, 1990). The failure to retrieve knowledge about the relevance of a behavioral outcome to one's goals may also underlie behaviors involving health risks, conformity, and domestic violence.

Despite the importance of the issue to explaining human functioning, the cognitive processes by which individuals become aware of preconsciously activated knowledge relevant to a goal are not well understood. Past research on cognitive processes is suggestive, however, of a number of factors that might influence the likelihood of becoming aware of such knowledge. The present model posits that the likelihood of becoming aware of preconsciously activated knowledge about the relevance of a consequence to a relational goal is positively related to two factors: (a) the level of activation of knowledge about the relevance of the consequence to the relational goal, and (b) available processing capacity.

Level of Activation of Goal-Relevant Knowledge. As noted earlier, the *likelihood* of activating preconscious knowledge about the relevance of a consequence to a relational goal increases with the level of activation of the goal and level of activation of the consequence. The same factors will influence the level of activation of knowledge about the relevance of the consequence to the goal. That is, when the relational goal or consequence are activated to a higher level, more activation will summate on beliefs representing an intersection between the goal and consequence.[2]

Evidence consistent with the view that individuals are more likely to become aware of preconscious knowledge when it is activated to a higher level comes from experiments employing a priming paradigm. For instance, Higgins, Rholes, and Jones (1977) found that the manner in which subjects interpreted ambiguous behaviors of a target person was influenced by which traits were primed in an earlier "unrelated" task. In their study, it is reasonable to assume that the primed trait was activated preconsciously when participants began the second "unrelated" experiment. It might be speculated that, when they processed the ambiguous behaviors, activation spread from the behaviors to multiple traits that could be attributed to the target, raising the preconscious level of activation of each. As the primed trait was already activated, the additional activation from the behaviors would have caused it to become activated more highly than unprimed traits. Thus, the results are consistent with the view that persons are more likely to become aware of knowledge if it is activated to a higher level preconsciously. In a related study, Bargh, Bond, Lombardi, and Tota (1986) showed that chronically accessible traits are more likely to be retrieved than less accessible traits in interpreting ambiguous behaviors of a target. In the latter experiment, it is likely that reading the behaviors caused a number of possible traits to become activated preconsciously. If a chronically accessible trait received the same amount of activation as a less accessible one, it would have become activated to a relatively higher level preconsciously. Hence, the Bargh et al. results also suggest that individuals are more likely to become aware of knowledge activated preconsciously when it is activated to a higher level.

It should be noted that, in these experiments, knowledge activated preconsciously reached conscious awareness only after receiving external stimulation from the processing of the ambiguous behaviors. The present model posits that preconscious knowledge about the relevance of a consequence to a relational goal is more likely to come to mind if it is activated to a higher level based solely on internal sources of activation. A specific assumption of the model is that the likelihood of becoming aware of the

---

[2]The activation level of knowledge about the relevance of a consequence to a goal will also be a function of these two factors in cases where a directly activated consequence already contains knowledge about the relevance of the message component to a goal. In such cases, the consequence will receive activation both from the message component and from the preconsciously activated goal. If the relational goal is activated to a higher level more activation will summate on the consequence.

relevance of a consequence to a goal will be higher if the consequence is activated to a higher level. Experiments on creative problem solving provide evidence consistent with this claim. A number of experiments suggest that the likelihood of becoming spontaneously aware of the relevance of available information to the goal of solving a problem is greater when the accessibility of that information has been raised in an apparently unrelated manipulation. In a well-known study by Maier (1931), subjects were asked to figure out how to tie two hanging cords together. The likelihood of thinking of a "pendulum" solution to the problem was greater when the experimenter provided a hint (by putting an unreachable cord in slight motion) even for subjects who were not consciously aware that a hint had been given (Lindsay & Norman, 1972). Similarly, Higgins and Chaires (1980) found that subjects were more likely to spontaneously think of a solution to the Duncker (1945) candle problem when an earlier, seemingly unrelated study primed the tendency to think of two objects involved in the problem (a box and the tacks that it held) as serving separate functions.

Available Processing Capacity. The second factor that influences the likelihood of becoming aware of knowledge about the relevance of a consequence to a relational goal is the amount of conscious processing capacity available. In general, individuals should be less likely to become aware of negative (or positive) relational outcomes when competing demands on capacity are greater. During a conversation, available capacity could be reduced by formulating and maintaining a more complex message plan (Berger, Karol, & Jordan, 1989; Greene & Ravizza, 1995) or processing a more complex topic. Capacity may also be reduced by physiological factors such as arousal or fatigue. Whereas the model predicts that the likelihood of becoming aware of negative relational outcomes will be poorer when arousal brought on by anger or apprehension are present, it also predicts that this problem will be lessened when the relational goal is accessible for the individual or the consequence is accessible due to frequency or recency of activation.

Message Revision

The awareness that a message consequence will conflict with a relational goal may or may not lead to cognitive editing. A speaker might become aware that a consequence will realize one goal (e.g., self-image enhancement) while conflicting with another (e.g., protecting the other's ego) and decide to produce the message nonetheless. If a decision is made to edit a message, the processing leading to a revised message plan could take one of two forms.

Suppose the speaker became aware that a message consequence would conflict with a goal to protect the other's ego. At that point, he or she might maintain a conscious representation of the latter goal. Activation spreading from this goal and current features could activate a schema containing a relational goal and features matched (or partially matched) to those in the current situation. Linguistic behaviors activated by the schema could then be integrated into the current message plan. A second possibility is that the negative outcome anticipated might be attributed to a feature of the situation that was not attended to when the initial message plan was formulated (e.g., low speaker status). An attentional focus on this feature in the context of the primary goal and other features could lead to the activation of a more highly differentiated schema containing current features as well as the "low speaker status" feature (Meyer, 1990). Behaviors activated by this schema could then be incorporated into the existing plan. A third possibility, of course, is that the speaker will be unable to retrieve behaviors for addressing the relational goal given the current context, in which case, the plan might be abandoned or produced nonetheless.

An Illustration of the Model's Assumptions

The model's assumptions will be illustrated by considering the case where a speaker has decided to express a difference of opinion on a political issue. Upon entering the conversation, the speaker might activate a schema containing a metagoal to be socially appropriate and the contextual information that the episode is a conversation. Activation from this schema will raise the preconscious level of activation of multiple relational goals. It will be assumed that the speaker's accessible relational goals are a goal to make a good impression and a goal to protect the other's ego and, hence, that these goals become activated to the highest level preconsciously.

Once the speaker is consciously maintaining a goal to express a difference of opinion, activation spreading from that goal and current situational features (e.g., that the hearer is well-known and liked) will activate a situation schema containing some degree of match to the current goal and features. Activation spreading from the schema might activate speech acts such as a disagreement and assertion. These acts will interact with the speaker's current thoughts to produce a tentative conceptual plan for the message. For instance, the speaker might decide to indicate that he or she thinks the hearer is wrong and then assert his or her own belief.

The speaker will then activate a plan to produce the first speech act. This representation contains a goal to produce a disagreement, current features, and a vague, conceptual representation of propositional content. Activation from this structure will raise the preconscious level of activation of syntactic structures and words corresponding to the conceptual plan. At the same time, activation spreading from the goal to produce a disagreement and current features will activate a situation schema containing similar cognitive elements. Activation spreading from the latter schema will raise the preconscious level of activation of behaviors that have been employed by the speaker in the past to disagree with a hearer who is well-known and liked. These behaviors might include words ("disagree," "wrong"), phrases ("no way," "I beg to differ"), nonverbal gestures (head movement, eye behavior), paralinguistic cues (pitch), and qualifiers ("I think"). Behaviors activated in this manner will, via bottom-up processing, interact with the preliminary representation of propositional content to produce an initial message plan for the first speech act.

Suppose the initial message plan is "I think you're wrong." Activation spreading from a conscious representation of this plan will cause action-consequence associations to become activated. These might include the following: (a) using the speech act, disagreement, will convey that I hold an opinion different from the hearer's and allow me to appear knowledgeable, (b) asserting that the hearer is "wrong" will cause the hearer to appear ill-informed and make me appear insensitive, and (c) saying "I think" will convey a provisional attitude. Once the latter consequences become activated, activation spreads from each consequence to associated beliefs, with more activation being sent by more highly activated consequences. The likelihood of activating knowledge about the relevance of each consequence to a relational goal will be greater if the consequence is more highly activated and the goal more highly activated. As the relational goals activated to the highest level preconsciously are a goal to protect the other's ego and an impression goal, the speaker should be most likely to activate knowledge about the relevance of consequences to the latter goals (assuming consequences relevant to each goal are activated to about the same level). For example, activation spreading from "will cause the hearer to appear ill-informed" could activate the beliefs "being ill-informed is an undesirable trait" and "implying that someone has an undesirable trait can hurt their self-esteem." This path of activation might intersect with behaviors already primed by the preconsciously activated goal to protect the other's ego. One such belief might be, "avoid saying things that would hurt the other's self-esteem." At that point, knowledge about the relevance of the consequence to a goal to protect the other's ego is activated preconsciously. Simultaneously, activation spreading from other consequences (e.g., "would allow me to appear knowledgeable," "will make me appear insensitive") may intersect with behaviors primed by the preconsciously activated impression-management goal. If the "appear knowledgeable" consequence is more highly activated than the "appear insensitive" consequence, the knowledge that the message would realize an impression goal would be more highly activated than the knowledge that it would conflict with an impression goal.

The likelihood that the speaker will become aware of knowledge about the relevance of a consequence to a goal will depend on the level of activation of the same knowledge and available capacity. If the knowledge that the message conflicts with a goal to protect the other's ego is more highly activated than the knowledge that it would realize (or conflict with) an impression goal, the speaker would be more likely to become aware of the former. If capacity were available, the speaker might become aware of numerous relational outcomes. Having anticipated a negative relational outcome, the speaker might edit the message by employing one of the editing methods described earlier.

The foregoing discussion describes how a relational outcome might be anticipated following the formulation of the initial speech act in a plan with multiple acts. Consequences of a message plan might also be anticipated at an earlier stage following the formulation of an overall plan. Alternatively, speakers might formulate message plans with multiple speech acts before anticipating relational outcomes.

IMPLICATIONS FOR INDIVIDUAL DIFFERENCES

One assumption of the model is that the likelihood of detecting that a message plan conflicts with a relational goal will be greater if the goal is accessible for the speaker than if not. When a relational goal is accessible, the likelihood that it will be activated to a conscious level prior to the formulation of a preliminary message plan is also greater. It is speculated that these effects of goal accessibility may underlie a number of individual differences in communication behavior that appear to be consistent across situations. As noted earlier, Hample and Dallinger (1987a) found the criteria employed to reject message strategies to be related to interpersonal orientation, verbal aggressiveness, and gender. The present framework implies that these findings might reflect differences in the preconscious accessibility of relational goals which influence the ability to detect that a message will conflict with a relational goal in situations where the speaker would prefer to avoid such consequences.

It is speculated that the effects of goal accessibility on cognitive editing might also underlie behavioral differences associated with such constructs as conversational narcissism (Vangelisti, Knapp, & Daly, 1990), construct differentiation (Burleson, 1987; Wilson, 1990, 1995), self-monitoring (Snyder, 1987), affinity-seeking (Bell & Daly, 1984) and assertiveness. For example, behaviors characteristic of conversational narcissists may be influenced by the fact that such persons are more likely to become aware of how a message will accomplish a highly accessible self-image enhancement goal than of how it will conflict with a less accessible relationship-management goal. In developing the Cognitive Rules Model, Wilson (1990) speculated that persons higher in construct differentiation might possess more chronically accessible cognitive rules linking situational features to supporting goals (but see Wilson, 1995). One implication of the current model is that the tendency of more differentiated persons to produce more person-centered messages (Burleson, 1987) may reflect differences in the accessibility of relational goals that influence the likelihood of detecting in advance that a message consequence will conflict with the goal. Consistent with this possibility, Waldron and Applegate (1994) found a positive correlation between construct differentiation and the use of plan editing in a verbal disagreement task. Similarly, the propensity of low self-monitors to act in a "principled and honest" manner may be due partly to the fact that they are more likely to anticipate the relevance of messages to an accessible identity goal than to a less accessible impression-management goal. The differences might be reversed for high self-monitors. Although a study by Hample and Dallinger (1987b) suggested that the effect of self-monitoring on editing standards may depend on gender and the situation, Smith, Cody, LoVette, and Canary (1990) found that low self-monitors (especially males) were less likely to endorse influence strategies involving the manipulation of feelings, referent influence, or coercive influence.

FUTURE RESEARCH

To date, little attention has been devoted to the nature of the cognitive structures and processes that underlie the ability to detect that a message consequence will conflict with a relational goal. This framework is intended as a preliminary model of these processes. Future research on the cognitive processes underlying cognitive editing will no doubt lead to refinements or perhaps major revisions of the above assumptions.

The foregoing model predicts that the ability to detect that a message will conflict with a relational goal should be greater when the goal is more accessible, the consequence has been thought about or experienced frequently, and a greater amount of capacity is available. A necessary condition for accumulating evidence relevant to the first of these predictions is the development of methods for measuring individual differences in the accessibility of relational goals. Although some information pertinent to such differences might be obtained by employing thought-listing techniques (Hample & Dallinger, 1994; Waldron & Applegate, 1994) or self-ratings of goal importance, more direct measures of the accessibility of a cognitive construct can be obtained by employing a reaction time methodology. Thus, data pertinent to differences in goal accessibility might be measured by employing methods similar to those used to measure the accessibility of constructs in the self-schema (Markus, 1977) or the accessibility of attitudes (Fazio, Sanbonmatsu, Powell, & Kardes, 1986).

A central prediction of the model is that individuals should be more likely to become aware of relational outcomes related to more accessible relational goals. Data bearing on this prediction might be obtained via thought-listing techniques based on videotaped conversations (Waldron & Applegate, 1994) or think-aloud computer conferencing. Such differences might also be reflected in the time required to think of a reason for rejecting a computer-presented message known to conflict with a relational goal.

An additional prediction of the model is that speakers should be more likely to become aware of relational outcomes related to more accessible consequences. One means of testing this prediction would be to manipulate the accessibility of expected consequences via experimental techniques. The model's claims regarding the effects of processing capacity on cognitive editing would also seem a fruitful area for future research. Although past research has indicated that the increased cognitive load associated with addressing a relational goal has a negative impact on fluency (Greene & Ravizza, 1995), there is a need to better understand how other demands on capacity influence both the likelihood of consciously addressing a relational goal and the likelihood of detecting unwanted relational outcomes.

REFERENCES

Ajzen, I., & Fishbein, M. (1980). *Understanding attitudes and predicting social behavior.* Englewood Cliffs, NJ: Prentice-Hall.

Anderson, J. R. (1983). *The architecture of cognition.* Cambridge, MA: Harvard University Press.

Bargh, J. A. (1994). The four horsemen of automaticity: Awareness, intention, efficiency, and control in social cognition. In R. S. Wyer, Jr. & T. K. Srull (Eds.), *Handbook of social cognition: Vol. 1. Basic processes* (pp. 1–40). Hillsdale, NJ: Lawrence Erlbaum Associates.

Bargh, J. A., Bond, R. N., Lombardi, W. J., & Tota, M. E. (1986). The additive nature of chronic and temporary sources of construct accessibility. *Journal of Personality and Social Psychology, 50,* 869–878.

Bell, R. A., & Daly, J. A. (1984). The affinity-seeking function of communication. *Communication Monographs, 51,* 91–115.

Berger, C. R. (1988). Planning, affect, and social action generation. In L. Donohew, H. E. Sypher, & E. T. Higgins (Eds.), *Communication, social cognition and affect* (pp. 93–116). Hillsdale, NJ: Lawrence Erlbaum Associates.

Berger, C. R. (1995). A plan-based approach to strategic communication. In D. E. Hewes (Ed.), *The cognitive bases of interpersonal communication* (pp. 141–179). Hillsdale, NJ: Lawrence Erlbaum Associates.

Berger, C. R., Karol, S. H., & Jordan, J. M. (1989). When a lot of knowledge is a dangerous thing: The debilitating effects of plan complexity on verbal fluency. *Human Communication Research, 16,* 91–119.

Bock, J. K. (1982). Toward a cognitive psychology of syntax: Information processing contributions to sentence formulation. *Psychological Review, 89,* 1–47.

Bock, J. K. (1987). Co-ordinating words and syntax in speech plans. In A. W. Ellis (Ed.), *Progress in the psychology of language* (Vol. 3, pp. 337–390). Hillsdale, NJ: Lawrence Erlbaum Associates.

Burleson, B. R. (1987). Cognitive complexity. In J. C. McCroskey & J. A. Daly (Eds.), *Personality and interpersonal communication* (pp. 305–349). Newbury Park, CA: Sage.

Cody, M. J., Canary, D. J., & Smith, S. W. (1994). Compliance-gaining goals: An inductive analysis of actors' goal types, strategies, and successes. In J. A. Daly & J. M. Wiemann (Eds.), *Strategic interpersonal communication* (pp. 33–90). Hillsdale, NJ: Lawrence Erlbaum Associates.

Craik, F. I. M., & Lockhart, R. S. (1972). Levels of processing: A framework for memory research. *Journal of Verbal Learning and Verbal Behavior, 11,* 671–684.

Dell, G. S. (1985). Positive feedback in hierarchical connectionist models. *Cognitive Science, 9,* 3–23.

Dell, G. S. (1986). A spreading-activation theory of retrieval in sentence production. *Psychological Review, 93,* 283–321.

Dell, G. S., & Reich, P. A. (1981). Stages in sentence production: An analysis of speech error data. *Journal of Verbal Learning and Verbal Behavior, 20,* 611–629.

Dillard, J. P. (1990). The nature and substance of goals in tactical communication. In M. J. Cody & M. L. McLaughlin (Eds.), *The psychology of tactical communication* (pp. 70–90). Clevedon, Avon, England: Multilingual Matters.

Dillard, J. P., Segrin, C., & Harden, J. M. (1989). Primary and relational goals in the production of interpersonal influence messages. *Communication Monographs, 56,* 19–38.

Duncker, K. (1945). On problem solving. *Psychological Monographs, 58* (Whole No. 270).

Fazio, R. H., Sanbonmatsu, D. M., Powell, M. C., & Kardes, F. R. (1986). On the automatic activation of attitudes. *Journal of Personality and Social Psychology, 50,* 229–238.

Greene, J. O. (1984). A cognitive approach to human communication: An action-assembly theory. *Communication Monographs, 51,* 289–306.

Greene, J. O., & Lindsey, A. E. (1989). Encoding processes in the production of multiple-goal messages. *Human Communication Research, 16,* 120–140.

Greene, J. O., & Ravizza, S. M. (1995). Complexity effects on temporal characteristics of speech. *Human Communication Research, 21,* 390–421.

Hample, D., & Dallinger, J. M. (1987a). Individual differences in cognitive editing standards. *Human Communication Research, 14,* 123–144.

Hample, D., & Dallinger, J. M. (1987b). Self-monitoring and the cognitive editing of arguments. *Central States Speech Journal, 38,* 152–165.

Hample, D., & Dallinger, J. M. (1992). The use of multiple goals in cognitive editing of arguments. *Argumentation and Advocacy, 28,* 109–122.

Hample, D., & Dallinger, J. M. (1994, July). *Why are persuasive messages less polite after rebuffs?* Paper presented at the annual meeting of the International Communication Association, Sydney, Australia.

Higgins, E. T., & Chaires, W. M. (1980). Accessibility of interrelational constructs: Implications for stimulus encoding and creativity. *Journal of Experimental Social Psychology, 16,* 348–361.

Higgins, E. T., Rholes, W. S., & Jones, C. R. (1977). Category accessibility and impression formation. *Journal of Experimental Social Psychology, 13,* 141–154.

Holland, J. H., Holyoak, K. J., Nisbett, R. E., & Thagard, P. R. (1986). *Induction: Processes of inference, learning, and discovery.* Cambridge, MA: MIT Press.

Lazarus, R. S. (1991). *Emotion and adaptation.* New York: Oxford University Press.

Lindsay, P. H., & Norman, D. A. (1972). *Human information processing: An introduction to psychology.* New York: Academic Press.

Maier, N. R. F. (1931). Reasoning in humans. II. The solution of a problem and its appearance in consciousness. *Journal of Comparative Psychology, 12,* 181–194.

Mandler, G. (1984). *Mind and body: Psychology of emotion and stress.* New York: Norton.

Marcel, A. J. (1983). Conscious and unconscious perception: Experiments on visual masking and word recognition. *Cognitive Psychology, 15,* 197–237.

Markus, H. (1977). Self-schemata and processing information about the self. *Journal of Personality and Social Psychology, 35,* 63–78.

Marwell, G., & Schmitt, D. R. (1967). Dimensions of compliance-gaining behavior: An empirical analysis. *Sociometry, 30,* 350–364.

McClelland, J. L., & Rumelhart, D. E. (1985). Distributed memory and the representation of general and specific information. *Journal of Experimental Psychology: General, 114,* 159–188.

Meyer, J. R. (1990). Cognitive processes underlying the retrieval of compliance-gaining strategies: An implicit rules model. In J. P. Dillard (Ed.), *Seeking compliance: The production of interpersonal influence messages* (pp. 57–73). Scottsdale, AZ: Gorsuch Scarisbrick Publishers.

Meyer, J. R. (1992). Fluency in the production of requests: Effects of degree of imposition, schematicity and instruction set. *Journal of Language and Social Psychology, 11,* 232–251.

Meyer, J. R. (1994). Formulating plans for requests: An investigation of retrieval processes. *Communication Studies, 45,* 131–144.

Meyer, J. R. (1996). Retrieving knowledge in social situations: A test of the Implicit Rules Model. *Communication Research, 23,* 581–611.

Motley, M. T. (1986). On replicating the slip technique: A reply to Sinsabaugh and Fox. *Communication Monographs, 53,* 342–351.

Motley, M. T., Baars, B. J., & Camden, C. T. (1981). Syntactic criteria in prearticulatory editing: Evidence from laboratory-induced slips of the tongue. *Journal of Psycholinguistic Research, 5,* 503–522.

Motley, M. T., Baars, B. J., & Camden, C. T. (1983). Experimental verbal slip studies: A review and an editing model of language encoding. *Communication Monographs, 50,* 79–101.

Motley, M. T., Camden, C. T., & Baars, B. J. (1979). Personality and situational influences upon verbal slips: A laboratory test of Freudian and prearticulatory editing hypotheses. *Human Communication Research, 5,* 195–202.

Neisser, U. (1967). *Cognitive psychology.* New York: Appleton-Century-Crofts.

O'Keefe, B. J., & Shepherd, G. J. (1987). The pursuit of multiple objectives in face-to-face persuasive interactions: Effects of construct differentiation on message organization. *Communication Monographs, 54,* 396–419.

O'Keefe, D. J. (1990). *Persuasion: Theory and research.* Newbury Park, CA: Sage.

Smith, S. W., Cody, M. J., LoVette, S., & Canary, D. (1990). Self-monitoring, gender and compliance-gaining goals. In M. J. Cody & M. L. McLaughlin (Eds.), *The psychology of tactical communication* (pp. 91–135). Clevedon, Avon, England: Multilingual Matters.

Snyder, M. (1987). *Public appearances, private realities: The psychology of self-monitoring.* New York: Freeman.

Vangelisti, A. L., Knapp, M. L., & Daly, J. A. (1990). Conversational narcissism. *Communication Monographs, 57,* 251–274.

Waldron, V. R., & Applegate, J. L. (1994). Interpersonal construct differentiation and conversational planning: An examination of two cognitive accounts for the production of competent verbal disagreement tactics. *Human Communication Research, 21,* 3–35.

Wilson, S. R. (1990). Development and test of a cognitive rules model of interaction goals. *Communication Monographs, 57,* 81–103.

Wilson, S. R. (1995). Elaborating the cognitive rules model of interaction goals: The problem of accounting for individual differences in goal formation. In B. Burleson (Ed.), *Communication yearbook 18* (pp. 3–25). Thousand Oaks, CA: Sage.

5

THE GENERATION OF DECEPTIVE MESSAGES: LAYING THE GROUNDWORK FOR A VIABLE THEORY OF INTERPERSONAL DECEPTION

Steven A. McCornack
Michigan State University

Despite nearly 25 years of research, deceptive communication remains a scholarly domain devoid of viable theory. Of the four theories and conceptual frameworks advanced thus far (i.e., Bradac, Friedman, & Giles, 1986; Buller & Burgoon, 1996; Hocking & Leathers, 1980; McCornack, 1992), only Information Manipulation Theory (McCornack, 1992; see also McCornack, Levine, Solow-czuk, Torres, & Campbell, 1992; Lapinski, 1995; Sahlman & Canary, 1995), and Interpersonal Deception Theory (Buller & Burgoon, 1996; see also Buller & Burgoon, 1991; Buller, Burgoon, White, & Ebesu, 1994; Burgoon, Buller, Guer-rero, Afifi, & Feldman, 1996) have spawned programmatic lines of research related to deceptive message production. Both theories, however, are decid-edly deficient, albeit in different ways. Information Manipulation Theory (IMT; McCornack, 1992) proposes that deceptive messages derive from speakers "transforming" relevant information (p. 6), but it fails to explicate this pur-ported transformation process. IMT also confounds three distinct, significant issues within the same discussion: deceptive message production, deceptive message characteristics, and recipient interpretation of such messages (for a detailed critique of IMT, see Jacobs, Dawson, & Brashers, 1996). More impor-tantly, IMT is not actually a *theory* at all: It provides no testable propositions or falsifiable hypotheses, hence, fails to meet the established criteria for viable social scientific theory (i.e., Popper, 1959).

In contrast, Interpersonal Deception Theory (IDT; Buller & Burgoon, 1996) provides a copious set of formal propositions regarding traditional decep-tion variables (e.g., suspicion, relational familiarity, behavioral leakage, etc.).

In addressing deceptive messages, IDT assumes a production process similar to that hinted at by IMT, one in which deceivers "strategically control the information in their messages" (Buller et al., 1994, p. 36; see also Burgoon et al., 1996). Also similar to IMT, this process is never explicated, although Buller et al. (1994) suggest that a hierarchical, multistep cognitive process might be involved, in which deceivers "confront communicative situations and decide whether to provide the truth or to alter information," then "decide how to manage information" (p. 36).

Despite the volume and scope of theoretical claims made, IDT fails to address many basic issues related to interpersonal deception, including the production mechanisms responsible for deceptive message encoding, and the cognitive processes underlying deceptive message interpretation (for a detailed critique of IDT, see Depaulo, Ansfield, & Bell, 1996a). In addition, many of the propositions presented by IDT, such as "deception displays change over time," are vague and nonfalsifiable (Levine & McCornack, 1996b). Consequently, IDT does "not meet the criteria [for theory] described by philosophers of science" (DePaulo et al., 1996a, p. 4).

The result of this dearth of coherent, viable theories is that deceptive communication is an area ripe for new theory development. Before such development can commence, however, three preliminary tasks must be accomplished. First, the theoretical domain in which new theories will be embedded must be specified.[1] Second, the characteristics of deceptive communication that merit theoretical explanation must be identified. Third, a set of coherent, parsimonious, yet profound issues of concern must be distinguished, issues that ultimately will form the rationale for theory generation.

The goal of this chapter is to lay the groundwork for future theory development in the area of deceptive communication by attempting to accomplish two of these three tasks. I begin by briefly describing the tension between hopeful myths and extant data that exists in the field of deception. I then identify and discuss three critical characteristics of deceptive communication for which any viable theory of interpersonal deception must account. Finally, I raise two compelling concerns that I believe should drive future theory development. I do not propose new theory in this chapter; I leave it to future scholars to identify the particular domain in which they

---

[1]For example, IMT was embedded within the domain of pragmatics, specifically, conversational implicature (i.e., Grice, 1975). However, because IMT was conceptually underspecified, it failed to capitalize on the potential richness that such an embedding could have engendered (Jacobs et al., 1996). IDT was not embedded within an extant theoretical domain, consequently, "no central explanatory mechanism is ever described" (DePaulo et al., 1996a, pp. 2–3). Instead, IDT combined an ad hoc assortment of "assumptions from the study of deception and interpersonal communication to move beyond individual and internal psychological processes to dyadic and external communicative patterns that defy explanation by a single intrapsychic behavioral, or interpersonal mechanism" (Buller et al., 1994, p. 36).

wish to embed their theories. However, I agree with Hewes and Planalp (1987) that "an understanding of the individual's knowledge, cognitive capacities and emotion is the necessary point of departure for building adequate theories of communication" (p. 172). And, as shall become clear throughout this chapter, I also believe that the most provocative questions confronting deception scholars necessarily will require the adoption of a cognitive approach in order to answer them.

HOPEFUL MYTHS AND EXTANT DATA

The deception literature is replete with intuitive conceptualizations and an abundance of data with which to test them. All too often, however, deception scholars have allowed "intuitive but debatable assumptions about the manner in which dishonesty is manifested in communication and discovered by communication partners" (Fiedler & Walka, 1993, pp. 199–200) to guide their theory construction and research designs. For example, consider one of the root claims of IDT (Buller & Burgoon, 1996), that deceivers exhibit more strategic and nonstrategic behaviors than do truthtellers (see IDT, Proposition 3). Such a claim is the evolutionary product of more than two decades of argument regarding deceivers' ability to strategically control behavioral displays (e.g., Ekman, 1985; Ekman & Friesen, 1969; Hocking & Leathers, 1980; Stiff & Miller, 1986). Although intuitive, this proposition is problematic on at least two counts. First, as a predictive claim it is nonfalsifiable (Levine & McCornack, 1996b). Second, as a descriptive claim, it represents an imprecise depiction of extant data. The suggestion that "deceivers engage in greater strategic activity designed to manage information, behavior, and image [than do truthtellers]" (Buller & Burgoon, 1996, Proposition 3) implies that deceivers systematically display behaviors designed to appear truthful, suppress behaviors that appear duplicitous, and adapt/adjust this behavioral display based on recipient feedback (see Buller & Burgoon, IDT Propositions 13 and 14, 1996; see also Buller, Strzyzewski, & Comstock, 1991). However, Levine and McCornack (1996a) have documented that across studies, deceptive sources do *not* strategically adapt their behaviors to appear honest when they are questioned by message recipients. DePaulo and her colleagues (see DePaulo & Kirkendol, 1988) repeatedly have demonstrated that deceptive sources who attempt strategic behavioral control actually are perceived as *more* duplicitous than sources who do not attempt such "strategizing," a finding they have labeled the motivational impairment effect.

The claim that deceptive message sources "display more nonstrategic arousal cues" (IDT, Proposition 3) than truthtellers also proves problematic. This claim derives from the assumption that deceivers experience significant, deception-based arousal that subsequently is exhibited in terms of uncontrollable (i.e., nonstrategic) behavioral cues (i.e., Ekman & Friesen, 1969; Hocking & Leathers, 1980). However, assuming such a simple and straightforward connection between the encoding of deception, physiological arousal, and behavioral output obscures the complex interrelationship between context, cognition, arousal, and message generation that occurs within real-life deceptive encounters (Fiedler & Walka, 1993). As Kraut (1978) noted, it is perilous for deception researchers "to treat verbal and nonverbal cues associated with deception as if they were analogous to cues associated with emotion and, thereby, underestimate the importance of context in providing them with meanings" (p. 389). Kraut concluded that "it is unlikely that any behaviors are invariably linked to deception attempts" (p. 389). As Fiedler and Walka (1993) elaborate,

> Although there is, of course, some evidence that some physiological indicators are correlated with lying under some conditions, we lack strong and cogent evidence for the specific emotional and cognitive processes supposed to mediate the physiological manifestations. The available evidence from laboratory studies under restrictive conditions . . . is hardly sufficient to support the universal assumption that everyday liars in social contexts in fact experience and reveal stress and guilty feelings most of the time. (p. 200)

Scholars also should be skeptical regarding a simple deception → arousal → behavioral cue relationship "because communication analyses show that lies and their derivatives (politeness, excuses, exaggerations, distractions, concealing, etc.) are quite common and telling the 'pure truth' seems to be the exception rather than the rule in real-life communication" (Fiedler & Walka, p. 200).

My goal with this illustration is not to criticize IDT per se, but to illustrate how the field of deceptive communication is rife with tension between hopeful myths and extant data. A powerful set of intuitive assumptions (i.e., "hopeful myths") regarding the nature of deception function to guide research designs and hypotheses, and bias interpretation of data (see, e.g., Levine & McCornack's (1996a) analysis of the behavioral adaptation myth). Hopeful myths that are treated by the majority of scholars as deception truths include the following:

1. the encoding of deceptive messages entails active, strategic, and detailed cognitive processing,
2. the encoding of deceptive messages requires greater cognitive load than the encoding of truthful messages,
3. the encoding of deceptive messages is more physiologically arousing than than the encoding of truthful messages,

4. there is an identifiable and consistent set of deception-arousal-based behavioral cues that deceivers "leak" when encoding deceptive messages,

5. human beings are innately capable of deception detection, and

6. deceptive messages have specifiable characteristics that render them distinct from truthful messages.

To ensure continued worship of this mythic pantheon, deception researchers utilize experimental methods that reify their assumptions into truths. The typical deception study forces sources to either baldly lie or baldly tell the truth (or design messages with specific deceptive or truthful characteristics), regarding artificial (i.e., experimenter-chosen) message content, allows them at least some time (or forewarning) prior to the production of their message, then places them within a highly arousing context (i.e., live interaction with stranger/friend/romantic partner, experimental room, videotape camera present and operative, and experimenter observing), for the "natural" interaction that then is observed and recorded. Message recipients typically are made aware that *something* peculiar is about to transpire (and often are informed that deception will be the particular peculiarity in question), then are instructed to pay close attention to source behaviors, and to ask certain questions at certain times. Researchers then claim strong empirical support for the strategic, demanding, arousing, detectable, and distinct nature of deception.

I believe that the time has come for deception researchers to bury their old gods, or at least challenge their authority (see, e.g., Fiedler & Walka, 1993; Levine & McCornack, 1996a). Communication scholars should embrace the observable characteristics of naturalistic deception, and set about generating viable theories that explain these characteristics. It is to these characteristics that I now turn.

CHARACTERISTICS OF DECEPTIVE COMMUNICATION

The field of deceptive communication is now so broad that it is impossible to dig up all "new caches of literature" (Hyman, 1989, p. 134). Correspondingly, there are an indefinite number of characteristics one could choose to focus on in a theoretical analysis. In the following discussion, I focus on four characteristics that I find particularly provocative and profound. They form an elegant paradox that, as of yet, has received little empirical attention or theoretical recognition: deception is at once *cognitive, ubiquitous, casual,* and *successful.*

The Cognitive Nature of Deceptive Communication

Scholars routinely conceptualize deceptive communication as an event defined by two critical, cognitive characteristics: speaker intentionality, and the generation of false beliefs in a recipient (see Levine, 1994, for a detailed analysis of deception definitions). As DePaulo, Kashy, Kirkendol, Wyer, and Epstein (1996b) explain,

> the self that is presented to others in everyday social life is characteristically an edited and packaged one. In nondeceptive presentations, the editing serves to specify and highlight the aspects of the self that are most relevant to the interaction at hand, without being designed to mislead. In comparison, the defining characteristic of the deceptive presentation is that it is *purposefully designed* to *foster a false impression.* (p. 4; emphasis added)

The conception of deception as intentional false-belief generation is shared by cognitive scientists, philosophers, psychologists, and communication researchers. Each of these domains is briefly discussed.

In explicating their speech-act-based language production model, Cohen and Perrault (1979) briefly noted the relationship between deception, belief generation, and multiple levels of belief-embeddedness. As they describe, "if AGT1 successfully lied to AGT2, he would have to be able to believe some proposition P, while believing that AGT2 believes that AGT1 believes P is false. . . . Hence, AGT1 would need at least three levels [of belief embedding]. . . . If AGT2 believes AGT1 has lied, he would need four levels" (p. 183). Airenti, Bara, and Colombetti (1993) expanded on this notion in their work addressing behavior games in conversation. To illustrate the Airenti et al. argument, suppose that Rupert and Katrinka are engaged in a conversation, and through this conversation come to share belief *P*. As Airenti et al. noted, Rupert and Katrinka sharing belief *P* in common potentially can give rise to Rupert believing that Katrinka believes *P*, Rupert believing that Katrinka believes that Rupert believes *P*, and so on, ad infinitum (p. 213). As they also described, "such finite nests of beliefs play an important role in nonstandard communicative situations, particularly in cases of deceit" (p. 213).

The notion that deception is integrally tied to belief-embedding has been explicated in greater detail by philosophers interested in intentional systems. Dennett (1987) described,

> a *first-order* intentional system has beliefs and desires (etc.) but no beliefs and desires *about* beliefs and desires. . . . A *second-order* intentional system is more sophisticated; it has beliefs and desires (and no doubt other intentional states) about beliefs and desires (and other intentional states)—both those of others and its own. . . . A *third-order* intentional system is one that is capable of such states as . . . *X wants Y to believe* that *X believes* he is alone." (p. 243; emphasis in original)

Deceptive communication would appear to require at least second-order intentionality. As Hyman (1989) argued, "to intentionally deceive someone, the deceiver must be a second-order intentional system . . . The deceiver must have beliefs about the intended victim's beliefs" (p. 141).

The relationship between deception, belief-embedding, and assumptions of intentionality is illustrated by an example provided by Dennett (1987). In his discussion of whether vervet monkeys can be considered intentional systems, Dennett described an incident in which two rival bands of vervets were fighting over territory:

> one of the losing side monkeys, temporarily out of the fray, seemed to get a bright idea: it suddenly issued a leopard alarm (in the absence of any leopards) leading *all* the vervets to take up the cry and head for the trees—creating a truce and regaining the ground his side had been losing. . . . If this act is not just a lucky coincidence, then the act is truly devious, for it is not simply a case of the vervet uttering an *imperative* "get into the trees" in the expectation that *all* the vervets will obey, since the vervet . . . should not *expect* a rival band to honor *his* imperative. So either the leopard call is *considered* by the vervets to be informative—a *warning*, not a *command*—and hence the utterer's credibility but not authority is enough to explain the effect, or our utterer is more devious still: he *wants* the rivals to *think* they are *overhearing* a command *intended* (of course) only for his folk. (p. 248; emphasis in original)

This example clearly demonstrates the fundamental link between cognition and deception. Not only is deception defined a priori as an act requiring at least second-order intentionality, but communicative acts that function deceptively, such as the vervet leopard call, require (or at least beg) post hoc appeal to cognitive concepts (e.g., intentionality, belief-embeddedness) to render them explicable, *even if those acts are performed by nonhumans* (see Dennett, 1987, for further discussion).

Psychologists have studied the link between cognition, belief-embeddedness, and deception by examining childrens' ability to lie (see DePaulo, Stone, & Lassiter, 1985, pp. 350–360, for a summary of research on children and deception). There is some debate regarding the precise age at which children acquire the cognitive skills necessary to be able to successfully deceive. Hyman (1989) suggested that children may possess the necessary cognitive skills at around age five, but require several additional years of experience and practice "before they can apply their deceptive competence effectively" (p. 144). However, there is little debate that the cognitive skills in question involve second-, third-, and fourth-order intentionality (i.e., the capacity to recognize multiple levels of belief-embeddedness). As Hyman described, "only in early adolescence does the child fully appreciate the possibility that, given the same information, the other person can still construe the situation differently," hence "it is not until early adolescence that children achieve the capacity for intentional deception" (Hyman, 1989, p. 144; see also Chandler, 1988; DePaulo et al., 1985).[2]

An excellent illustration of Hyman's argument is the work of Peskin (1992), examining 3-, 4-, and 5-year-olds' ability to conceal information. Children selected a sticker that they liked the best, one that was moderately liked, and one that was disliked. They subsequently interacted with two puppets, the "bad puppet" and the "good puppet." Children were told prior to the interaction that the puppets would get to choose stickers, that the "good puppet never chooses the sticker you really like, because he doesn't want you to be sad," whereas the "bad puppet always chooses the one that you really like, because he doesn't care if you're sad" (see Peskin, p. 89). Children were prompted to "think of what you can do or say so that he [the bad puppet] doesn't choose the one you want" (p. 89). Children then interacted with the puppets over a series of four trials. Each time, the puppets asked the children "which sticker do you like?" In a separate condition, children experienced the same procedure, except that they acted out the role of a third puppet, a "friend," rather than voicing their own desires.

Peskin found that only a few of the 3-year-olds hid their preferences for the desired sticker, despite the fact that upon revealing their feelings, "the bad puppet seized the desired sticker, leaving a disappointed child with the disliked sticker, trial after trial" (p. 86). Three-year-olds also failed to show any demonstrable learning across trials: they repeatedly would reveal their desired sticker to the bad puppet, knowing that the bad puppet subsequently would take the sticker away. Whether children were expressing their own opinions or role-playing the "friend" puppet had no significant effects. Several 3-year-olds did attempt to physically prevent the bad puppet from taking the desired sticker following their disclosure. As Peskin (1992) describes, "although 3-year-olds did not understand that they could manage someone's actions by manipulating the person's mental state, they did understand that these actions could be affected by physical obstruction" (p. 87). In her conclusion, Peskin explicitly links her findings with conceptions of belief-embeddedness: "in concealing their intentions, children had to represent the problem not only as a first-order mental state (bad puppet falsely *thinks*) but as a second-order or embedded mental state (bad puppet falsely *thinks* I *want* Sticker X) or even a third order mental state (friend *wants* bad puppet to falsely *think* he or she *wants* Sticker X)" (p. 88).

Compared to cognitive scientists, philosophers, and psychologists, communication scholars have devoted little effort toward addressing the cognitive skills necessary for deception. The only detailed treatment of this issue

---

[2]Young children *can* identify and distinquish between intentional deception and intentional truth, however. Bussey (1992) found that preschoolers who read a series of hypothetical vignettes correctly identified nearly 70% of lies and truthful statements involving misdeeds presented in the vignettes.

is provided by Bradac et al. (1986), in their treatise on deception and propositional communication. They argued that "communicative actions are . . . contextualized, and a very important aspect of communication context is the Speaker's *beliefs about* the Hearer, including beliefs about the latter's beliefs concerning the former" (p. 127; emphasis in original). Bradac et al. defined communication accuracy as whether hearers construe utterances in ways that match speakers' topical beliefs. Consequently, a speaker's view of communicative accuracy involves third-order intentionality: "*accuracy* refers to a belief regarding the correctness of Hearer's belief regarding Speaker's belief" (p. 131; emphasis in original).

Bradac et al. then link their discussion of communication accuracy to deception, through the following example:

> Suppose Speaker's topical belief is, *John loves Sara*, and suppose further that Speaker believes that Hearer always infers the opposite of what Speaker's utterance denotes. Speaker believes the statement "he adores Sara," is relevant to the belief. Speaker believes that this utterance can be interpreted by Hearer in only one way: namely, as *Speaker believes John despises Sara*. Then, Speaker's intention to utter "He adores Sara" would constitute the belief state "falsehood." (p. 136; emphasis in original)

As Bradac et al. noted, this example underscores the fact that deception is not simply a cognitive act rooted in higher-order intentionality. Rather, deception involves the *exploitation* of the very belief-embeddedness that forms the foundation for accurate communication.

Taken as a whole, the works of scholars across divergent disciplines demonstrate the fundamentally cognitive nature of deception. At its core, deception derives from a profoundly complicated relationship between higher order intentionality, belief states, and message forms.

The Ubiquitous, Casual Nature of Deceptive Communication

Deceptive discourse, as it occurs within everyday conversations, is both ubiquitous and casual. Consider findings from two studies analyzing naturally occuring deception. Turner, Edgley, and Olmstead (1975) had 130 respondents generate a verbatim record of an important relationship conversation. Respondents then reviewed and evaluated each of the verbal expressions that they had recorded, distinguishing those expressions that were "completely honest" from those in which they had presented something other than the truth. Turner et al. found that of 870 utterances recorded across 130 significant relational encounters, 61.5% were deceptive (i.e., expressions rated by sources as not completely honest). In addition, "of the 130 encounters studied, there were no cases in which an actor was honest throughout the entire conversation; however, there were numerous encounters that contained no honest conversation at all" (pp. 72–73). Of the 61.5% of utterances identified as deceptive, less than one sixth were outright lies.[3] The most common deceptive message form did not involve the generation and presentation of false information at all: Complete concealment comprised 32% of deceptive messages analyzed.

The most comprehensive analysis to date of naturalistic deception is the work of DePaulo et al. (1996b). They conducted two separate studies focusing exclusively on lies (i.e., as opposed to other deceptive message forms), in which they "asked participants to keep records of all of their social interactions, and all of the lies that they told during those social interactions, every day for a week" (p. 3). Respondents reported the types of lies, the quality of the interaction, the seriousness of the lie, their arousal state at the time of the deception, and the target's reaction to the lie. Respondents also completed post hoc measures at the end of the week regarding whether the target had discovered the lie. Across the two studies that they conducted, DePaulo et al. found that college students reported lying "in approximately one out of every three of their social interactions, and people from the community lied in one out of every five social interactions" (p. 16). They also found that the naturally occurring lies reported by their respondents

> were generally not very serious ones. They noted that they put little effort into planning them, and did not worry much about the possibility of being caught. Instead, at the time of their lies, they reported that they expected to be believed. . . . We are not suggesting that all of the lies of everyday life are little lies of little consequence; there was variability in all of our measures. However, the majority of them do seem to fit just that description. (p. 30)

In their analysis of the characteristics of lies, they describe how their results

> underscore our contention that the lies of everyday life are mostly "light" lies that are not associated with much rumination or distress and that are generally successful. Participants said . . . that the level of distress they felt before, during, or after they told their lies was not high. (p. 24)

Taken as a whole, results from studies of naturally occuring deception suggest several conclusions. First, deception is ubiquitous to interaction. Messages that significantly control information in a fashion so as to mislead listeners constitute a substantial portion of natural discourse (Turner et al., 1975). Second, the types of deceptive messages typically studied by experi-

---

[3]Turner et al. (1975, p. 74) note that 30.7% of deceptive acts were lies. However, better than 50% of the acts coded as "lies" were not "exploitative prevarications" (p. 74), but were white lies. Thus, lying constituted less than 15% of the conversationally deceptive acts coded.

mental deception researchers (i.e., bold-faced lies) constitute a small minority of naturally occuring deceptive message forms (Turner et al., 1975). The vast majority of deceptive messages involve subtle and complex combinations of truthful and deceptive information (Turner et al., 1975; see also McCornack, 1992). Third, when one narrows the analytical focus exclusively to lies, one finds that lies told in conversations characteristically are casual (DePaulo et al., 1996b). Unlike lies in experimental settings, where sources are confronted with unfamiliar content, suspicious recipients, observing experimenters, and operative videocameras, the average conversational lie is *unplanned*, *unarousing*, and *insignificant* (DePaulo et al., 1996b).

Dilemmas

The facts that deception comprises a significant portion of natural discourse (Turner et al., 1975), and typically is casual (DePaulo et al., 1996b) pose two perplexing dilemmas for scholars interested in generating viable deception theory. First, these findings underscore the lack of ecological validity present in current theories. For example, IDT (Buller & Burgoon, 1996) depicts deception as involving "strategic moves and countermoves by deceivers and deceived" (Buller et al., 1994, p. 36). It presumes that deception involves a "very self-conscious deliberative process that is protracted in time and characterized by moves and countermoves. It is peopled by suspicious interrogators out to trap their quarry, and vigilant liars alert to any cues to skepticism in their targets" (DePaulo et al., 1996a, p. 11). Such a conceptualization bears little resemblance to naturalistic deception (DePaulo et al., 1996a; DePaulo et al., 1996b). This begs the question, how did such a conceptualization emerge in the first place? A likely explanation is that it is an artifact of experimental settings. As Eagley and Chaiken (1993) described,

> Most often laboratory subjects are constrained by an implicit demand that they "do their job" by paying attention to the materials that they are given and dutifully processing them on a relatively systematic basis. By fulfilling this obligation, laboratory subjects ensure that attentional and reception processes operate at a relatively constant, high level. The importance of these processes is consequently underestimated, and the importance of effortful, elaborative processing of message content is overestimated. (p. 685)

I am not suggesting that experimental methods are inappropriate as the basis for deception knowledge generation. As DePaulo et al. (1996a) noted, both interactive and noninteractive experimental paradigms are useful for answering certain questions about the nature of deceptive communication; particularly when the questions entail isolating the effect of a specific independent variable upon a specific dependent measure. I am suggesting that deception scholars should not equate interactive designs with natural discourse (e.g., Buller & Burgoon, 1996).

Second, a common assumption of many cognitive theories is that "people prefer less effortful to more effortful modes of information processing," because "people are economy-minded souls who wish to satisfy their goal-related needs in the most efficient ways possible" (Chaiken, Liberman, & Eagly, 1989, p. 220). People utilize cognitive strategies that emphasize efficiency; "the capacity-limited thinker searches for rapid adequate solutions, rather than slow accurate solutions" (Fiske & Taylor, 1991, p. 13). At the same time, scholars have presumed that deception is generally more cognitively demanding than truthtelling (Greene, O'Hair, Cody, & Yen, 1985; Zuckerman & Driver, 1985). Taken together, these assumptions beg a second dilemma related to the ubiquitous, casual nature of deception: How can the prevalence of deception in everyday discourse, and the ease with which it is produced, be reconciled with the claim that humans are cognitive misers? The answer, I suspect (and discuss in detail later), is that contrary to previous opinion, *deception possesses fundamental cognitive efficiency advantages over truthtelling within certain contexts.*

The Successful Nature of Deceptive Communication

If one assumes that the principal perlocutionary intent of deceptive communication is to generate false beliefs in listeners, one must conclude that deceptive messages typically are successful in rendering their desired effects. This claim is supported by three different forms of evidence. First, experimental studies of deception repeatedly have demonstrated that lie detection accuracy ranges between 45% and 60% (DePaulo et al., 1985; see also Kraut, 1980). Although heralded as evidence confirmatory of humans' innate ability to detect deception, the more surprising aspect of this finding is that detection accuracy is so *low*, given that experimental settings ensure that respondents' "attentional and reception processes operate at a relatively constant, high level" (Eagley & Chaiken, 1993). The fact that subjects, within highly controlled settings, fail to detect between 40% and 55% of lies suggests that deception often succeeds. Second, this claim is supported more strongly by data examining naturalistic deception. Across their two studies, DePaulo et al. (1996b) found that the vast majority of everyday lies remained undetected. Third, although data suggest that humans are not particularly adroit *lie* detectors, lies constitute only a small minority of deceptive message forms (i.e., less than 15%, according to Turner et al., 1975), a message form that should be among the easiest of deceptive messages to detect, given the blatant manipulations of information that occur within them (McCornack, 1992). Consequently, the claim that deceptive communication typically is successful appears warranted.

Dilemma

Given the successful nature of most deceptive discourse, one of the most provocative dilemmas confronting future theorists is why message recipients "generally believe in other people's truthfulness and accept the content of their communications at face value" (DePaulo et al., 1985, p. 326). I believe that the answer to this dilemma lies in the examination of two factors: the cognitive/information-processing limitations of human beings, and the relationship between speaker cognitions, message meaning, and hearer cognitions that underlies successful deception.

For nearly 100 years, scholars have recognized the link between human inferential processes and the identification of deceptive messages. For example, in his discussion of deception and illusionists, Jastrow (1900) argued that "our perceptions [of deceptive stimuli] are not based directly on sensory inputs, but rather on inferences that we unconsciously make from these inputs . . . the sensory input provides some constraints, but the perceiver automatically corrects for any deficiencies in the data by interpreting the inputs in terms of strong assumptions and expectations" (cited in Hyman, 1989). Until recently, most deception researchers echoed Jastrow's (1900) sentiments, assuming a model of deception recipients as naive scientists, "carefully applying sophisticated rules of inference to the behaviors of others" (Hilton, Fein, & Miller, 1993, p. 507). In the past decade, however, the notion of perceiver as active information processor has become replaced with the notion of perceiver as cognitive miser (Hilton et al., 1993; see Fiske & Taylor, 1991). Most recent models of the attributional processes underlying deceptiveness judgments share in common "the image of a perceiver who initially accepts behavior at face value and then corrects that inference for any extenuating circumstance" (Hilton et al., 1993, p. 508). As Hilton et al. go on to explain, "to the extent that conscious, deliberative thought is implicated in the inference process, it is implicated primarily during the later stages, occurs only when perceivers have sufficient cognitive resources, and is usually limited to a consideration of situational factors (e.g., constraint, strong situational press) that modify the initial inference" (p. 508).

The most common approach that deception researchers have adopted for exploring recipient cognitive miserliness is to examine the cognitive heuristics that influence deceptiveness judgments (e.g., Fiedler & Walka, 1993; Levine & McCornack, 1994; Stiff, Miller, Sleight, Mongeau, Garlick, & Rogan, 1989). Although heuristics undoubtedly influence deception judgments, there is reason to believe that humans' deficiency as lie detectors derives from more deeply rooted cognitive processes related to knowledge representation. Specifically, there is strong evidence that *humans initially cognitively represent processed information as true, then subsequently re-assess that information in terms of veracity.* In a brilliant series of studies, Gilbert, Krull, and Malone (1990) compared Cartesian and Spinozan models of knowledge representation.

Descartes argued that units of knowledge perceived by individuals initially are represented in the mind without reference to truth or falsity, and only subsequently are submitted to a rational analysis. In contrast, Spinoza argued that decoded ideas initially are mentally represented as true, with some ideas subsequently undergoing a reanalysis that results in them being unaccepted (i.e., rerepresented as false; see Gilbert et al., p. 601). These two competing models of cognitive knowledge representation give rise to competing empirical predictions related to the processing of true and false propositions (see Gilbert et al., Figure 1, p. 602). Specifically,

> the Spinozan hypothesis asserts that rejecting an idea requires the extra step of unaccepting or "tagging" a mental representation as false. If this is so, then people should initially accept both true and false ideas [as true] upon comprehension but, when the processing of the idea is interrupted, should not be able to go on and unaccept or tag false ideas. As such, [cognitive] interruption should cause Spinozan systems to mistake false ideas for true ones, but not vice versa. (p. 602)

To test the Spinozan hypothesis, Gilbert et al. (1990) conducted a series of experiments in which subjects were confronted with information about which they had no prior knowledge (i.e., nonsense statements in the Hopi Native American language, deceptive facial expressions of an unknown man, characteristics of a fictitious animal called "the furry glark"). Upon being presented with the information, subjects were informed that the information was either true or false. However, during some of the information presentations, subjects' processing of the presentation was interrupted by an auditory tone. Subjects were instructed to push a response button immediately upon hearing this tone. Subjects subsequently recalled the truth or falsity of the initially presented information.

The pattern of results across the three studies was clear and consistent. When cognitive processing of information identified as being true or false was interrupted, individuals subsequently (when asked to recall the truth or falsity of the information) erred in the direction of assuming that the information was true: "Interruption caused an increase in the percentage of false propositions that were misidentified as true, . . . but not vice versa" (p. 604). Consequently, the Spinozan hypothesis was supported.

Gilbert et al. (1990) explicitly link their findings to the inability of humans to detect deception. They argued, "in the course of a single day, everyone is exposed to a variety of deceptive communications, ill-conceived opinions, and erroneous facts, many of which they must comprehend, remember, and yet somehow manage not to believe" (p. 611). However, humans as information processors "easily accept all information before it is assessed, and then laboriously recode the information that is subsequently found to be false" (p. 612). As they described in their conclusion, the human tendency toward initially representing ideas as true may be economical and it may be adaptive, but any system that uses it will err on the side of belief more often than doubt. That human beings are, in fact, more gullible than they are suspicious should probably "be counted among the first and most common notions that are innate in us." (p. 612)

Deceptive communication is successful not simply because humans err in processing information in directions that benefit deceivers, however, but also because it involves an extremely complicated decoding task for recipients. If one conceives of deceptive communication as acts the goal of which is to generate false beliefs, then detecting deception becomes an act in which a recipient must not simply *identify* the relationship between message meaning and speaker belief (i.e., Speaker A is using utterance X to convey to me that she believes Y), but *recognize that relationship as erroneous* (i.e., Speaker A is using utterance X to convey to me that she believes Y, but she actually believes Z). Such a decoding process poses not just an exceedingly difficult cognitive task for recipients, but an exceedingly difficult *pragmatic* task as well. As Bradac et al. (1986) elaborate,

there is no necessary connection between overt utterances and underlying beliefs. This not only makes it possible for Speaker to lie, evade, etc., but also makes it impossible for Hearer to know with *certainty* where a given utterance accurately or inaccurately represents Speaker's propositional belief. Indeed, as many Speakers represent their beliefs extremely idiosyncratically and in ways that conventional Hearers find at best ambiguous, efforts at lie detection are very hazardous. In other words, only Speaker can know for sure whether s/he has lied or told the truth. (p. 129)

COMPELLING CONCEPTUAL CONCERNS

Given the fact that deceptive communication characteristically is cognitive, ubiquitous, casual, and successful, a number of compelling conceptual concerns immediately arise, concerns that I believe should drive the development of future deception theory. Given space limitations, I address only two of these: the relationship between deceptive message production and cognitive load, and how deceptive messages are generated.

The Generation of Deceptive Messages and Cognitive Load

Deception scholars have assumed a priori that "it is more cognitively difficult to fabricate a plausible and convincing lie consistent with everything the observer knows or might find out than to tell the truth" (Vrij, Semin, & Bull,

1996, p. 546), an assumption heretofore referred to as the "cognitive load hypothesis" (i.e., CLH). The rationale underlying the CLH is comprised of two assumptions. First, deceivers "must construct a message from scratch and the content of the message must be both internally consistent and compatible with what the listeners already know" (Zuckerman & Driver, 1985, p. 133). Consequently, deception is more cognitively demanding than truthtelling, because "unlike truthful communications, deceptive messages are constructed in the deceiver's mind" (p. 139). Second, the cognitive process involved in the encoding of deception is assumed to be "generally more [cognitively] difficult because of the number of constraints placed upon the formulation of the lie" (Greene et al., 1985, p. 341).

When subjected to close scrutiny, each of these assumptions proves faulty. The argument that deceptive messages are distinct because they are cognitively constructed "from scratch" implies that truthful messages are not cognitively constructed from scratch, but are the product of a generation process utilizing prefabricated message forms, a claim at odds with contemporary models of message production (e.g., Lambert, 1992; Lambert & O'Keefe, 1990; O'Keefe & Lambert, 1995). Likewise, the claim that deceptive messages are distinct because they must be "internally consistent and compatible with what the listeners already know" suggests that truthful messages are constructed without regard to internal consistency and recipient knowledge, a claim equally at odds with extant literature (Hovy, 1990). The claim that there are inherently "more constraints" (cognitive and/or contextual) upon the formulation of deceptive messages fails to recognize the expediency of deception for achieving cognitive and contextual goals. As Turner et al. (1975) described, deception is viewed by relationship partners "as a very efficacious means of controlling information for whatever purposes they had in mind; it prevents communication of discourse which could embarrass, spoil presentation of self, insult the other, or be offensive in some way" (p. 74).

Putting aside (for the moment) the tenuous assumptions upon which the CLH is founded, the CLH entails that certain behavioral symptoms indicative of increased cognitive load should occur with greater frequency when sources lie than when they tell the truth (Burgoon, Kelley, Newton, & Keeley-Dyreson, 1989). This logical entailment creates the possibility of empirically testing the CLH, albeit indirectly. If deceivers display more behavioral cues indicative of and solely attributable to cognitive load than do truthtellers, we reasonably can conclude that deception generates greater cognitive load than does truthtelling. Zuckerman and Driver (1985) tested this prediction in their meta-analysis of 45 deception studies, by examining the effects of deception upon four cues indicative of increased cognitive load: longer response latencies, increased speech hesitations, increased pupil dilation, and decreased use of illustrators. They found no support for the CLH. Across the studies they analyzed, "only speech hesitations and pupil dilation were related to deception and these relationships can be accounted for by the arousal factor [rather than the cognitive load factor]" (p. 139). However, Zuckerman and Driver refused to accept their own meta-analytic results as disconfirmation of the CLH, and instead argued that the presence of significant effects for two factors not initially predicted as being related to load (i.e., decreased response length, increase in irrelevant information) constituted confirmatory evidence "that deception involves more complex cognitive processing [than does truthtelling]" (p. 139).[4]

The most direct empirical test of the CLH yet conducted is the work of Greene et al. (1985). They had respondents either lie or tell the truth about a vacation that they had taken, while interacting with an experimental confederate. Sources were allowed to prepare their responses in advance. During the interaction, the confederate asked the respondent an initial question about her or his vacation, then immediately probed the respondent by asking, "Oh, really? What did you do there?" (see Greene et al., p. 349). Near the end of the interaction, the confederate suddenly confronted the source with an additional probe, "Listen, you said that you went to ___. What were the people there like?" (Greene et al., p. 349). Source behaviors were videotaped and subsequently coded.

Related to the CLH, Greene et al. (1985) predicted that liars would exhibit longer response latencies and less eye contact than would truthtellers when confronted with spontaneous probes. Greene et al. found only marginal support for their predictions. Liars did not exhibit significantly longer response latencies than truthtellers when confronted with the initial probe, nor did they exhibit significantly less eye contact, although the means for both effects were in the predicted directions. They also found that liars confronted with the subsequent probe did not exhibit significantly longer response latencies, although they did exhibit decreased eye contact. Similar to Zuckerman and Driver (1985), Greene et al. did not interpret their nonsignificant results as evidence disconfirming the CLH, but rather, argued that "these result indicate support for the proposed relation of deception and cognitive load" (p. 357).

---

[4]In my opinion, this is a clear-cut example of how hopeful myths regarding deception function to bias interpretation of data. Rather than accept their results at face value as disconfirmatory of the CLH, Zuckerman and Driver (1985) immediately assume that the *data* must be suspect, and search for other, unpredicted effects that allow their (intuitively-based) hypothesis to remain viable. Hence, the deception-myth-based biasing process functions as follows: (a) start with a priori conceptual assumption rooted in deception myth, (b) make specific, empirical predictions regarding expected effects based on this assumption, (c) conduct empirical test of prediction, (d) generate results that provide explicit disconfirmation of the predicted effect, (e) rather than rejecting the prediction (or the myth-based assumption that gave rise to it), conduct immediate search for other, nonpredicted effects or evidence that may constitute potential confirmation of the disconfirmed prediction, (f) claim confirmation for the predicted effect.

The Greene et al. (1985) results should be interpreted with caution, however, given a confound in their design. Greene et al. manipulated cognitive load through the use of interrogative probes. Numerous studies have documented that interrogative probes cause deceptive message sources to exhibit cues indicative of arousal (see Levine & McCornack, 1996a). Consequently, we cannot claim with any certainty that the one significant effect found by Greene et al. related to the CLH (i.e., decreased eye contact subsequent to the second probe), derived from cognitive load, rather than increased arousal due to probing.

More recently, Vrij et al. (1996) compared attempted control versus cognitive load explanations for the behavioral cues associated with deception. Similar to the findings of DePaulo examining the motivational impairment effect (see DePaulo & Kirkendol, 1988), Vrij et al. found that deceptive sources (compared to truthtellers) reduced the number of hand/finger and foot/leg movements that they exhibited. Sources also reported that lying "required more mental effort" than truthtelling. These results offer little direct evidence in support of the CLH, however. Of the five cues previously identified as symptomatic of cognitive load (i.e., response latencies, eye contact, pupil dilation, speech hesitations, illustrators), Vrij et al. examined only one (i.e., illustrators, described as "gestures"), but found no significant effect for deception upon this behavior (see Table 2, p. 553). The only significant load-related effect found was the effect for lying upon the degree of self-perceived "mental effort" reported. Given that sources either told the truth or constructed a lie regarding possession of a set of headphones (p. 548), this effect is neither surprising nor informative regarding the CLH (i.e., constructing a spontaneous lie regarding headphone possession will obviously entail more perceived effort than headphone truthtelling).

Taken as a whole, the Zuckerman and Driver (1985), Greene et al. (1985), and Vrij et al. (1996) results offer minimal support for the premise that deception is more cognitively demanding than truthtelling. These results do not constitute the type of robust effects one would anticipate, if deception truly is more cognitively taxing than truthtelling. Nor do they constitute the type of results one should count as *compelling* evidence supporting the CLH. Given the lack of support for the CLH, deception scholars need to carefully reassess the core assumptions underlying this hypothesis. *Why* should deception be more cognitively demanding than truthtelling? Particularly within the types of goal-complex contexts that characteristically give rise to deception (see Metts & Chronis, 1986; McCornack, 1992), why should the manufacturing and presentation of information *specifically designed to satisfy complex contextual demands* be *more* cognitively demanding than the retrieval and presentation of information that is contextually problematic? To address these questions, I return to the conceptual underpinnings of the CLH.

The CLH derives from speculation regarding the comparative cognitive demands of the messages typically generated within deception experiments:

bold-faced lies (i.e., BFLs) versus bold-faced truths (i.e., BFTs). On an intuitive level, a BFL *should* require more cognitive effort than generating a BFT. Whereas the production of a BFT requires retrieval of relevant information, formation of that information into a message, and presentation of that information, the production of a BFL requires a more demanding initial cognitive step: generation of false information that adequately meshes with the context. However, there are numerous reasons why scholars should reject the BFT/BFL comparison as the basis for general predictions regarding deception and cognitive load. First, the vast majority of message forms in natural discourse are neither BFT nor BFL, but something "in-between" (McCornack, 1992; Turner et al., 1975). For example, both Turner et al. (1975) and McCornack (1992) found that BFL's comprise only a small portion of the deceptive messages constructed by sources; most deceptive messages involve subtle and complex packaging of both false and truthful elements. Second, assuming that the generation of truthful messages entails simple retrieval and disclosure of information neglects an enormous and varied literature addressing the normative constraints related to bald disclosure (e.g., Brown & Levinson, 1978; Goffman, 1955; O'Keefe, 1988). Particularly within complicated relational situations, most truthful messages do not simply dump all salient information, but rather, attach additional, conventional face-maintaining devices, or provide explicit contextualizing phrases (O'Keefe, 1988, 1990; O'Keefe & Lambert, 1989). Consequently, the vast majority of truthful messages do not entail a simple "lump and dump" production process. Rather, truthful message generation likely entails a complicated cognitive process in which sources retrieve relevant information from memory, recognize that unedited disclosure likely would result in significant negative outcomes (given contextual demands), then generate a truthful message that presents the information in a face-maintaining package. This suggests that the relevant, ecologically valid comparison between truthful versus deceptive message generation is not BFT versus BFL, but *packaged truth* (PT) versus *packaged deception* (PD).

The PT/PD comparison immediately begs a vastly different description of corresponding cognitive load. Neither PT nor PD is *innately* more demanding, because each is potentially difficult and taxing, or efficient and expedient, *depending on the context*. For contexts in which non-face-threatening content is made relevant for disclosure, sources generating PTs (or even BFTs) face fewer cognitive demands than sources generating PDs (or BFLs). However, PDs or BFLs generally will not be produced within such contexts (i.e., when there are no contextual consequences attached to truthtelling, sources generally generate truthful messages; see McCornack, 1992; Metts & Chronis, 1986). Within the types of contexts that provoke deception—contexts in which *face-threatening* or *potentially damaging* content is made relevant for disclosure—sources generating PTs must retrieve relevant information, recognize the penalties associated with unadulterated disclosure, then decipher a way in which the truth can be palatably packaged. By contrast, sources generating PDs retrieve relevant information, recognize the penalties associated with unadulterated disclosure, then fabricate information perfectly suited toward reconciling contextual demands. Rather than deception being "more difficult because of the number of constraints placed upon the formulation of the lie" (Greene et al., p. 341), *truthtelling faces more constraints in terms of how it can be formulated.* One can creatively deceive in any number of ways so as to meet contextual demands, whereas truthtellers face limited degrees of freedom that constrain the appropriate packaging of information (i.e., they must disclose certain information elements in certain ways in order for their utterance to conventionally be considered "honest"). Consequently, PD becomes a potentially efficacious cognitive alternative, in terms of the creative freedom it allows the source (i.e., the different ways information and messages can be adapted to fit contexts).

The radically increased degrees of freedom provided by PD does create an associated cognitive cost, however: the potential for combinatorial explosion. As Pavitt (1991) described,

> as the number of symbols in the environment increases, the number of possible combinations of these symbols that can appear in the condition of the production grows exponentially. As a result, the number of productions needed to perform a task may increase extremely quickly given any increase in the number of symbols in the data base. Unless the designer has done an exemplary job of organizing the production list and conflict resolution strategy, the number of productions may be too large to be searched in a feasible amount of time. This problem is called "combinatorial explosion." (p. 218)

Hence, although deceivers can adapt information to fit contextual demands in whatever fashion they see fit, this freedom evokes increased cognitive load related to which exact information will be manufactured and presented.

To illustrate the PT/PD comparison, consider the Committed Chris scenario (McCornack, 1992). Respondents confronted with this scenario are provided with 10 root pieces of relevant information: (1) you have known Chris for a long time, (2) this has been the closest relationship in which you have been involved, (3) recently your feelings toward Chris have begun to change, (4) Chris has been pressuring you for a firmer commitment, (5) you want to date other people, (6) the two of you have been fighting recently, (7) Chris has been behaving very jealously, (8) unbeknownst to Chris, you have been dating someone else, (9) this other relationship has been fun, (10) this other relationship recently has become sexual. Respondents then are informed that one night they are out with Chris, and Chris suddenly says, "you seem really distant recently, is there something wrong?"

Chris's query immediately establishes as relevant the 10 information units provided to respondents, although respondents likely will weight the comparative relevance of different information units differently (O'Keefe & Lambert, 1989). Virtually no one discloses all 10 units without attached, face-maintaining linguistic devices, however; even "completely truthful" messages typically exploit syntactic and semantic resources to blunt the blow (see McCornack, 1992, message examples 1–3). Consequently, consider the respective cognitive demands confronting the message source who opts to present PT in the Committed Chris scenario, versus the message source who opts to present PD. Let us also presuppose (to provide a precise, controlled comparison) that both sources share the following desired end-state characteristics: temporarily maintain relationship with Chris, keep Chris happy, temporarily maintain outside relationship, keep self happy. The message source generating PT faces extremely limited degrees of freedom in designing her message, limitations that create a challenging cognitive task. She not only must access the information units relevant to the query, but then also must (a) determine how these units can be packaged in a fashion so as to maintain the expressive order (Goffman, 1955); a demanding task, given that disclosure of many of the relevant units (e.g., units 3, 5, 8, 9, 10) by definition will disrupt the expressive order, and (b) determine how these units can be packaged in a fashion so as to achieve the desired end state (i.e., maintain both current relationships, keep self and Chris happy), all the while maintaining the integrity of the information as *honest*. The source producing PD faces no such constraints. Upon retrieving the relevant information and recognizing the ill fit between disclosure, expressive order, and desired end state, he simply manufactures information that immediately achieves the desired end-state and maintains the expressive order: For example, "No Chris, there isn't anything wrong, I'm just stressing about exams!" However, he *is* confronted with a new and bewildering cognitive task: determining which false information is best suited toward remedying the context (e.g., do I say "there isn't anything wrong, I am just stressing about exams," or do I say "I haven't been feeling well the past few days, I think it's the flu"?).

Deception as Problem Solving

The foregoing discussion suggests that deception is a potentially efficient means for achieving desired end-states, although it is not without cognitive costs. As such, deception can be considered a particular communicative class of problem-solving activities. Within contexts in which individuals possess face-threatening information that is made contextually relevant for disclosure (through query or other causes), "any rational agent will seek to avoid these face-threatening acts, or will employ certain strategies to minimize the threat" (Brown & Levinson, 1978, p. 73). As Brown and Levinson argued, communicators within such contexts "will take into consideration the relative weightings of (at least) three wants: (a) the want to communicate the content of the FTA x, (b) the want to be efficient or urgent, and (c) the want to maintain H's face to any degree. Unless (b) is greater than (c), S will want to minimize the threat of his FTA" (p. 73). Some communicators resolve communicative dilemmas by choosing to not disclose FTAs. The payoff for such a choice is "that S avoids offending H at all with this particular FTA" (p. 77), while the cost is that "S also fails to achieve his desired communication" (p. 77). However, if the source does not desire to disclose the information in the first place, but is contextually expected or required to do so, deception becomes a desirable solution for dealing with FTAs. As DePaulo et al. (1996b) described,

> many of the same goals that motivate nondeceptive presentations also motivate deceptive ones. These include the claiming of desired identities, the support of other people's claims to desired identities, and the exchange of enhancing and supportive emotions, preferences, and opinions. When reality is kind . . . then these goals can be accomplished nondeceptively; *but under less propitious circumstances, it becomes more tempting to lie.* (p. 4; emphasis added)

Conceptualizing deception as problem solving immediately suggests that a fruitful literature in which to embed future theoretical work may be the extant problem-solving literature (e.g., Barr, Cohen, & Fiegenbaum, 1989; Ernst, 1987; Hayes-Roth, 1985; Newell & Simon, 1972; Nii, 1989). Briefly described, problem-solving models are conceptual schemes that formally specify and organize the reasoning steps and domain knowledge needed to construct solutions to particular problems (Nii, 1989). Within a problem-solving model, "*reasoning* refers to a computational process whereby needed information is inferred from what is already known" (Nii, p. 4). Problem-solving models typically posit some form of "problem space" (Newell & Simon, 1972), a domain in which all information relevant to the problem solution resides. As Lambert (1992) stated,

> the problem space is a symbolic representation of a problem that encodes the current state and the goal state. Operators are abstract actions that map one problem state onto another. Using means–ends analysis as a control strategy, operators are chosen whose application to the problem reduces the difference between the current state and the goal. Thus, problem-solving proceeds by applying a sequence of operators that trace a path through problem space from current state to goal state, and that sequence of operators is the problem solution. (pp. 6–7)

Problem-solving models typically take one of three forms: backward reasoning, forward reasoning, or opportunistic. In backward reasoning problem-solving models, the problem-solving process entails moving backward through the problem space from the desired end state to be achieved toward the initial state. In forward reasoning models, the inference steps are applied from initial state toward the end state. In opportunistic reasoning models, however, "pieces of knowledge are applied either backward or forward at the most 'opportune' time" (Nii, 1989, p. 4).

One type of opportunistic problem-solving model with potential applications for deceptive message production is the blackboard model of problem solving. Within such models, the solution space is organized into multiple, application-dependent hierarchies. As Nii (1989) elaborated,

> Information at each level in the hierarchy represents partial solutions and is represented by a unique vocabulary that describes the information. Opportunistic reasoning is applied within this overall organization of the solution-space and task-specific knowledge; that is, which module of knowledge to apply is determined dynamically, one step at a time, resulting in the incremental generation of partial solutions. The choice of a knowledge module is based on the solution state (particularly the latest additions and modifications to the data structure containing pieces of the solution) and on the existence of knowledge modules capable of improving the current state of the solution. (1989, p. 5)

Perhaps the most distinct feature of blackboard models is that during each step in the solution-generation process, either forward- or backward-reasoning methods may be utilized. As Nii (1989) describes, this allows such models to encompass reasoning processes that are "event driven, goal driven, model driven, expectation driven, and so forth" (p. 5). This makes blackboard models particularly well-suited for problems that can be solved in multiple ways, involve noisy and unreliable data, require the integration of diverse information in solution-generation, mandate the cooperation of many independent or semiindependent pieces of knowledge in solution-generation, may require (or entail) multiple reasoning methods, and (may) require incremental and evolutionary solution construction (Nii, p. 70).

The application of a blackboard problem-solving model to deception suggests intriguing possibilities related to the reasoning processes and production mechanisms underlying deceptive message generation. Because the focus of blackboard models is upon the interaction between partial solutions generated at different levels in the production hierarchy, utilizing both forward- and backward-reasoning processes, it allows for the "interleaved planning" (Hovy, 1990) that is characteristic of (and necessary in order to explain) human discourse, including deception. As Hovy (1990) explained,

> when we speak, we do not try to satisfy only one or two goals, and we operate (often, and with success) with conflicting goals for which no resolution exists.

> We usually begin to speak before we have planned out the full utterance, and then proceed while performing certain planning tasks in bottom-up fashion. (p. 166)

As an illustration of how such a model potentially might be applied to deception, consider the following message example responding to Committed Chris, excerpted from McCornack (1992):

> Chris, yeah, there is something wrong. We have been fighting all the time! Your jealousy is getting way out of hand. You're pressing me to commit, and I just don't think I'm ready yet. I've been feeling recently like I want to date other people. *Don't think that I would ever do something like that without telling you, because I wouldn't!* It's just my feelings toward you have begun to change (message example #13, p. 11; emphasis in original)

The only account that contemporary deception theories can offer regarding the cognitive processes responsible for this message is that the source mysteriously "managed" information (Buller & Burgoon, 1996), "manipulated" information (McCornack, 1992), or worse yet, that this message is the product of a cognitively invoked "deception type" (e.g., "half-truth"). Application of blackboard problem-solving principles suggests a vastly different, albeit speculative and metaphorical, account. The message source, reasoning opportunistically, begins to "solve the situation" by disclosing relevant information, utilizing forward reasoning. Partial solutions to the "problem" are generated simultaneously, and outputted online as verbal behavior. Because the current state is dominated by the contextual demand "say what is wrong," the source begins his message by disclosing "there is something wrong." Utilizing forward reasoning, the source then specifies information relevant to the "wrongness" that exists (e.g., "we have been fighting," "your jealousy"). As additional thoughts relevant to wrongness become activated and disclosed as partial solutions, the current state demand of "say what is wrong" eventually evokes the thought (and subsequent disclosure of) "I want to date other people." At this point, however, backward reasoning from a desired end-state characteristic (i.e., keep Chris happily ignorant of my dalliance) activates a new microproblem within the macroproblem of message generation: Disclosure of desire to date others may cause Chris to infer that dating others has already occured, an outcome substantially discrepant from the desired end state of "keep Chris happily ignorant." As a solution to this new problem, the source immediately attempts attenuation of a recipient inference *that has not yet occurred*, by generating and presenting false information: "Don't think I would ever do something like that without telling you . . ."

As even this coarsely articulated and speculative example illustrates, conceiving of deceptive message production as problem solving suggests rich possibilities for addressing the observable characteristics of deceptive messages, and the reasoning processes underlying their production. However, no prior attempt has been made on the part of deception researchers to link deception with problem solving models. The only direct empirical evidence that we have of a link between problem solving and deception derives from the work of Hovy (1990), modeling natural language production.

Hovy's principal concern was generating a language program capable of producing varied linguistic output to different recipients within different contexts based upon identical input. For example, given the following information input,

> First Jim bumped Mike once, hurting him. Then Mike hit Jim, hurting him. Then Jim hit Mike once knocking him down. Then Mike hit Jim several times, knocking him down. Then Jim slapped Mike several times, hurting him. Then Mike stabbed Jim. As a result Jim died. (Hovy, 1990, p. 175)

human speech producers can generate an indefinite number of relevant messages, depending upon context and recipient. One can say, "Oh, did you hear that Mike killed Jim the other night? They got in a heinous scrap, and Mike stuck him with this gnarly blade!"; one can say, "Yes, Officer, they exchanged blows a number of times prior to the actual occurrence of the knifing," or an indefinite number of alternative messages (see p. 176). However, most language production programs are capable only of operating from "a fixed correspondence between topic representation types on the one hand and grammatical rules and lexical elements on the other" (p. 175), consequently, they are incapable of adapting inputted content in flexible ways when designing outputted messages.

In response to this concern, Hovy (1990) designed PAULINE, a language program that incorporates a host of pragmatic factors related to message design (e.g., conversational atmosphere, speaker status, hearer status, speaker–hearer relationship, interpersonal goals, rhetorical goals; see pp. 160–163). Of relevance to the present discussion is what occurred when Hovy had PAULINE generate messages describing caucus results in three pragmatically different scenarios. In the first scenario, neither interlocutor had strong opinions about the results, and the level of formality was colloquial (see p. 191). In the second, the hearer was a friend, although they each had conflicting opinions about the results (p. 191). In the third scenario, however, the context had several complicated elements. Not only did the two interactants have strongly different opinions (i.e., PAULINE was a Carter support and hearer was a Kennedy supporter), but the hearer was PAULINE's boss, the interaction was over the phone, the interaction was under time constraints, and PAULINE's desire was to not anger the boss and to reaffirm the boss's social dominance (pp. 191–192). In response to this pragmatic configuration, PAULINE chose to withhold disclosure of information about the election results altogether. Subsequent investigation determined that PAULINE "chose" to white lie because of haste: given the pressured nature of the interaction (as a programmed contextual factor), PAULINE could not activate strategies involving indirect (and face-maintaining) disclosure of the information, and consequently concealed the information. Deception by omission became the most efficient solution to the problem. As Hovy (1990) described, "the goal to present the topic only in mitigated (implicit opinion) form couldn't be satisfied, and no sentence could be generated" (p. 192).

Implications and Applications

Conceiving of deception as problem solving, and embedding deception theory within the problem-solving literature, suggests a number of implications and applications. First, such a conceptualization underscores the radically simplistic nature of the CLH. Neither truthtelling nor deception is *inherently* more cognitively demanding, although both potentially *are* cognitively demanding, albeit for different reasons (i.e., truthtelling frequently entails format constraints that give rise to restricted degrees of freedom, whereas deception invites the potential for combinatorial explosion). Second, conceiving of deception as problem solving suggests potential, precise tests for the CLH. To the degree to which current state factors, desired end-state characteristics, and generated message forms vary, the corresponding cognitive load associated with truth versus deception also should vary. For example, contexts in which the presentation of BFT poses no dilemmas for sources, and in which sources are forced to generate BFLs regarding unfamiliar message content, should result in greater cognitive load being associated with the generation of BFLs. Contexts in which the presentation of BFT would entail face-related negative outcomes should result in greater cognitive load being associated with the generation of PT than with BFL or PD.

Third, the adoption of a problem-solving perspective calls into question traditional assumptions regarding deceptive intent, the planning antecedent to deceptive message production, and the arousal associated with deception. If many deception forms derive from opportunistic problem solving rather than a priori decision to deceive, sources generating deceptive messages may perceive their message output as deceptive parallel with, or even immediately subsequent to, the presentation of the message that constitutes the problem solution. Sources within conversational settings generate deceptive forms as contextual problem solutions so quickly and efficiently that recognition of their conventionally deceptive nature may occur only ad hoc or post hoc. Such an account would go far in explaining DePaulo et al.'s (1996b) finding that liars in naturalistic settings typically experience little arousal or guilt during and after their lies.

Challenging the notion that deceptive intent is a necessary precursor for deceptive communication may strike readers as both counterintuitive and radical. However, reconsider Hovy's (1990) findings related to PAULINE. Within the boss/employee context, PAULINE behaved in an unquestionably duplicitous fashion: "she" actively concealed relevant information. At the same time, PAULINE's deceptive behavior could not possibly have derived from deceptive intent: Intent to deceive was not included as a part of her program. PAULINE generated *unequivocally deceptive communicative behavior with the absolute absence of deceptive intent.*

One cannot overstate the significance of the PAULINE finding as it relates to current conceptualizations of deception. Virtually all current deception theory and research is predicated upon the assumption that deception begins with a priori intent to deceive; intent that then is mapped onto deceptive acts. This assumption forms the foundation for corresponding assumptions regarding the association between deception, arousal, and behavioral cues. Assuming a problem-solving orientation would call this foundational assumption into question. As is obvious, a narrow band of contexts would result in sources generating intent to deceive, particularly those contexts that allow for preparation, involve significant outcomes, and/or involve potentially incriminating information (e.g., relationship lies regarding fidelity, police interrogations of guilty criminals, etc.). However, the vast majority of *everyday* deceptions would *not* necessarily derive from such intents. Consequently, most deceptive acts would not generate significant levels of arousal, generate corresponding behavioral leakage, nor be addressable by conventional deception theories such as IDT (Buller & Burgoon, 1996).

How Are Deceptive Messages Generated?

When one moves from using problem solving as a metaphor (as in my previous discussion) to using problem solving as the mechanistic basis for a posited message production model, one immediately is confronted with a host of limitations inherent to such models. Many problem-solving-based models of message production are founded on the assumptions that speaker intentions are mapped onto speech act forms (e.g., Cohen & Perrault, 1979), and that these act forms are mapped onto sentence types (O'Keefe & Lambert, 1995). Speech acts become the operators within the problem-solving space that change one intentional state to another (Lambert, 1992). As Cohen and Perrault (1979) described, "given an initial set of beliefs and goals, the speech act operator definitions and plan construction inferences should lead to the generation of plans for those speech acts that a person could issue appropriately under the same circumstances" (p. 179). The mapping procedure of intentions onto speech acts, and speech acts onto sentence forms, utilizes a process described by O'Keefe and Lambert (1995) as "functional indexing." Certain abstract forms at each stage in the production process (e.g., intentions <↔> speech acts <↔> sentences <↔> phonemes <↔> etc.) are indexed to certain other forms at the adjacent level of hierarchical abstraction, based on the predicated functions of the forms. For example, if one's intention is to "request", abstract forms at the next level in the production hierarchy (i.e., speech acts) that are indexed accordingly are activated. Once the particular speech act request has been selected, specific message forms that are indexed to the functions served by "requesting" are activated, and the message best suited toward accomplishing these functions is selected. This happens at all levels of the production hierarchy, including sentence (utterance) construction. As O'Keefe and Lambert (1995) described,

> each word is indexed by its grammatical function (noun, verb, determiner) and by its meaning. Once words are chosen, morphemes and phonemes must be chosen to fill the slots in the words' representations. Once phonemes are chosen, articulatory patterns must be chosen to produce the relevant sounds. At each level there is a choice to be made, and the dilemma of choice is always resolved in the same way, by indexing choices in terms available at the highest adjacent level of abstraction. (pp. 56–57)

There are numerous problems associated with message-production models that use functional indexing schemes (Lambert, 1992; O'Keefe & Lambert, 1995), but I shall limit my discussion to two. First, these models typically draw upon Searle's Speech Act Theory (Searle, 1965, 1969, 1975), and correspondingly assume the straightforward and unproblematic mapping of speaker intentions onto speech acts, and speech acts onto message forms. Adopting principles from Searle's SAT is an obvious choice for programmers generating production models to make, as Searle posits a fixed, constitutive-rule-governed relationship between intent, speech acts, and message forms, that lends itself well to computer program writing. However, as both Levinson (1981) and Streek (1980) have noted, the relationship between speaker intent, speech acts, and message forms is anything but fixed and rule-governed (see Lambert, 1992, pp. 13–21, for a detailed discussion of this issue). The speech act that is performed often is not defined a priori by speaker intent (and corresponding constitutive rules), but retroactively by the nature of the recipient's response (Levinson, 1981; Streek, 1980). Multiple acts can be mapped onto the same utterance (see Levinson, pp. 98–99), and multiple speakers producing multiple utterances can jointly produce a single speech act (see Streek, p. 140). Functional-indexing schemes, which assume fixed and identifiable intention/act/message relations, cannot account for the extremely fluid relationship that exists between intentions, acts, and messages as they actually are generated by human interactants, even by programming in contextual parameters (e.g., Hovy, 1990).

A second, related problem is that "the indexing that is required [by functional indexing models] in order to enable rational choice among forms depends on there being a decontextualized relationship between form and function" (O'Keefe & Lambert, 1995, p. 57). However, speaker intents, speech acts, and message forms are never not in a context, consequently their interrelationship always will be context-determined, though typically stable within a particular context (Fish, 1978). "That's a nice one" said to a clerk while pointing at a lettuce inside a produce store will count as a request, while the same utterance (presented with identical nonverbal function indicators) said to a friend outside of the store while looking through the window will count as a compliment regarding the quality of the produce (see Levinson, 1981, pp. 112–113). Alternatively, the greeting "Hi!" exchanged between two lovers immediately after meeting each other in the morning will count as a greeting, whereas the same "Hi!" exchanged immediately after lovemaking will count not as a greeting per se, but as a flouting of the prepartory conditions underlying greeting (see Searle, 1965, p. 239) in order to convey the message, "Wow, our passionate coupling certainly transported us to a different plane!" (see Streek, pp. 144–145). As these two examples demonstrate, message forms are not indexed to speech acts based on an abstract and immutable constitutive rule-set, but are indexed based on context. As O'Keefe and Lambert (1995) argued,

> to put it bluntly, decontextualized linguistic forms have no functional significance. It is a truism to say that the meaning of a form depends on the context of its use. At the level of discourse acts or message features, the evidence shows that the form-function relationship is mediated by reasoning from context-specific beliefs. (p. 57)

Production models predicated upon functional indexing schemes also pose additional, interesting dilemmas when applied to deceptive-message production. The only account such models can offer for explaining deception is to suggest that deceptive intents are mapped onto deceptive acts, which then are mapped onto deceptive message forms. This immediately begs the question, does deception involve a separate message-production mechanism than truthtelling? There are two possible answers, neither of which is particularly satisfactory. The first is to suggest that truthful intents, truthful speech acts, and truthful message forms all have corresponding deceptive counterparts that exist separately in some type of parallel but distinct deceptive message-production mechanism. This appears to be the model that is tacitly endorsed by current deception researchers, given their claims that deception involves an identifiably distinct process (varying along multiple behavioral dimensions) from truthtelling. However, truthful messages can be used to deceive, through the generation of deceptive implicatures (Jacobs et al., 1996). This suggests that deceptive intents can be mapped onto truthful acts and truthful message forms so as to render deceptive perlocutionary effects, which would seem to undermine the "separate mechanism" hypothesis. A second possibility is that deceptive intents, deceptive acts, and deceptive messages exist side by side with their truthful counterparts within the same production mechanism (or knowledge units), but simply are indexed as distinct. Although somewhat more plausible, it does beg two additional problems. First, it invites combinatorial explosion, as each and every message (and act, and intent) generated will be the product of selection not just between a set of potential truthful alternatives, but from the entire set of deceptive and truthful alternatives available. Second, the notion that truthful and deceptive messages are indexed separately does not mesh well with examples such as the previously discussed Committed Chris message, in which truthful and deceptive elements were *blended* within the *same* message.

As a consequence of these problems, I believe that deception scholars should be reticent to embrace holistic-functional models of message design that posit functional indexing schemes as the basis for message production (see Lambert, 1992, O'Keefe & Lambert, 1995, for additional discussion). Instead, scholars interested in accounting for deceptive message production should examine models that provide for the fundamentally situated nature of message meaning, and that potentially could account for the cognitive and casual nature of deception described earlier.

An Alternative Model

When one confronts the cognitive, ubiquitous, casual, and successful nature of deceptive message production, one is faced with an apparent paradox: How can people so casually generate messages that exploit such apparent cognitive complexities as multiple levels of belief embeddedness, yet do it so quickly, frequently, and successfully? Although it is not my goal with this chapter to propose theory (i.e., my goal is to raise questions that need to be answered), I do wish to briefly highlight a theoretical approach to message production that shows promise in being able to resolve this paradox. This approach is the local management model of message design recently proposed by O'Keefe and Lambert (1995). As they describe their model in detail elsewhere, I shall briefly note some of the key features of their model, and discuss its potential (and the potential of analogous models) for explaining the cognitive, casual nature of deception.

O'Keefe and Lambert (1995) conceptualize communication as a problem-solving activity. However, rather than viewing solution-generation as a process governed by higher order plans and goals, solution-generation involves "the organization of situated beliefs and the movement of [attentional] focus through belief structures" (p. 68), rooted in a parallel distributed processing (i.e., PDP) architecture of cognition (see Rumelhart, McClelland, & the PDP Research Group, 1986). PDP models assume that the mind is comprised of complex networks of interconnections that operate in a parallel fashion (see Rumelhart et al., 1986, for details). They offer a vastly different depiction of the cognitive processes underlying communication. Whereas standard models of cognition and message production typically would "represent a communicative goal as a discrete symbol, a PDP model can represent a goal as a pattern of activation over many units, where each unit represents the degree of presence or absence of a specific thought" (O'Keefe & Lambert, 1995, p. 69).

O'Keefe and Lambert link PDP with the model of speech production proposed by the Research Group in Language and Cognition at the University of Mannheim, Germany (i.e., Hoppe-Graff, Herrmann, Winterhoff-Spurk, & Mangold, 1985), while maintaining their focus on communication as problem solving. The result is a blended model, one in which

> message design begins with a pattern of activated thoughts that correspond to a goal. Activation of the goal state initiates message generation, the selection and transformation of situated knowledge; the goal maps to a message by way of the message generator. Output of the message generator is evaluated by the activity model to determine whether its utterance would bring about the desired effect; if so, the message is uttered. If not, the activity model propagates an error message back through the message generator, changing the weights in that network. The process is repeated until the system is satisfied with the chosen message (perhaps because no more time is available). (O'Keefe & Lambert, p. 78)

Similar to problem-solving models in general, the local-management model (O'Keefe & Lambert, 1995) casts doubt upon the entire premise on which deception research and theory has been founded: that deception derives from a priori intent to deceive, and this intent gives rise to arousal which is detectable via behavioral output. Rather than deceptive messages being the product of deceptive intents mapped onto deceptive strategies mapped onto deceptive messages, most "everyday" deceptive messages may be the product of a very different process: the activation and expression of relevant thoughts. For example, when faced with a problematic relationship context, relevant truthful thoughts are activated. Thoughts linked with these initial truthful thoughts also become activated (e.g., as in the Committed Chris example, "there is something wrong" → "we've been fighting" → "your jealousy" → etc.), and the message generator forms them into potential message units. However, if the activity model perceives a mismatch between the activated thoughts, the perceived consequences of uttering these thoughts as message units, and the desired end state, it will send "an error message back through the message generator, changing the weights in that network" (p. 78). The result will be that alternative thoughts better suited for achieving the end state will be activated (i.e., deceptive thoughts). These alternative, false thoughts will (in turn) activate additional, associated, false thoughts. At this point in the message design process, both truthful and false thoughts remain activated. However, as processing continues, the thoughts that "win out" (in terms of degree of activation that ultimately will result in the thoughts being formatted into verbal messages and presented) will be those that are evaluated by the activity model as bringing about the desired end state.[5] Given that most relational partners' disclosures are guided by the principle "say what is good for the relationship" (Turner et al., 1975), false information should frequently receive greater levels of activation than truthful information, and subsequently be disclosed.

Adopting a PDP-based local management model of deceptive message production suggests at least three implications. First, a significant portion of relationship discourse should be deceptive. This meshes well with the Turner et al. (1975) finding that only 38.5% of utterances produced in significant relationship conversations were truthful. Second, many forms of "relational deception" may not derive from deceptive intents, but (ironically) honest intents, honesty being defined by relational partners as fidelity to the maintenance of a relationship (Turner et al., 1975). Third, such a model could potentially reconcile the degrees of freedom dilemma described earlier. Although individuals early in youth should find all forms of deception challenging to construct, over time this difficulty should be replaced with relative ease. As O'Keefe and Lambert (1995) described, "over time, the weights in the message generator will be trained to meet the expectations of the activity model. Hence reflections and practice should lead to quicker message planning, because fewer iterations should be required to satisfy the activity model" (p. 78). Once an individual has a fair amount of experience with designing deceptive messages, and has stored a corresponding repository of false information from which such messages can be constructed (as well as knowledge regarding the efficacy of deception), deception will become an efficient cognitive alternative to packaging problematic truths. Although second-order intentionality is necessary to *initially* conceive of and enact deception, once the cognitive competence to conceive of belief-embeddedness is achieved, it likely would not be consciously relevant as the basis for everyday deception generation (i.e., deceptive messages may be generated almost automatically, rather than as the product of careful, conscious thought and planning).

---

[5]I would like to thank Dr. Tim Levine for originally bringing this point to my attention.

SUMMARY AND CONCLUSIONS

The goal of this chapter was to articulate several key issues related to deceptive message production. Although a number of concerns were discussed, four key points that were raised merit final emphasis through repetition. First, most deception research performed to date has little to do with naturalistic deception, and much to do with comparisons between two narrow bands of artificial discourse: experimentally constructed, bold-faced lies versus experimentally constructed, bold-faced truths. As a consequence, contemporary deception theory and research suffers from an appalling lack of ecological validity. Second, scholars interested in generating new theory must account for the apparently paradoxical characteristics of everyday interpersonal deception. Third, careful scrutiny of the cognitive processes underlying deceptive message production suggests that many of the assumptions upon which the field of deception has been founded are questionable. Fourth, the most provocative and challenging questions confronting deception scholars are cognitive in nature, and consequently will mandate turning to domains not normally linked with deception (e.g., cognitive science, artificial intelligence, problem solving) in order to generate answers.

The exploration of deceptive message production from a cognitive perspective will entail a fundamental paradigm shift in deception research. Scholars must be willing to abandon the hopeful myths that have guided so much of our prior research. In addition, no single explanatory framework likely will account for the entire process. Rather than generating theories that attempt to account for all of interpersonal deception (and end up explaining little), theorists should focus on parsing out particular facets of the deception process, and developing parsimonious, coherent explanatory accounts for these facts.

ACKNOWLEDGMENTS

The author would like to thank Dr. Tim Levine, Dr. Kelly Morrison, Dr. Bella DePaulo, and Annemarie Hodges for their helpful suggestions regarding this chapter, and Amy Janan Johnson for her assistance.

REFERENCES

Airenti, G., Bara, B. G., & Combetti, M. (1993). Conversation and behavior games in the pragmatics of dialogue. *Cognitive Science, 17*, 197–256.
Barr, A., Cohen, P. R., & Feigenbaum, E. A. (1989). *The handbook of artificial intelligence, Volume IV*. Reading, MA: Addison-Wesley.

Bradac, J., Friedman, E., & Giles, H. (1986). A social approach to propositional communication: Speakers lie to hearers. In G. McGregor (Ed.), *Language for hearers* (pp. 127–151). Oxford: Pergamon Press.

Brown, P., & Levinson, S. (1978). Universals in language usage: Politeness phenomena. In E. Goody (Ed.), *Questions and politeness* (pp. 56–311). Cambridge, England: Cambridge University Press.

Buller, D. B., & Burgoon, J. K. (1991, August). *The language of interpersonal deception: Falsification, equivocation, and concealment.* Paper presented at the International Conference on Language and Social Psychology, Santa Barbara, CA.

Buller, D. B., & Burgoon, J. K. (1996). Interpersonal deception theory. *Communication Theory.*

Buller, D. B., Burgoon, J. K., White, C. H., & Ebesu, A. S. (1994). Interpersonal deception VII: Behavioral profiles of falsification, equivocation, and concealment. *Journal of Language and Social Psychology, 13,* 366–395.

Buller, D. B., Strzyzewski, K. D., & Comstock, J. (1991). Interpersonal deception I: Deceivers' reactions to receivers' suspicions and probing. *Communication Monographs, 58,* 25–40.

Burgoon, J. K., Buller, D. B., Guerrero, L. K., Afifi, W. A., & Feldman, C. M. (1996). Interpersonal deception XII: Information management dimensions underlying deceptive and truthful messages. *Communication Monographs, 63,* 50–69.

Burgoon, J. K., Kelley, D. L., Newton, D. A., & Keeley-Dyreson, M. P. (1989). The nature of arousal and nonverbal indices. *Human Communication Research, 16,* 217–255.

Bussey, K. (1992). Lying and truthfulness: Children's definitions, standards, and evaluative reactions. *Child Development, 63,* 129–137.

Chandler, M. (1988). Doubt and developing theories of mind. In J. Astington, P. Harris, & D. Olson (Eds.), *Developing theories of mind.* New York: Cambridge University Press.

Chaiken, S., Liberman, A., Eagly, A. H. (1989). Heuristic and systematic information processing within and beyond the persuasion context. In J. S. Uleman & J. A. Bargh (Eds.), *Unintended thought.* New York: Guilford.

Cohen, P. R., & Perrault, C. R. (1979). Elements of a plan-based theory of speech acts. *Cognitive Science, 3,* 177–212.

Dennett, D. C. (1987). *The intentional stance.* Cambridge, MA: MIT Press.

DePaulo, B. M., Ansfield, M. E., & Bell, K. L. (1996a). Theories about deception and paradigms for studying it: A critical appraisal of Buller and Burgoon's interpersonal deception theory and research. *Communication Theory.*

DePaulo, B. M., Kashy, D. A., Kirkendol, S. E., Wyer, M. M., & Epstein, J. A. (1996b). Lying in everyday life. *Journal of Personality and Social Psychology.*

DePaulo, B. M., & Kirkendol, S. E. (1988). The motivational impairment effect in the communication of deception. In J. Yuille (Ed.), *Credibility assessment* (pp. 50–69). Belgium: Kluwer.

DePaulo, B. M., Stone, J. I., & Lassiter, G. D. (1985). Deceiving and detecting deceit. In B. R. Schlenker (Ed.), *The self and social life* (pp. 323–370). New York: McGraw-Hill.

Eagly, A. H., & Chaiken, S. (1993). *The psychology of attitudes.* New York: Harcourt Brace Jovanovich.

Ekman, P. (1985). *Telling lies.* New York: Berkley Books.

Ekman, P., & Friesen, W. V. (1969). Nonverbal leakage and clues to deception. *Psychiatry, 32,* 93–94.

Ernst, G. (1987). Means-ends analysis. In S.C. Shapiro, D. Eckroth, & G. A. Vallasi (Eds.), *Encyclopedia of artificial intelligence* (pp. 578–584). New York: Wiley.

Fiedler, K., & Walka, I. (1993). Training lie detectors to use nonverbal cues instead of global heuristics. *Human Communication Research, 20,* 199–223.

Fish, S. E. (1978). Normal circumstances, literal language, direct speech acts, the ordinary, the everyday, the obvious, what goes without saying, and other special cases. *Critical Inquiry, 4,* 243–265.

Fiske, S. T., & Taylor, S. E. (1991). *Social cognition* (2nd ed.). New York: McGraw-Hill.

Gilbert, D. T., Krull, D. S., & Malone, P. S. (1990). Unbelieving the unbelievable: Some problems in the rejection of false information. *Journal of Personality and Social Psychology, 59,* 601–613.

Goffman, E. (1955). On face work: An analysis of ritual elements in social interaction. *Psychiatry, 18,* 319–345.

Greene, J. O., O'Hair, H. D., Cody, M. J., & Yen, C. (1985). Planning and control of behavior during deception. *Human Communication Research, 11,* 335–364.

Grice, H. P. (1975). Logic and conversation. In P. Cole & J. L. Morgan (Eds.), *Speech acts* (pp. 41–58). New York: Academic Press.

Hayes-Roth, B. (1985). A blackboard architecture for control. *Artificial Intelligence, 26,* 251–321.

Hewes, D. E., & Planalp, S. (1987). The individual's place in communication science. In C. Berger & S. Chaffee (Eds.), *Handbook of communication science* (pp. 147–183). Newbury Park, CA: Sage.

Hilton, J. L., Fein, S., & Miller, D. T. (1993). Suspicion and dispositional inference. *Personality and Social Psychology Bulletin, 19,* 501–512.

Hocking, J. E., & Leathers, D. G. (1980). Nonverbal indicators of deception: A new theoretical perspective. *Communication Monographs, 47,* 119–131.

Hoppe-Graff, S., Herrmann, T., Winterhoff-Spurk, P., & Mangold, R. (1985). Speech and situation: A general model for the process of speech production. In J. Forgas (Ed.), *Language and social situations* (pp. 81–95). New York: Springer-Verlag.

Hovy, E. H. (1990). Pragmatics and natural language generation. *Artificial Intelligence, 43,* 153–197.

Hyman, R. (1989). The psychology of deception. *Annual Review of Psychology, 49,* 133–154.

Jacobs, S., Dawson, E. J., & Brashers, D. (1996). Information manipulation theory: A replication and assessment. *Communication Monographs, 63,* 70–82.

Jastrow, J. (1900). *Fact and fable in psychology.* Cambridge, MA: Riverside Press.

Kraut, R. E. (1978). Verbal and nonverbal cues in the perception of lying. *Journal of Personality and Social Psychology, 36,* 380–391.

Kraut, R. E. (1980). Humans as lie-detectors: Some second thoughts. *Journal of Communication, 30,* 290–216.

Lambert, B. L. (1992, November). *Functional abstraction and plan-based models of message production.* Paper presented at the annual meeting of the Speech Communication Association, Chicago.

Lambert, B. L., & O'Keefe, B. J. (1990, November). *Modelling message design.* Paper presented at the annual meeting of the Speech Communication Association, Chicago.

Lapinski, M. K. (1995). *Deception and the self: A cultural examination of information manipulation theory.* Unpublished master's thesis, University of Hawaii at Manoa.

Levine, T. R. (1994, November). *Conceptualizing interpersonal and relational deception.* Paper presented at the annual meeting of the Speech Communication Association, New Orleans, LA.

Levine, T. R., & McCornack, S. A. (1994, June). *Behavioral adaptation and heuristic message processing explanations of the probing effect.* Paper presented at the annual meeting of the International Communication Association, Sydney, Australia.

Levine, T. R., & McCornack, S. A., (1996a). A critical analysis of the behavioral adaptation explanation of the probing effect. *Human Communication Research, 22,* 575–588.

Levine, T. R., & McCornack, S. A. (1996b). Can the BAE explain the probing effect? *Human Communication Research, 22,* 604–613.

Levinson, S. C. (1981). Some pre-observations on the modelling of dialogue. *Discourse Processes, 3,* 133–154.

McCornack, S. A. (1992). Information manipulation theory. *Communication Monographs, 59,* 1–16.

McCornack, S. A., Levine, T. R., Solowczuk, K. A., Torres, H. I., & Campbell, D. M. (1992). When the alteration of information is viewed as deception: An empirical test of information manipulation theory. *Communication Monographs, 59,* 17–29.

Metts, S., & Chronis, H. (1986, May). *Relational deception: An exploratory analysis*. Paper presented at the annual meeting of the International Communication Association, Chicago, IL.

Newell, A., & Simon, H. A. (1972). *Human problem solving*. Englewood Cliffs, NJ: Prentice-Hall.

Nii, H. P. (1989). Blackboard systems. In A. Barr, P. R. Cohen, & E. A. Feigenbaum (Eds.), *The handbook of artificial intelligence, Volume IV* (pp. 1–82). Reading, MA: Addison-Wesley.

O'Keefe, B. J. (1988). The logic of message design: Individual differences in reasoning about communication. *Communication Monographs, 55*, 80–103.

O'Keefe, B. J. (1990). The logic of regulative communication: Understanding the rationality of message designs. In J. P. Dillard (Ed.), *Seeking compliance: The production of interpersonal influence messages* (pp. 87–104). Scottsdale, AR: Gorsuch Scarisbrick.

O'Keefe, B. J., & Lambert, B. L. (1989, November). *Effects of message design logic on the communication of intention*. Paper presented at the annual meeting of the Speech Communication Association, San Francisco.

O'Keefe, B. J., & Lambert, B. L. (1995). Managing the flow of ideas: A local management approach to message design. In B. R. Burleson (Ed.), *Communication yearbook 18* (pp. 54–82). Thousand Oaks, CA: Sage.

Pavitt, C. (1991). An analysis of artificial intelligence based models for describing communicative choice. *Communication Theory, 1*, 204–224.

Peskin, J. (1992). Ruse and representations: On children's ability to conceal information. *Developmental Psychology, 28*, 84–89.

Popper, K. R. (1959). *The logic of scientific discovery*. New York: Routledge.

Rumelhart, D. E., McClelland, J. L., & the PDP Research Group (Eds.). (1986). *Parallel distributed processing: Explorations in the microstructure of cognition: Vol. 1., Foundations*. Cambridge: MIT Press.

Sahlman, J. M., & Canary, D. J. (1995, November). *Effects of information manipulation on attributions of deceptive intent*. Paper presented at the annual meeting of the Speech Communication Association, San Antonio, TX.

Searle, J. (1965). What is a speech act? In M. Black (Ed.), *Philosophy in America* (pp. 221–239). Ithaca, NY: Cornell University Press.

Searle, J. (1969). *Speech acts: An essay in the philosophy of language*. Cambridge, England: Cambridge University Press.

Searle, J. (1975). Indirect speech acts. In P. Cole & J. L. Morgan (Eds.), *Syntax and semantics, Volume 3: Speech acts* (pp. 59–82). New York: Academic Press.

Stiff, J. B., & Miller, G. R. (1986). Come to think of it . . . Interrogative probes, deceptive communication, and deception detection. *Human Communication Research, 12*, 339–357.

Stiff, J. B., Miller, G. R., Sleight, C., Mongeau, P., Garlick, R., & Rogan, R. (1989). Explanations for visual cue primacy in judgments of honesty and deceit. *Journal of Personality and Social Psychology, 56*, 1–10.

Streek, J. (1980). Speech acts in interaction: A critique of Searle. *Discourse Processes, 3*, 133–154.

Turner, R. E., Edgley, C., & Olmstead, G. (1975). Information control in conversations: Honesty is not always the best policy. *Kansas Journal of Sociology, 11*, 69–85.

Vrij, A., Semin, G. R., & Bull, R. (1996). Insight into behavior displayed during deception. *Human Communication Research, 22*, 544–562.

Zuckerman, M., & Driver, R. E. (1985). Telling lies: Verbal and nonverbal correlates of deception. In A. W. Siegman & S. Feldstein (Eds.), *Multichannel integrations of nonverbal behavior* (pp. 129–147). Hillsdale, NJ: Lawrence Erlbaum Associates.

6

NEW DIRECTIONS IN RESEARCH ON AGING AND MESSAGE PRODUCTION

Susan Kemper and Mary Lee Hummert
University of Kansas

Message production begins with the formulation of a message and includes steps of syntactic encoding, lexical selection, and discourse planning prior to the final step of phonological production. Errors, reflecting attentional lapses, processing limitations, and execution problems, can arise at any stage of production. Normative aging processes, arising from general slowing of cognitive processes (Salthouse, 1992), reductions of working memory capacity (Light, 1991), or a breakdown of inhibitory processes (Hasher & Zacks, 1988), may exacerbate such production problems; specific diseases, such as Alzheimer's disease and other progressive dementias, may also affect message production. On the other hand, maintenance of or increases in social knowledge, for example, wisdom (Simonton, 1990; Smith & Baltes, 1990), may be related to improved discourse planning on the part of older persons. This chapter examines what is currently known about how normal aging affects message production and reviews available research on how Alzheimer's disease affects message production. It must be noted at the outset that research on aging and message production has, like the study of production processes in general, lagged behind studies of message comprehension and memory because of the difficulties inherent in experimentally manipulating production processes. The chapter concludes by considering the criteria for an adequate model of message production in aging.

GENERAL CHARACTERISTICS OF MESSAGE PRODUCTION

Models of language production (Bock, 1987; Dell, 1986; Garrett, 1988; MacKay, 1987) have tended to focus on two issues: the modularity of syntactic, semantic, and/or pragmatic processes; and serial versus hierarchical accounts of language production. Modularity (Fodor, 1982) or autonomy theory holds that message production involves a sequence of processing stages or levels. Typically four properties are ascribed to this sequence of processing stages: (a) each stage corresponds to a distinct linguistic rule system, (b) each stage involves a discrete representational system, (c) processing flows unidirectionally through the sequence of stages, and (d) each stage may be characterized by independent constraints on the rules, representations, or processing operations at that stage. Consider, for example, Garrett's (1988) account of speech errors. He noted that speech errors may reflect at least three distinct phenomena:

1. at the level of lexical selection, word substitutions and fusions may occur, resulting in the production of hybrids such as "dreeze" from "draft" and "breeze," or "caking" from "cooking" and "baking" or self-corrected errors such as "and a letter about myself . . . picture of myself";

2. at the level of syntactic encoding, word and morpheme shifts and exchanges may occur, producing "he go backs" rather than "he goes back," or "I would hear one if I knew it" rather than "I would know one if I heard it";

3. finally, at the level of phonological encoding, sound deletions, substitutions, anticipations, and perseverations may occur, resulting in "I thought the park was trucked" rather than "I thought the truck was parked" or "because of band hadwriting" instead of "because of bad handwriting" or "that's what Tomsky was chalking about" instead of "that's what Chomsky was talking about."

Although messages are produced "one word at a time" (Bloom, 1975), message structure is inherently hierarchical. A number of phenomena are typically discussed to illustrate this tension between serial and hierarchical accounts. First, languages impose arbitrary conventions regarding the ordering of linguistic units at all levels. Compare the English "Daddy threw a ball" with its Turkish equivalent *"Babam topu verdi"* (i.e., "Daddy ball threw"). English typically uses SUBJECT-VERB-OBJECT whereas Turkish canonically uses SUBJECT-OBJECT-VERB order. Second, word-order variation is also permitted to indicate subtle differences in meaning or focus, but language-specific constraints on linear order must also be observed; in English, datives and objects can alternate in the linear sequence for some verbs such as *give* (compare "Mary gave a cookie to me" to "Mary gave me a cookie") but not for others such as *donate* ("Mary donated a million dollars to me" vs. "Mary donated me a million dollars"). Third, human languages are characterized by their ability to permit infinite variation; one means by which such variation is achieved is through recursion or the embedding of one linguistic unit inside another. Clauses can be embedded within clauses through a variety of formal devices including relative clauses, "The baby smiled at the woman *who held him*"; gerundive clauses, "*The baby's smiling* brought a smile to the woman's face"; infinitive clauses, "The woman tried *to get* the baby *to smile*"; and subordinate clauses, "*After the woman picked up the baby*, he smiled." Fourth, word-order variation and clause embedding create the possibility that long-distance dependencies will occur. For example, in English, verbs must agree with their subjects in person and number; this constraint is violated in "Efforts to make English the official language is gaining strength throughout the U.S." (*The New Yorker*, November 17, 1986, p. 94); although the verb *is gaining* agrees with the immediately preceding noun *language*, the grammatical subject of the sentence is the plural noun *Efforts*. Fifth, the interpretation of the scope of quantifiers also is influenced by word-order variation and clause embedding. Compare "Everyone in this room speaks two languages" to "Two languages are spoken by everyone in this room." Whereas the first sentence implies only that each individual is fluent in two languages, the second implies that they are fluent in the *same* two languages. Finally, ambiguities can arise whenever the linear sequence can be assigned to multiple hierarchical structures. The sequence "The boy chased the dog with two bones" could be interpreted as indicating that the boy had two bones by attaching the prepositional phrase to the verb phrase ([[chased $_V$] [the dog $_{NP}$] [with two bones $_{PP}$] $_{VP}$]) or that the dog had two bones by attaching the prepositional phrase to the object noun phrase ([[chased $_V$] [the dog [with two bones $_{PP}$] $_{NP}$] $_{VP}$]).

Although these problems of modularity and serialization have been central in discussions of formal production models, they have received little attention from researchers concerned with the effects of normal or pathological aging. Word-finding problems and other disfluencies are highly salient to older adults and are often noted by others (Bayles & Tomoeda, 1991; Lubinski, Morrison, & Rigrodsky, 1981; Ryan & Burk, 1974; Ryan & Heaven, 1988; Ryan & Johnson, 1987; Ryan & Laurie, 1990; Sunderland, Watts, Baddeley, & Harris, 1986). Yet there is far too little research on how aging affects many aspects of speech production. For instance, little is known about how aging affects speech errors at syntactic, semantic, and phonological levels; how word order variation, quantifier scope, and attachment ambiguities are affected by normal and pathological aging; and how discourse planning may show positive as well as negative effects of normal aging. More critically, there is far too little research that attempts to distinguish the effects of normal aging processes from those due to diseases and pathologies, especially progressive dementias such as Alzheimer's disease. What is known is summarized next. We consider first the research on syntactic encoding, lexical selection, and discourse planning in normal aging, and then examine research on disorders of message production.

AGE-RELATED CHANGES IN MESSAGE PRODUCTION

Syntactic Encoding

The syntax of the speech of older adults appears simplified in comparison to that of young adults (Benjamin, 1988; Cooper, 1990; Davis, 1984; Kemper, 1992; Kemper, Kynette, Rash, Sprott, & O'Brien, 1989; Kemper, Rash, Kynette, & Norman, 1990; Kynette & Kemper, 1986; Shewan & Henderson, 1988; Ulatowska, Freedman-Stern, Weiss-Doyle, Macaluso-Haynes, & North, 1983; Walker, Roberts, & Hedrick, 1988). Although sentence length in words remains constant, older adults show a reduction in their use of complex syntactic constructions such as those involving subordinate and embedded clauses. Older adults favor coordinate or right-branching constructions, for example, "She's awfully young to be running a nursery school for our church," over left-branching constructions, for example, "The gal who runs a nursery school for our church is awfully young." During the production of the left-branching constructions (in which the embedded clause occurs to the left of the main clause), the form of the subject "the gal" must be retained and the grammatical form of the main clause verb "is" (which must agree with its subject in person and number) must be anticipated while the embedded clause "who runs a nursery school for our church" is being produced. Each clause is produced sequentially in the right-branching construction (in which the embedded clause occurs to the right of the main clause).

Older adults' use of complex sentences is also affected by task demands. During undemanding interpersonal conversation or simple picture-description tasks, older adults may be able to use complex syntactic constructions with some ease (Glosser & Deser, 1992; Walker et al., 1988). But as task demands increase, complex syntax may trade-off with other task demands such as constructing elaborate narrative plots (Kemper, 1990; Kemper et al., 1990).

Working memory limitations appear to affect adults' ability to produce complex syntactic constructions. Kemper et al. (1989) reported that the mean number of clauses per utterance (MCU), a general measure of the complexity of adults' language, is positively correlated with the adults' backward digit span using the WAIS subtest (Wechsler, 1958). Further, Kemper and Rash (1988) calculated Yngve depth (Yngve, 1960), a measure of the working memory demands of sentence production, and found that it was positively correlated with WAIS digit span as well as with MCU. This line of research, therefore, suggests that working memory limitations may affect older adults' production, as well as comprehension, of complex syntactic constructions.

Lexical Selection

Word-finding problems are among the most frequent complaints of older adults. Pauses, circumlocutions, "empty speech" such as pronouns lacking clear referents, and substitution errors during spontaneous speech may all reflect age-related impairments in accessing and retrieving lexical information (Cohen, 1979; Obler, 1980; Ulatowska, Cannito, Hayashi, & Fleming, 1985). It appears that older adults have difficulty accessing lexical information, especially the phonological form of words (Burke, MacKay, Worthley, & Wade, 1991). Consequently, tip-of-the-tongue experiences, in which familiar words are temporarily irretrievable, are more common for older adults than for young adults and less often resolved by retrieval of the intended word. Word-finding problems are also apparent in controlled tasks such as those requiring word retrieval in response to definitions (Bowles, Obler, & Albert, 1987; Bowles, Obler, & Poon, 1989; Bowles & Poon, 1981, 1985), pictures (Albert, Heller, & Milberg, 1988; Nicholas, Obler, Albert, & Goodglass, 1985), or category cues (Howard, Shaw, & Heisey, 1986; Obler & Albert, 1981) as well as during picture and video description tasks (Heller & Dobbs, 1993).

Name retrieval is a particularly troubling wording-finding difficulty for older adults (Burke & Laver, 1990; Cohen, 1994; Cohen & Faulkner, 1986). This selective deficit for proper names seems not to reflect specific changes in the cognitive system (Cohen, 1994), but instead the interaction of low levels of cognitive activation in older persons, for example, cognitive slowing or working memory deficits, and the lexical distinctiveness of proper names (Bruce & Young, 1986; Burton & Bruce, 1992; Cohen, 1992). That is, because proper names have fewer semantic associations than other words and because proper names are highly similar phonologically, normative word-finding difficulties experienced by older persons are increased whenever the desired word is a proper name.

Discourse Planning

Discourse encompasses a variety of communication skills, ranging from opening and closing conversations, maintaining and shifting topics, and telling stories, to establishing and modifying personal relationships, conveying individual and group identity, gaining and avoiding compliance, and being polite, saving "face" or giving offense. To date, little research has examined older adults' discourse skills.

There is some evidence that discourse skills increase with age: Older adults create elaborate narrative structures that include hierarchically elaborated episodes with beginnings describing initiating events and motivating states, developments detailing the protagonists' goals and actions, and endings summarizing the outcomes of the protagonists efforts; evaluative codas are often attached to older adults' narratives which assess the contemporary significance of these stories (Kemper & Anagnopoulos, 1989; Kemper et al., 1990; Pratt, Boyes, Robins, & Manchester, 1989; Pratt & Robins, 1991). Narrative stories told by older adults are evaluated more positively, preferred by listeners, and are more memorable than those told by young adults (Kemper & Anagnopoulos, 1989; Kemper et al., 1990; Pratt et al., 1989; Pratt & Robins, 1991).

Other discourse skills appear to be vulnerable to aging. Older adults often have difficulty with referential communication tasks. In one such referential communication task, Hupet, Chantraine, and Nef (1993) tracked how dyads of young and older adults formulated mutually acceptable labels for abstract drawings. The older adults benefited less from repetition of the task than the young adults; whereas the young adults added new information to previously used descriptions, the older adults tended to supply totally new labels. The older adults' problems with this task may have resulted from forgetting of the old labels from trial to trial or from their inability to inhibit irrelevant thoughts or associations, including the new descriptions.

In a series of studies, Kemper and her colleagues (Kemper, Othick, Gerhing, Gubarchuk, & Billington, 1996; Kemper, Othick, Warren, Gubarchuk, & Gerhing, 1996; Kemper, Vandeputte, Rice, Cheung, & Gubarchuk, 1995) have compared young–young, old–old, and young–old dyads on a referential communication task involving giving map directions. Whereas young adults spontaneously adopt a simplified speech style when addressing older adults versus age-equivalent peers, older adults do not appear to code-switch. This may be due to a number of factors, including:

1. Older adults may not be sensitive to the same situational cues that elicit code-switching from the young adults;

2. Older adults may not be able to vary their grammatical complexity or semantic content while simultaneously executing the complex task;

3. Older speakers may have "optimized" their speech to peers as a result of extensive practice at communicating with other older adults and adults experiencing communicative problems; hence, shifting to a non-optimal speech style when addressing younger adults would not be an appropriate strategy;

4. Older adults may be unwilling to shift to a simplified speech style when they are addressing peers since this form of speech may resemble patronizing talk (Ryan, Hummert, & Boich, 1995) or secondary baby talk (Caporael,

1981); although older listeners performed better with the young persons who used simplified speech, they rated their personal communicative competence lower when they were paired with a young person than with an older person (Kemper et al., 1996). This may reflect negative self-assessments of their own communicative competence which were triggered by the perception that they were the recipients of patronizing speech.

The discourse of young and older adults differs in other ways. For instance, dyads of older adults mix talk about the past along with talk about the present to achieve a shared sense of meaning and personal worth which is lacking in the discourse of young adults (Boden & Bielby, 1986). In addition, conversations with older adults are often marked by "painful self-disclosures" of bereavement, ill-health, immobility, and assorted personal and family problems (Coupland, Coupland, & Giles, 1991). Painful self-disclosures may serve several different goals for communicators (Coupland, Coupland, & Grainger, 1991; Shaner, 1996), for example, maintaining "face" by contrasting personal strengths and competencies with past problems and limitations, and coping with personal losses and difficulties. Yet painful self-disclosures also maintain and reinforce negative age stereotypes about the elderly as weak and disabled (Shaner, 1996). Consequently, such self-disclosures can suppress conversational interactions and limit the quality of intergenerational communication (Nussbaum, Hummert, Williams, & Harwood, 1996). Age disclosure on the part of the older partner is another conversational practice noted by Coupland, Coupland, and Grainger (1991). Like painful self-disclosures, age disclosures may lead to unsatisfactory intergenerational interactions by emphasizing the differences between older and young partners.

A final discourse style often presumed to accompany aging is verbosity, or repetitive, prolonged, off-target speech. However, recent research (Arbuckle & Gold, 1993; Arbuckle, Gold, & Andres, 1986; Gold, Andres, Arbuckle, & Schwartzman, 1988; Gold & Arbuckle, 1992; Gold, Arbuckle, & Andres, 1994) has suggested that verbosity is not a general characteristic of older adults but is an extreme form of talkativeness that results from intellectual decline associated with frontal lobe impairments (see Arbuckle & Gold, 1993, for a review of these issues). Frontal lobe impairments disrupt inhibitory processes and lead to perseverative behaviors on other tasks. Verbosity can be characterized as involving a loss of the ability to inhibit competing responses; hence, an age-related loss of frontal lobe function may lead to increased verbosity among older adults. Verbosity, like talk of the past, painful self-disclosures and age disclosures, may disrupt social interactions and lead to a loss of interpersonal contact and social support. Unlike the other discourse practices of older adults, however, verbosity appears to reflect changes in message-production processes that lie at the juncture between normal and pathological aging.

DISORDERS OF MESSAGE PRODUCTION

Message production is disrupted by a number of age-related diseases and disorders: discourse impairments are observed for adults with sensorineural hearing loss (presbycusis); motor speech disorders of the positioning and timing of articulatory mechanisms (apraxia) and speech disturbances due to weakness or slowing of neuromuscular systems (dysarthria) may result from a variety of diseases such as Parkinson's; expressive or receptive impairments following brain lesions (aphasia) often result from stroke and other forms of neurological trauma. Recently, attention has shifted to the examination of disorders of message production arising from senile dementia of the Alzheimer's type as well as other forms of dementia.

Communication problems are often the first symptoms of a progressive dementia such as Alzheimer's disease and communication problems are frequently noted by spouses and other family members (Bayles & Tomoeda, 1991; Orange, 1991; Rau, 1991). Clinical markers of the onset of Alzheimer's disease are difficult to distinguish from nonclinical age-related lapses of attention or memory, "benign senescent forgetfulness" or "non-pathological age-associated memory impairments" (Huppert, 1994; Kral, 1962). Distinguishing normative age-related changes to message production from non-normative or pathological changes may be important for the early diagnosis, hence possible treatment, of Alzheimer's disease and related disorders.

The Regression Hypothesis claims that the breakdown of language is the inverse of its acquisition (Jackson, 1958; Jakobson, 1941/1968). Typically, the Regression Hypothesis is put forth to account for aphasia disorders (Dennis & Wiegel-Camp, 1979; Grodzinsky, 1990; Lesser, 1978) but it has more recently been advanced as an account of the effects of normal aging on language. In its strongest form, the Regression Hypothesis claims that the development of linguistic competence in childhood is mirrored by the dissolution of linguistic competence in adulthood (Emery, 1985, 1986).

The Regression Hypothesis has been most carefully examined in the domain of syntactic production. Although studies of the speech of adults with dementia reveal that older adults with dementia are less likely to spontaneously produce complex grammatical forms than healthy peers, their speech does not evidence a progressive degeneration into "baby talk." Compare the following extracts from children (extracts 1 and 2) and dementing adults (extracts 3 and 4) who were asked to relate an oral story in response to a picturebook, *Frog, Where Are You?* (Mayer, 1969). While there are many similarities (e.g., the use of ambiguous or nonspecific pronouns and the omission of causal or temporal connectives), the extracts from the children and the dementing adults also differ with regards to a number of characteristics (e.g., text cohesiveness, event sequencing, the provision of details, the inclusion of inferences about motivational states, the construal of agency, and causality, the occurrence of word-finding problems, and the nature and function of metalinguistic comments to the listener).

Extract from a 3-year-old: (1)
. . . the frog got away, and then, look what happened. He tried to go in, but see, he didn't, couldn't go in! And then, he licked the boy, and he was mad! And then, some bees came out of the tree, and then he tried to get the bees, but he couldnt. And then he looked into the hole, and see, there's a mouse coming! And then he climbed a tree—tried to climb the tree but look what happened. Owl came out . . . (Berman & Slobin, 1994)

Extract from a 9-year-old: (2)
. . . the dog falls out of the window—the dog had got the jar stuck on his head, and he falls out of the window and it breaks and the little boy picks it up. And they start calling after the frog and the dog starts sniffing some bees. And then he looks in a hole, and the dog's looking at this beehive. And then some gopher comes up and then the dog's still looking at that beehive. So then the beehive falls and all the bees are—they start chasing after him, and he um, the little boy climbs up a tree and looks into a hole, and an owl flies out, and he falls off the tree . . . (Berman & Slobin, 1994)

Extract from a mildly demented adult: (3)
. . . he's falling . . . out of the window. But the dog is OK. They're going to the the woods . . . barking. There's a house for . . . for the insects . . . buzz. It's a . . . I just can't remember. He's barking at them. He . . . He . . . I don't know. Is he trying to scare the bees? Now they're back in the woods. He's up in a tree. . . . (Kemper, unpublished data)

Extract from a moderately demented adult: (4)
. . . I don't know. The dog . . . he's out. Trees. What's this? [points to wasps' nest]. He wants it. Now he's going to hide in there, I guess. . . . (Kemper, unpublished data)

Although there have been no formal, comparative studies of the speech of children versus that of dementing adults, it is likely that the similarities between language acquisition in childhood and the nature of language breakdown in dementia arise from different underlying mechanisms and principles, a view that is inconsistent with the Regression Hypothesis.

Syntactic production appears to be buffered from the effects of Alzheimer's disease (Bates, Harris, Marchman, Wulfeck, & Kritchevsky, 1995; Blanken, Dittman, Haas, & Wallesch, 1987; Kemper et al., 1993; Kemper & Lyons, 1994; Kempler, 1991; Kempler, Curtiss, & Jackson, 1987; Kempler & Zelinski, 1994; Lyons et al., 1993). Some simplifications of syntax may result but their speech does not appear to become agrammatic. For example, Kemper et al. (1993) examined single sentences produced by older adults undergoing a neurological examination as part of the Mini-Mental State

Examination (Folstein, Folstein, & McHugh, 1975). The adults were classified as nondemented or diagnosed with probable Alzheimer's disease and rated as very mildly, mildly, or moderately demented. The sentences were evaluated for propositional content, length, and grammatical form. The sentences produced by the moderately demented adults were shorter and simpler, both in content and form, than those produced by the nondemented and very mildly demented adults. Despite these differences, the sentences from the moderately demented adults were just as grammatical as the sentences from the nondemented and mildly demented adults. Whereas the nondemented adults might produce a sentence such as "I was walking in the rose garden today before coming to the hospital," the moderately demented adults might produce "Today the sun is shining." This retention of basic syntactic structure with the progression of Alzheimer's disease is evidence for the modularity of syntax as an autonomous or separate module, although the decline in content and length indicates that cognitive limitations associated with Alzheimer's disease also affect language production.

In contrast, semantic and lexical processes do appear to be disrupted by Alzheimer's disease. Two hypotheses have been put forth to account for these disruptions. Some researchers have concluded that the structure of semantic knowledge is destroyed by Alzheimer's disease (Abeysinghe, Bayles, & Trosset, 1990; Butters, Granholm, Salmon, Grant, & Wolfe, 1987; Butters, Salmon, & Heindel, 1990; Chan et al., 1993; Chan, Butters, Salmon, & McGuire, 1993; Chertkow, Bub, & Seidenberg, 1989; Eustache, Cox, Brandt, Lechevalier, & Pons, 1990; Hodges, Salmon, & Butters, 1992; Martin, 1987; Troster, Slamon, McCullough, & Butters, 1989). As a result, performance on verbal-fluency tasks, such as generating exemplars of categories or words beginning with a specific letter, is impaired; picture and object naming is hindered; and word associations are destroyed. Others have concluded that the semantic network of adults with Alzheimer's dementia is intact but becomes inaccessible (Nebes, 1989, 1992; Nebes & Rady, 1990). From this perspective, semantic priming in reaction-time tasks involving word naming and lexical decisions is preserved.

Many of the impairments to discourse which have been observed in adults with Alzheimer's dementia may stem from their gross word-finding problems whereas other problems may stem from attentional deficits and cognitive confusions. The heavy use of deictic terms such as *this* and *that*, the loss of specific reference and loss of cohesion, the prevalence of vague terms and "empty speech," a loss of detail, an increase in repetition and redundancy, and confusing shifts in topic and focus have all been noted as characteristic of the speech of adults with Alzheimer's disease (Bayles, 1982; Bayles, Boone, Tomoeda, Slauson, & Kaszniak, 1989; Bayles & Kaszniak, 1987; Bayles, Tomoeda, & Boone, 1985; Garcia & Joanette, 1994; Hier, Hagenlocker, & Shindler, 1985; Hutchinson & Jensen, 1980; Nicholas, Obler, Albert, &

Helm-Esterbrooks, 1985; Ripich & Terrell, 1988; Ripich, Terrell, & Spinelli, 1983; Ulatowska, Allard, & Donnell, 1988; Ulatowska & Chapman, 1991).

Other discourse-level communication problems have also been linked to Alzheimer's disease. Whereas healthy older adults follow a story grammar in telling personal narratives, relating setting information, complications, the protagonists' actions, and a resolution, the spontaneous narratives of adults with Alzheimer's disease characteristically supply only setting information (Ulatowska et al., 1988; Ulatowska & Chapman, 1991) unless they are prompted by their conversational partner (Kemper, Lyons, & Anagnopoulos, 1995). The ability to use or follow a familiar script, or a series of temporally and causally linked events such as *eating in a restaurant, going to a movie,* or *holding a wedding,* is also impaired by Alzheimer's disease (Grafman et al., 1991; Harrold, Anderson, Clancy, & Kempler, 1990), as are spontaneous turn-taking, topic initiation, topic maintenance, topic shifting, conversational repairs, and speech acts, such as requesting, asserting, clarifying, and questioning (Bayles & Kaszniak, 1987).

A breakdown of self-awareness and metalinguistic skills may contribute to the discourse problems of adults with Alzheimer's dementia; Hamilton (1994a, 1994b) has suggested that the progression of Alzheimer's disease is indicated by an erosion of metalinguistic skills marked by declines in requests for clarification, references to memory problems, and self-evaluation of skills and abilities. By carefully tracing communication breakdowns during a series of conversations spanning 4½ years between herself and Elsie, a woman with Alzheimer's disease, Hamilton was able to elucidate four stages to the deterioration of communication:

Stage 1: Elsie was an active participant in the conversations, but one who was bothered by word-finding problems as well as memory lapses; she was aware of her communication problems and attempted to deal with them through excuses, circumlocutions, and other metalinguistic comments. Turn-taking, joking, and speech formalisms were preserved.

Stage 2: Elsie remained an active participant in the conversations, but her awareness of and responses to her memory lapses and word-finding problems had disappeared. Perseverations and excessive repetitions had begun to appear.

Stage 3: Elsie's participation in the conversation was markedly reduced, perseverations were common, and formulaic language, for example, "ready-made" conversational routines, predominated and neologisms frequently occurred. Politeness markers, expressions of appreciation, and joking routines had disappeared from Elsie's conversation.

Stage 4: Elsie had become a passive participant; lexical language was lost, replaced by a limited repertoire of nonverbal responses, *uhhuh, mhn, mm Hm, mmm, hmm?* Elsie was able to draw upon this repertoire to request

repetitions and clarifications, take a turn during the conversation, and indicate her interest in her surroundings.

As others have noted, end-stage Alzheimer's disease is often characterized by mutism, inappropriate nonverbal vocalizations, and frequent failures to respond to others (Lamar, Obler, Knoefel, & Albert, 1994).

TOWARD A THEORY OF MESSAGE PRODUCITON IN AGING

From the research reviewed, it is clear that normal aging, and to a greater
extent age-related disorders, create a number of message-production difficulties for older persons. These range from the name-retrieval problems
experienced by most older adults to the mutism of those in the latter stages
of dementia. At the same time, some message-production processes are
preserved (e.g., syntax) or even improved (e.g., narrative skills) with age.
The effects of normal aging on message production seem to be distinct from
the effects of progressive dementias such as Alzheimer's disease. Further,
there is little evidence to suggest that the consequences of normal aging on
message production lead to reductions in communication competence in
everyday interactions (Ryan, 1991). These observations suggest two key
questions that must be addressed in an adequate theory of message production in aging. First, paraphrasing Rabbitt's (1977, p. 623) comment on the
effects of cognitive aging on problem solving, "How, in spite of declining
cognitive and physical resources, do most old people preserve such relatively good communication?" Second, "What message-production difficulties
distinguish normal from pathological aging?" The first question can be conceptualized as the Resources/Competence Dilemma and the second as the
Normal/Pathological Dilemma.

The Resources/Competence Dilemma

Despite problems with word retrieval and declines in working memory and
processing speed, older persons sometimes produce more effective messages than younger ones, for example, the more interesting narratives discussed earlier in this chapter (Kemper et al., 1990). A recent study by
Hummert, Shaner, Garstka, and Henry (1996) revealed another way in which
the messages of older speakers may be judged as more effective than those
of younger ones. Young, middle-aged, and elderly participants delivered
persuasive messages to two elderly targets, one portrayed as active, sociable, intelligent, etc. (i.e., a positive stereotype of aging), and one portrayed
as sad, hopeless, lonely, etc. (i.e., a negative stereotype of aging; see Hum-

mert, Garstka, Shaner, & Strahm, 1994). The resulting messages were classified as affirming (respectful, appropriate, nondirective), patronizing/nurturing (analogous to secondary baby talk) or patronizing/directive (explicitly controlling, cold, condescending). The majority of elderly participants gave affirming messages to both targets. In contrast, middle-aged and young speakers delivered more patronizing messages of both types, particularly to the negatively stereotyped target. The elderly speakers, more than the young and middle-aged, were successful at constructing messages to meet the dual goals of persuasion and face preservation.

What developmental processes might account for the better performance of older speakers in comparison to younger ones in the narrative and persuasion tasks? Possibilities include both practical knowledge and motivational explanations. In the case of narratives, older persons, more than younger ones, might be expected to: have access to more interesting life experiences simply due to having lived longer; have more practice in delivering narratives; have developed story scripts for especially significant life events that have been modified and improved through repeated tellings; come from a cohort in which oral storytelling is more valued. Practical knowledge may also account for the older adults' abilities to integrate task and relational goals more effectively than younger persons. That is, a lifetime of experience in persuasion may have honed older persons' skill in accomplishing multiple goals.

Practical knowledge of the types just described fit the definition of wisdom advanced by Smith and Baltes (1990): expert knowledge about fundamental life matters. Contrary to popular beliefs, wisdom has not been shown to increase with age, primarily because it is dependent on experience in particular contexts or with certain tasks: Young and old adults with equivalent experience are judged equally on wisdom (Smith & Baltes, 1990; Smith, Staudinger, & Baltes, 1994; Staudinger, Smith, & Baltes, 1992). On the other hand, unlike working memory and processing speed, wisdom does not decline with age. Wisdom, therefore, suggests the potential for growth in the aging mind and may provide an avenue to compensate for biological decline (Baltes & Staudinger, 1993). An adequate theory of message production in aging must address this potential of wisdom.

Heckhausen and Schulz' (1995) life-span theory of control offers a motivational explanation for the observed communicative competence of older adults. Two types of control behaviors are available to individuals: primary-control behaviors that are directed at the external world, attempting to change it to meet the desires and needs of the individual; and secondary-control behaviors which center on internal processes and are designed to minimize losses in, preserve, and expand levels of primary control. Although primary control is the preferred method across the lifespan, developmental capabilities and constraints may require a shift from primary to secondary control at different points in the lifespan. As Heckhausen and Schulz show, old age may lead to general physical decline with its associated health problems and functional disabilities (i.e., to severely reduced opportunities for primary control). Whereas this may necessitate a shift from primary to secondary control mechanisms focused on emotional coping (e.g., distancing, downward comparisons, etc.; see Folkman, Lazarus, Pimley, & Novacek, 1987), it may also involve an increased emphasis on communication as both the sole remaining form of primary control and as a way of enacting secondary control interpersonally (e.g., coping, life review).

The ways in which primary and secondary control motivations influence the messages of older adults, however, may not always result in optimal interactions. Although these motivations may be lead to interesting narratives and sensitivity to multiple goals in conversation, they may also engender painful self-disclosures, age disclosures, and other communicative behaviors that interfere with intergenerational communication. As Heckhausen and Schulz (1995) stated, for older adults,

> not only because of declining powers, but also because of the changing ratio of lifetime spent to lifetime remaining, there is an increasing emphasis on the interpretation of the past rather than on planning future changes. Tracking personal consistency . . . , constructing one's personal life story . . . , and interpreting life's successes and failures are high-priority tasks in old age. Most of these can be viewed as serving secondary control needs to enhance selectivity and buffer the negative effects of losses . . . (p. 291)

Unfortunately, while these behaviors may be functional from a psychological perspective, some may be viewed as disfunctional (incompetent) from a communication perspective. Life review, enacted interpersonally, may be competent interpersonally if it is in the form of an interesting narrative; on the other hand, it may be viewed negatively if in the form of painful self-disclosures. An adequate theory of message production in aging must also consider this motivational explanation as an influence on both competent and disfunctional interpersonal messages.

Our focus in this discussion of the resources/competence dilemma has centered on the ways in which practical knowledge and control motivations may influence discourse planning, and in so doing, also compensate for declines in the mechanics of cognition (i.e., memory, processing speed, word retrieval). Paradoxically, the cognitive constraints on message production may themselves contribute to older adults' communicative competence at a basic level. That is, messages that are shorter, less grammatically complex, and delivered at a slower rate should be easier for listeners of all ages to comprehend than longer, more complex messages delivered at faster rates. This paradox too should be incorporated into any model of message production in aging.

The Normal/Pathological Dilemma

While one task of the model of message production in aging is to account for the co-occurrence of declines in production resources with the maintenance of communication competence, the other task is to define the boundaries of normal and pathological aging. This is particularly important for progressive disorders such as age-related dementias or Parkinson's disease. Unlike aphasias that can be traced to a specific and acute biological trauma, these disorders begin slowly. Longitudinal research involving normal and impaired older persons offers the most promise of illuminating these boundaries.

A recent study (Snowdon et al., 1996) provides tantalizing cues. This study is part of an ongoing epidemiological study of risk factors for Alzheimer's disease, the Nun Study, directed by Dr. David Snowdon of the University of Kentucky. Snowdon and his colleagues examined autobiographies written by the study participants at approximately age 20 and their health, physical function, and cognitive ability approximately 60 years later. The participants, 678 members of the School Sisters of Notre Dame religious congregation, were all born before 1917; since 1988 they have been undergoing periodic assessments of their health, physical function, and cognitive ability, and all have agreed to postmortem brain donation for neuropathological examination. Snowdon et al.'s study of the autobiographies found that two measures, one of grammatical complexity and one of idea content, were predictive of cognitive impairment in late life, and the idea-content measure was predictive of Alzheimer's neuropathology. In other words, those nuns whose autobiographies exhibited a simplified style at age 20 (e.g., "There are ten children in the family, six boys and four girls. Two of the boys are dead. I attended St. James grade and high school and made my First Holy Communion in June 1921.") were at greater risk for the development of cognitive impairment 60 years later and at greater risk for the development of Alzheimer's disease. In contrast, nuns whose early autobiographies were written in a more elaborated, complex style (e.g., "The happiest day of my life so far was my First Communion Day which was in June nineteen hundred and twenty when I was but eight years of age, and four years later in the same month I was confirmed by Bishop D. D. McGavick.") were more likely to have intact cognitive skills in late life and to show little of the neuropathology characteristic of Alzheimer's disease after death. A number of interpretations of this finding are possible: (a) it may be that individuals with reduced linguistic ability exhibit the signs of Alzheimer's disease at younger ages since they lack many of the linguistic skills critical to the assessment and diagnosis of dementia; (b) Alzheimer's disease may be a lifelong process whereby neuropathological damage gradually accumulates and, hence, an early sign of the disease may be reduced linguistic ability in young adulthood; or (c) reduced linguistic ability in young adulthood may make individuals more vulnerable to the onset of the disease later in life because they fail to develop resistant, neurologically complex brains as a result of reduced cognitive and social stimulation throughout adulthood. Ongoing analysis of language-production data from these nuns may help to distinguish among these interpretations. Incorporated into a model of message production in aging, this information may help to refine criteria for the early diagnosis of Alzheimer's and related dementias and may help ensure that individuals receive appropriate interventions and treatments as they are developed.

CONCLUSIONS

Research on message production in aging reveals a number of conflicting findings. Cognitive processing deficits in working memory, processing speed, inhibitory mechanisms, etc., yield clear performance differences between young and old adults on measures of grammatical complexity and word retrieval. Age-related diseases such as Alzheimer's disease may also affect production, but distinguishing these effects from those of normal aging is difficult. Finally, semantic memory, basic syntactic processes, and practical knowledge are maintained or improved in old age, resulting either in no performance differences between young and old adults or differences which favor the older speakers. These findings call for a theory of message production that can account for (a) the discrepancy between declines in cognitive production resources available to older adults and their maintenance of communicative competence, and (b) the boundaries between normal and pathological aging. Research on message production in aging should be directed towards these two requirements of the theory. For example, research on language processing has shown that older listeners develop strategies to mitigate the effects of cognitive and sensory deficits on their processing of spoken language, for example, through an increased reliance on prosody as an interpretational aid (Stine & Wingfield, 1987; Wingfield, Wayland, & Stine, 1992). However, there have been no comparable studies of compensatory production strategies used by older adults. Wisdom and control motivations offer promising possibilities as compensatory strategies. Likewise, longitudinal research on normal and impaired populations will provide insight into the initial stages of Alzheimer's dementia and related disorders. These lines of research and the resulting theory of message production in aging should offer a comprehensive developmental picture of the aging individual, one which acknowledges both the growth and decline in communication processes that accompany aging.

ACKNOWLEDGMENTS

Preparation of this chapter was supported by Grant AG09952 from the National Institute on Aging to S. Kemper and Grant AG09433 from the National Institute on Aging to M. L. Hummert.

REFERENCES

Abeysinghe, S. C., Bayles, K. A., & Trosset, M. W. (1990). Semantic memory deterioration in Alzheimer's subjects: Evidence from word association, definition, and associate ranking tasks. *Journal of Speech and Hearing Research, 33,* 574–582.

Albert, M. S., Heller, H. S., & Milberg, W. (1988). Changes in naming ability with age. *Psychology and Aging, 3,* 173–178.

Arbuckle, T., & Gold, D. P. (1993). Aging, inhibition, and verbosity. *Journal of Gerontology: Psychological Sciences, 48,* P225–P232.

Arbuckle, T. Y., Gold, D., & Andres, D. (1986). Cognitive functioning of older people in relation to social and personality variables. *Psychology and Aging, 1,* 55–62.

Baltes, P. B., & Staudinger, U. M. (1993). The search for a psychology of wisdom. *Current Directions in Psychological Science, 2,* 75–80.

Bates, E., Harris, C., Marchman, V., Wulfeck, B., & Kritchevsky, M. (1995). Production of complex syntax in normal aging and Alzheimer's disease. *Language and Cognitive Processes, 10,* 487–539.

Bayles, K. A. (1982). Language function in senile dementia. *Brain and Language, 16,* 265–280.

Bayles, K., Boone, D. R., Tomoeda, C., Slauson, T., & Kaszniak, A. W. (1989). Differentiating Alzheimer's patients from the normal elderly and stroke patients with aphasia. *Journal of Speech and Hearing Disorders, 54,* 74–87.

Bayles, K. A., & Kaszniak, A. W. (1987). *Communication and cognition in normal aging and dementia.* Boston: College-Hill.

Bayles, K. A., & Tomoeda, C. K. (1991). Caregiver report of prevalence and appearance order of linguistic symptoms in Alzheimer's patients. *The Gerontologist, 31,* 210–216.

Bayles, K. A., Tomoeda, C., & Boone, D. R. (1985). A view of age-related changes in language function. *Developmental Neuropsychology, 1,* 231–264.

Benjamin, B. J. (1988). Changes in speech production and linguistic behavior with aging. In B. Shadden (Ed.), *Communication behavior and aging* (pp. 163–181). Boston: Williams & Wilkins.

Berman, R. A., & Slobin, D. I. (1994). *Relating events in narrative: A crosslinguistic developmental study.* Hillsdale, NJ: Lawrence Erlbaum Associates.

Blanken, G., Dittman, J., Haas, J.-C., & Wallesch, C.-W. (1987). Spontaneous speech in senile dementia and aphasia: Implications for a neurolinguistic model of language production. *Cognition, 27,* 247–275.

Bloom, L. (1975). *One word at a time.* The Hague: Mouton.

Bock, J. K. (1987). Coordinating words and syntax in speech plans. In A. Ellis (Ed.), *Progress in the psychology of language* (pp. 337–390). London: Lawrence Erlbaum Associates.

Boden, D., & Bielby, D. D. (1986). The way it was: Topical organization in elderly conversation. *Language and Communication, 6,* 73–89.

Bowles, N. L., Obler, L. K., & Albert, M. L. (1987). Naming errors in healthy aging and dementia of the Alzheimer type. *Cortex, 23,* 519–524.

Bowles, N. L., Obler, L. K., & Poon, L. W. (1989). Aging and word retrieval: Naturalistic, clinical, and laboratory data. In L. W. Poon, D. C. Rubin, & B. A. Wilson (Eds.), *Everyday cognition in adulthood and late life* (pp. 244–264). New York: Cambridge University Press.

Bowles, N. L., & Poon, L. W. (1981). The effect of age on speed of lexical access. *Experimental Aging Research, 7,* 417–425.

Bowles, N. L., & Poon, L. W. (1985). Aging and the retrieval of words in semantic memory. *Journal of Gerontology, 40,* 71–77.

Bruce, V., & Young, A. (1986). Understanding face recognition. *British Journal of Psychology, 77,* 305–327.

Burke, D. M., & Laver, G. D. (1990). Aging and word retrieval: Selective age deficits in language. In E. A. Lovelace (Ed.), *Aging and cognition: Mental processes, self-awareness, and interventions* (pp. 281–300). New York: Elsevier-North Holland.

Burke, D. M., MacKay, D. G., Worthley, J. S., & Wade, E. (1991). On the tip of the tongue: What causes word finding failures in young and older adults. *Journal of Memory and Language, 30,* 542–579.

Burton, A. M., & Bruce, V. (1992). I recognize your face but I can't remember your name: A simple explanation? *British Journal of Psychology, 83,* 45–60.

Butters, N., Granholm, E., Salmon, D. P., Grant, I., & Wolfe, J. (1987). Episodic and semantic memory: A comparison of amnesic and demented patients. *Journal of Clinical and Experimental Neuropsychology, 9,* 479–497.

Butters, N., Salmon, D. P., & Heindel, W. C. (1990). Processes underlying the memory impairments of demented patients. In E. Goldberg (Ed.), *Contemporary neuropsychology and the legacy of Luria* (pp. 99–126). Hillsdale, NJ: Lawrence Erlbaum Associates.

Caporael, L. (1981). The paralanguage of caregiving: Baby talk to the institutionalized aged. *Journal of Personality and Social Psychology, 40,* 876–884.

Chan, A. S., Butters, N., Paulsen, J. S., Salmon, D. P., Swenson, M., & Maloney, L. (1993). An assessment of the semantic network in patients with Alzheimer's disease. *Journal of Cognitive Neuroscience, 5,* 254–261.

Chan, A. S., Butters, N., Salmon, D. P., & McGuire, K. A. (1993). Dimensionality and clustering in the semantic network of patients with Alzheimer's disease. *Psychology and Aging, 8,* 411–419.

Chertkow, H., Bub, D. N., & Seidenberg, M. (1989). Priming and semantic memory loss in Alzheimer's disease. *Brain and Language, 36,* 420–446.

Cohen, G. (1979). Language comprehension in old age. *Cognitive Psychology, 11,* 412–429.

Cohen, G. (1992). Why is it difficult to put names to faces? *British Journal of Psychology, 81,* 287–297.

Cohen, G. (1994). Age-related problems in the use of proper names in communication. In M. L. Hummert, J. M. Wiemann, & J. F. Nussbaum (Eds.), *Interpersonal communication in older adulthood: Interdisciplinary theory and research* (pp. 40–57). Newbury Park, CA: Sage.

Cohen, G., & Faulkner, D. (1986). Memory for proper names: Age differences in retrieval. *British Journal of Developmental Psychology, 4,* 187–197.

Cooper, P. V. (1990). Discourse production and normal aging: Performance on oral picture description tasks. *Journal of Gerontology: Psychological Sciences, 45,* P210–P214.

Coupland, J., Coupland, N., & Giles, H. (1991). My life in your hands: Processes of intergenerational self-disclosure. In N. Coupland, J. Coupland, & H. Giles (Eds.), *Language, society, and the elderly* (pp. 75–108). Oxford, England: Basil Blackwell.

Coupland, J., Coupland, N., & Grainger, K. (1991). Intergenerational discourse: Contextual versions of ageing and elderliness. *Ageing and Society, II,* 189–208.

Davis, G. A. (1984). Effects of aging on normal language. In A. L. Holland (Ed.), *Language disorders in adults: Recent advances* (pp. 79–111). San Diego: College-Hill Press.

Dell, G. S. (1986). A spreading-activation theory of retrieval in sentence production. *Psychological Review, 93,* 283–321.

Dennis, M., & Wiegel-Camp, C. A. (1979). Aphasic dissolution and language acquisition. *Studies in Neurolinguistics, 4,* 211–224.

Emery, O. (1985). Language and aging. *Experimental Aging Research, 11,* 3–60.

Emery, O. (1986). Linguistic decrement in normal aging. *Language and Communication, 6,* 47–64.

Eustache, F., Cox, C., Brandt, J., Lechevalier, B., & Pons, L. (1990). Word association responses and severity of dementia in Alzheimer's disease. *Psychology Reports, 66,* 1315–1322.

Fodor, J. A. (1982). *Modularity of mind.* Cambridge, MA: MIT Press.

Folkman, S., Lazarus, R. S., Pimley, S., & Novacek, J. (1987). Age differences in stress and coping processes. *Psychology and Aging, 2,* 171–184.

Folstein, M. F., Folstein, S. E., & McHugh, P. R. (1975). Mini-Mental State: A practical method for grading the cognitive state of patients for the clinician. *Journal of Psychiatric Research, 12,* 189–198.

Garcia, L. J., & Joanette, Y. (1994). Conversational topic-shifting analysis in dementia. In R. L. Bloom, L. K. Obler, S. de Santi, & J. S. Ehrlich (Eds.), *Discourse analysis and applications: Studies of adult clinical populations* (pp. 161–184). Hillsdale, NJ: Lawrence Erlbaum Associates.

Garrett, M. F. (1988). Processes in language production. In F. J. Newmeyer (Ed.), *Linguistics: The Cambridge survey, III: Language: Psychological and biological aspects* (pp. 69–96). Cambridge, England: Cambridge University Press.

Glosser, G., & Deser, T. (1992). A comparison of changes in macrolinguistic and microlinguistic aspects of discourse production in normal aging. *Journal of Gerontology: Psychological Sciences, 47,* 266–272.

Gold, D., Andres, D., Arbuckle, T., & Schwartzman, A. (1988). Measurement and correlates of verbosity in elderly people. *Journal of Gerontology: Psychological Sciences, 43,* 27–33.

Gold, D. P., & Arbuckle, T. Y. (1992). Interactions between personality and cognition and their implications for theories of aging. In E. A. Lovelace (Ed.), *Aging and cognition: Mental processes, self-awareness, and interventions* (pp. 351–377). Amsterdam: North-Holland.

Gold, D. P., Arbuckle, T. Y., & Andres, D. (1994). Verbosity in older adults. In M. L. Hummert, J. M. Wiemann, & J. F. Nussbaum (Eds.), *Interpersonal communication in older adulthood: Interdisciplinary theory and research* (pp. 107–129). Thousand Oaks, CA: Sage.

Grafman, J., Thompson, K., Weingartner, H., Martinez, R., Lawlor, B. A., & Sunderland, T. (1991). Script generation as an indicator of knowledge representation in patients with Alzheimer's disease. *Brain and Language, 40,* 344–358.

Grodzinsky, Y. (1990). *Theoretical perspectives on language deficits.* Cambridge, MA: MIT Press.

Hamilton, H. (1994a). *Conversations with an Alzheimer's patient.* Cambridge, England: Cambridge University Press.

Hamilton, H. (1994b). Requests for clarification as evidence of pragmatic comprehension difficulty: The case of Alzheimer's disease. In R. L. Bloom, L. K. Obler, S. de Santi, & J. S. Ehrlich (Eds.), *Discourse analysis and applications: Studies in adult clinical populations* (pp. 185–200). Hillsdale, NJ: Lawrence Erlbaum Associates.

Harrold, R. M., Anderson, E. S., Clancy, P., & Kempler, D. (1990). Script knowledge deficits in Alzheimer's disease. *Journal of Clinical and Experimental Neuropsychology, 12,* 397.

Hasher, L., & Zacks, R. T. (1988). Working memory, comprehension, and aging: A review and a new view. In G. H. Bower (Ed.), *The psychology of learning and motivation* (Vol. 22, pp. 193–226). New York: Academic Press.

Heckhausen, J., & Schulz, R. (1995). A life-span theory of control. *Psychological Review, 102,* 284–304.

Heller, R. B., & Dobbs, A. R. (1993). Age differences in word finding in discourse and nondiscourse situations. *Psychology and Aging, 8,* 443–450.

Hier, D. B., Hagenlocker, D., & Shindler, A. G. (1985). Language disintegration in dementia: Effects of etiology and severity. *Brain and Language, 25,* 117–133.

Hodges, J. R., Salmon, D. P., & Butters, N. (1992). Semantic memory impairment in Alzheimer's disease: Failure of access or degraded knowledge? *Neuropsychologia, 30,* 301–314.

Howard, D. V., Shaw, R. J., & Heisey, J. G. (1986). Aging and the time course of semantic activation. *Journal of Gerontology, 41,* 195–203.

Hummert, M. L., Garstka, T. A., Shaner, J. L., & Strahm, S. (1994). Stereotypes of the elderly held by young, middle-aged, and elderly adults. *Journal of Gerontology: Psychological Sciences, 49,* P240–P249.

Hummert, M. L., Shaner, J. L., Garstka, T. A., & Henry, C. (1996, November). *"Arthur, Arthur, Arthur, are you nuts?": Types of patronizing messages to older adults.* Paper presented at the annual meeting of the Speech Communication Association, San Diego, CA.

Hupet, M., Chantraine, Y., & Nef, F. (1993). References in conversation between young and old normal adults. *Psychology and Aging, 8,* 339–346.

Huppert, F. A. (1994). Memory function in dementia and normal aging—Dimension or dichotomy? In F. A. Huppert, C. Brayne, & D. W. O'Connor (Eds.), *Dementia and normal aging* (pp. 291–330). Cambridge, England: Cambridge University Press.

Hutchinson, J. M., & Jensen, M. (1980). A pragmatic evaluation of discourse communication in normal elderly and senile elderly in a nursing home. In L. K. Obler & M. L. Albert (Eds.), *Language and communication in the elderly* (pp. 59–73). Lexington, MA: D. C. Heath.

Jackson, J. H. (1958). Evolution and dissolution of the nervous system. In J. Taylor (Ed.), *Selected writings of John Hughlings Jackson* (pp. 191–212). New York: Basic Books.

Jakobson, R. (1941/1968). *Child language, aphasia, and phonological universals.* The Hague: Mouton.

Kemper, S. (1990). Adults' diaries: Changes made to written narratives across the life-span. *Discourse Processes, 13,* 207–223.

Kemper, S. (1992). Language and aging. In F. I. M. Craik & T. A. Salthouse (Eds.), *Handbook of aging and cognition* (pp. 213–270). Hillsdale, NJ: Lawrence Erlbaum Associates.

Kemper, S., & Anagnopoulos, C. (1989). Language and aging. In R. B. Kaplan (Ed.), *Annual review of applied linguistics* (Vol. X, pp. 37–50). Los Angeles: American Language Institute.

Kemper, S., Kynette, D., Rash, S., Sprott, R., & O'Brien, K. (1989). Life-span changes to adults' language: Effects of memory and genre. *Applied Psycholinguistics, 10,* 49–66.

Kemper, S., LaBarge, E., Ferraro, R., Cheung, H. T., Cheung, H., & Storandt, M. (1993). On the preservation of syntax in Alzheimer's disease: Evidence from written sentences. *Archives of Neurology, 50,* 81–86.

Kemper, S., & Lyons, K. (1994). The effects of Alzheimer's disease on language and communication. In M. L. Hummert, J. M. Wiemann, & J. F. Nussbaum (Eds.), *Interpersonal communication in older adulthood: Interdisciplinary theory and research.* Newbury Park, CA: Sage.

Kemper, S., Lyons, K., & Anagnopoulos, C. (1995). Joint story-telling by Alzheimer's patients and their spouses. *Discourse Processes, 20,* 205–217.

Kemper, S., Othick, M., Gerhing, H., Gubarchuk, J., & Billington, C. (1996). *Practicing speech accommodations to older adults.* Unpublished manuscript.

Kemper, S., Othick, M., Warren, J., Gubarchuk, J., & Gerhing, H. (1996). Facilitating older adults' performance on a referential communication task through speech accommodations. *Aging, Neuropsychology, and Cognition, 3,* 37–55.

Kemper, S., & Rash, S. (1988). Speech and writing across the life-span. In M. M. Gruneberg, P. E. Morris, & R. N. Sykes (Eds.), *Practical aspects of memory: Current research and issues* (pp. 107–112). Chichester, England: Wiley.

Kemper, S., Rash, S. R., Kynette, D., & Norman, S. (1990). Telling stories: The structure of adults' narratives. *European Journal of Cognitive Psychology, 2,* 205–228.

Kemper, S., Vandeputte, D., Rice, K., Cheung, H., & Gubarchuk, J. (1995). Speech adjustments to aging during a referential communication task. *Journal of Language and Social Psychology, 14,* 40–59.

Kempler, D. (1991). Language changes in dementia of the Alzheimer type. In R. Lubinski (Ed.), *Dementia and communication* (pp. 98–113). Philadelphia: Decker.

Kempler, D., Curtiss, S., & Jackson, C. (1987). Syntactic preservation in Alzheimer's disease. *Journal of Speech and Hearing Research, 30,* 343–350.

Kempler, D., & Zelinski, E. M. (1994). Language and dementia in normal aging. In F. A. Huppert, C. Brayne, & D. O'Connor (Eds.), *Dementia and normal aging* (pp. 331–365). Cambridge, England: Cambridge University Press.

Kral, V. A. (1962). Senescent forgetfulness: Benign and malignant. *The Canadian Medical Association Journal, 86,* 257–260.

Kynette, D., & Kemper, S. (1986). Aging and the loss of grammatical forms: A cross-sectional study of language performance. *Language and Communication, 6,* 43–49.

Lamar, M. A. C., Obler, L. K., Knoefel, J. E., & Albert, M. L. (1994). Communication patterns in end-stage Alzheimer's disease: Pragmatic analyses. In R. L. Bloom, L. K. Obler, S. de Santi, & J. S. Ehrlich (Eds.), *Discourse analysis and applications: Studies in adult clinical populations* (pp. 216–235). Hillsdale, NJ: Lawrence Erlbaum Associates.

Lesser, R. (1978). *Linguistic investigations in aphasia.* New York: Elsevier.

Light, L. (1991). Memory and aging: Four hypotheses in search of data. In M. R. Rosenzweig & L. W. Porter (Eds.), *Annual review of psychology* (Vol. 42, pp. 333–376). Palo Alto, CA: Annual Reviews.

Lubinski, R., Morrison, E. B., & Rigrodsky, S. (1981). Perception of spoken communication by elderly chronically ill patients in an institutionalized setting. *Journal of Speech and Hearing Disorders, 46,* 405–412.

Lyons, K., Kemper, S., LaBarge, E., Ferraro, F. R., Balota, D., & Storandt, M. (1993). Language and Alzheimer's disease: A reduction in syntactic complexity. *Aging and Cognition, 50,* 81–86.

MacKay, D. G. (1987). *The organization of perception and action.* New York: Springer-Verlag.

Martin, A. (1987). Representation of semantic and spatial knowledge in Alzheimer's patients: Implications for models of preserved learning in amnesia. *Journal of Clinical and Experimental Neuropsychology, 9,* 191–224.

Mayer, M. (1969). *Frog, where are you?* New York: Dial Press.

Nebes, R. D. (1989). Semantic memory in Alzheimer's disease. *Psychological Bulletin, 106,* 377–394.

Nebes, R. D. (1992). Cognitive dysfunction in Alzheimer's disease. In F. I. M. Craik & T. A. Salthouse (Eds.), *Handbook of cognitive aging* (pp. 373–446). Hillsdale, NJ: Lawrence Erlbaum Associates.

Nebes, R. D., & Rady, C. B. (1990). Preserved organization of semantic attributes in Alzheimer's disease. *Psychology and Aging, 5,* 574–579.

Nicholas, M., Obler, L., Albert, M., & Goodglass, H. (1985). Lexical retrieval in healthy aging. *Cortex, 21,* 595–606.

Nicholas, M., Obler, L. K., Albert, M. L., & Helm-Esterbrooks, N. (1985). Empty speech in Alzheimer's disease and fluent aphasia. *Journal of Speech and Hearing Research, 28,* 405–410.

Nussbaum, J. F., Hummert, M. L., Williams, A., & Harwood, J. (1996). Communication and older adults. In B. R. Burleson (Ed.), *Communication yearbook 19* (pp. 1–47). Newbury Park, CA: Sage.

Obler, L. K. (1980). Narrative discourse style in the elderly. In L. K. Obler & M. L. Albert (Eds.), *Language and communication in the elderly* (pp. 75–90). Lexington, MA: Heath.

Obler, L., & Albert, M. (1981). Language and aging: A neurobiological analysis. In D. Beasley & G. Davis (Eds.), *Aging: Communication processes and disorders* (pp. 107–121). New York: Grune & Stratton.

Orange, J. B. (1991). Perspectives of family members regarding communication changes. In R. Lubinski (Ed.), *Dementia and communication* (pp. 168–187). Philadelphia: Decker.

Pratt, M. W., Boyes, C., Robins, S., & Manchester, J. (1989). Telling tales: Aging, working memory, and the narrative cohesion of storytellers. *Developmental Psychology, 25,* 628–635.

Pratt, M. W., & Robins, S. L. (1991). That's the way it was: Age differences in the structure and quality of adults' personal narratives. *Discourse Processes, 14,* 73–85.

Rabbitt, P. (1977). Changes in problem-solving in old age. In J. E. Birren & K. W. Schaie (Eds.), *Handbook of the psychology of aging* (pp. 606–625). New York: Van Nostrand Reinhold.

Rau, M. T. (1991). Impact on families. In R. Lubinski (Ed.), *Dementia and communication* (pp. 152–167). Philadelphia: Decker.

Ripich, D. N., & Terrell, B. Y. (1988). Patterns of discourse cohesion and coherence in Alzheimer's disease. *Journal of Speech and Hearing Disorders, 53,* 8–15.

Ripich, D. N., Terrell, B. Y., & Spinelli, F. (1983). Discourse cohesion in senile dementia of the Alzheimer type. In R. H. Brookshire (Ed.), *Clinical aphasiology conference proceedings* (pp. 316–321). Minneapolis, MN: BRK Publishers.

Ryan, E. B. (1991). Normal aging and language. In R. Lubinski (Ed.), *Dementia and communication: Clinical and research issues* (pp. 84–97). Toronto: B. C. Decker.

Ryan, E. B., & Burk, K. W. (1974). Perceptual and acoustic correlates of aging in the speech of males. *Journal of Communication Disorders, 7,* 181–192.

Ryan, E. B., & Heaven, R. K. B. (1988). The impact of situational context on age-based attitudes. *Social Behavior, 3,* 105–117.

Ryan, E. B., Hummert, M. L., & Boich, L. H. (1995). Communication predicaments of aging: Patronizing behavior toward older adults. *Journal of Language and Social Psychology, 14,* 144–166.

Ryan, E. B., & Johnson, D. G. (1987). The influence of communication effectiveness on evaluations of younger and older adult speakers. *Journal of Gerontology, 42,* 163–164.

Ryan, E. B., & Laurie, S. (1990). Evaluations of older and younger adult speakers: Influence of communication effectiveness and noise. *Psychology and Aging, 5,* 514–519.

Salthouse, T. A. (1992). *Mechanisms of aging-cognition relations in adulthood.* Hillsdale, NJ: Lawrence Erlbaum Associates.

Shaner, J. L. (1996). *Painful self-disclosures of older adults: Judgments of perceived motivations and discloser characteristics.* Unpublished doctoral dissertation, Department of Communication Studies, University of Kansas, Lawrence, KS.

Shewan, C. M., & Henderson, V. L. (1988). Analysis of spontaneous language in the older normal population. *Journal of Communication Disorders, 21,* 139–154.

Simonton, D. K. (1990). Creativity and wisdom in aging. In J. E. Birren & K. W. Schaie (Eds.), *Handbook of the psychology of aging* (pp. 320–329). New York: Academic Press.

Smith, J., & Baltes, P. B. (1990). Wisdom-related knowledge: Age/cohort differences in response to life-planning problems. *Developmental Psychology, 26,* 494–505.

Smith, J., Staudinger, U. M., & Baltes, P. B. (1994). Occupational settings facilitating wisdom-related knowledge: The sample case of clinical psychologists. *Journal of Consulting and Clinical Psychology, 62,* 989–999.

Snowdon, D. A., Kemper, S., Mortimer, J. A., Greiner, L. H., Wekestein, D. R., & Markesbery, W. R. (1996). Cognitive ability in early life and cognitive function and Alzheimer's disease in late life: Findings from the nun study. *Journal of the American Medical Association, 275,* 528–532.

Staudinger, U. M., Smith, J., & Baltes, P. B. (1992). Wisdom-related knowledge in a life review task: Age differences and the role of professional specialization. *Psychology and Aging, 7,* 271–281.

Stine, E. L., & Wingfield, A. (1987). Process and strategy in memory for speech among younger and older adults. *Psychology and Aging, 2,* 272–279.

Sunderland, A., Watts, K., Baddeley, A. D., & Harris, J. E. (1986). Subjective memory assessment and test performance in the elderly. *Journal of Gerontology, 41,* 376–384.

Troster, A. I., Slamon, D. P., McCullough, D., & Butters, N. (1989). A comparison of the category fluency deficits associated with Alzheimer's and Huntington's disease. *Brain and Language, 37,* 500–513.

Ulatowska, H. K., Allard, L., & Donnell, A. (1988). Discourse performance in subjects with dementia of the Alzheimer type. In H. Whitaker (Ed.), *Neuropsychological studies of nonfocal brain damage* (pp. 108–131). New York: Springer-Verlag.

Ulatowska, H. K., Cannito, M. P., Hayashi, M. M., & Fleming, S. G. (1985). Language abilities in the elderly. In H. K. Ulatowska (Ed.), *The aging brain: Communication in the elderly* (pp. 125–139). San Diego: College-Hill.

Ulatowska, H. K., & Chapman, S. B. (1991). Discourse studies. In R. Lubinski (Ed.), *Dementia and communication* (pp. 115–132). Philadelphia: Decker.

Ulatowska, H. K., Freedman-Stern, R., Weiss-Doyle, A., Macaluso-Haynes, S., & North, A. J. (1983). Production of narrative discourse in aphasia. *Brain and Language, 19,* 317–334.

Walker, V. G., Roberts, P. M., & Hedrick, D. L. (1988). Linguistic analyses of the discourse narratives of young and aged women. *Folia Phoniatica, 40,* 58–64.

Wechsler, D. (1958). *The measurement and appraisal of adult intelligence.* Baltimore: Williams & Wilkins.

Wingfield, R., Wayland, S. C., & Stine, E. A. L. (1992). Adult age differences in the use of prosody for syntactic parsing and recall of spoken sentences. *Journal of Gerontology: Psychological Sciences, 47*, P350–P356.

Yngve, V. (1960). A model and a hypothesis for language structure. *Proceedings of the American Philosophical Society, 104*, 444–466.

7

A SECOND GENERATION
ACTION ASSEMBLY THEORY

John O. Greene
Purdue University

The impetus for this chapter derives from two characteristics of theory building, both affect-laden, but of very different hedonic tone. On one hand, few pursuits are as satisfying as making theory—there is an immense pleasure associated with attempting to "carve nature at its joints." Conversely, publication of a theory results in a tension between that relatively static public statement and the much more dynamic conceptualization of the system in question that exists in the mind of the theorist. With respect to the particular case at hand, while I would retain the general framework and certain key features of the original version of action assembly theory (Greene, 1983, 1984), other aspects of that formulation have become less and less adequate characterizations of my own understanding of the output system. Some of the changes from the original version of the theory have been introduced, though not in any systematic way, in subsequent publications (e.g., Greene, 1994, 1995a, 1995b; Greene & Geddes, 1993), while others, such as the conception of the assembly process articulated here, have not been presented in any previous article. Together, these changes constitute a second generation action assembly theory (AAT2) that differs in several important respects from the original.

A SECOND GENERATION ACTION ASSEMBLY THEORY

Overview

Just as in the original version (Greene, 1984, p. 289), the focus of AAT2 is human behavior, broadly construed, but with particular emphasis on the sorts of verbal and nonverbal behaviors that people produce in interactions with others. Elsewhere (Greene, 1994) I have developed the concept of human behavior more fully, and here I shall simply note that from the perspective of AAT2, behavior is seen to be an inherently creative, multifunctional complex comprised of a very large number of elemental units, or features. The theory, then, is an attempt to specify the mechanisms by which output, so conceived, is produced, moment-by-moment, during ongoing interactions.

From its inception, specification of the mechanisms of the output system in action assembly theory was guided and constrained by four ubiquitous properties of social behavior (see Greene, 1983, 1995b). Briefly, these are, first, that behavior is at once creative and yet comprised of recurrent elements. Second, people act on the basis of the meanings they attach to inputs such that as one's interpretation of the social setting, behavior of the other, and so on, changes, so too will the responses that the individual exhibits. Third, while behavior ultimately consists of a very large number of efferent commands specifying motor movements, our phenomenal experience of behavioral control involves much more abstract action specifications. And, finally, while aspects of our social behavior are often deliberate and planful, it is also possible to behave automatically, with little conscious monitoring.

From the outset, then, the idea was to develop a model of the output system, using these four phenomena as a point of departure for specifying the properties of that system. In keeping with the general approach of cognitive science (see Churchland, 1988; Flanagan, 1984; Gardner, 1987), the development of such a model involved describing the structural and processual mechanisms of the system, cast primarily in functional rather than neurophysiological terms (see Churchland, 1988).

In both the original version of the theory and that presented here, the fundamental structural unit of the output system is the *procedural record*—a long-term memory structure which preserves elemental features of action. These procedural records are brought to bear in behavioral production via two processes: an *activation* process in which particular behavioral features are retrieved from memory, and an *assembly* process by which activated features are integrated, or organized, to form a coherent representation of action-to-be-taken. This collocation of behavioral features constitutes the *output representation*—the configuration of features comprising an individual's behavior at any moment. These four constructs, two structural and two processual, comprise the rudimentary elements of action assembly theory. The details of the theory, then, are given by the specific characteristics and properties ascribed to these components.

Because the concern of AAT2 is with explicating the nature of the mechanisms that constitute the behavioral-production system (i.e., the mechanisms by which the output representation is formed), the theory simply assumes a set of perceptual, interpretive, and motivational processes. Rather than seek to explicate the input side of the system, the theory posits two structures that result from the operation of the processes that fall outside its purview. The first of these, the *situational representation*, is the momentary configuration of situational features produced by the operation of perceptual and interpretive mechanisms. The second, the *goal representation*, is the configuration of goals and functional ends resulting from the operation of the motivational system. These structures stand in a functionally interactive relationship with the output representation in the sense that they serve as inputs to the behavioral-production system, and, at the same time, are subject to the influences of the operation of that system.

Representation of Behavioral Specifications: Procedural Records

The concept of procedural records, structural units of long-term-procedural memory, occupies a central place in action assembly theory. In the earliest version of the theory (Greene, 1983, 1984) procedural records were treated in much the same way as productions in standard production-system architectures (see Davis & King, 1977; Neches, Langley, & Klahr, 1987), with the exception that rather than consisting of condition—action rules, procedural records were seen to consist of action feature—outcome feature pairs.

Several attendant properties of this original conception of procedural records merit note in the present context. The first of these, *multiple code systems*, concerns the fact that the symbolic representations of features of action and outcomes in various procedural records are represented in a number of distinct formats or codes that vary in level of abstraction. To clarify, the claim is not that there are symbolic elements within a single code system that vary in level of abstraction (e.g., lexical items in a natural-language-based code). Rather, the idea is that there are multiple representational formats, some abstract (e.g., propositional codes), some intermediate (e.g., lexical, phonetic codes) and still other very concrete, low-level specifications (e.g., motoric codes). A second property ascribed to procedural records in the original version of the theory was that, following standard treatments of production systems, each record was held to be characterized by some level of *strength* where strength was a function of the recency and frequency with which the record had been activated. A third key idea concerned the *elemental* nature of the action specifications contained in each record. By this I mean that each procedural record was held to represent a single action specification, where a person's behavior at any moment was seen to consist of a very large number of such features. Thus, a procedural record cast at the level of lexical items may contain the representation of a single word; at a lower level, a record might represent a single phonological element, and at a lower level still, records may represent motor routines, or even portions of motor routines, for producing particular sounds. Finally, the structural properties of procedural records reflected the principle of *modularity* in that each record was held to be structurally independent of other records.

These latter two properties, elemental representation and modularity, were qualified to some degree in the original version of the theory by the inclusion of a second long-term memory structure which effectively served to combine behavioral features from multiple procedural records. According to the theory, *unitized assemblies* of procedural records are formed when a group of procedural records is repeatedly activated and assembled to form a portion of the output representation. In this way, the theory provided for links between records such that a single structure might contain more than one behavioral feature.

In subsequent treatments and extensions of the theory (e.g., Greene, 1989a, 1989b) the original production-system-based conception of procedural records underwent a pair of minor revisions. In these later papers the conception of procedural records was cast in associative network terms and also expanded to include a third type of symbolic element, situational features. Thus, procedural records came to be viewed as network structures comprised of nodes and associative pathways, where the nodes represented three types of symbolic elements: features of action, outcomes, and situations. The adoption of network terminology preserved the properties of multiple code systems, strength, and qualified elemental representation and modularity, although strength was now seen to be a characteristic of the individual associative links comprising a record.

Procedural Records in AAT2. In AAT2, the procedural record remains the basic structural unit of long-term-procedural memory, but the conception of these structures has undergone some refinements. Among these refinements is that while the notion of procedural records as associative network structures is retained from the earlier version of the theory, the treatment of the nature of the links themselves has been sharpened by distinguishing two general types of pathways between nodes.

One standard conception of structural relations in long-term memory is to view them as content-free pathways that develop between nodes as a result of the concurrent activation or processing of those nodes. Such a conception has its roots in the long tradition of associationist views of learning and memory (see Voss, 1979), and we can point to a number of more modern models in both cognitive (e.g., Hayes-Roth, 1977; Raaijmakers & Shiffrin, 1981) and social psychology (e.g., Markus & Smith, 1981; Srull, Lichtenstein, & Rothbart, 1985) that invoke such notions. Alternatively, structural links themselves may be considered to have symbolic content that defines relationships between nodes (see Brachman, 1979; Woods, 1975), as in common models of semantic memory (e.g., Anderson, 1976; Collins & Loftus, 1975).

One of the developments in AAT2, then, is to explicitly incorporate both of these classes of structural relations.[1] On one hand, "associative links" reflect *connections* between nodes established via concurrent processing. Thus, when driving my car the set of behavioral features for depressing the clutch may become associated with another set of features for letting up on the accelerator while making a gear change. In contrast, "symbolic links" preserve semantic (i.e., meaning-based) *relationships* between nodes. In the realm of procedural memory such relationships may be represented by symbolic content that corresponds to such natural-language-based concepts as "results in," "leads to," and "in order to." Still in my car, I may rely on a procedural record that expresses something like "push in the clutch *in order to* change gears." Following standard network conceptions, both types of links are held to be characterized by a strength parameter where strength is a function of the recency and frequency with which the link has been instantiated.

One of the chief implications of distinguishing associative and symbolic links is to suggest different processes of procedural record formation.[2] Whereas associative links are formed simply as a result of concurrent processing, symbolic links are formed by encoding some meaningful relationship between nodes. Further, while both types of links are characterized by strengthening, it is possible that the time course of strengthening for the two classes of links is different. An associative link instantiated n times may have less (or more) strength than a symbolic link activated the same number of times. Similarly, decay in linkage strength as a result of disuse may be characterized by different functions. Finally, there is the possibility that,

---

[1]As an evolutionary kluge the human mental system has in all likelihood developed to take advantage of multiple representational and structural formats (see J. Anderson, 1990), an idea consistent with the principle of multiple code systems discussed earlier. With respect to structural links, the development of higher mental processes may have augmented more primitive associative links by permitting the establishment of symbolic links as well.

[2]It is important to note that in many cases nodes are likley to be linked by *both* types of pathways. An individual may have made use of an action–outcome association many times before ever establishing a symbolic relationship between those nodes. Conversely, a person may have encoded a symbolically based link between some action feature and an outcome feature, and through use, acquire an associative link as well.

given equal strength, the time course of activation propagation and subsequent decay in level of activation (see below) will not be the same for the two types of links.

Beyond the explicit incorporation of distinct types of associative pathways, a second refinement in the conception of procedural records in AAT2 is to further relax the principles of elemental representation and modularity found in earlier versions. Strict application of these principles suggests a production-like conception of procedural records (i.e, structurally independent units, each containing a single action feature). However, the implication of bringing associative network assumptions to bear in specifying the nature of procedural records is to suggest a more complex and "noisier" structural unit, something more similar to the conception of "unitized images" proposed by Raaijmakers and Shiffrin (1981).

Specifically, one can imagine a continuum defined at one end by strict modularity and elemental representation and at the other by perfect connectivity (i.e., a network structure in which every node is connected to every other node by pathways of equal strength). The particular range of this continuum occupied by procedural records is a function of two countervailing forces. On one hand, on the assumption that an associative link is formed whenever two nodes are concurrently activated, associative link formation will tend to drive network structures away from modularity and elemental representation and toward greater connectivity. At the same time, decay in the strength of associative pathways pushes procedural records away from connectivity in the direction of simpler, more modular entities. The upshot is that as a conceptual entity, the procedural record becomes a memory structure with imprecise boundaries. The current view is that memory is partitioned into procedural records in the sense that associations within a record are stronger and more numerous than the associations between records (see Raaijmakers & Shiffrin, 1981).

One final development in the specification of structural representations in long-term memory concerns combinations of multiple behavioral features. As previously noted, the original version of action assembly theory did not reflect pure elemental representation in that it provided for the emergence of unitized assemblies of multiple behavioral features as a result of the formation of associative links between features due to repeated activation and assembly.

In AAT2, two types of structurally based, and one content-based, combination of behavioral features are specified. With respect to structurally based combinations, as in the original version of the theory, associative links may develop between multiple behavioral features. Similarly, symbolic links between action features may be established when a person encodes some relationship between them (e.g., first do x and then do y). Again, both of these types of links are characterized by a strength parameter. Finally, although it may be obvious, we should note that the symbolic specification of a unitary action feature comprising any node may itself be a combination of elemental features which are represented in other nodes. Perhaps the simplest and most obvious example would be a routinized string of words represented as a node while other nodes represent the individual words comprising that string.

Selection of Behavioral Specifications: The Activation Process

The conception of a long-term memory repository containing a very large number of procedural records raises the question of how particular behavioral features are selected for use in behavioral production. Contrasted with the original version of action assembly theory, AAT2 reflects two changes in thinking about the selection of behavioral features. The original version of the theory offered a rudimentary approach to the problem of selection by invoking an activation construct (Greene, 1984). That is, at any moment, each procedural record is held to be characterized by some level of activation, where this activation level is a function of the degree of match between the current contents of the situational and goal representations on one hand, and the outcome features and situational features represented in the record, on the other (see Greene, 1989b).[3] The result is that the behavioral features most likely to be highly activated, and hence, to be used in behavioral production (see the following discussion of the assembly process), are those relevant to current goals and conditions.

AAT2's adoption of a more complex, "noisier" procedural record suggests that some refinements are needed in the conception of the selection process. Relaxing the elemental-representation assumption means that activation of procedural records cannot, in and of itself, suffice as an account of feature selection. If records contain multiple behavioral features, then activating a record does not solve the problem of how selection is made among the various features represented in that record. In AAT2 the problem of selection of behavioral features in complex (i.e., nonelemental) network structures is handled simply by treating the individual node, rather than the record as a whole, as the site of activation. This is a straightforward move, but one necessitated by the shift in the conception of the nature of procedural records.

In a procedural record comprised of nodes and symbolic and associative relations, any particular node representing a behavioral feature may be connected to outcome features, situational features, and other behavioral

---

[3]The speed of activation propagation along associative and symbolic links is held to be a function of the strength of those links.

features. The activation level of that node at any particular moment, then, will be a function of the sum of the activation arriving at that node from other activated nodes, with the limitation that there is some upper boundary on the maximum level of activation that a node may attain.

This notion of summation of activation impinging upon individual behavioral-feature nodes is, of course, just one side of the dynamics of activation. At the same time, activation must be governed by a decay mechanism that drives the activation of a node back toward resting levels. While the original version of action assembly theory did little more than acknowledge such a mechanism, AAT2 accords a central role to decay in activation level.

Just as the shift from the procedural record to the individual behavioral-feature node as the site of activation follows from the reconceptualization of the nature of procedural records, this shift in prominence accorded to decay is the outgrowth of a reconceptualization of the assembly process. In the original version of the theory, activation provided only a partial solution to the problem of selection because the theory held that, due to the parallel nature of the activation process, at any moment a large number of records might be highly activated. Thus, the problem of selection among activated behavioral features remained. The earlier version of the theory resolved the question of selection among activated features by positing a serial assembly process in which features were incorporated into the output representation, one at a time, based on level of activation. In contrast, AAT2 no longer incorporates a serial assembly mechanism (see discussion to follow), and instead, assumes a very large decay parameter which rapidly drives the activation of a node back toward resting levels.

Integration of Behavioral Specifications: The Assembly Process

The most important developments in AAT2 have to do with the conceptions of the assembly process and the output representation. It is the assembly process by which activated behavioral features are combined, or integrated, to form the configuration of output specifications that constitute a person's behavior, both internal representations and attendant overt manifestations, at any moment.

In the original version of the theory, assembly is held to be fundamentally serial, capacity-limited, and primarily top-down. The theory posits a hierarchical output representation comprised of levels of varying abstractness in behavioral specifications (see Greene, 1984). The serial nature of assembly, then, is given by the proposition that it proceeds by incorporating into each level of the output representation, one at a time, the most highly activated behavioral feature appropriate to that level; the exception being those cases where unitized assemblies of procedural records permit larger complexes of behavioral specifications to be added all at once.

The original version of the theory further specifies that assembly makes demands upon a pool of processing resources. That is, the theory invokes the common conception of limited processing capacity (see Kahneman, 1973; Navon, 1984; Norman & Bobrow, 1975) and posits that it is the capacity-demanding property of assembly that gives rise to performance limitations under conditions where assembly is required.

Finally, the third key attribute of the assembly process in the original version of the theory is the notion of downward constraint setting. That is, higher levels of the output representation constrain the behavioral specifications that can be formulated at lower levels. Thus, an utterance-representation specification to produce a particular word will constrain the content of the sensorimotor representation by requiring the formulation of motor programs for production of that word.

The top-down, constraint-setting property of the assembly process is mitigated by two additional provisions of the original theory. First, within the constraints imposed by higher levels of the output representation, lower levels remain relatively autonomous in their execution of higher order commands. Thus, a particular higher order specification may be executed in a variety of ways. Second, the theory permits the development of structural relations among procedural records at different levels of abstraction such that activation of a lower level record might influence more abstract action specifications.

Assembly in AAT2. Despite the fact that they are definitive attributes of assembly in the original version of the theory, assembly in AAT2 is neither serial, capacity-limited, nor top-down. The approach toward the nature of assembly in AAT2 is to posit a new structural construct, "coalitions," and to treat assembly as a process of coalition formation.

In simplest terms, a coalition is a momentary assemblage of activated behavioral features that could be said to "fit" together.[4] Thus, a behavioral-feature node representing a syntactic frame with slots for a noun and a verb might coalesce with a particular activated noun and verb. In a very general sense, coalitions may be thought of as having "horizontal" and "vertical" dimensions. The horizontal dimension reflects an assemblage of behavioral features in the same representational code. For example, at a fairly abstract propositional level, a coalition might represent an actor–action pairing. At a lower level, a horizontal coalition may correspond to a string of words. The vertical dimension, in contrast, reflects an assemblage across levels of

---

[4]Coalitions, as momentary assemblages of activated action specifications that reside in the output representation, are distinguished from the structural combinations of behavioral features (i.e., action features linked by semantic and/or associative links) stored in long-term memory. Such combinations of features from long-term memory may, of course, come to constitute all or part of a coalition.

representational codes. Thus, a particular abstract concept (e.g., automobile) may coalesce with a given word (e.g., "car"), and with motor-program specifications for pronouncing that word.

This process of combining activated behavioral features to form a coalition is held to be massively interactive and parallel. Thus, a given behavioral feature may coalesce with any of a number of other activated features represented either in the same code format or in other codes. Further, at any moment, there are likely to be a large number of coalitions, some consisting of a single pair of features while others are comprised of a very large number of action specifications.

As noted earlier, AAT2 assumes that the activation level of a behavioral-feature node is subject to very rapid decay. However, the effect of coalition formation is to augment the activation level of all the features comprising the coalition. Thus, features that coalesce with others do not decay as rapidly as those that fail to find their way into coalitions. The image of behavioral production in AAT2, then, is of a very rapid process of coalition formation where multiple, and potentially competing, coalitions "recruit" activated features, each additional feature resulting in a more extensive output specification and incrementing the activation level of the coalition. A person's behavior at any moment, then, is nothing more nor less than the constellation of coalitions operating at that time.

Again, one implication of this conception of coalition formation is to do away with the serial assembly process specified in the original version of the theory. Further, AAT2 invokes no conception of limited, general purpose processing resources. Rather, performance limitations are seen to arise from the dynamics of decay in activation level and coalition building (see the later discussion of "executive processes"). Finally, AAT2 no longer relies on the sort of top-down, constraint-setting property of assembly given in the earlier formulation. Indeed, according to AAT2, lower level specifications may actually drive the formation of more abstract coalitions (see Harley, 1984), as in the case, say, where a word leads to the formulation of an idea, or where a motor specification corresponding to a gesture prompts production of a word.

The processes of coalition building that give rise to such "bottom-up" effects are no different than those that underlie typical top-down influences. In either case, nodes which remain activated longer are able to recruit other action specifications. Thus, lower level features will drive coalition formation when those lower level nodes stay activated long enough to form coalitions. From the perspective of AAT2, then, behavioral production typically has the *appearance* of being fundamentally top-down because the activating conditions of higher level feature nodes change more slowly than those of lower level nodes, causing more abstract nodes to remain activated longer.

The Output Representation

In the original version of action assembly theory, behavioral production proceeds as activated behavioral features are written into the output representation—the contents of which comprise the individual's behavior, both overt and covert, motoric and mental, at any particular moment. Two properties of the output representation are especially important in the original formulation. First, the output representation is divided into a number of hierarchical levels, and second, the collocation of features within each level constitutes a unit of inherent size, or extensivity.

With respect to the first of these properties, the original version specifies four major levels of the output representation:

1. the *interactional representation*—a plan-like structure consisting of current state, goal state and one or more transition steps linking the two,
2. the *ideational representation*—specifying the ideational content of a single transition,
3. the *utterance representation*—containing a specification of words and their order, and
4. the *sensorimotor representation*—where motor programs for speech and other overt responses are assembled.

On the issue of unit size, the interactional representation is assumed to vary in its extensivity (i.e., the number of transitions), although presumably there is some upper bound imposed by processing-capacity limitations. In contrast, the ideational and utterance representations are held to be of specific and fixed size—the ideational representation specifying a single transition, or move, and the utterance representation a single clause.

The Output Representation in AAT2. In the original version of the theory, levels and unit size are treated as inherent properties of a cognitive structure (i.e., the output representation). In contrast, the approach of AAT2 is to treat these as aspects of cognitive *content* rather than structure. Thus, the output representation is no longer conceived as being comprised of multiple, hierarchical levels. There *is* a hierarchical aspect to the output representation, but this derives from various levels of abstraction in representational codes of activated behavioral features (see the earlier discussion of procedural records), rather than from the structural properties of the output representation itself.

Similarly, the transitions and clauses that constitute units of verbal production (see Bock, 1982; Boomer, 1978; Fromkin, 1971; Greene & Cappella, 1986) are viewed in AAT2 as arising from the content of procedural records, and, as such, are held to have been acquired in the course of message-production-skill development.[5] One obvious example of such content-based units would be syntactic frames for various utterance types (see Clark & Clark, 1977). More generally, treating the units of message production as manifestations of cognitive content rather than inherent properties of the output representation suggests that there may, in fact, be a variety of output units that can be discerned in verbal messages of one sort or another (see Chafe, 1980, 1990; Gee & Grossjean, 1984; Levelt, 1989; van Dijk & Kintsch, 1983).

Executive Processes

To this point my approach toward exposition of AAT2 has been to trace shifts in the conception of various structural and processual components specified in the earlier version of the theory. In the remaining two sections I want to focus on elements of AAT2 that received little or no attention in the original version. The first of these concerns what might be termed "executive processes," including planning, rehearsal, editing, monitoring, and so on.

AAT2 treats such executive processes in terms of the application of procedural records that, like all action specifications, are invoked by the occurrence of particular activating conditions. That is, rather than posit some executive system or dedicated planning, monitoring, editing, etc. systems, executive functions are viewed as acquired cognitive activities represented as action features of procedural records.[6] These procedures are invoked by, and in turn apply over, the content of the output, goal, and situational representations. Via application of executive processes, a person may manipulate his or her own behavior, evaluate and/or reformulate goals, and explore alternative construals of the situation, his or her interlocutors, and their behavior.

Central to AAT2's characterization of executive processes is the reciprocal influence of conscious awareness and activation level. On one hand, features, or more likely, configurations of features, in the output, goal, and situational representations become conscious when they are highly activated for some period of time (see Carr, 1979; Chafe, 1980; Underwood, 1979). The resulting state of consciousness may itself constitute a portion of the activating conditions for procedural records related to various executive

---

[5]This is not to suggest that unit size is arbitrary or that units of any size might be acquired. Rather, the requirements of listening and comprehension, the time course of decay in activation levels, manipulation of the physical structures involved in verbal production, or even patterns of respiration in speech may contribute to the development of units of particular extensivity.

[6]One implication of the treatment accorded executive processes in AAT2 is that the theory invokes no homunculus—no "little man in the head" overseeing the operation of the rest of the system.

processes.[7] Thus, for example, to become aware of some goal may serve to invoke procedures for planning in pursuit of that goal.

At the same time that activation leads to conscious awareness, the application of executive procedures effectively augments the activation level of the features to which those procedures are applied, and hence, serves to slow their decay back toward resting levels. To continue the example of planning to accomplish some goal, evoking executive procedures should allow the individual to keep possible courses of action activated while their potential outcomes are evaluated.

The effects of application of executive procedures, then, are held to be threefold. First, because they are themselves behavioral features and subject to the same processes of activation and assembly as other sorts of behavioral specifications, the application of executive procedures involves their incorporation into the output representation as features of the individual's cognitive activity at that moment. Second, as activated behavioral features, executive procedures augment the activation level of the coalitions to which they are applied. Thus, situational and intraindividual factors that lead to activation of "monitoring" procedures for keeping track of one's own behavior allow a person to do just that by keeping the coalitions of features that constitute that behavior highly activated, and, hence, conscious. Finally, execution of executive procedures involves the manipulation of the content of the output, goal, and situational representations as the procedure (i.e., covert rehearsal, planning, editing, etc.) is carried out. Thus, activation of "rehearsal" procedures allows the individual to traverse a sequential ordering of certain message features; "editing" allows a person to compare a coalition representing attributes of his or her current behavior with some other configuration of desirable attributes of behavior, and so on.

The characterization of executive processes in AAT2 has number of noteworthy implications. First, as previously noted, the fact that executive processes are represented as components of procedural records suggests that they are subject to the same processes of acquisition, strengthening, activation (and decay in activation level), and assembly as other action features. As a result, it should be possible to illuminate the dynamics governing the use of executive procedures via recourse to the properties of these underlying processes.

A second implication derives from the notion that features become conscious when they are highly activated for some period of time and that the resulting state of conscious awareness may itself serve as part of the acti-

---

[7]This should not be taken to imply that executive processes are brought into play *only* under conditions of consciousness. Rather, the assertion is simply that conscious awareness constitutes a portion of the activating conditions for certain executive procedures. It is almost certainly the case that some executive procedures are both activated and executed in the absence of conscious awareness.

vating conditions for various executive procedures. We should expect, then, that among the conditions that will serve to invoke executive procedures are problems in assembly. For example, a coalition comprised of relatively abstract features may be unable to recruit requisite lower level content for actually implementing the more abstract action specifications. In such cases of failure in vertical coalition building, the abstract coalition that otherwise would have made its contribution to the stream of behavior and subsequently decayed, may become conscious, thereby invoking a set of executive processes. In much the same way, impediments to the horizontal dimension of coalition building, such as difficulty in integrating features or coalitions, may cause one or more of those action specifications to enter conscious awareness. As we have seen, once a feature (or coalition of features) becomes conscious, the application of executive procedures may cause that feature to remain activated, with the possible effect that the assembly problem will be overcome as new records are activated.

A third implication of AAT2's approach to executive processes is to identify the application of such procedures as a source of processing limitations in the output system. As noted previously, AAT2 invokes no conception of a limited pool of processing resources. However, limitations in a person's ability to execute multiple tasks, or to do so with rapidity, are seen to arise, in part, as a result of the application of executive processes.[8] By augmenting the activation level of certain coalitions, executive procedures bias the content of the output representation. In other words, the coalitions to which the executive procedures are applied will tend to dominate the output representation and overwhelm other coalitions. As a result, an individual may be slow to execute tasks that would have been handled by other coalitions, or indeed, may not exhibit any overt action in response to certain inputs.

The Neurophysiological Substrate

The prevailing approach of cognitive science is to pursue explanation via functional terms (i.e., by describing the structures and processes of noncorporeal "mind" that give rise to the phenomena of interest; see Flanagan, 1984; Gardner, 1987). As noted at the outset of this chapter, the original version of action assembly theory reflects just such a functional orientation. More recently, however, I have argued that theories of human action should incorporate both functional and physiological constructs and, moreover,

---

[8]The point being made here is actually a special case of a more general principle that extends beyond application of executive procedures. The more general claim is that performance on multiple tasks will degrade when coalitions relevant to various tasks cannot be integrated. In such cases, the coalition(s) relevant to one task may come to dominate the content of the output representation and overwhelm the behavioral features activated in pursuit of other responses.

that theories of the output system should seek to explicate the nature of the joint interplay of the functional and physiological domains in behavioral production (Greene, 1994). As a move in this direction, AAT2 incorporates a set of claims about the physiological instantiation of the theory's functional machinery and the impact of the physiological realm on the activation and assembly processes.

Again, it is important to emphasize that the theoretical constructs of AAT2 discussed thus far (e.g., feature nodes, associative and symbolic links, activation, coalition building, etc.) are functional, not neurophysiological, constructs. However, the theory assumes the instantiation of these functional structures and processes in the hardware and physiological processes of the brain. More specifically, on the assumption that the cortex is comprised of networks of densely interconnected neurons (see Edleman, 1987; Palm, 1990; Roland, 1993), the key point of contact between the functional and physiological realms is to identify coalition building as the establishment of patterns of excitation and inhibition within and between these neural networks.

The conception of coalitions as patterns of activity in neural networks suggests a number of ways in which physiological factors can be seen to impact the functional processes of activation and assembly. In the space remaining I want to focus on two of these, the first of which, at the risk of oversimplifying, can be thought of as being primarily processual and the latter as being primarily structural.

Cortical Activation. Beginning with the work of Yerkes and Dodson (1908) in the early part of this century, researchers have suggested that an individual's performance on a variety of cognitive and motor tasks is an inverted-U function of "arousal" level, and a number of theories have been advanced to account for this phenomenon (e.g., Easterbrook, 1959; Hebb, 1955; Humphreys & Revelle, 1984; Kahneman, 1973; Malmo, 1959, 1975). However, it is also the case that the issue of the relationship between physiological arousal and performance is characterized by considerable controversy (see, e.g., Anderson, 1990; Neiss, 1990). It has been suggested, for example, that the conception of "arousal" is a vague and excessively broad construct (Neiss, 1988), and that evidence purporting to demonstrate a relationship between various measures or manipulations of arousal, on one hand, and performance levels on the other, may, in fact, be subject to alternative interpretations (Näätänen, 1973; Neiss, 1988). It does appear, however, that certain brain structures, most notably those comprising the ascending reticular activating system, serve to heighten cortical activation, either in a diffuse fashion or more locally, (see Malmo, 1959, 1975; Tucker & Williamson, 1984) and that performance is curvilinearly related to level of activity in these systems (see Andreassi, 1989).

The earlier discussion of the activation process in AAT2 indicated that the level of activation of a behavioral-feature node is the sum of the activation arriving at that node from associated outcome, situational-feature, and other behavioral-feature nodes. As a result, those behavioral features most appropriate to current goals and conditions tend to be most highly activated at any particular time. From the perspective of AAT2, the effect of increases in the activity of central arousal systems is to augment the activation level of behavioral-feature nodes.[9] That is, all nodes are characterized at any moment by some level of activation that is a function of the degree to which their activating conditions are met. The impact of increasing the level of activity in physiological activating systems is to heighten the activation of every node (or at least every node represented in the neural structures stimulated by a given arousal system).

Increasing the activity of physiological activating systems, then, should have the effect of driving the activation of the most relevant nodes toward their maximal value, thereby improving performance by facilitating the formation of coalitions around such features. With additional increases in the activity of central arousal systems, however, even less relevant nodes will be activated to the extent that they too are able to recruit coalitions. The effect of the presence of less relevant, competing, or even inappropriate coalitions, should be to degrade task performance. The overall implication is to produce the familiar inverted-U function via a single mechanism. In light of the claim that features become conscious when they are highly activated for some period of time, we should expect that the concomitant phenomenal experience of heightened arousal would be the intrusion of extraneous or distracting cognitions.

Cortical Density. A second avenue by which physiological factors may come to impact behavioral production is suggested by two characteristics of the behavior of older adults. First, among the most ubiquitous features of human behavior is a general slowing of responses in old age, a phenomenon that has been demonstrated in a variety of task domains (see Birren, Woods, & Williams, 1980; Cerella, Poon, & Williams, 1980; Salthouse, 1985) and that extends to the realm of verbal message production (e.g., Duchin & Mysak, 1987; Liss, Weismer, & Rosenbek, 1990; Ramig, 1983; Smith, Wasowicz, & Preston, 1987). Second, it is generally observed that the elderly are at a disadvantage relative to younger adults in the acquisition of new skills (e.g., Denney, 1982; Hashtroudi, Chrosniak, & Schwartz, 1991; Strayer & Kramer, 1994). This effect, too, appears to extend to the realm of message production (see Hupet, Chantraine, & Nef, 1993).

---

[9]In addition to the sort of nonspecific physiological factors under discussion here, specific physiological states may constitute activating conditions for particular behavioral features (see Greene, 1989b, note 2).

Various accounts of behavioral slowing have been advanced (see Light, 1988; Salthouse, 1985; Welford, 1984), but the approach of AAT2 is to identify the source of slowing as a decrease in synaptic density, an idea that has been suggested by a number of theorists (e.g., Birren et al., 1980; Cerella, 1990; Rabbitt, 1990). This claim follows from two considerations. First, it is fairly well established that the density of synaptic connections in the brain diminishes with advancing age (see Coleman & Flood, 1987; Haug et al., 1983; Huttenlocher, 1990; Ivy, MacLeod, Petit, & Markus, 1992), and second, the effect of decreasing connections in a network structure is to slow the rate of information processing (see Cerella, 1990). Thus, the locus of age-related slowing is held to be a direct result of a decrease in cortical density. In a similar fashion, the performance deficits that accompany decreases in network density (see McClelland, 1986) suggest that such age-related changes might underlie observed skill-acquisition deficits in the elderly.

CONCLUSION

My aim here has been to sketch the general framework of a second generation action assembly theory by tracing the conceptual shifts and refinements that differentiate this theory from the original version of AAT. Just as was the case for AAT (see Greene, 1995a), many of the details of the theory, especially those concerning the dynamics of coalition formation, must await empirical investigation. As a final comment, then, I would emphasize that coalition formation has both cognitive and social dimensions. Clearly, AAT2 suggests a large number of research questions that focus on the functional and physiological factors that influence the course of action assembly. At the same time, there is a need for research examining the role of one's interlocutor(s) in facilitating (or impeding) coalition formation and the emotional, interactional, and relational implications of such events.

ACKNOWLEDGMENTS

The author wishes to thank Glenn G. Sparks and Marianne S. Sassi for their helpful comments during preparation of this chapter.

REFERENCES

Anderson, J. A. (1990). Hybrid computation in cognitive science: Neural networks and symbols. *Applied Cognitive Psychology, 4,* 337–347.

Anderson, J. R. (1976). *Language, memory, and thought.* Hillsdale, NJ: Lawrence Erlbaum Associates.

Anderson, K. J. (1990). Arousal and the inverted-U hypothesis: A critique of Neiss's "Reconceptualizing Arousal." *Psychological Bulletin, 107,* 96–100.

Andreassi, J. L. (1989). *Psychophysiology: Human behavior and physiological response* (2nd ed.). Hillsdale, NJ: Lawrence Erlbaum Associates.

Birren, J. E., Woods, A. M., & Williams, M. V. (1980). Behavioral slowing with age: Causes, organization, and consequences. In L. W. Poon (Ed.), *Aging in the 1980s: Psychological issues* (pp. 293–308). Washington, DC: American Psychological Association.

Bock, J. K. (1982). Toward a cognitive psychology of syntax: Information processing contributions to sentence formulation. *Psychological Review, 89*, 1–47.

Boomer, D. S. (1978). The phonemic clause: Speech unit in human communication. In A. W. Siegman & S. Feldstein (Eds.), *Nonverbal behavior and communication* (pp. 245–262). Hillsdale, NJ: Lawrence Erlbaum Associates.

Brachman, R. J. (1979). On the epistemological status of semantic networks. In N. V. Finder (Ed.), *Associative networks: Representation and use of knowledge by computers* (pp. 3–50). New York: Academic Press.

Carr, T. H. (1979). Consciousness in models of human information processing: Primary memory, executive control and input regulation. In G. Underwood & R. Stevens (Eds.), *Aspects of consciousness* (Vol 1, pp. 123–153). London: Academic Press.

Cerella, J. (1990). Aging and information processing rate. In J. E. Birren & K. W. Schaie (Eds.), *Handbook of the psychology of aging* (3rd ed., pp. 201–221). San Diego: Academic Press.

Cerella, J., Poon, L. W., & Williams, D. M. (1980). Age and the complexity hypothesis. In L. W. Poon (Ed.), *Aging in the 1980s: Psychological issues* (pp. 332–340). Washington, DC: American Psychological Association.

Chafe, W. L. (1980). The development of consciousness in the production of a narrative. In W. L. Chafe (Ed.), *The pear stories: Cognitive, cultural, and linguisitc aspects of narrative production* (pp. 9–50). Norwood, NJ: Ablex.

Chafe, W. (1990). Some things that narratives tell us about the mind. In B. K. Britton & A. D. Pellegrini (Eds.), *Narrative thought and narrative language* (pp. 79–98). Hillsdale, NJ: Lawrence Erlbaum Associates.

Churchland, P. M. (1988). *Matter and consciousness: A contemporary introduction to the philosophy of mind* (Rev. ed.). Cambridge, MA: Bradford.

Clark, H. H., & Clark, E. V. (1977). *Psychology and language: An introduction to psycholinguistics.* New York: Harcourt, Brace, Jovanovich.

Coleman, P. C., & Flood, D. G. (1987). Neuron numbers and dendritic extent in normal aging and Alzheimer's disease. *Neurobiology of Aging, 8*, 521–544.

Collins, A. M., & Loftus, E. F. (1975). A spreading-activation theory of semantic processing. *Psychological Review, 82*, 407–428.

Davis, R., & King, J. (1977). An overview of production systems. In E. W. Elcock & D. Michie (Eds.), *Machine intelligence 8* (pp. 300–332). New York: Halsted Press.

Denney, N. W. (1982). Aging and cognitive changes. In B. B. Wolman (Ed.), *Handbook of developmental psychology* (pp. 807–827). Englewood Cliffs, NJ: Prentice-Hall.

Duchin, S. W., & Mysak, E. D. (1987). Disfluency and rate characteristics of young adult, middle-aged, and older males. *Journal of Communicative Disorders, 20*, 245–257.

Easterbrook, J. A. (1959). The effect of emotion on cue utilization and the organization of behavior. *Psychological Review, 66*, 183–201.

Edelman, G. M. (1987). *Neural Darwinism: The theory of neuronal group selection.* New York: Basic Books.

Flanagan, O. J., Jr. (1984). *The science of the mind.* Cambridge, MA: Bradford.

Fromkin, V. (1971). The non-anomalous nature of anomalous utterances. *Language, 47*, 27–52.

Gardner, H. (1987). *The mind's new science: A history of the cognitive revolution.* New York: Basic Books.

Gee, J. P., & Grossjean, F. (1984). Empirical evidence for narrative structure. *Cognitive Science, 8*, 59–85.

Greene, J. O. (1983). *Development and initial tests of an action assembly theory.* University of Wisconsin-Madison.

Greene, J. O. (1984). A cognitive approach to human communication: An action assembly theory. *Communication Monographs, 51,* 289–306.

Greene, J. O. (1989a). Action assembly theory: Metatheoretical commitments, theoretical propositions, and empirical applications. In B. Dervin, L. Grossberg, B. J. O'Keefe, & E. Wartella (Eds.), *Rethinking communication, Vol. 2: Paradigm exemplars* (pp. 117–128). Newbury Park, CA: Sage.

Greene, J. O. (1989b). The stability of nonverbal behaviour: An action–production approach to problems of cross-situational consistency and discriminativeness. *Journal of Language and Social Psychology, 8,* 193–220.

Greene, J. O. (1994). What sort of terms ought theories of human action incorporate? *Communication Studies, 45,* 187–211.

Greene, J. O. (1995a). Production of messages in pursuit of multiple social goals: Action assembly contributions to the study of cognitive encoding processes. In B. R. Burleson (Ed.), *Communication yearbook 18* (pp. 26–53). Thousand Oaks, CA: Sage.

Greene, J. O. (1995b). An action assembly perspective on verbal and nonverbal message production: A dancer's message unveiled. In D. E. Hewes (Ed.), *The cognitive bases of interpersonal communication* (pp. 51–85). Hillsdale, NJ: Lawrence Erlbaum Associates.

Greene, J. O., & Cappella, J. N. (1986). Cognition and talk: The relationship of semantic units to temporal patterns of fluency in spontaneous speech. *Language and Speech, 29,* 141–157.

Greene, J. O., & Geddes, D. (1993). An action assembly perspective on social skill. *Communication Theory, 3,* 26–49.

Harley, T. A. (1984). A critique of top-down independent levels models of speech production: Evidence from non-plan-internal speech errors. *Cognitive Science, 8,* 191–219.

Hashtroudi, S., Chrosniak, L. D., & Schwartz, B. L. (1991). Effects of aging on priming and skill learning. *Psychology and Aging, 6,* 605–615.

Haug, H., Barmwater, R., Eggers, R., Fischer, D., Kuhl, S., Sass, N.-L. (1983). Anatomical changes in aging brain: Morphometric analysis of the human prosencephalon. In J. Cervos-Navarro & H.-I. Sarkander (Eds.), *Brain aging: Neuropathology and neuropharmacology* (pp. 1–12). New York: Raven Press.

Hayes-Roth, B. (1977). Evolution of cognitive structures and processes. *Psychological Review, 84,* 260–278.

Hebb, D. O. (1955). Drives and the C.N.S (Conceptual nervous system). *Psychological Review, 62,* 243–254.

Humphreys, M. S., & Revelle, W. (1984). Personality, motivation, and performance: A theory of the relationship between individual differences and information processing. *Psychological Review, 91,* 153–184.

Hupet, M., Chantraine, Y., & Nef, F. (1993). References in conversation between young and old normal adults. *Psychology and Aging, 8,* 339–346.

Huttenlocher, P. R. (1990). Morphometric study of human cerebral cortex development. *Neuropsychologia, 28,* 517–527.

Ivy, G. O., MacLeod, C. M., Petit, T. L., & Markus, E. J. (1992). A physiological framework for perceptual and cognitive changes in aging. In F. I. M Craik & T. A. Salthouse (Eds.), *The handbook of aging and cognition* (pp. 273–314). Hillsdale, NJ: Lawrence Erlbaum Associates.

Kahneman, D. (1973). *Attention and effort.* Englewood Cliffs, NJ: Prentice-Hall.

Levelt, W. J. M. (1989). *Speaking: From intention to articulation.* Cambridge, MA: MIT Press.

Light, L. L. (1988). Language and aging: Competence versus performance. In J. E. Birren & V. L. Bengston (Eds.), *Emergent theories of aging* (pp. 177–213). New York: Springer.

Liss, J. M., Weismer, G., & Rosenbek, J. C. (1990). Selected acoustic characteristics of speech production in very old males. *Journal of Gerontology: Psychological Sciences, 45,* 35–45.

Malmo, R. B. (1959). Activation: A neurophysiological dimension. *Psychological Review, 66,* 367–386.

Malmo, R. B. (1975). *On emotions, needs, and our archaic brain.* New York: Holt, Rinehart & Winston.

Markus, H., & Smith, J. (1981). The influence of self-schemata on the perception of others. In N. Cantor & J. F. Kihlstrom (Eds.), *Personality, cognition, and social interaction* (pp. 233–262). Hillsdale, NJ: Lawrence Erlbaum Associates.

McClelland, J. L. (1986). Resource requirements of standard and programmable nets. In J. L. McClelland & D. E. Rumelhart (Eds), *Parallel distributed processing: Explorations in the microstructure of cognition, Vol. 1: Foundations* (pp. 460–487). Cambridge, MA: MIT Press.

Näätänen, R. (1973). The inverted-U relationship between activation and performance: A critical review. In S. Kornblum (Ed.), *Attention and performance IV* (pp. 155–174). New York: Academic Press.

Navon, D. (1984). Resources—A theoretical soup stone? *Psychological Review, 91,* 216–234.

Neches, R., Langley, P., & Klahr, D. (1987). Learning, development, and production systems. In D. Klahr, P. Langley, & R. Neches (Eds.), *Production system models of learning and development* (pp. 1–53). Cambridge, MA: MIT Press.

Neiss, R. (1988). Reconceptualizing arousal: Psychobiological states in motor performance. *Psychological Bulletin, 103,* 345–366.

Neiss, R. (1990). Ending arousal's reign of error: A reply to Anderson. *Psychological Bulletin, 107,* 101–105.

Norman, D. A., & Bobrow, D. G. (1975). On data-limited and resource-limited processes. *Cognitive Psychology, 7,* 44–64.

Palm, G. (1990). Cell assemblies as a guideline for brain research. *Concepts in Neuroscience, 1,* 133–147.

Raaijmakers, J. G. W., & Shiffrin, R. M. (1981). Search of associative memory. *Psychological Review, 88,* 93–134.

Rabbitt, P. (1990). Applied cognitive gerontology: Some problems, methodologies and data. *Applied Cognitive Psychology, 4,* 225–246.

Ramig, L. A. (1983). Effects of physiological aging on speaking rates. *Journal of Communication Disorders, 16,* 217–226.

Roland, P. E. (1993). *Brain activation.* New York: Wiley-Liss.

Salthouse, T. (1985). *A theory of cognitive aging.* Amsterdam: North-Holland.

Smith, B. L., Wasowicz, J., & Preston, J. (1987). Temporal characteristics of the speech of normal elderly adults. *Journal of Speech and Hearing Research, 30,* 522–529.

Srull, T. K., Lichtenstein, M., & Rothbart, M. (1985). Associative storage and retrieval processes in person memory. *Journal of Experimental Psychology: Learning, Memory, and Cognition, 11,* 316–345.

Strayer, D. L., & Kramer, A. F. (1994). Aging and skill acquisition: Learning—Performance Distinctions. *Psychology and Aging, 9,* 589–605.

Tucker, D. M., & Williamson, P. A. (1984). Asymmetric neural control systems in human self-regulation. *Psychological Review, 91,* 185–215.

Underwood, G. (1979). Memory systems and conscious processes. In G. Underwood & R. Stevens (Eds.), *Aspects of consciousness* (Vol. 1, pp. 91–121). London: Academic Press.

van Dijk, T. A., & Kintsch, W. (1983). *Strategies of discourse comprehension.* New York: Academic Press.

Voss, J. F. (1979). Organization, structure, and memory: Three perspectives. In C. R. Puff (Ed.), *Memory organization and structure* (pp. 375–400). New York: Academic Press.

Welford, A. T. (1984). Between bodily changes and performance: Some possible reasons for slowing with age. *Experimental Aging Research, 10,* 73–88.

Woods, W. A. (1975). What's in a link: Foundations for semantic networks. In D. G. Bobrow & A. Collins (Eds.), *Representation and understanding: Studies in cognitive science* (pp. 35–82). New York: Academic Press.

Yerkes, R. M., & Dodson, J. D. (1908). The relation of strength of stimulus to rapidity of habit-formation. *Journal of Comparative Neurology of Psychology, 18,* 459–482.

8

FRAMING MESSAGE PRODUCTION RESEARCH WITH FIELD THEORY

Dale Hample
Western Illinois University

Shortly after Kurt Lewin's death in 1947, Edward Tolman estimated that when the history of 20th-century psychology was written, Freud's and Lewin's names would stand above all the others. Lewin, however, no longer seems quite so current as Freud. Many of Lewin's own primary ideas have seeped into the social sciences and become general currency, without specific attribution. The connections between Lewin and his extraordinary group of students have been obscured by time. Few other than those with a serious interest in the history of psychology know that he or those working with him developed group dynamics, cognitive dissonance theory, the first studies of autocractic/democratic/lassiez faire leadership, social exchange theory, gatekeeper phenomena, the Zeigarnik effect, or action research. Nor is it simple, even on reviewing his life's work, to give an easy summary (see Marrow, 1969, for a full length intellectual biography). A proponent of individual case studies, he generated standard quantitative experiments; an advocate of applied research, he wrote theoretical papers with explicit logical and mathematical derivations; a leading figure in the Gestalt approach to perception, he wrote on conditioned reflexes and Freudian psychodynamics; a prolific empirical researcher, he elaborated an epistemology he learned at the feet of Cassirer; a professor on two continents who sought work on a third, he did some of his most valuable work chatting in coffee houses; often called the father of academic social psychology, he is also the ancestor of encounter groups. In a recent and welcome "great man" sort of history of Communication, Rogers (1994, chap. 8) devoted a full chapter to

Lewin, without mentioning field theory, this chapter's topic. In studying Lewin, we are all like the blind men examining the elephant. Perhaps I will be forgiven for not discussing any of the contributions Rogers does.

Instead, I wish to explore field theory, Lewin's most elaborated and consuming theoretical project. This essay has three main parts: an intial sketch of field theory, the record of its application to message production studies, and an indication of several ways in which field theory can sharpen our conceptual understanding of current research problems.

FIELD THEORY

In this first section, I offer a brief outline of field theory, concentrating on those features that seem to have special applicability to the study of message production.[1] Field theory can be understood as being a metatheory (Gold, 1992). It is a system of fundamental commitments to the study of human action, as well as a specification of the sorts of variables that should figure into a theory of some particular behavioral domain.

Fundamental Commitments

Lewin concerned himself with what he calls "psychological behavior," actions that are controlled by the actor, things that are done on purpose. Although many passages in Lewin's work give the impression that this viewpoint restricts him to the study of consciously controlled behavior, unconscious cognition is also admissible (Deutsch, 1954), which is fortunate for those studying communication (Hample, 1987). Still, a simple conditioned reflex appears to be outside the scope of the theory. The actor must be in control of his or her actions for them to come within the purview of field theory. Thus, we might properly analyze a person's public speech in Lewinian terms, but would have to pass by issues such as lexical storage or the physiology of hearing; speech errors, such as word or syllable transposition, would probably be omitted as well, depending on one's theoretical account (e.g., Motley, Baars, & Camden, 1983).

---

[1]The key primary source is Lewin (1951), but Lewin (1935) and Lewin (1936) are also informative for their details. Barker, Dembo, and Lewin (1941) is important for its examination of frustration and aggression, but the key theoretical chapters are reprinted in Lewin (1951). The standard secondary resource is Deutsch (1954). Leeper (1943) is a very detailed summary and critique, for which Lewin apparently had some respect. Current Lewinian research is reliably to be found in the issues of *Journal of Social Issues* and in recent compilations of work reported at the Society for the Advancement of Field Theory (Stivers & Wheelan, 1986; Wheelan, Pepitone, & Abt, 1990). In addition to Marrow's (1969) biography, Ash (1992) should be consulted for a detailed history of the Iowa years.

The starting point for analysis of psychological behavior is therefore the actor's perspective. A person can only behave in response to, or in pursuit of, things of which he or she is aware, consciously or unconsciously. Lewin certainly acknowleged that a person's life may be affected by factors unknown to him or her (e.g., a person might not be successful in a job application because the organization had just decided to downsize), but a person will only act in regard to things that are in view. The actor's perspective is captured in the idea of "life space," which is the situation as the person sees it.

Behavior, according to Lewin, is a joint function of the person and the perceived environment: $B = f(P, E)$. The life space may or may not include the person, since we sometimes behave without any particular self-awareness, and, at other times, with a clear focus on self. Because social scientists often conduct experiments in which they specify some part of the situation for their participants (e.g., "your goal is to persuade your partner"), we should carefully notice that the experimenter's instructions are only relevant to psychological behavior insofar as they are endorsed and understood by the participant.

Although I wait until the next subsection to indicate the sorts of elements that should be expected to appear in life spaces, we should note here that the life space itself is a momentary, ephemeral thing. It exists and controls behavior only in the instant. "Instant" is itself defined from the actor's perspective. It might actually be a second or two, as when a father idly picks up a softball and tosses it back to his daughter. It might be an hour, as when a distance runner trains. Or it might be a month, for an advertising campaign. What is important, however, is to notice that neither past nor future enter into this, except insofar as they are brought into the moment of action by the actor. A previous experience might alter the present perception, or a future-oriented ambition might direct current behavior, but only if they are salient at the time of action. This, of course, puts Lewin at odds with Freud, and also offers his solution to the problem of teleology. For us, it has implications for how we will understand goals, enduring personality traits, immediately prior utterances, and past patterns of action, among other things.

Finally, we should notice an important distinction Lewin makes, between the "planes of reality" and "irreality." For the most part, we have been implictly discussing the plane of reality to this point. This is the life space in which a person acts, and it contains goals, obstacles, the person, and so forth. It is the phenomenal world of action. The plane of irreality, however, is the life space of wishes, imagination, and plans. A person might, in the plane of irreality, project certain lines of action, but might, in the plane of reality, find him or herself distracted into doing something else. The two planes might be nearly isomorphic, as when a person plans and then executes a particular series of actions. Or the planes might be poorly coordinated with one another, as when a person daydreams about playing major league baseball while taking notes on a lecture. The degree of coordination between the planes is an empirical and variable matter. Much research on planning, however, seems to take for granted that the two life spaces will be nearly isomorphic (cf. Greene, 1990).

Likely Elements of the Life Space

Because the life space is nothing more than the actor's unique perception, external analysts cannot insist that any particular thing be included. However, certain elements are expectable, or at least possible, and those are specified by field theory. Those that seem to be of special interest to those of us interested in message production are the person, locomotion, goals, obstacles, barriers, climate, and plans. Though any of these can be thought about (hence being part of the plane of irreality), the discussion will treat all of these except plans as being located within the plane of reality.

The person is the actor. The actor may or may not be a salient part of the life space, depending on the degree of self-focus the actor has. At one extreme, a behavior might be performed without any sensitivity to its effects on self. In contrast, a person might be extremely self-conscious while acting. This does not depend primarily on the behavior in question. One player can hit a forehand volley in tennis automatically, concentrating only on the ball and court position, and another person might be focused mainly on the bend of his or her elbow during a similar stroke. Public speaking instructors have long been sensitive to the fact that some students are so self-conscious that they can hardly speak at all, while others perform freely and comfortably. Awareness of self is a continuous variable. People can be more or less conscious of themselves, so that we might have one person vaguely noticing that an errant utterance is awkward, while another person feels more intensely that an objectively equivalent mistake has been too revealing, has made it impossible to continue speaking, and has destroyed own face.

In Lewinian terms, behavior is technically called "locomotion," because action is conceived as movement of the person from one region of the life space to another. As we will see momentarily, life spaces are dynamic systems of forces, pushing and pulling people in various directions. Each region has a valence and a force. When the life space is out of equilibrium, the person moves in such as way as to restore balance.

Goals are regions that have positive valences, and obstacles are negative regions. Actors are drawn toward goals and repelled from obstacles. So a person wanting to ask another for a date (the goal, a positive attraction) while avoiding the chance of embarrassment (the obstacle, a repulsion) might form an indirect message that includes a nunhurtful means of refusal (e.g., "If you're not busy, maybe we could go out"). This is a simplified (though possible) example. In a real life space, the actor might be reacting to several goals and obstacles at once. The object is to move in such a way as to occupy the goal regions, satiating and so eliminating their attraction; the obstacles disappear as well, once the task is finished. Notice that the actor might perform several actions on the way to a goal. Each of these actions is a region to be occupied, and each will have its own valence and strength, often derivative from the main goal being sought. Thus a goal might be seen as having subgoals, and so we should expect a succession of locomotions, unless the goals overlap so that a single action could result in occupying more than one region at a time.

Barriers are quite a different sort of thing than obstacles. Every region has a boundary, which separates it from surrounding regions. Some of these boundaries are easy to pass through, but some offer resistance. A barrier is a boundary that is hard to penetrate. Achieving locomotion into the goal region "greetings" is ordinarily not very difficult, and we say "hello" effortlessly. However, an adolescent asking for a first date might find the boundary around "request a date" to be almost impassable; this second person is faced with a barrier. For our present purposes, the most important barriers are those around goal regions. Passing through a barrier requires force of some sort; the more resistant the barrier, the more effort or repetition is required. Obstacles encourage a person to move away from a region, but boundaries require that a person push through.

There is one complication, however. When an obstacle completely surrounds a goal region, then the obstacle acts somewhat like a boundary. While no unusal amount of energy may be required to pass through the obstacle region (merely some willingness to endure the effects of the negative valence), nonetheless the obstacle cannot be avoided. This observation leads to a tentative suggestion about one difference between obstacles and boundaries. At the risk of oversimplifying: People understand obstacles, but find barriers to be mysteries. For example, suppose a person has repeatedly failed to get employment after being interviewed. In one case, the person might understand that she is too aggressive in conversation, and thereby perceive an obstacle to successful interviewing. In the other case, an equally aggressive person does not realize that he is too pushy, or have any idea why his interviews are failures; this second person is faced with a barrier. The key to this suggestion is to recall that the life space must be seen from the viewpoint of the actor. If a person is aware of a problem, it is an obstacle and will have an obstacle's effects on locomotion. But if a goal is simply hard to achieve, and for no apparent reason, then the actor is confronted with a barrier. Locomotion will differ in these two cases, the obstacle-oriented person moving around a negatively valenced region, and the barrier-confronted actor moving with more force, or doing the action repeatedly.[2]

---

[2]I cannot help wondering if bad date-requesting behavior might not be related to imperceptiveness about reasons for being turned down.

Every life space has a climate, a feel about it. The effect of a climate is to facilitate some actions and/or to make others less likely. This may be a very general effect, as when a high level of communication apprehension makes a person not want to speak at all. Or it may be more specific: Cooperative conflict climates encourage trustful action, while competitive climates generate more threats (Deutsch, 1973). A person's affective state (more precisely, the life space's climate) may be an important factor influencing both locomotion and the elements in the plane of irreality.

Finally, then, we arrive at plans, which are actions projected in the plane of irreality. The whole life space may be experienced both immediately and cognitively (i.e., in both the planes of reality and irreality). The person's thoughts and imaginings about the situation, as it is or as it might be, are the elements of the irreal life space. As noted earlier, the planes of reality and irreality may be closely coordinated, nearly irrelevant to one another, or somewhere in between. The plane of irreality is especially important to message production research when we have reason to suppose that a person might be planning his or her messages (e.g., Berger, 1995), rather than generating them mindlessly (Langer, 1978).

EMPIRICAL WORK ON MESSAGE PRODUCTION, FROM A LEWINIAN PERSPECTIVE

One of the great merits of field theory is its ability to integrate research done in different research traditions. Here, I want to cover essentially the same conceptual ground as in the first section, but concentrate only on message production. This displays, incidentally, field theory's status as a metatheory: It is a theory about what needs to be included in a theory of, in this case, message behavior. As we shall see, the Lewinian approach permits us to see connnections among research projects concerned with goals, obstacles, plans, affect, and other topics.

The Locomotion

The locomotion of interest in this chapter is message production. This is, however, not an unambiguous concept. As D. O'Keefe (1987) has shown, messages can be described in an indefinitely large number of accurate ways, and this implies that we can have an equally large number of theories about messages. In this matter, then, the researcher's task is not to be right, but to be reasonable.

I think of messages as being systematic collections of verbal and/or nonverbal behaviors that are intended to stimulate someone else. Message production is the process by which those behaviors are generated or selected. But these are only general conceptualizations; in practice, the research I review is much more limited.

In the first place, field theory's sole focus on psychological behavior obviously omits things like the motor control of speech (Levelt, 1989), the grammatical capabilities "wired into" humans (Chomsky, 1965), and any other processes or structures not under the actor's control. This restriction leaves unclear the applicability of field theory to automated cognitive processes, which are nonetheless under some general intentional control, and which might have been acquired with effortful awareness in the first place (Greene, 1995; Kellermann, 1992). These limitations mean that a field-theory approach is not going to account for certain aspects of messages and their production, but this is true of any theory.

The second set of limitations is not inherent, and is no more than a recognition that the research reviewed in this section has dealt with only certain sorts of messages. The work I've done within an explicit Lewinian frame has, as it happens, been limited to persuasive messages, often in conflict situations. These messages have been spoken or (less often) written, and usually have been produced as part of a laboratory-sited conversation.

A similar limitation has to do with selective message description. Messages are represented in research as collections of features. For instance, one study might report the effects of language intensity, and another might analyze the appearance of self-initiated repairs. The fact of the actual messages recedes into the background of the research, and the messages' only operational existence is as transparent vehicles for intensity or repair. The descriptions and codings become avatars for the messages themselves. My own research has generally looked at messages' sophistication, their politeness, their relevance to possible goals, and related issues. I have not examined messages' validity, topical coherence, production latency, other-adaptiveness, or any of the indefinitely large number of other features that we might well wish to know about.

Perception of the Life Space

Because people produce messages in response to the environment they believe they occupy, field theory directs us to try to understand how people view their life spaces. Although other research traditions have pursued similar questions (e.g., Miller, Cody, & McLaughlin, 1994), three particular issues have arisen here: the differentiation with which the life space is perceived, the focal life space, and the actor's expectations for the life space.

Differentiation. Lewin (1951, p. 116) says that differentiation refers to the number of parts one perceives in a whole. This conceptualization is more general, but otherwise quite consistent with, constructivists' understanding of interpersonal construct differentiation (Burleson & Waltman, 1988). Several sorts of differentiation have been studied in this research program, since the life space is, and contains, several wholes worthy of examination. The general idea is that a person will not be able to respond to anything not perceived in the life space, thus making his or her differentiation for goals, obstacles, and so forth, a kind of perceptual upper limit on the sophistication with which he or she can function. A person who only notices one goal cannot, except by accident, satisfy three.

Several studies in the research program have made use of interpersonal construct differentiation to represent the detail with which a person perceives his or her life space. This is a standard variable, with a nice empirical record. Furthermore, it may well stand in for differentiation in general, due to the salience of target persons in communication and the reality that we cannot be maximally differentiated for everything at once. In a conflictive or persuasive situation, it is reasonable to suppose that the actor may regard the other person as an important element of the psychological field.[3] Therefore, people with higher interpersonal construct differentiation (assuming equivalent motivation and so forth) ought to produce more sophisticated messages, and this has generally proved to be the case (Applegate, 1990).

However, looking at things in a Lewinian frame has immediately suggested some other approaches to differentiation. For instance, a first question might be, What, and how many things, do people perceive in their life spaces? The question is obviously too broad for a definite answer to be given, but a sample approach may be illuminating. In a study summarized in Hample (1994), 85 people were interviewed immediately after having written messages requesting that a target person either keep a secret or quit smoking. In the interviews, people mentioned their instrumental goal 5.4 times, twice as often as any of the other goals we coded for: relationship maintenance (1.8 times), protection of own self-image (1.5 times), or protection of the target person's self-image (1.8 times). And on average, 3.9 obstacles of one sort or another were mentioned. In other words, about 14.4 positively or negatively valenced regions in the participants' life spaces were found in the interviews. Since no allowance was made for duplications, this figure may be somewhat high as a summary of overall differentiation. But

---

[3]Notice that this is an assumption that is likely to be wrong in some cases. For instance, some people take conflicts so personally that they may be entirely focused on self to the exclusion of the other; some persuaders simply blurt out what they think, making their differentiation for the other irrelevant. But these sorts of exceptions do not invalidate the general strategy of having the researcher make an informed judgment about what is likely to be in the life space for most people. Individual case studies will always be more illuminating on a person-by-person basis, and statistical generalizations will always be attenuated by exceptions. Serious problems only arise when the researcher is substantially wrong about what to look for.

other researchers might have found different goals to code in the interviews. Nor does this figure of 14.4 take into account explicit mentions of self (70 times, on average) or other (50 times), and these are also likely to be relevant to the life space. At any rate, an effort to produce an overall index of life space differentiation may eventually prove useful in predicting the quality of messages produced in response to those life spaces.

A second approach to differentiation begins by noticing that the target person is only one likely component of the life space. Perhaps attention to some other element would generate a more direct representation of differentiation. Hample (1993) compared the usual measure of interpersonal construct differentiation with two measures of differentiation for messages. One, modeled on Daly, Bell, Glenn, and Lawrence (1985), counted the constructs people used in a single essay comparing good and bad conversations. The other measure was constructed more analogously to the Role Category Questionnaire: Respondents described a good conversation, then a bad one, and their constructs were counted. The two new instruments were nicely associated with one another ($r = .57$), and each correlated with the RCQ ($r = .37$ and $r = .29$, respectively). However, none of the three predicted message design logic, the measure of message sophistication used in that study. While this last result is discouraging, the general association between differentiation and design logic is modest and inconsistent (Cortes, Larson, & Hample, 1992; Hample, 1993; Lenkaitis, Fritz, & Hample, 1992; B. O'Keefe, 1988), so further work on other sorts of differentiation might still be in order.

The last new approach to differentiation takes into account Lewin's admonition that only the life space in the instant will predict behavior. In Hample (1996), both trait and state interpersonal construct differentiation were assessed. The trait measure was obtained in the usual way, with the Role Category Questionnaire. The state measure consisted of counting the constructs applied to self and other in a structured interview. People were individually shown 30 second intervals of a conversation they had just completed, and asked a number of questions at each interval. While the "state" measure is certainly not a pure one (it is, after all, collected after the message, not during it), it should prove more relevant to the messages than the trait measure. In fact, that is what happened: Only the state measure predicted perception of obstacles or editorial behavior. Interestingly, the trait and state measures of differentiation are correlated, but only at a moderate level ($r = .26$). Trait differentiation may predict the degree of fineness one is capable of perceiving, but state differentiation ought to be more reflective of actual perceptiveness.

Focal Life Space. The second perceptual issue brought to the fore by the Lewinian paradigm is the recognition that respondents in most of our studies are actually confronted with several life spaces at once. In the study that most explicitly explores this (Hample, Alajmi, Klein, Ward, & White, 1997), we asked pairs of respondents to compose a persuasive note to a third person, and to think aloud and together as they did so. This task potentially involves several life spaces, from the viewpoint of participant A: A's own life space, which recognizes the reality that he or she is participating in an experiment, probably to help out the friend who recruited him or her; A's role-playing life space, in which A writes a fictional note to a target person; the actual life space in which A and B join together in writing the note; A's perception of the life space of the target person; and perhaps A's understandings of B's various life spaces as well. While all of these intersect, more or less, on the task of writing a persuasive note, they are not the same life space at all. Each environment has different goals and obstacles, for instance, and each involves A in a different role. Each life space has a different force-field dynamic, and encourages different locomotion.

Although space limitations prevent anything like a full analysis, parts of a single transcript offer a modest illustration of the multiplicity of life spaces. The two participants are asking the target person to drop a suit of clothes off at a dry cleaners. J is the one actually writing down the note.

> 30   T: Yesterday ((pause)) Beautiful penmanship.
> 31   J: THANK you ((still writing)) yesterday.

The "yesterday's" represent what is being written to the third party, and presumably reference something T and J regard as useful or important in their estimate of the target person's life space. T's compliment in 30, however, is oriented only to the life space shared by T and J. We suspected, as a matter of fact, that T was flirting with J at this point.

> 50   T: Say I won- I know you won't mind doing this since I do everything for you ((laughs))
> 51   J: WOULD? you mind (6.0) dropping
> 52   T: ((overtalking)) flatter her again
> 53   J: I haven't finished the letter yet just a minute- would you mind dropping off (2.0) dropping only has one "p" doesn't it? (4.0) off the suit (5.0) for Saturday night.

Lines 50 and 51 indicate what is being proposed or written in the note, and again are oriented to the absent target person, and his or her life space. Note, however, that in 51, by ignoring the proposal that T and J claim a substantial debt of favors paid, J pointedly does not do any uptake of T's suggestion in 50, nor does she share in his laughter. We thought that by this point, J also thought T was flirting, and was putting a stop to it. In 52, T returns to task, orienting to the target person's life space, since flattery requires orientation to a positively valenced region in someone else's (perceived) perceived environment. Flattery is obviously a plan of T's (he had mentioned it earlier, at 20), and so T is here attempting to translate an element from his own plane of irreality to the planes of reality for all the life spaces in which the persuasive note exists. In 53, J orients only to the writing of the note, and exhibits concern for accurate spelling. Perhaps good spelling is part of J's self-image and is therefore an attractive part of her personal life space; perhaps she is trying to make a good impression on the target person, and is therefore orienting to the life spaces she shares with the target person; perhaps she is concerned about her relationship with T, and wishes to appear businesslike; or perhaps she is worried about the reaction of the only people who will actually read the note, the experimenters, one of whom recruited her to be in the study. We did not conduct the sort of close interviews needed to resolve this last matter (or our suspicions about flirting), but the simple fact of these various and reasonable interpretations shows that we will not properly account for J's behavior (or her joint behavior with T) without knowing what life space she is orienting to, and at what moment.

Thus, we arrive at the concept of the focal life space. Most of our experiments require some role-playing on the part of our respondents, as, for instance, when we ask them to pretend that they are persuading, informing, comforting, etc., someone else. We almost always assume that the observed behaviors (the messages, the evaluations, the reactions) are to be explained by the fictional life spaces we have asked our respondents to imagine, and we typically ignore the actual life space of participating in a study. This is an example of experimenters assuming that they know which life space is focal, which goals are in play, and which obstacles are salient. The experimenters may be right, of course, but they might also have it wrong from time to time. A field-theoretic orientation makes it difficult to skip over this interpretive step in understanding the results of a study. People act in response to the life space(s) they think is pertinent, their focal environment may be labile throughout the experiment, and they may or may not take on the assigned task in exactly the way the experimenter intends. These are all basic lessons from field theory.

Expectations About the Life Space. People do not enter their life spaces as blank slates. They have expectations that are influenced by personality traits, among other things (such as explicit information or relevant experience). For instance, an extroverted person will see a party full of strangers as an opportunity to make new friends, while a shy person will see the same room as a promise of hurtful experience. Traits can therefore be at least partly understood as perceptual predispositions, since they can summarize how people think they will act or feel in a situation.

The trait we have worked with most often in Lewinian terms is "taking conflict personally" (TCP). This is a set of feelings about conflict: Interpersonal arguments are felt to be punishing, aversive, personally directed, stressful, and so forth (Hample & Dallinger, 1995). People who score highest on TCP are also those who find a particular conflict to have been in fact most aversive and personally directed (Hample, Dallinger, & Fofana, 1995). So people feel what they expect to feel in their life spaces.

A recent study has taken this idea further, to show how affective expectations predict cognitive understandings of the life space (Hample, Dean, Johnson, Kopp, & Ngoitz, 1997). After assessing participants' TCP levels, we asked them to describe the steps in a typical face-to-face conflict. We found systematic differences between people high and low in TCP. High personalizers expect angry feelings to appear sooner, believe that physical violence is more likely, and are less likely to anticipate a period of calm after the conflict is over. While there are many commonalities between high and low personalizers, there remain substantial differences in what they think will happen, when it will happen, and how it will feel.

To summarize this rather lengthy section: Field theory insists that we try to see the life space as the actor does. The claim that situation affects messages has been a verity in communication research for several thousand years, but the Lewinian approach suggests several new considerations. Message producers can be differentiated for things other than people, they may flit from one focal life space to another, and their expectations about life spaces predict their feelings and thoughts while occupying them.

Climate

Every life space has a climate, a feel, an atmosphere, and these can affect message production. Just as we consider traits to be generalized expectations about life spaces, so we regard personality states as affective summaries of a situation's climate. Here, too, our research has been focused on TCP.

Trait TCP is consistently associated with the desire to avoid conflict (Dallinger & Hample, 1995; Hample & Dallinger, 1995). People who take conflict personally wish to avoid arguments, and do not plan to pursue their interests very hard. However, once they are engaged in an interpersonal conflict, they actually behave more aggressively than people who personalize less. This effect was intially found for trait TCP (Hample & Dallinger, 1993). A second study (Hample, Dallinger, & Nelson, 1995), however, discovered that trait TCP was less predictive of aggressiveness than the other person's arguing behaviors. The most recent paper on this point (Hample, Dallinger, & Fofana, 1995) finds that state TCP, assessed immediately after the conflict, is a far better predictor of behavior than is trait TCP.

Our reading of these results is that people who have a predisposition to personalize conflict generally find a way to do so. Inasmuch as they expect conflicts to be aversive, their natural wish is to avoid them. But once involved, they feel the negative affect they expected, they perform or perceive the aggressive conflict steps mentioned in the previous section, and they feel frustrated and unhappy. For personalizers, the climate of a conflict is very likely to be pressured, hurtful, and personal. This makes them more likely to see a need for self-defense and to think that aggression is the norm. Thus, high personalizers are more likely to raise their voices, issue challenges, and disagree during the interaction (Hample, Dallinger, & Fofana, 1995). Given the relationship between own and other's behavior, these actions not only represent the personalizer's projection of the climate, but will call out reactions to reinforce the climate as well. This all increases the chance that the climate will cycle destructively, confirming the person's initial aversion to conflict.

Goals and Obstacles

Goals and obstacles are valenced regions in the life space, differing only in that goals are attractive and obstacles are repulsive. Although this is a conceptually clear distinction, in practice the difference can be obscured unless the actor's perspective is respected. For instance, one message producer might have the goal of maintaining the other's self-image, while another person might regard possible damage to the other's self-image as an obstacle. This is not a distinction without a difference. In the first case, the message might well have positive face-work features, designed to make the target person feel good. In the second case, the speaker might simply try to avoid any reference at all to the other person. Thus, if maintaining the other's image is a goal, we might observe the message, "Please help me move the couch. I know you're strong." But if other's face is simply an obstacle to be avoided, we might hear something simpler, such as, "Help me with the couch, okay?" From the viewpoint of an external analyst, obstacles can generally be phrased as goals: not insulting the other becomes maintaining other's face, not making grammatical errors becomes speaking clearly, and so forth. Many goals can be rephrased as obstacles, too. But it is not the analyst's viewpoint that matters. The actor's perspective is in control of the actor's messages.

Nonetheless, experimenters can often make informed judgments about what are potentially available as goals or obstacles. Though some may reject an experimental instruction, it is reasonable to suppose that most participants told to write a persuasive note in fact intend to do so. And as Brown and Levinson (1987) have argued, face and politeness are omnipresent in all interactions (also see B. O'Keefe, 1992). The most valid investigative design in this respect is to elicit each participant's perceived life space, and notice what regions are present, and what their valences are. But only case studies permit such a procedure without substantial shortcuts. In practice, we will probably continue to make reasonable guesses as to what our respondents are thinking, and to check those guesses against our results, and against the outcomes of the occasional case studies.

Think-aloud protocols are useful triangulations (Ericsson & Simon, 1984). For instance, a number of studies yield the conclusion that persuaders attend to the following goals and obstacles while producing messages: persuasive effectiveness, self-image, other's self-image, relationship maintenance, truth, and relevance (for a summary, see Hample & Dallinger, 1990). When think-aloud protocols were examined for evidence of these considerations, most of them were clearly present (Hample, 1991). Both the protocols and the general research program, however, have had difficulty accounting for use of the truth and relevance goals. This suggests, in retrospect, that these are not actively attractive regions in the life space; they may only be obstacles around which people easily navigate, and they may be rare ones at that. Relevance, in particular, is so automatically accomplished that it is taken for granted, and seems therefore not to appear in the life spaces at all.

Normally when we observe that a message has served some goal or avoided some obstacle, we assume that the message producer was aware of that consideration, and adapted the message to it. A moment's reflection will reveal the leaps in this reasoning, however. A person might repeat or reshape a message he or she heard somewhere else (think of an adolescent male learning pickup lines from the movies), and so produce a message that is more sophisticated than the speaker understands. Or a person might simply speak in a conventional way, being polite without noticing. If we can mistakenly "put our foot in our mouth," we can accidentally produce a deft message, too.

Some effort to analyze this situation empirically was made in Hample (1996).[4] Participants were interviewed after a conflictive conversation, and the interviews were coded for mentions of obstacles and sensitivity to instrumental goals. Participants estimated their own effectiveness and appropriateness. The conversations were rated on similar dimensions. If people are adapting their messages in detail, competently, and on purpose, we ought to find substantial correlations between the message ratings and the interview and self-report data. However, this is not what the results indicate. The message effectiveness rating does not correlate with interview mentions of the instrumental goal ($r = .11$, ns), although it does predict the self-effectiveness rating ($r = .23$, $p < .05$). Coders' estimates of actual conversational

---

[4]Several of these results are reported here for the first time, although they are based on the Hample (1996) data set. The correlations are based on sample sizes ranging from 58 to 60.

appropriateness are not associated with own-appropriateness estimates (r = .04, ns); nor are the more specific ratings of the message's positive orientation to self (r = .02, ns), other (r = −.04, ns), or relationship (r = .03, ns) predicted by own-appropriateness ratings. Ratings of conversational truth and relevance work do not predict sensitivity to these issues during the interviews (r = .14, ns). Mention of obstacles during the interviews does not predict the messages' rated appropriateness (r = −.05, ns) or effectiveness (r = .03, ns).

By and large, these are not encouraging results. Of course, the fault may lie in the design of the study or the measurement of the variables, though these procedures meet our normal disciplinary standards, and other results in the study are sensible. Generally, these results suggest that we be wary about attributing awareness of goals or obstacles to speakers on the sole ground that their messages function to satisfy the goals or avoid the obstacles. There are other possibilities, and we need to explore them (Greene, 1990).

However, it would be misleading to end this section without noticing the most fundamental finding about goals, obstacles, and messages: Goals and obstacles have an important influence on message content and form. Readers are certainly aware of the substantial body of research on persuasive tactics (see Kellermann & Cole, 1994, for an exhaustive review). That we do not have a complete list of the sorts of persuasive appeals, and may never have, should not obscure the central fact that all the types of content and form (altrusitic appeals, promises, and so forth) appear appropriately and predictably in the service of persuasive goals. Even more finely grained work has been done on "the obstacle hypothesis," which says that a request will be formed so as to address the most likely obstacle to its being granted (Francik & Clark, 1985; Roloff & Janiszewski, 1989). So to ask a favor in contemplation that the target person might be too busy to perform it, one might say, "If you have a moment, could you pick up my mail for me?" If we know an actor's goals, and know what obstacles are perceived, we can make some general predictions about what will be said, and how it will be said. In this connection, the more limited obstacles literature seems further along than the work on persuasive tactics.

Barriers

Readers will recall that a barrier is the relatively impenetrable boundary around a region in the life space, normally an attractive region. If the actor knows the reason that a goal region is difficult to move into, then an obstacle is perceived. But if the locomotion is impeded for no apparent reason, then he or she is confronted with a barrier. We have just reviewed how message producers will try to maneuver around an obstacle. But a barrier must be breached.

The most pertinent literature on this point is concerned with what we call the "rebuff phenomenon" (Hample & Dallinger, 1994). This is the common finding (e.g., Bisanz & Rule, 1990; deTurck, 1985) that persuaders are more aggressive in their messages after they have been rejected one or more times. Critically, a nearly universal feature of the studies demonstrating the rebuff phenomenon is that persuaders are not given a reason for their message's failure: the actors are simply told, "it didn't work; what would you say now?" While some actors may naturally imagine a reason for the failure, meaning that they face an obstacle, the studies generally provide so little information about the target person that it seems reasonable to suppose that persuaders act as though they face a barrier. Barker, Dembo, and Lewin (1941) showed that children's natural reactions to barriers were either to become more aggressive, or to withdraw. Since the studies rarely permit respondents to withdraw, what we typically find is that second and third efforts are less polite and more forceful.

We think that there are two leading explanations for this result, and we have explored one of them. One possibility is repertoire exhaustion: People run out of polite things to say, and find themselves using messages that they would not normally produce as the persuasive encounter continues. The other explanation, the one we studied (Hample & Dallinger, 1994), is that people become frustrated and therefore more aggressive. We gave people equivalent lists of things to say initially, after one rebuff, and after a second rebuff. Participants either endorsed the messages or indicated why they would not say them. We found that people were less choosy about their messages as they went through the sequence, and they made less use of what we call person-oriented reasons for suppression. That is, they were less likely to object to a message on the grounds that it would damage the other's self-image or might harm the relationship between speaker and hearer. This finding is quite consistent with field theory's explanations of how actors respond to the presence of a barrier.

Planning

While important work has been done on the effects of anxiety on message production (e.g., McCroskey & Richmond, 1987), I wish to concentrate here on the other main research project concerning the plane of irreality, planning. Plans are usually held to mediate between goals and actions. This is the GPA model of message production implicit in most work, and nicely explained in Dillard (1990): goals cause plans, which cause action. In field theory, this relationship is not quite so straightforward, since the mediation involves a coordination of the planes of reality and irreality. This coordination might be so clear as to make the planes isomorphic, but it might also be absent, or flawed in some way (see Greene, 1990).

In his unusually expansive discussion of message planning, Berger (1995) observes that plans may be implemented, adapted, or abandoned. Abandonment occurs because of what Berger calls "goal blockage," and which we might analyze as a barrier or perhaps an obstacle. Berger and diBattista (1993) have explored what happens when a nicely planned message is met by what in Lewinian terms is a barrier. Their participants were asked to give local directions to confederates, who, without elaboration, said they did not understand, and asked for additional help. Direction givers tended to repeat the same message over again, but in a louder and slower voice. This supports what Berger calls the "hierarchy hypothesis," which states that people will make the simplest possible alterations to their plans when faced with initial failure. The similarity of this result to the rebuff phenomenon is noticeable; in fact, if one assumes that aggression is simpler than politeness, these may be the same sort of effect. Berger and diBattista's results suggest, at any rate, that plans tend to stay in place if at all possible.

The relationship between goals and plans is an interesting one that may deserve more attention that is usually accorded. The GPA model tends to see the connection as unproblematic, and perhaps it often is. However, there are other possibilities, many deriving from the likelihood of multiple goals in human interaction. We have long known, for instance, that a person may perceive two incompatible goals, resulting in an approach–approach conflict (Deutsch, 1954). In such a case, the person might plan to reach one goal region, and ignore the other (see B. O'Keefe & Shepherd, 1987).

But suppose that we see evidence in the message of a person having, in fact, pursued multiple goals (e.g., B. O'Keefe, 1988). Lewin typically used little diagrams to illustrate life spaces, and an attempt to sketch out a multiple-goal environment immediately encounters ambiguity. I see at least three possibilities, each with different implications for the resulting message (Hample, 1992). First, the goals may overlap, so that they have a common region. In this case, a single locomotion can move the actor into that region, satiating all the goals. Second, the goals may not overlap at all. In this case, the actor must move first to one goal region, then to the next. While all the goals may eventually be satisfied, we will see a sequence of achievement. The third possibility is similar in some ways to the second. Here, the speaker attains the one perceived goal, and then immediately notices another. On moving into the second goal region, the actor then perceives a third goal, and so forth. This case also results in a sequence of messages. The difference between possibilities two and three is this: In case two, the actor's planes of reality and irreality initially include all the goals, while in case three, we have a succession of life spaces, each with a new goal. Case two might have a single coherent message, moving from one objective to the next. Case three might have a series of disjointed messages, with inconsistencies possible among them. The issue, of course, is what the actor perceives as the interaction unfolds, for this is all that can affect the planning.[5]

WHAT DOES FIELD THEORY HAVE TO OFFER THE STUDY OF MESSAGE PRODUCTION?

Field theory takes a particular point of view regarding message production. It has clear biases, which are not shared by every current research program. It offers a specific definition of the behavior within its scope, but omits actions that others might wish to study. And it has implications that are not obvious in other approaches. Field theory's initial attraction for me was that it simply seemed to integrate a lot of material that I thought was relevant to the study of message production, but essentially unconnected. After working in a Lewinian paradigm for several years, however, I have found that it is not so neutral as it first seemed. It shapes thought and points us in particular directions. In closing this chapter, let me mention some of those ideas.

Though several theorists are working on their own particular approaches to message production, my reading of the literature at large is that the GPA model (Dillard, 1990) is in conceptual control of the community project. Most of the work has been done in the general area of persuasion, but one can see GPA in either the forefront or background of research on other sorts of messages as well: affinity seeking (Daly & Kreiser, 1994), information acquisition (Berger & Kellermann, 1994), and comforting (Burleson, 1994), for instance.

Perhaps the most obvious distinction between the GPA model and field theory is that the Lewinian approach includes more things. One might suppose that GPA researchers could begin to consider the ways goals differ in their ease of achievement. However, it is not easy to see how they might add climate, emotions, obstacles, or personality to the model, except as ad hoc variables. Nor does differentiation of any sort immediately come into play. In fact, situation as a whole is a sort of exogenous variable in the GPA model, a "given" setting within which goals stimulate the plans that control action.

---

[5]Mention of "interaction" brings us to a problem, not only with field theory, but with much of the work on planning. Field theory is obviously centered on one person's perceptions, and planning research, with the important exception of Bruce and Newman (1978), typically has the same single-actor emphasis. The problem is that we know that conversations are emergent, rather than coauthored. That is, each partner in a dyad does not produce half of a conversation. Instead, each participates in something that grows between them. In our studies of planning, and message production generally, we need somehow to move beyond (without abandoning) our research on essentially isolated individuals. The work mentioned above, using dual think-aloud protocols, was our attempt to start in this direction, but we are frankly not very far along.

The Lewinian approach has greater scope. Goals, plans, and actions are obviously present in field theory, just as they are in GPA. However, the Lewinian interest in how the life space is perceived makes a home for work on memory organization packets (MOPS; Kellermann, 1995) and imagined interactions (Honeycutt & Zagacki, 1988). Differentiation becomes a central issue, not simply the leading variable in one school of thought. Emotions, especially as they bear on anxieties, mood, and frustration, are clearly integrated into this framework, rather than being the sort of thing one has to issue periodic calls for attention to (Dillard & Wilson, 1993; see Bohner & Schwartz, 1993, and Metts & Bowers, 1994). And climate leaves the specialized domains of small group and organizational research to rejoin interpersonal communication at large.

A further benefit of field theory is its insights into various phenomena. "Multiple goals" becomes a specific set of ideas, not the overly simple concept it seems to be at present. Differentiation appears in field theory as a general construct, and is no longer restricted to one application. Barriers and obstacles are distinguished, leading to an explanation of why people become more polite when confronted with an obstacle, but ruder when they encounter a barrier (Hample & Dallinger, 1994). The whole idea of the plane of irreality gives plans a cognitive home, and emphasizes the problem of examining the coordination of intention and action.

But at the same time that field theory gives coherence to a broader range of concepts, it limits how we look at them. We are to focus on the actor's perspective, excluding what B. O'Keefe (1992) calls rational models of message production. Our measurements should, to the degree possible, examine the moment of production, not its past or future. We need to recalibrate and reconceptualize so that we begin looking to states rather than traits as explanatory resources. Field theory sites itself within one person's perceptual home, making it hard to study conversational and other phenomena that are conjointly produced. These are all costs imposed by the Lewinian framework.

A final issue is whether field theory can be falsified. Several factors make this rather impracticable. First, as a metatheory, it has a huge domain, which is unlikely to be plumbed with any degree of completeness. Second, even in its application to message production, the theory is open to a substantial variety of variables and operationalizations. How many goals are there, for instance, or how many climates? That these problems are not unique to field theory is beside the point. No handful of investigations is likely either to disconfirm the theory, or to demand its application.

So the decision to make use of Lewin's insights is a free one. Its attractions are its integrative and suggestive potentials. These seem to me to overbalance its insistence on the moment of one actor's perception. Others may agree.

REFERENCES

Applegate, J. L. (1990). Constructs and communication: A pragmatic integration. *Advances in Personal Construct Psychology, 1,* 203–230.

Ash, M. G. (1992). Cultural contexts and scientific change in psychology: Kurt Lewin in Iowa. *American Psychologist, 47,* 198–207.

Berger, C. R. (1995). A plan-based approach to strategic communication. In D. E. Hewes (Ed.), *The cognitive bases of interpersonal communication* (pp. 141–179). Hillsdale, NJ: Lawrence Erlbaum Associates.

Berger, C. R., & Kellermann, K. (1994). Acquiring social information. In J. A. Daly & J. M. Wiemann (Eds.), *Strategic interpersonal communication* (pp. 1–32). Hillsdale, NJ: Lawrence Erlbaum Associates.

Barker, R., Dembo, T., & Lewin, K. (1941). *Frustration and regression: An experiment with young children.* Iowa City: University of Iowa Press.

Bisanz, G. L., & Rule, B. G. (1990). Childrens' and adults' comprehension of narratives about persuasion. In M. J. Cody & M. L. McLaughlin (Eds.), *The psychology of tactical communication* (pp. 48–69). Philadelphia: Multilingual Matters.

Bohner, G., & Schwarz, N. (1993). Mood states influence the production of persuasive arguments. *Communication Research, 20,* 696–722.

Brown, P., & Levinson, S. C. (1987). *Politeness: Some universals in language usage.* Cambridge, England: Cambridge University Press.

Bruce, B., & Newman, D. (1978). Interacting plans. *Cognitive Science, 2,* 195–233.

Burleson, B. R. (1994). Comforting messages: Features, functions, and outcomes. In J. A. Daly & J. M. Wiemann (Eds.), *Strategic interpersonal communication* (pp. 135–162). Hillsdale, NJ: Lawrence Erlbaum Associates.

Burleson, B. R., & Waltman, M. S. (1988). Cognitive complexity: Using the role category questionnaire measure. In C. H. Tardy (Ed.), *A handbook for the study of human communication* (pp. 1–35). Norwood, NJ: Ablex.

Chomsky, N. (1965). *Aspects of the theory of syntax.* Cambridge, MA: MIT Press.

Cortes, C., Larson C., & Hample, D. (1992, November). *Message design logic, interpersonal construct differentiation, and gender for Mexican and American nationals.* Paper presented at the annual meeting of the Speech Communication Association, Chicago.

Dallinger, J. M., & Hample, D. (1995). Personalizing and managing conflict. *International Journal of Conflict Management, 6,* 287–289.

Daly, J. A., Bell, R. A., Glenn, P. J., & Lawrence, S. (1985). Conceptualizing conversational complexity. *Human Communication Research, 12,* 30–53.

Daly, J. A., & Kreiser, P. O. (1994). Affinity seeking. In J. A. Daly & J. M. Wiemann (Eds.), *Strategic interpersonal communication* (pp. 109–134). Hillsdale, NJ: Lawrence Erlbaum Associates.

deTurck, M. A. (1985). A transactional analysis of compliance-gaining behavior: Effects of noncompliance, relational contexts, and actors' gender. *Human Communication Research, 12,* 54–78.

Deutsch, M. (1954). Field theory in social psychology. In G. Lindsey (Ed.), *Handbook of social psychology* (pp. 181–222). Reading, MA: Addison-Wesley.

Deutsch, M. (1973). *The resolution of conflict: Constructive and destructive processes.* New Haven, CT: Yale University Press.

Dillard, J. P. (1990). The nature and substance of goals in tactical communication. In M. J. Cody & M. L. McLaughlin (Eds.), *The psychology of tactical communication* (pp. 70–91). Philadelphia: Multilingual Matters.

Dillard, J. P., & Wilson, B. J. (1993). Communication and affect: Thoughts, feelings, and issues for the future. *Communication Research, 20,* 637–646.

Ericsson, K. A., & Simon, H. A. (1984). *Protocol analysis: Verbal reports as data.* Cambridge, MA: MIT Press.

Francik, E. P., & Clark, H. H. (1985). How to make requests that overcome obstacles to compliance. *Journal of Memory and Language, 24,* 560–568.

Gold, M. (1992). Metatheory and field theory in social psychology: Relevance or elegance? *Journal of Social Issues, 48,* 67–78.

Greene, J. O. (1990). Tactical social action: Towards some strategies for theory. In M. J. Cody & M. L. McLaughlin (Eds.), *The psychology of tactical communication* (pp. 31–47). Philadelphia: Multilingual Matters.

Greene, J. O. (1995). An action-assembly perspective on verbal and nonverbal message production: A dancer's message unveiled. In D. E. Hewes (Ed.), *The cognitive bases of interpersonal communication* (pp. 51–85). Hillsdale, NJ: Lawrence Erlbaum Associates.

Hample, D. (1987). Communication and the unconscious. In B. Dervin & M. J. Voigt (Eds.), *Progress in communication sciences* (Vol. 8, pp. 83–121). Norwood, NJ: Ablex.

Hample, D. (1991, November). *Cognitive editing in the production of conversational utterances.* Paper presented at the annual meeting of the International Communication Association, Chicago.

Hample, D. (1992, September). *Field theory applied to message production.* Paper presented at the biennial meeting of the Society for the Advancement of Field Theory, Philadelphia.

Hample, D. (1993, November). *Messages' design logic, goals, and face-work, and their associations with conversational and personal construct differentiation.* Paper presented at the annual meeting of the Speech Communication Association, Miami Beach.

Hample, D. (1994, September). *A field theory of message production: The empirical record to date.* Paper presented at the biennial meeting of the Society for the Advancement of Field Theory, Ann Arbor.

Hample, D. (1996, May). *A theoretical and empirical effort to describe message production.* Paper presented at the annual meeting of the International Communication Association, Chicago.

Hample, D., Alajmi, N., Klein, M., Ward, S., & White, J. (1997, May). *Dual think-aloud protocols of message production.* Paper presented at the annual meeting of the International Communication Association, Montreal.

Hample, D., & Dallinger, J. M. (1990). Arguers as editors. *Argumentation, 4,* 153–169.

Hample, D., & Dallinger, J. M. (1993). The effects of taking conflict personally on arguing behavior. In R. E. McKerrow (Ed.), *Argument and the postmodern challenge* (pp. 235–238). Annandale, VA: Speech Communication Association.

Hample, D., & Dallinger, J. M. (1994, July). *Why are persuasive messages less polite after rebuffs?* Paper presented at the annual meeting of the International Communication Association, Sydney, Australia.

Hample, D., & Dallinger, J. M. (1995). A Lewinian perspective on taking conflict personally: Revision, refinement, and validation of the instrument. *Communication Quarterly, 43,* 297–319.

Hample, D., Dallinger, J. M., & Fofana, J. (1995). Perceiving and predicting the tendency to personalize arguments. In S. Jackson (Ed.), *Argumentation and values* (pp. 434–438). Annandale, VA: Speech Communication Association.

Hample, D., Dallinger, J. M., & Nelson, G. K. (1995). Aggressive, argumentative, and maintenance arguing behaviors, and their relationship to taking conflict personally. In F. H. van Eemeren, R. Grootendorst, J. A. Blair, & C. A. Willard (Eds.), *Proceedings of the Third ISSA Conference on Argumentation, vol. III: Reconstruction and application* (pp. 238–250). Amsterdam: SicSat.

Hample, D., Dean, C., Johnson, A., Kopp, L., & Ngoitz, A. (1997, May). *Conflict as a meta-MOP in conversational behavior.* Paper presented at the annual meeting of the International Communication Association, Montreal.

Honeycutt, J. M., & Zagacki, K. S. (1988). Imagined interaction as an element of social cognition. *Western Journal of Communication, 52,* 23–45.

Kellermann, K. (1992). Communication: Inherently strategic and primarily automatic. *Communication Monographs, 59,* 288–300.

Kellermann, K. (1995). The conversation MOP: A model of patterned and pliable behavior. In D. E. Hewes (Ed.), *The cognitive bases of interpersonal communication* (pp. 181–221). Mahwah, NJ: Lawrence Erlbaum Associates.

Kellermann, K., & Cole, T. (1994). Classifying compliance gaining messages: Taxonomic disorder and strategic confusion. *Communication Theory, 4,* 3–60.

Langer, E. J. (1978). Rethinking the role of thought in social interaction. *New Directions in Attribution Research, 2,* 35–58.

Leeper, R. W. (1943). *Lewin's topological and vector psychology: A digest and critique.* Eugene: University of Oregon Press.

Lenkaitis, J. L., Fritz, K. L., & Hample, D. (1992). *Politeness, gender, and message design logic.* Paper presented at the annual meeting of the Speech Communication Association, Chicago.

Lewin, K. (1935). *A dynamic theory of personality.* New York: McGraw-Hill.

Lewin, K. (1936). *Principles of topological psychology.* New York: McGraw-Hill.

Lewin, K. (1951). *Field theory in social science.* New York: Harper & Row.

Levelt, W. J. M. (1989). *Speaking: From intention to articulation.* Cambridge, MA: MIT Press.

Marrow, A. J. (1969). *The practical theorist: The life and work of Kurt Lewin.* New York: Basic Books.

McCroskey, J. C., & Richmond, V. P. (1987). Willingness to communicate. In J. C. McCroskey & J. A. Daly (Eds.), *Personality and interpersonal communication* (pp. 129–156). Newbury Park, CA: Sage.

Metts, S., & Bowers, J. W. (1994). Emotion in interpersonal communication. In M. L. Knapp & G. R. Miller (Eds.), *Handbook of interpersonal communication* (2nd. ed., pp. 508–541). Thousand Oaks, CA: Sage.

Miller, L. C., Cody, M. J., & McLaughlin, M. L. (1994). Situations and goals as fundamental constructs in interpersonal communication research. In M. L. Knapp & G. R. Miller (Eds.), *Handbook of interpersonal communication* (2nd. ed., pp. 162–198). Thousand Oaks, CA: Sage.

Motley, M. T., Barrs, B. J., & Camden, C. T. (1983). Experimental verbal slip studies: A review and an editing model of language encoding. *Communication Monographs, 50,* 79–101.

O'Keefe, B. J. (1988). The logic of message design: Individual differences in reasoning about communication. *Communication Monographs, 55,* 80–103.

O'Keefe, B. J. (1992). Developing and testing rational models of message design. *Human Communication Research, 18,* 637–649.

O'Keefe, B. J., & Shepherd, G. J. (1987). The pursuit of multiple objectives in face-to-face persuasive interaction: Effects of construct differentiation on message organization. *Communication Monographs, 54,* 396–419.

O'Keefe, D. (1987, November). *Message description.* Paper presented at the annual meeting of the Speech Communication Association, Boston.

Rogers, E. M. (1994). *A history of communication study.* New York: Free Press.

Roloff, M. E., & Janiszewski, C. A. (1989). Overcoming obstacles to interpersonal compliance: A principle of message construction. *Human Communication Research, 16,* 33–61.

Stivers, E., & Wheelan, S. (Eds.). (1986). *The Lewin legacy: Field theory in current practice.* New York: Springer-Verlag.

Wheelan, S. A., Pepitone, E. A., & Abt, V. (Eds.). (1990). *Advances in field theory.* Newbury Park, CA: Sage.

INTERINDIVIDUAL COHERENCE AND COORDINATION

TOWARD A THEORY OF INTERACTIVE
CONVERSATIONAL PLANNING

Vincent R. Waldron
Arizona State University West

Conversation is, among other things, the process by which our plans for the future and our memories of the past are grounded in the reality of the present. Our goals for where we want our selves and our relationships to be in some near or distant future, no matter how fuzzy or contingent, get played out in the messages we create during our interactions. Conversation is one means, arguably the primary social means, of getting from here to there. Our past comes to bear too, as we retrieve memories of previous encounters and replay the social routines that guide us in many of our interactions with others. Understanding this blending of the pasts and futures of two people, through an interactive process that looks sometimes complex and open-ended, and other times ritualized and predictable, is what I see as the central task of message-production theories.

In this chapter, I argue that planning can be central in such theories, because planning is the process by which past and future are integrated with communicative action. The contributions of planning theorists to the understanding of message production can be summarized within three approaches or traditions. These contributions are already considerable, particularly within the tradition which examines preconversational planning, or *planning for* conversation. This body of literature demonstrates convincingly that the cognitive structures and processes developed by an individual from his or her previous social experiences facilitate the preparation and production of conversational messages. However, in keeping with the forward-looking theme of this volume, I spend comparatively little space reviewing this established work, so that I might look more closely at developments within two emerging approaches to conversational planning. Both of these have the potential to move cognition-based theorizing closer to the interactive, social realm of message production. One such approach, which I call the conversational planning perspective, examines planning *during* conversation in an effort to gain a better understanding of how plans are used in the process of conversation. As with the preconversational planning approach, the focus here is primarily on the individual and his or her cognitive activities, but theoretically and methodologically, research in this tradition grapples with the problem of how planning facilitates the production of messages which are responsive to the relatively unique qualities of interaction—high cognitive workload, time-limited information processing, adaptation, multitasking. A third approach, which I call the *interactive* perspective, moves the study of conversational planning to relatively new theoretical ground by considering planning a process of mutual construction and coordination of action plans, rather than simply a process of individual-level cognition. The verbal and nonverbal messages that allow dyadic partners to coordinate their plans and move through conversational time toward some future state are the focus of this approach. To some extent, "conversation about planning" rather than "planning about conversation" is what this research tradition seeks to understand. This approach has yet to be implemented seriously in empirical studies of communication, yet I take it as one of my objectives to delineate some of the conceptual underpinnings and research questions which might form the starting place for a theory of interactive planning.

This chapter begins with a brief overview of key concepts found in the planning literature. In the second section I present a defense of plan-based theories of message production, responding in part to criticisms (some my own) of cognitive approaches to communication research. I conclude this section by advocating aggressive pursuit of all three of the planning approaches described above. In the third section, I review key contributions of the preconversational planning literature, trusting that the interested reader will find more detailed treatments readily available (e.g., Berger, 1995). The fourth section reviews the "planning-during conversation" tradition, identifies types of online planning, reviews the effects of online planning on conversational outcomes, presents a study which documents the shifting priorities interactants assign to conversational goals and plans. Finally, the conceptual origins of a dyadic, interactive theory of planning are identified and key research themes associated with this new area of planning research are explored.

PLANNING THEORY: A BRIEF INTRODUCTION

Cognitive and social scientists have for many years embraced the importance of plans and planning processes in their attempts to account for human performance of complex tasks, including the production and understanding of messages (Berger, 1995; Galambos, Abelson, & Black, 1986; Hammond, 1989; Kreitler & Kreitler, 1987; Miller, Galanter, & Pribram, 1960; Sacerodoti, 1977). After reviewing numerous definitions of the plan concept, Berger (1988a) defined plans as mental representations of actions (not actions themselves), organized to facilitate achievement of one or more goals. Similarly, conversational plans have been operationalized as units of thought that take an actor–action–goal structure (Waldron, Cegala, Sharkey, & Teboul, 1990). The integral link between goals and plans is a constant in the planning literature. However, the link is not a simple one. Plans are not predetermined paths leading straight toward some singular endpoint. Cognitive scientists (e.g., Robertson & Zachary, 1990) and communication researchers (e.g., Dillard, 1990) have long recognized that social action is oriented to multiple, changing, and sometimes conflicting goals. Moreover, communicators have not just explicit goals, but also implicit ones of which they may be unaware at any given moment in conversation. Thus plan-goal relations are multifaceted, fleeting, conflicted, partially subconscious, and susceptible to even subtle variation in the constellation of objectives pursued by interactants. Not surprisingly, most theorists view plans as flexible and embedded, in that they specify not just one, but potentially numerous, behavioral paths at multiple levels of abstraction.

The process of planning includes the cognitive operations of searching for, constructing, evaluating, deploying, and revising plans (Hayes-Roth & Hayes-Roth, 1979; Sacerodoti, 1977; Stefik, 1981a, 1981b). Planning is typically described as a fundamental process connecting cognition with future action (Sacerodoti, 1977). This process may yield plans that are implemented in action or only considered hypothetically (e.g., Edwards, Honeycutt, & Zagacki, 1988). Planning may involve "filling-in" the details of an existing abstract plan (top-down planning) or inductive construction of plans based on cues from the environment (bottom-up planning). Conversation no doubt involves both types of planning processes, but the need to conserve cognitive resources probably yields a preference for top-down planning, in which general plans that have "worked" in similar conversations, are implemented when possible and adjusted to the needs of the current situation (Berger, 1988a). Interactants probably start most conversations with only general goals and vague plans (Newman, 1990). The general plan for "asking a favor from a friend" is accessed in each favor-request situation, but the specific request tactics are adjusted as the conversation progresses and the friend's response to the request is evaluated.

The preference for efficiency points to the presence of constraints, or overriding "metagoals," in planning processes. Numerous researchers have identified the preservation of cognitive resources as one such planning constraint (e.g., Wilenski, 1983). Communication researchers frequently identify the need to be "socially appropriate" as another constraint, or metagoal (see Berger, 1995 for an extensive summary). This metagoal of preserving the face of self and other (Goffman, 1959) limits planning options to some degree and sometimes conflicts with the goal of being efficient. Competent interactants appear to be those who cognitively and tactically "manage" the potential conflicts between these metagoals (Cegala & Waldron, 1992; Kellermann & Berger, 1984; Waldron, 1990; Waldron et al., 1990).

As do most cognitive theorists, communication researchers who study planning assume humans are limited information processors who can attend to only some of their goals and plans at any given moment. This limited capacity becomes problematic when processing demands are high, as is the case in many message-production situations. This seems partially true during strategic conversation where multiple cognitive operations (listening, searching memory, constructing action, monitoring the partner) happen simultaneously or in rapid succession. Of course, conversation can also be rather simple and routinized. But, under complex conditions, individuals must make adjustments to conserve resources by processing more efficiently or allowing performance to degrade as the cognitive system "catches up" with processing demand. The limited cognitive capacity assumption by itself allows researchers to account for gross variations in performance in high and low demand situations. But the explanatory value of this notion is limited and perhaps too prominent in cognitive theories of communication. I say this because I presume that cognitive demands are *always* high in the types of complex conversation which message production researchers most want to understand. Planning theories are most helpful in this pursuit when they account for how interactants manage to produce messages, often highly effective ones, *despite* the high cognitive workload.

PLANNING APPROACHES TO MESSAGE PRODUCTION: A RATIONALE

This chapter is written at a time when cognitive approaches to message production enjoy widespread influence but also are receiving increased critical scrutiny within the communication discipline. Planning and other cognitivist theories have been criticized as inadequate accounts for complex human thinking generally (e.g., Dreyfus & Dreyfus, 1986) and communication specifically (Baxter, 1992; McPhee, 1995). From interpretive and "social" perspectives, cognitive theories of message production can be criticized for promulgating a reductionist view of communication, where the cognitive systems and architectures are themselves imbued with inordinate power to cause changes in communication behavior, with little acknowledgment of the larger social forces that shape interaction, the importance of social context in framing the meaning of communicative acts for participants, or the capacity of interactants to use cognitive operations in a purposeful manner. What I describe in this chapter as an interactive approach to planning is in part an attempt to show how planning research can be linked more directly to the social and purposeful behavior which we typically associate with conversation.

In offering a different kind of criticism, I have argued previously (Waldron, 1995) that the study of cognitive processes is most useful to the communication discipline when it contributes to the development of *communication*, rather than cognitive theory. Although this claim appears obvious, my reading of the typical cognitively oriented study is that minimal communication measures (e.g., pause duration, disfluency rates) are collected almost as an afterthought to test models of what is happening inside the heads of interactants. In some cases, the theoretical principles tested by these researchers are intended to generalize to the interactive realm, but for purposes of experimental conrol, noninteractive measures are used. This is possibly the case with Greene's program of research on action assembly theory (for a recent review see Greene, 1995). However, in arguing for a "requirement-centered" approach, I have suggested that cognitively oriented communication research might reasonably begin with analysis of conversational situations from the standpoint of a communication theory. This theoretical analysis yields some indication of the message processes required for interactants to function in that situation. Researchers might (or might not) infer from these message requirements that certain types of cognitive operations "ought to be" present. The collection of data about these cognitive operations then functions to test the deductions drawn from the communication theory.

For example, politeness theory (Brown & Levinson, 1978) and its descendants (Lim & Bowers, 1991) contends that competent interactants attend to certain face wants as they construct messages in face-threatening situations. Researchers have examined messages for evidence of the expected face support with mixed success (Baxter, 1984; Craig, Tracy, & Spisak, 1986). However, the production of face-supporting messages implies any number of cognitive operations, each of which might be studied to extend the theory and account for the success or failure of interactants to produce messages sufficiently responsive to the partner's face concerns. In routinized situations, the cognitive requirements may simply involve activation of a well-worn script that specifies the appropriate form of politeness.

More complex situations may require the interactant to recognize and interpret the conversational plans of the partner as a means of predicting where he or she intends to direct the conversation. For example, if one can predict relatively quickly that a friend is steering the conversation to a future point where the requesting of a favor is likely, one can, in the interim, plan acceptance or denial strategies that are adapted to this particular friend and his or her unique face considerations. In this case, "thinking ahead" may be the key cognitive operation that determines whether sophisticated or rudimentary face support is provided.

This example, almost incidentally, points to the potential importance of planning processes in one communication theory. The justification for studying planning processes is obvious in other examples. Constructivists claim that competent communication involves an ability to take into account the multiple goals and perspectives of others (Applegate, 1990). From this theoretical point of view, "person-centered" arguments are those that recognize the unique qualities of the other party. In fact, person-centered messages have been rated as more adaptable and persuasive in several studies (Applegate, 1990). Taking this notion into the realm of conversation, person-centered messages are presumably those that incorporate information derived from the partners' previous utterances, among other sources. In fact, Waldron and Applegate (1994) reasoned that during verbal disagreements, person-centered messages (conversational turns) were those that acknowledged the partners' previous arguments and integrated them with arguments offered by the self. The cognitive operations implied by this behavioral pattern are: construction of one's own plan of argument; recognition of the other's plan; updating of own plans with new actions; and, in some cases, creation of novel plans to meet unexpected arguments or circumstances.

Based on these few examples, it appears research on conversational planning might contribute directly to the development of communication theory. However, critics might question whether planning models overemphasize strategic and mindful aspects of interaction. As Kellermann (1992) notes, strategic communication is "voluntary, controllable, directioned, chosen, and purposeful" (p. 292), but not necessarily mindful. Indeed, strategic communication is probably organized around goals and plans without the interactants' continuous and full cognitive involvement in the goal-setting and planning processes. Conversational planning need not be a deliberate, highly engaged mental process. However, planning *is* prominent in strategic conversation, if the self-reports of interactants themselves are to be believed. I found in one study of information-seeking interactions between strangers, that 44% of 2,273 self-reported conversational cognitions related to conversational goals and the plans used to achieve them (Waldron, 1990). Similar results were found in a more recent study of safe-sex conversations among peers (Waldron, Caughlin, & Jackson, 1995).

In sum, planning theories have gathered enough cross-disciplinary momentum in recent decades to spark considerable research by communication scholars studying message production processes. Through analysis of the planning processes and plan qualities mentioned only briefly thus far, theorists have attempted to account for variation in message production and specify how goals are linked to actions. From the perspective of message-production research, planning approaches are promising in that they move beyond the simple description of message variation to specify some of the factors that account for such variation.

THE PRECONVERSATIONAL PLANNING APPROACH

Research in the preconversational planning tradition has been discussed extensively elsewhere (Berger, 1988a, 1995) so I provide only a brief review here. To some extent, the metaphor guiding this approach is "plan as program," in the sense that preconversational plans are characterized as preloaded sets of instructions which vary in terms of their complexity and specificity, are stored in memory, "accessed" and "deployed" when conversations of a particular type are anticipated. Within this tradition, emphasis is placed on describing the structure of plans and testing models of the planning processes underlying message production. In some cases, response latencies, disfluencies and other low-level speech behaviors are measured as indicators of cognitive functioning. (To extend the plan-as-program metaphor, this approach is akin to the use of computer response time as an indicator of processing load.) In other studies, planning indices are linked with messages at the tactical level. Briefly summarized, the contributions of this research relate to attributes of communication plans and the processes of searching for and formulating plans.

Plan Attributes

At least three previously acknowledged qualities of plans have been investigated for their effects on message production. First, conversational plans have most frequently been conceptualized in terms of *plan complexity*. In a study of date-request planning, Berger (1988a) operationalized plan complexity as the number of planned actions and the number of contingency statements included in plans. Plan length and the number of distinct arguments contained in a plan were measures of plan complexity in a persuasion study (Berger, Karol, & Jordan, 1989). Presumably, interactants who can access greater numbers of hypothetical actions (e.g., more potential arguments) should experience increased tactical flexibility and an increased likelihood of discovering a course of action which facilitates self and partner goals. In this regard, the characteristics of hypothetical plans have been linked to communication skills (Edwards et al., 1988). In general, Berger's (1988a, 1988b, 1989) studies show that plan complexity is *negatively* associated with measures of verbal fluency. Perhaps the process of searching through plan options inhibits message production at this level (Berger, 1995). This may not be the case at more abstract levels of message production. In studies of online planning (discussed in the next section), plan complexity appears to *facilitate* the production of information seeking and verbal disagreement tactics (Waldron, 1993; Waldron & Applegate, 1994).

Plan specificity, a second attribute, is the extent to which conversational plans are fully articulated. Conversational plans clearly vary in abstractness (Berger, Knowlton, & Abrahams, 1996; Waldron et al., 1995), with some providing only vague blueprints for future action and others specifying a concrete set of behavioral steps. Interactants who can think of only abstract courses of action ("argue the point," "be friendly") may be stymied by the need to produce specific responses during conversational situations. Plans that specify more concretely the actions needed for integration ("argue the point by telling him the statistic I read in the paper," "be friendly by summarizing all the good points he made") are more likely to assist interactants in moving the conversation toward desired future states (Waldron, 1993).

In addition to these structural features of plans, *plan quality* is another important attribute of communicative plans. Berger (1988a) has found evidence that the plan sophistication or content of plans has potential social consequences, as evidenced in his studies of date-request situations and in correlations between plan quality and measures of loneliness (Berger & Bell, 1988).

Plan Search and Formulation

Several studies have examined how planners search through previous plans for one that can be used in the current situation. In studies of planning sources, Berger and Jordan (1992) found that in producing messages for new situations, interactants search for action plans used in past episodes, aggregations of past episodes, or imagined episodes. When old plans don't fit current circumstances well, interactants prefer to make changes at the lowest level of abstraction (changing the details) rather than higher levels (replacing the whole plan with a new one), a propensity consistent with the resource-preserving "hierarchy principle" (Berger et al., 1996).

Conclusion: The Preconversational Planning Approach

The research in this tradition highlights the importance of the past, represented in the form of recalled plans, in shaping the quality of messages produced in the present. The already substantial work done from this perspective suggests that the attributes of plans recalled from memory and the constraints imposed on the planning process by cognitive resource limitations are likely to impact message behavior and have social consequences. Interestingly, the effects of planning attributes may be more pronounced at abstract levels of message behavior (tactics), where interactants are likely to be aware of their message choices and (perhaps) more likely to use their plans in a purposeful way to manage the conversational goals of themselves and their partners. This decidedly social interpretation of the results reported earlier, along with Berger's work on the adaptation of plans, encourages planning researchers to look more closely at planning during conversation.

THE CONVERSATIONAL PLANNING APPROACH

Research in this tradition moves the study of planning closer to the interactive realm by trying to study plans in the flow of conversation. This research builds on the first tradition but assumes that conversation has unique properties that may significantly alter the planning process (Waldron & Cegala, 1992). From a metaphorical perspective, plans are viewed as attempts by individuals to channel and impose partial order on a stream of conversational events that changes continually in its speed, intensity, and composition. The online process of planning the next few conversational moves is assumed to be the primary cognitive focus of interactants. This process is no doubt aided by preconversational planning processes, but it is assumed to be more dynamic and accommodative. Like the preconversational perspective, the level of analysis here is the individual. However, in a step toward interactive planning the degree to which conversational partners' previous utterances are incorporated into one's own plans becomes a point of consideration. In addition, rather than consider single plans, this approach makes it possible to study multiple plans as they emerge, are adapted, and discarded as conversation unfolds.

Types of Online Planning

Building on planning work in the cognitive sciences, Waldron (1990, 1993; Waldron & Applegate, 1994) has delineated multiple types of planning that are likely to occur while conversation is underway. First, planning might be "knowledge-based" in the sense that interactants' stock of prefabricated actions (i.e., arguments) is the sole source of current plans. Interactants simply implement preplanned actions with little attempt to adapt to the partner, the partner's utterances, or other current conversational conditions. Second, planning may be "accommodative" in that prefabricated plans or plan components can be adapted to the unique requirements of the current situation and partner (cf. Hammond, 1989). The incorporation of current information about conversational conditions and the editing (if necessary) of off-the-shelf-plans for these conditions define this approach (for a discussion of cognitive editing, see Hample & Dallinger, 1987).

Third, interactants might at times use a more creative, proactive variety of planning to construct relatively novel action sequences. Such planning would be most useful in conversations where previous experience is not directly applicable, where partner behavior is not highly predictable, and where the rules and goals of conversation are viewed as at least somewhat negotiable. The major planning task is not to select the behavior sequence that best meets a familiar set of current conversational requirements and goals (as in knowledge-based planning), but instead to consciously determine goals for the near or long term conversational future and construct hypothetical action sequences which move self and other toward those goals. As with accommodative planning, editing of plans to reflect changes in goals and conversational conditions should be a prominent part of creative planning.

Planning Effects

One advantage of taking measures of planning during conversation is that such measures can be linked empirically with desireable and undesirable conversational outcomes. In some conversational situations, online planning (at least the highly deliberate, resource-intensive variety) might actually result in negative outcomes. Excessive use of resources for planning may divert resources away from other cognitive operations (e.g., attending to the partner) and may result in processing delays manifested in unacceptably long pauses or disfluencies. In fact, studies document both facilitating and debilitating effects of online planning. In a series of studies examining how peers discuss AIDS, Waldron et al. (1995) reasoned that interactants who produced higher numbers of plans and those who produced more specified plans would be better able to guide safe-sex discussions. The authors determined that successful conversations were those in which participants discussed AIDS prevention strategies not in general terms (e.g., "use safe sex") but in terms of concrete behavioral steps ("use latex condoms"). Peer discussion leaders were asked to elicit this kind of concrete discussion from their partners (rather than simply offer the information themselves). Success was further operationalized with a coding system that gave the leader "points" for each concrete prevention behavior elicited from the partner. As expected, discussion leaders were more successful when their plans for eliciting discussion were specific rather than general. The raw number of planned actions also correlated positively with the measure of conversational success. The results of the Waldron et al. study suggested that planning "pays off" by increasing speakers' ability to progress beyond simple questioning strategies to more complex and effective conversational management approaches. In addition, when initial strategies failed, complex planners were able to "fall back" on alternate approaches. In this context, the practical benefits of planning approaches seem supported. Waldron et al. (1995) suggested that AIDS educators might find it fruitful to improve the quantity and quality of the plans people bring to safe-sex discussions.

In contrast, planning effects were mixed in data collected during earlier studies (Waldron, 1990, 1993). Working from the self-reported plans of interactants seeking socially "sensitive" information from partners, Waldron linked the quality of online plans with the achievement of information seeking and social appropriateness (based on partner ratings) goals. Results indicated that interactants who reported simple, direct plans ("just ask for the information") were perceived as less appropriate by their partners than those who constructed more complex indirect action sequences (gradual manipulation of the conversation so the desired information was volunteered, not requested). However, this group often failed to acquire the sensitive information. Waldron (1990) concluded that excessively complex plans might actually inhibit conversational success under high workload conditions (depending on how "success" is defined). However, Cegala and Waldron (1992) demonstrated that when conversational success was operationalized as a combination of effectiveness (information-seeking success) *and* perceived conversational appropriateness, planning was a key determinant of positive outcomes.

Tracking Changes in Plans and Goals

By gathering data about planning processes as they occur online, researchers can better explain how plans and goals change in their nature and importance. The complex relations between plans and goals can also be scrutinized. Recent cognitive work on the properties of conversation confirms the notion, popular in the communication literature for some time, that conversational goals are multiple and fluid (Clark & Delia, 1979; Dillard, 1990). For cognitive scientists, developing models of the goal-management process represents a key roadblock to the development of next-generation interactive computer systems (Robertson & Zachary, 1990). Research in the planning-during-conversation tradition can contribute meaningfully here by describing how interactants shift the priorities associated with their conversational goals and plans, the nature of these shifts, and the conversational events which prompt priority shifting. Here I briefly relate the results of an as yet unpublished study (Waldron, 1996), predicated on the assumption that conversational planning is oriented toward the achievement of interpersonal goals, and shaped by the continuous changing of the importance and relative priority attached to such goals. The study attempted to collect empirical evidence documenting these changes, including qualitative data regarding the mental and conversational triggers for adjustments in plans and goals.

Method. Building on a series of previous investigations (Cegala & Waldron, 1992; Waldron et al., 1990), this study examined the goals and plans used by interactants to encourage their partners to reveal socially sensitive information about their religious or political beliefs. A cued-recall method was used to assess interactants' reconstructed conversational cognitions and their ratings of goal importance. After completing 8-minute conversations, subjects were separated and instructed to watch one copy of the videotaped conversation. An experimenter stopped the tape after every 30 seconds of conversation. At each tape stop, participants were instructed to describe any thought or feeling they recalled experiencing during the interval. Participants rated the importance of five types of interpersonal goals (Dillard, 1990): arousal management, relational, management of self-identity, management of other identity, and information seeking. Ratings were keyed to a 10-point semantic differential scale anchored by the words *unimportant* and *important*.

The means and standard deviations for the importance ratings were computed for each minute of the conversation. To identify shifts in goal priorities, the mean interval-to-interval change in importance (and the standard deviation) for each goal type was computed. When a change exceeded in magnitude the standard deviation of this measure, it was considered substantive and subjected to further analysis. The "triggers" for the substantive changes were investigated qualitatively by having three independent coders read the self-reported cognitions associated with each 30-second interval, which included a substantive goal change. Coders simultaneously observed the videotape for that interval. Each made a holistic judgment regarding the apparent reason for the goal adjustment and then recorded the behavioral indicators (if any) that lead them to make this judgment. The three coders then discussed their judgments, reviewed the videotape when necessary, and came to a consensus. Through this iterative process of examining self-reports, watching tapes, and critical discussion, the research team created a taxonomy of reasons for shifts in goal and plan priorities. The conversations were sampled randomly and subjected to this review process until extensive redundancy in the behavioral and self-report data was encountered.

Results. Several general observations were derived from the review of the goal-shift data. First, approximately 30% of the 30-second intervals involved a significant shift in goal importance. About 55% of these intervals involved multiple shifts (e.g., the instrumental goal increased and identity and relational goals decreased).

With regard to the triggers for shifts in the importance of goals, qualitative review of the self-report and behavioral data indicated that *planning confusions* often accompanied goal adjustments. Confusions were uncertainties about which actions to deploy in the conversational future. Confusions were indicated by self-reported uncertainty and by behavioral indicators of uncertainty (awkward pauses, self-interruptions). One interactant who had been engaging in considerable "forced" and apparently aimless small talk, recalled, *"I was becoming worried about how I was going to talk about what I was supposed to talk about."* Another reported that she was *"thinking a lot about what to talk about next . . . how am I going to get info. about her reasons for her religion?"* Confusions prompted increases in the importance rating of the instrumental goal (and frequently, the arousal-management goal). In addition, planning confusions were associated with a concomitant increase in the importance ratings for self-identity goals.

Blocked plans typically involved noncooperation by the partner. They had the effect of bringing the instrumental goal to the foreground, and were often associated with decreases in the rated importance of the other-identity goal. Some typical self-reports: *"I was wishing I could initiate the conversation and say what I wanted to say . . . she seemed to have to control the topic"; "I was wanting to get to the topic of politics soon, but she was still dwelling on her own feelings."* Behaviorally, these shifts were associated with increasingly direct questioning, longer turns, and interruptions of partner talk.

Goal achievement, particularly achievement of the instrumental (information-seeking) goal, was implicated as a cause of changes in goal importance. Behaviorally, these shifts were accompanied by decreased questioning, by topic manipulations which ceded conversational control to the partner, ("So, what can we talk about next") and by decreased nonverbal immediacy. One individual recalled, *"I had gotten some info. about her religion, but I feel like I really want to get to know her . . ."* Another noted, *"My discussion had reached a roadblock. I had the information I wanted . . . and when she asked about me, I knew she wanted to talk about something else. I let the conversation go."* Acquisition of the desired information typically lead to decreases in importance of the instrumental goal. The decrease was often accompanied by decreased importance of the arousal-management objective and by increases in the importance of relational or identity objectives.

Partner rule violations included perceived invasions of privacy and partner behaviors judged to be inconsistent with the rules pertaining to relevance, quantity, quality, or style of conversation between strangers (cf. Grice, 1975): *"She was being rather inquisitive about my personal life."; "He wasn't too discrete."; "Wondering why she is talking religion??? Bizarre!"*).

Plan assessments (sometimes in concert with partner rule violations) were also associated with increased importance of relational and identity goals.

The partner's behavior prompted speculation about the partner's plans or goals (*"How can she not like Com? What is she getting at?"; "I just realized she is trying to find out religious information about me"*) or the partner's psychological or emotional commitment to his/her plans (*"She seemed eager to tell me about her job"; "She was nervous to talk about her religious beliefs"; "I think she felt the information she was giving me was important to her."*).

Cognitive *Engagements/disengagements* occurred during intervals in which the importance of all or most goals changed. In engagement, the interactant appeared verbally and nonverbally to be highly interested in the topic or the partner (*"I was excited to find out she was in campus crusade . . . I was very glad to meet another Christian"; "Curious why he left New York . . ."*). In disengagement, interactants appeared to be mentally removed from the conversation, either because a conversational topic had prompted them to dwell privately on a subject or because they were uninterested in the conversation: (*"Bored!"; "Thinking about my wedding day"; "Thinking about the hell . . . we went through in our lives then"*).

The results of the study confirm the complexity of goal-plan relations. The frequent and multidirectional changes in conversational goals, and the qualitative data indicating these changes were triggered by planning confusions, blocked plans, plan assessments, and goal achievement (among other things), are evidence that plans and goals are closely linked. The unmistakable message in the aggregated qualitative and quantitative data implies not only that planning is a dynamic process, but that replanning and adustment of plans should be considered the norm in strategic conversation.

The factors prompting shifts in goal importance were varied, but largely consistent with existing theory. That interactants adjusted their goals in response to confusions, blocked plans, and goal achievement supports Berger's (1988a, 1995) theoretical framework outlining the relationship between goals, plans, and actions. The role of rules violations in prompting interactants to rethink relational and identity goals is consistent with work that emphasizes the cooperative nature of conversation (e.g., Grice, 1975) and the normal obligations of stranger relationships (e.g., Brown & Levinson, 1978). From the standpoint of cogntive theory, such incidents might prompt cognitive reinterpretation of the plans and meanings of the partner (Hewes, 1995). Finally, the prominence of partner assessment as a prelude to changes in goal importance is consistent with uncertainty reduction theory (Berger & Calabrese, 1975).

Conclusions: The Conversational Planning Approach

The planning-during-conversation perspective moves closer to an interactive approach to the study of message production. However, studying plans during conversation is difficult from a purely methodological standpoint.

Cognitive scientists have evolved any number of methods for documenting the thought processes used by persons performing complex tasks. The strengths and weaknesses of these approaches have been discussed elsewhere in the communication (Waldron & Cegala, 1992) and cognition literatures (Zachary, 1990). Here I simply conclude that admitting some degree of interactive *process* to the study of planning involves tradeoffs with which some researchers may be uncomfortable. One such tradeoff is the acceptance of self-report data as evidence of the cognitive operations of interactants. However, the need for methodological creativity is obvious if this research is to progress.

Aside from methodological challenges, this approach to planning is limited by its individualistic approach. Clearly, communicative action is partially determined by the individual plans of interactants. Yet the coordination and sequencing of behavior that defines conversation is essentially a dyadic social process. Moreover, it is in interaction itself, the mutual creation and sequencing of language *behaviors*, that plans are expressed, coordinated, modified, and constructed. Oddly, few communication researchers have studied plans at this most communicative level of analysis. We know little about the role of messages in the planning process. Moreover, cognitive scientists have recently come to the conclusion that communication is the critical missing link in recent attempts to model the next generation of cooperative computing systems (Robertson & Zachary, 1990). The interactive planning perspective, only in its infancy, moves issues of communication to the the foreground

TOWARD AN INTERACTIVE PLANNING APPROACH

Proposed in a complex model nearly two decades ago by Bruce and Newman (1978) the notion of "interactive planning" has been revisited recently as cognitive scientists have begun to grapple seriously with problems of cooperation and situated action (Greeno, 1993; Robertson, Zachary, & Black, 1990). Theorists working in the interactive planning tradition attempt to identify the planning features of natural conversation and incorporate them in models of interactive computing, story understanding, and cooperation (e.g., Bruce, 1983; Cawsey, 1993; Gibbs & Mueller, 1990; Newman, 1990; Newman & Bruce, 1986; Ponssard, 1990). Consistent with much of the work on story understanding at the time, Bruce and Newman (1978) developed a comprehensive but complex notation to represent the plans of characters in stories. Their work adds to the previous planning traditions by explicitly recognizing that stories (like conversations) are best understood not simply by referencing the goals and plans of single actors, but by understanding how actors react to the plans of other actors, and how plans gain meaning primarily in relation to the plans of other participants.

In distinguishing between single-actor and interacting plans, Bruce and Newman analyze the familiar story of "Hansel and Gretel" (Grimm, 1945). In the story, a reluctant woodcutter agrees to a plan proposed by his wife (the stepmother of the two children) to abandon their children in the forest. The plan is apparently designed to conserve the limited amount of food available to the impoverished household. Hansel overhears the plan and develops a counterplan, which involves gathering white pebbles and leaving them along the trail, so that he and his sister can find their way home.

This folktale can be partially understood in terms of the structure of Hansel's plan. He has a goal (returning home) and constructs a set of actions (collecting pebbles, dropping them, following them) to reach the goal. The parents' plan could be similarly reconstructed. However, as Bruce and Newman make clear, this analysis of single plans misses much of what makes the actors' behaviors significant in the context of the story. Hansel's plan *interacts* with the plan of the parents, in the sense that it is predicated on his understanding of their plan. For instance, he knows he must drop pebbles on the path, because he understands that the parents intend to bring the children to an unfamiliar part of the forest. This knowledge helps Hansel recognize that when his parents tell the children that the family will depart on a "wood chopping" expedition, they are in essence fabricating a plan, which disguises their "real" plan. For their part, the parents must be capable of maintaining this planning ruse as they prepare for the journey, walk through the woods, and then leave the children by the fire "to rest" while the parents cut wood. As the plans unfold and Hansel secretly drops his pebbles, he too engages in plan fabrication. When asked by his father why he is hesitating along the trail, he claims to be " . . . looking at my white cat. It is sitting on the roof wanting to say good-bye to me."

This simple story reveals much about what makes social interaction complex. The actors pursue multiple goals simultaneously. Their plans are interdependent and their overt actions are driven partially by the actor's understanding of the other's intentions, partially by literal plans, and partially by the need to "appear as if" certain plans are being conformed to, even when they are not. Bruce and Newman's early (1978) analysis of stories, when transferred to the realm of conversational planning, yields a refined understanding of how plans facilitate the production of competent strategic messages under interactive conditions. For example, we can see that discovering the plans of the partner can be an essential message-production task. Doing so allows us to select and sequence our own conversational moves in a complementary or contradictory manner. Perhaps more important, knowing the partner's plan—where he or she is headed, allows us to reallocate cognitive resources temporarily. No longer must we be fully

engaged in monitoring our partner's behavior to discern his or her intentions. Like Hansel, we can use these resources to construct a plan which
allows us to produce messages that meaningfully intersect with the partner's
unfolding plan, or in some cases undermines or redirects it to a goal more
suited to our purposes.

Early attempts at modeling interacting plans were suggestive, and the
concepts I discuss next are largely attributable to the work of cognitive
scientists like Bruce and Newman (1978). Yet the extent to which the interactive planning notion has been incorporated in subsequent research by
communication and cognitive science scholars has been somewhat disap-
pointing. One reason is that the social phenomena they attempted to capture
and the notations they used were so complex as to be discouraging to other
researchers. More important for our purposes here, the early work failed
to develop several aspects of social interaction that might more clearly
distinguish it from the two more individualistic planning traditions discussed
earlier. For example, in most models, planning remains primarily an individual-level activity. Bruce and Newman (1978) admit social interaction to the
planning process in a limited way by acknowledging that individuals incorporate the intentions and plans of others in their own plans. However, this
corresponds to what I called "accommodative" conversational planning in
discussing the conversational planning perspective (see also Suchman,
1990). Although clearly social, this type of planning is different from the
cooperative development of plans by two or more parties.

A second problem, which has received some research attention (Newman,
1986), but that requires more if we are to develop adequate models of
interactive planning, is the notion of "mutual knowledge." Discussed in more
detail shortly, and implied in the earlier analysis of "Hansel and Gretel" this
refers to the existence of conventional plans that are acquired through
socialization and assumed to be known by "everyone." Mutual knowledge
allows Hansel to explain his dallying on the trail by indicating that he was
looking at his cat on the roof. He didn't need to explain that the plan for
"looking from afar" requires one to slow down, stop, turn around, and peer
through the mist, etc. His parents supplied these steps, as he knew they
would. In fact, he counted on it. Due to the existence of mutual knowledge,
the ruse worked as intended.

A final problem in the early interactive planning work is that the processes
by which interactions among plans are constructed is left unexplained. Plans
do not by themselves "interact." People use communication to coordinate
their plans (or not). Not surprisingly, cognitive science researchers survey-
ing the state of the field place additional study of the coordinating mechanisms inherent in natural communication at the top of their agenda for badly
needed research (Robertson & Zachary, 1990).

Communication researchers with an interest in cognitive explanations for
message production should find encouragment in the fact that cognitive

scientists seem to be looking in our direction for answers. The problems with which they are struggling now are those communication researchers have long studied (the management of goals through discourse, the role of relationships in message selection; the communicative mechanisms which facilitate coordination). On the other hand, in our research we have yet to fully link cognitive constructs (like plans) to the interactive phenomena that currently challenge the cognitive sciences. Pushing message-production research in this direction would strengthen our theoretical accounts for variation in conversational behavior, and have the pleasant side effect of increasing the interdisciplinary relevance of communication research.

In the following pages, I identify some of the interactive planning concepts that will challenge us to think about planning as a dyadic process—a process evident in messages as well as cognitions.

The Discourse of Cooperative Planning

Researchers who view planning as a cooperative social process, rather than simply that which happens within the heads of individual interactants, will look closely at discourse for evidence of plan construction, modification, and adjustment. In some cases, "planning talk" is explicit and obvious. When interactants explicitly discuss how their conversation will proceed, they are in essence jointly constructing a plan. Explicit planning talk is most obvious in formal conversations, like job interviews. Here, the interviewer may lay out the action structure of the interviews: "First, we will talk about your education, then your job experience, and then your objectives for the future. . . ." This action plan usually includes a "slot" for the interviewer to interject his or her questions: "After each topic is covered we have time for you to ask me some questions." Before implementing the plan, the speaker may check with the listener to confirm that he or she understands how the conversation will unfold ("Does that sound OK to you?") and to seek modifications to the plan ("Are there any other topics you would like to cover?").

The importance of plans in these structured interactions is recognized implicitly in textbooks and other sources of interviewing advice. Interviewers are advised to use a structured series of questions to avoid "getting off track" and to minimize conversation that might be biasing or discriminatory. On the other hand, the dangers of plan rigidity are recognized when interviewers are advised to be flexible enough to ask unplanned questions, probe unclear answers, and respond to inquiries. Interviewees are warned against allowing interviewers to completely determine the interviewing plan. They are advised to contribute to the interview agenda, be prepared with their own set of questions, and make certain they steer the conversation toward some topics and away from others. "Steering" is a means of influencing the planning process.

Through *plan substitution*, interviewers can replace the interviewer's plan with one more to their own liking ("Before we start talking about objectives for this job, I'd like to take just a minute to review some of the details of my last position"). Plan substitutions generally require mutual consent about "where we are going" with the conversation, if only temporarily and at an abstract level. Once consent is obtained, the speaker is relatively free to fill in plan details. In this case, the speaker may talk at length about his or her last position or content him- or herself with a relatively abstract rendering of the major points.

Discovering Plans

To remain relevant in conversation, particularly if one is contemplating a topic change, speakers must determine the plans of their partner. Where is the conversation headed? What steps is he or she likely to take to get to that future point? At which intermediary step can I intervene or "branch" to a step in my own plans? Plan recognition is necessary for predicting the conversational future and finding a path that allows one to move conversation to desired outcomes. Waldron and Applegate (1994) found that those who accommodated the plans of others, verbally and cognitively, were more effective in achieving mutually agreeable solutions in verbal disagreements. Plan recognition is the first critical step in the process of reacting to and accommodating to the plans of others. But the role of planning in coordination is obvious not just in plan recognition itself but in the metacommunication used by interactants to signal plans. The notion of "intended plan recognition" (Cohen, Perrault, & Allen, 1981; Zachary, 1990) implicates not just the receiver, but the speaker in the recognition process. Speakers signal their intentions to receivers and then assume that the speaker will recognize the plan and "fill in" the necessary actions. Consider a situation where two colleagues are speaking about a coworker. The speaker signals the listener to shut the door. The speaker assumes his or her plan to "tell secrets" about the coworker will be recognized by the listener. Having signaled the intention, the speaker can assume with some confidence that the listener will cooperate with the plan.

In turn, the listener can predict some of the conversational actions that may be forthcoming at both nonverbal (lowering of voices) and verbal (revelation of a shocking disclosure about the coworker) levels and plan a set of responses (a look of surprise; an exclamation like, "I can't believe it!"). The listener may prepare alternative plans too (e.g., a method of indicating discomfort at the telling secrets behind close doors). The point is that "advance notice" about plans allows both parties to gain some purchase on the evolving goals of the conversation and to reallocate cognitive resources to the task of creating and selecting subplans. This helps them coordinate their behaviors in the conversational future. The plan discovery and recognition process deserves further exploration by message-production researchers. How are plan intentions signaled? How confident are listeners in their interpretations of speaker plans? How confident are speakers that listeners will recognize their intentions? How do speakers and listeners "check" the accuracy of these interpretations? How does the degree of confidence associated with these estimates limit or enhance the interactants' ability to coordinate their plans and behaviors?

Plan Appropriation

It is tempting for cognitive researchers to view the process of plan coordination as simply a matter of uncovering the goals and plans existing within the heads of interactants. From this overly simple cognitive perspective communication is simply a matter of one speaker understanding the mental model of the other and then adapting his or her behavior to that model. However, this approach likely overestimates the degree to which individuals actually possess clearly articulated goals and plans which can be "discovered." Moreover, it focuses our attention inside the head rather than on social interaction, where plans are actually manifested. As Newman (1990) has explained, interaction is partially a process of deciding what our actions mean. Actions that I initiate in conversation with no apparent purpose may come to have meaning (or very new meaning) as they are incorporated into the plans of my partner. One process by which my partner redefines my actions by incorporating them into his or her plans is plan appropriation.

Newman (1990), whose planning work is partly concerned with the processes by which plans are altered through education and socialization, describes a plan-appropriation episode observed in a preschool. The example will be familiar to parents of young children. As part of their daily activity, the children were given crayons and paper and encouraged to draw. Most children were at the stage where this activity involved random doodling with little real intention of drawing a "picture" in the adult sense of the word. Newman observed the classroom teachers' interaction with these young students as they finished their drawing activity.

> Since the children did not have a plan from the beginning there was always an interesting negotiation between the teacher and the children as to whether the drawing was finished. Children would announce they were finished when other more interesting activities caught their attention . . . She would have a little discussion about what they had done before hanging it on the wall. She would generally initiate the discussion with an open-ended question, like "Can you tell me about your picture?" and follow up with more specific questions like, "What is this ?" The children would answer with a more simple description

like, "That's a moon" . . . Then the teacher would compliment the child for a
nice drawing and write his or her name on it. (p. 90)

Through this process of interacting with the child, the teacher in essence
appropriates the child's activities into her own planning scheme. Through
her questions, pointings, and compliments the teacher behaves toward the
child *as if* the child were truly drawing a picture. The child's initial behavior
appears to be planless, or at least oriented to goals other than picture-drawing. Yet, through repeated exposure to the teachers' postdrawing interactions, the child will probably learn to organize these activities as a picture-
drawing plan. More important, this scenario demonstrates that the actions
of children (and perhaps adults) can be incorporated in conversational
plans without the kind of conscious intent that we often associate with
planning. Too, the picture-drawing discussions speak directly to the social
nature of plans, in that the teacher is conveying societal expectations about
the structure of discussions on creating pictures. The young student learns
this set of conversational conventions implicitly, in the course of preschool
activities explicitly designed to encourage drawing and creative expression.

An analogous situation can be seen in adult conversations, where one
interactant unobtrusively steers conversation toward goals of which the
other is unaware. For example, one class of interactions involves the acquisition of social information that the partner is reluctant to provide (Kellermann & Berger, 1984; Cegala, 1981; Waldron, 1990). Depending on the context, conversations about religion, politics, sex, or perhaps one's salary,
qualify. Particularly (but not exclusively) among less intimate partners,
conversations about these topics are potentially face threatening, because
unwelcome questions have the potential to create embarrassment or overt
conflict. Yet at times such socially sensitive information is likely to be
desired by one's conversational partner. Perhaps a coworker of equal rank
to you feels he or she is underpaid. To confirm this suspicion, the coworker
must learn your salary. Company policy and your own modesty discourage
discussion of such financial details. How does the coworker obtain the
information without causing undue embarrassment to you? I have studied
the plans and information-seeking strategies used in situations like these
(Waldron, 1990; Cegala & Waldron, 1992) and found that skilled information
seekers construct fairly sophisticated plans which involve gradual manipulation of conversational topics.

Perhaps your coworker initiates the salary conversation by commenting
on recent newspaper coverage of a labor strike at a nearby manufacturing
plant. This leads to a discussion of worker's rights. You comment on the
growing divide between the salaries of CEOs and workers. This leads to a
discussion of injustice generally and the need for more competitive salaries
in your profession. Ultimately, the coworker discloses a feeling of bitterness

about his or her own salary and confides the yearly amount to you. Riding an emotional wave of worker solidarity and responding to an obligation to self-disclose, you exclaim: "That *is* low!", and reveal your own salary. Your coworker has obtained the needed information.

In this scenario, you launched into a conversation that you perceived to be idle chitchat. But your small talk was appropriated by the partner in the interests of obtaining a goal you did not know existed. Although this example seems far-fetched and perhaps unrealistically manipulative, it may be that the appropriation of conversational plans is a characteristic of successful strategic communication. It appears to be standard procedure in some kinds of occupational talk. Conversations with salespersons on used car lots come immediately to mind. The prevalence of plan appropriation, and the conversational tactics which allow it to happen are worth further investigation.

Plan Interpretation and Reinterpretation

Plans are sometimes easily interpreted and monolithic. At other times they are less easily deciphered, due either to the unintended ambiguities of language or by design of the speaker (Newman & Bruce, 1986). As evidence of the latter case, we know that our conversational partners sometimes hide their plans, perhaps to avoid culpability for their actions. A colleague recently related to me an account of a phone conversation that she had with a man she had met only briefly at a party. He had called a day or two afterward, to relate (apparently) that he had a good time at the party and to ask if she too had enjoyed it. Surprised at the call, uncertain about the man's name, but fairly sure he had been wearing a wedding ring at the party, my colleague answered in positive but vague terms. The caller proceeded to ask if he might "drop by" her office if he "happened" to be in her area in the near future. Puzzled, my colleague remained noncommittal as the phone conversation came to an awkward end. Afterward she spoke with several friends and coworkers to determine what the caller was "up to." Had the caller been asking to get better acquainted in a potentially romantic way or was he simply networking in an attempt to develop a business relationship? Or was some other plan afoot? The process of discerning the plans of others is partially a process of cognitive guesswork (Hewes, 1995). But, the detective work is often social, as past conversations are recounted by the participants or related to others, and actions are reinterpreted in light of newly discovered knowledge or motives. The search for the "real meaning" of past conversations is in effect an attempt to reevaluate our own goals and plans and those of our partners. The message processes used in plan discernment, the contexts which trigger plan reevaluation, the consequences when interactants reinterpret the plans of their conversational partners all require additional study. The extent to which this process of plan discernment and reevaluation is familiar (and, to me at least, it seems quite familiar) is evidence that we can participate in the plans of others but not be fully aware of them. More simply, planning is a process partially out of our control. Thus in searching beyond the cognitive processes of individuals for where planning really "is" we are encouraged to look at interaction itself.

CONCLUSION

In this chapter I have attempted to review three traditions of planning research that I see as particularly relevant to theories of message production. I have ordered them in terms of the degree to which they admit social processes, more specifically, conversational processes, as a central concern in their theorizing and methodological choice-making. I believe that all three traditions have contributed and will continue to contribute significantly to our understanding of how conversational behavior is produced. In using much of this space to advocate a move to more interactive models of planning, I have paid too little attention to the many researchers who have contributed meaningfully within more traditional planning paradigms. The planning literature is vast and I hope the reader takes seriously my references to more thorough treatments of the topic. In pushing cognitive communication researchers to study more closely the role of dyadic planning during conversation, I am directing them to ground that is already partially occupied. Discourse analysts inside the communication discipline (McClaughlin, 1984) and in related fields (e.g., Hobbs & Evans, 1980) have long explored the role of plans in organizing conversation. However, the closer linkage between cognitive and discourse theorists is likely to yield improved theorizing about how patterns of conversational behavior are produced and maintained.

As I have suggested previously (Waldron, 1995), now is an opportune moment for cognitively oriented communication researchers to ask some of the "hard questions" about the role of planning and other processes in interaction. This will require us (and our journals) to experiment with methods which better capture the complexities of cognition in process. In selecting research questions, choosing methods, and interpreting our results we will do well to question our assumption that communication is *primarily* accounted for by the properties of cognitive systems (McPhee, 1995), without discounting the significant contributions made by cognitive theorists thus far. Cognitive phenemona, like plans, are themselves shaped and even created through socialization and communication processes. They are outcomes of communication as well as antecedents to it. My own preference is that we study cognition as a means of confirming and extending communication theory. Doing so might encourage us to conduct more studies on the effects of communication on planning and fewer on the effects of planning on communication. Whatever our course, the widespread and interdisciplinary influence of planning approaches is evidence of their value in explaining how people (and machines) draw upon past experiences to facilitate their progress toward future goals. Given that conversation is a primary site for this integration of past and future, it seems highly likely that planning theory will figure prominently in our efforts to understand it more completely.

REFERENCES

Applegate, J. A. (1990). Constructs and communication: A pragmatic integration. In G. Neimeyer & R. Neimeyer (Eds.), *Advances in personal construct psychology* (Vol. 1, pp. 203–230). Greenwich, CT: JAI.

Baxter, L. E. (1984). An investigation of compliance gaining as politeness. *Human Communication Research, 10,* 427–456.

Baxter, L. (1992). Interpersonal communication as dialogue: A response to the "social approaches" forum. *Communication Theory, 2,* 330–336.

Berger, C. R. (1988a). Planning, affect, and social action generation. In L. Donohew, H. E. Sypher, & E. T. Higgins (Eds.), *Communication, social cognition, and affect* (pp. 93–115). Hillsdale, NJ: Lawrence Erlbaum Associates.

Berger, C. R. (1988b, May). *Communication plans and communicative performance.* Paper presented at the annual conference of the International Communication Association, New Orleans.

Berger, C. R . (1995). A plan-based approach to strategic communication. In D. E. Hewes (Ed.), *Cognitive bases of interpersonal communication* (pp. 141–180). Hillsdale, NJ: Lawrence Erlbaum Associates.

Berger, C. R., & Bell, R. A. (1988). Plans and the initiation of social relationships. *Human Communication Research, 15,* 217–235.

Berger, C. R., & Calabrese, R. J. (1975). Some explorations in initial interaction and beyond: Toward a developmental theory of interpersonal communication. *Human Communication Research , 1,* 99–112.

Berger, C. R., & Jordan, J. M. (1992). Planning sources, planning difficulty, and verbal fluency. *Communication Monographs, 59,* 130–149.

Berger, C. R., Karol, S. H., & Jordan, J. M. (1989). When a lot of knowledge is a dangerous thing: The debilitating effects of plan complexity on verbal fluency. *Human Communication Research, 16,* 91–119.

Berger, C. R., Knowlton, S. W., & Abrahams, M. F. (1996). The hierarchy principle in strategic communication. *Communication Theory, 6,* 111–142.

Brown, P., & Levinson, S. (1978). Universals of language usage: Politeness phenomena. In E. N. Goody (Ed.), *Questions and politeness: Strategies in social interaction* (pp. 56–289). Cambridge, England: Cambridge University Press.

Bruce, B. (1983). Plans and discourse. *Text, 3,* 253–259.

Bruce, B. C., & Newman, D. (1978). Interacting plans. *Cognitive Science, 2,* 196–233.

Cawsey, A. (1993). Planning interactive explanations. *International Journal of Man–Machine Studies, 38,* 169–199.

Cegala, D. J. (1981). Interaction involvement: A cognitive dimension of communication competence. *Communication Education, 30,* 109–121.

Cegala, D. J., & Waldron, V. R. (1992). A study of the relationship between communicative performance and conversation participants' thoughts. *Communication Studies, 43,* 105–125.

Clark, R. A., & Delia, J. G. (1979). Topoi and rhetorical competence. *The Quarterly Journal of Speech, 65,* 187–206.

Cohen, P., Perrault, C., & Allen, J. (1981). Beyond question-answering (Rep. No. 4644). Cambridge, MA: Bolt, Beranek, and Newman, Inc.

Craig, R. T., Tracy, K., & Spisak, F. (1986). The discourse of requests: Assessment of a politeness approach. *Human Communication Research, 12,* 437–468.

Dillard, J. P. (1990). A goal-driven model of interpersonal influence. In J. P. Dillard (Ed.), *Seeking compliance: The production of interpersonal influence messages* (pp. 41–56). Scottsdale, AZ: Gorsuch Scarisbrick.

Dreyfus, H. L., & Dreyfus, H. L. (1986). *Mind over machine: The power of human intuition and expertise in the era of the computer.* New York: Free Press.

Edwards, R., Honeycutt, J. M., & Zagacki, K. S. (1988). Imagined interaction as an element of social cognition. *Western Journal of Speech Communication, 52,* 23–45.

Galambos, J. A., Abelson, R. P., & Black, J. B. (1986). Goals and plans. In J. A. Galambos, R. P. Abelson, & J. B. Black (Eds.), *Knowledge structures* (pp. 101–102). Hillsdale, NJ: Lawrence Erlbaum Associates.

Gibbs, R., & Mueller, R. (1990). Conversation as coordinated, cooperative interaction. In S. P. Robertson, W. Zachary, & J. B. Black (Eds.), *Cognition, computing, and cooperation* (pp. 95–114). Norwood, NJ: Ablex.

Goffman, E. (1959). *The presentation of self in everyday life.* Garden City, NY: Doubleday Anchor.

Greene, J. O. (1995). An action-assembly perspective on verbal and nonverbal message production: A dancer's message unveiled. In D. E. Hewes (Ed.), *Cognitive bases of interpersonal communication* (pp. 51–86). Hillsdale, NJ: Lawrence Erlbaum Associates.

Greeno, J. (Ed.). (1993). Situated action [Special issue]. *Cognitive Science, 17*(1).

Grice, H. P. (1975). Logic and conversation. In P. Cole & J. Morgan (Eds.), *Syntax and semantics: Volume 3, Speech acts* (pp. 41–58). New York: Academic Press.

Hammond, K. (1989). *Case-based planning.* New York: Academic Press.

Hample, D., & Dallinger, S. M. (1987). Individual differences in cognitive editing standards. *Human Communication Research, 14,* 123–144.

Hayes-Roth, B., & Hayes-Roth, F. (1979). A cognitive model of planning. *Cognitive Science, 3,* 275–310.

Hewes, D. E. (1995). Cognitive processing of problematic messages: Reinterpreting to "unbias" texts. In D. E. Hewes (Ed.), *Cognitive bases of interpersonal communication* (pp. 113–140). Hillsdale, NJ: Lawrence Erlbaum Associates.

Hobbs, J. R., & Evans, D. A. (1980). Conversation as planned behavior. *Cognitive Science, 4,* 349–377.

Kellermann, K. (1992). Communication: Inherently strategic and primarily automatic. *Communication Monographs, 59,* 288–300.

Kellermann, K., & Berger, C. R. (1984). Affect and the acquisition of social information: Sit back, relax, and tell me about yourself. In R. Bostrum (Ed.), *Communication yearbook 8* (pp. 412–445). Newbury Park, CA: Sage.

Krietler, S., & Krietler, H. (1987). Plans and planning: Their motivational and cognitive antecedents. In S. L. Friedman, E. Skolnick, & R. R. Cocking (Eds.), *Blueprints for thinking: The role of planning in cognitive development* (pp. 110–178). New York: Cambridge University Press.

Lim, T., & Bowers, J. H. (1991). Facework: Solidarity, approbation, and tact. *Human Communication Research, 17,* 415–450.

McClaughlin, M. L. (1984). *Conversation: How talk is organized.* Beverly Hills, CA: Sage.

McPhee, R. D. (1995). Cognitive perspectives on communication: Interpretative and critical responses. In D. E. Hewes (Ed.), *Cognitive bases of interpersonal communication* (pp. 225–246). Hillsdale, NJ: Lawrence Erlbaum Associates.

Miller, G. A., Galanter, E., & Pribram, K. H. (1960). *Plans and the structure of behavior.* New York: Holt, Rinehart & Winston.

Newman, D. (1986). The role of mutual knowledge in perspective-taking development. *Developmental Review, 6,* 122–145.

Newman, D. (1990). Cognitive change by appropriation. In S. P. Robertson, W. Zachary, & J. B. Black (Eds.), *Cognition, computing, and cooperation* (pp. 84–94). Norwood, NJ: Ablex.

Newman, D., & Bruce, B. (1986). Interpretation and manipulation in human plans. *Discourse Processes, 9,* 149–196.

Ponssard, J. (1990). Self enforceable paths in extensive form games: A behavioral approach based on interactivity. *Theory and Decision, 29,* 69–83.

Robertson, S. P., & Zachary, W. (1990). Conclusion: Outline for a field of cooperative systems. In S. P. Robertson, W. Zachary, & J. B. Black (Eds.), *Cognition, computing, and cooperation* (pp. 399–414). Norwood, NJ: Ablex.

Robertson, S. P., Zachary, W., & Black, J. B. (Eds.). (1990). *Cognition, computing, and cooperation.* Norwood, NJ: Ablex.

Sacerodoti, E. D. (1977). *A structure for plans and behavior.* Amsterdam: Elsevier North-Holland.

Stefik, M. (1981a). Planning with constraints (MOLGEN: Part 1). *Artificial Intelligence, 16,* 111–139.

Stefik, M. (1981b). Planning and meta-planning (MOLGEN: Part 2). *Artificial Intelligence, 16,* 141–169.

Suchman, L. A. (1990). What is human-machine interaction? In S. P. Robertson, W. Zachary, & J. B. Black (Eds.), *Cognition, computing, and cooperation* (pp. 25–55). Norwood, NJ: Ablex.

Waldron, V. R. (1990). Constrained rationality: Situational influences on information acquisition plans and tactics. *Communication Monographs, 57,* 184–201.

Waldron, V. R. (1993, February). *Does planning payoff? Information acquisition success in peer discussions of AIDS.* Paper presented at the annual conference of the Western States Communication Association, Albuquerque, NM.

Waldron, V. R. (1995). Is the "Golden Age of Cognition" losing its luster? Toward a requirement-centered approach. In B. Burleson (Ed.), *Communication yearbook 18* (pp. 180–200). Thousand Oaks, CA: Sage.

Waldron, V. R. (1996). *Cognitive shifts during conversation: Tracking changes in the relative importance of conversational objectives and plans.* Arizona State University West. Manuscript submitted for review.

Waldron, V. R., & Applegate, J. A. (1994). Interpersonal construct differentiation and conversational planning: An examination of two cognitive accounts for the production of competent verbal disagreement tactics. *Human Communication Research, 21,* 3–35.

Waldron, V. R., Caughlin, J., & Jackson, D. (1995). Talking specifics: Facilitating effects of planning on AIDS talk in peer dyads. *Health Communication, 7,* 179–204.

Waldron, V. R., & Cegala, D. J. (1992). Assessing conversational cognition: Levels of cognitive theory and associated methodological requirements. *Human Communication Research, 18,* 599–622.

Waldron, V. R., Cegala, D. J., Sharkey, W. F., & Teboul, B. (1990). Cognitive and tactical dimensions of goal management. *Journal of Language and Social Psychology, 9,* 101–118.

Wilensky, R. (1983). *Planning and understanding: A computational approach to human reasoning.* Reading, MA: Addison-Wesley.

Zachary, W. W. (1990). Describing cooperation: Afterword to section I. In S. P. Robertson, W. Zachary, & J. B. Black (Eds.), *Cognition, computing, and cooperation* (pp. 115–120). Norwood, NJ: Ablex.

10

PRODUCING MESSAGES UNDER UNCERTAINTY

Charles R. Berger
University of California, Davis

Many have noted the seeming contradiction between the notions that communication between people is: (a) virtually automatic and effortless, and frequently carried out both fluently and successfully with only minimal forethought and planning, and (b) sometimes the product of considerable conscious deliberation, calculation and effort (Kellermann, 1992; Langer, 1978, 1992; Reddy, 1979). Reddy (1979) has argued that the English language itself biases people to think and talk about the process of communication in ways that suggest feelings and ideas are put into words that serve as the vessels to carry meaning from the head of one person to the head of another. This *conduit metaphor,* as Reddy terms it, implies that communication is automatic and effortless and when it fails, it is primarily the message producer's responsibility. It is message creators who fail to "put their thoughts into words," rather than recipients who fail to understand.

As an alternative to the *conduit metaphor*, Reddy argues that the *toolmaker's paradigm,* coupled with the postulate of radical subjectivity, provides a more useful and realistic framework from which to view communication. Under this rubric, he likens communicators to individuals living in a hypothetical primitive world with no formal language. These beings live in quite different physical environments and cannot see each other, but by means of a special device they can exchange rough sketches of implements they have constructed individually and found useful in their daily lives. The individuals inhabiting this communicative milieu must struggle to understand what it is their counterparts are trying to communicate to them, and they must, by necessity, rely heavily upon inferences both to interpret the strange symbols that appear on the sketches they receive and to fill in the many gaps left in these strange, opaque messages. When communication fails in this world, the message recipient is also strongly implicated in the problem. Within this perspective, the interpretative acumen of the message receiver assumes center-stage.

At least three important implications about the relationships among cognitive processes, message production, and communication flow from Reddy's analysis. First, within the context of the toolmaker's paradigm, uncertainty is endemic to the system. Message generators learn from their experience that message receivers are apt to have difficulty interpreting the sketches they send; consequently, message producers must pay very close attention to how they code their conceptions of their worlds. On the one hand, they must anticipate the problems message receivers will have understanding them; while on the other hand, their knowledge of their fellow interlocutors is extremely limited, including their knowledge of the symbols that message recipients will find understandable. On the other side of this communication equation, message recipients know they will be confronted with difficult-to-understand marks on the pieces of paper they receive. They must be prepared to deal with considerable ambiguity while trying to decode these symbols. Within this world, these chronic and fluctuating states of uncertainty suggest the potential viability of the assertion: *The probability of perfect communication is zero.*

Second, in order for communication to occur at all under the toolmaker's paradigm, both interactants must generate internal representations of each other's knowledge of both the environment within which they exist and the code systems they use to represent these environments. Without these cognitive representations, all is lost. Under the conduit metaphor, such internal representations are not prerequisites for communication because words themselves carry emotions, ideas, and thoughts from the message producer to the message consumer.

Finally, the toolmaker's paradigm implies that the cognitive structures and processes underlying the production of communicative action may be considerably more complex than those implied by production models that posit the automatic activation of such knowledge structures as procedural records, scripts, and plans as guides to action production. Under conditions of uncertainty, the mindless activation of such knowledge structures by goals and the resulting deployment of action sequences guided by these knowledge structures could lead to potentially disastrous consequences. Clearly, realistic models of message production must take into account the cognitive and communication processes by which these communicative uncertainties are recognized and dealt with by message producers. Given

Reddy's conception of communication, it seems foolhardy to assume that the cognitive processes underlying message production unfold as if message producers are absolutely certain of the effects their messages are likely to produce in those who receive them. In the remainder of this chapter, I focus primarily on the first of these implications, with special emphasis on the uncertainties that may bedevil message producers and how producers may cope with these uncertainties; however, in considering these issues, by necessity, the second and third implications will also receive some attention.

MESSAGE PLANNING IN UNCERTAIN COGNITIVE WORLDS

Although communication situations can be ordered with respect to the degree to which message producers are uncertain about what messages might be effective at accomplishing their instrumental and communication goals and doing so in a socially appropriate manner (Berger & Kellermann, 1983, 1994; Kellermann & Berger, 1984), even in the most routine social encounters involving individuals who are very well acquainted with each other, the taken-for-granted substrate of shared knowledge underlying their relationship may be disrupted. Individuals, their relationships with each other, and the contexts within which they interact are dynamic to the point that messages that may have been produced under conditions of considerable certitude at an earlier point in time may now be generated within a highly uncertain social interaction matrix. In fact, dramatic changes from what were predictable to what are now quite unpredictable interaction circumstances may present among the most challenging message production problems to communicators (Planalp & Honeycutt, 1985; Planalp, Rutherford, & Honeycutt, 1988).

Having acknowledged the fact that even mundane social encounters, that on the surface may seem to be highly predictable, may in fact become sites for uncertainty-ridden social interactions, attention now turns to an explication of uncertainty sources and how uncertainty may impinge on some of the cognitive processes subserving message production. In the latter section of this chapter, hedges for dealing with these uncertainties at the level of social action are considered, as well as the conditions under which these hedging devices are likely to be deployed.

Sources of Uncertainty

It is necessary to delineate specific sources of uncertainty that message producers may have to confront before considering how uncertainty influences message production processes. This is the case because uncertainty with respect to different aspects of the communication context and the individuals participating in it may affect message production process in different ways and at different points. Berger (1995a) has suggested a number of such sources of uncertainty, each of which is considered only briefly here.

Precondition Uncertainty. Included under this general rubric are uncertainties that arise from judgments about the ability of the parties to the communication situation to meet the basic prerequisites for carrying out verbal interaction. For example, when individuals encounter each other for the first time, they may be unsure of the linguistic capabilities of their co-interactants. The physical appearance of others with whom one is about to interact or the context within which an initial encounter takes place may suggest that the individuals about to be addressed for the first time do not share one's language, thus creating a situation in which a basic precondition for verbal communication is not met. Furthermore, even after the interaction has commenced, individuals may be uncertain concerning the degree to which their interaction partners understand their language. Being able to render a fluent greeting in a foreign language provides precious little diagnostic information concerning the overall linguistic capabilities of the individual providing such a greeting. As the interaction unfolds, suspicions about the ability of one's interaction partner to follow what one is saying may come to the fore.

Even when individuals interact with those who share their first language, marked discrepancies in education may act to cue uncertainties about the abilities of individuals with less education to understand their more highly educated counterparts. Messages containing a copious number of arcane words that are responded to by blank looks may give rise to considerable uncertainty concerning the degree to which one's interaction partner is following what is being said. Even if general linguistic competence is granted, conversational topics dealing with narrow and highly technical issues that take place between individuals with very different levels of knowledge about the domain under discussion may also give rise to uncertainties about the degree to which one is being understood. Here the problem is not with one's linguistic competence per se but instead concerns the degree to which one possesses the knowledge to understand the concepts under consideration.

Goals and Plans. Many models of action production and speech production presuppose that individuals have instrumental and communication goals for which they strive during their interactions with others. No attempt is made here to deal systematically with the problem of where these goals arise from in the first place (Wilensky, 1983). Although postulating a goal or goals as a starting point for such models is an understandable and perhaps necessary convenience, in the hurly-burly of social interaction, the goals of interaction partners may not be at all clear. Since message comprehension and interpretation are partially based on inferences about the goals one's interaction partner is pursuing and the plans being used to pursue them (Green, 1989), uncertainty with respect to the goals and plans of interaction partners may make it problematic for message producers to set their own goals. Furthermore, even if message producers do not entertain high levels of uncertainty about their partners' goals, they may harbor considerable uncertainty about the plans their partners are employing to achieve them. Because goals and plans may be dynamic over the course of a given social encounter, certitude regarding the states of these entities at one point in time does not necessarily imply continuing predictability over the course of the interaction. Goals and plans may transmute in unpredictable ways as interaction unfolds, leaving message generators bemused as a result (Berger, 1995b).

Affective States. In a wide variety of social interaction contexts, the current emotional state of one's message target may exert considerable influence on the kinds of messages one directs toward that individual. Under certain circumstances, for instance requesting a favor, an assessment leading to the inference that the target is not in a "good mood" at the present time may lead the potential requester to abandon the goal of making the request until the target is in a "better mood." Uncertainty with respect to the affective state of the potential recipient of a request may present significant message formulation problems to the person making the request. These problems may affect the content and structure of the messages produced by the requester, and they may determine whether the interaction itself continues.

Part of the reticence displayed by individuals to deliver bad news to others (the MUM effect) may in part be due to the fact that not knowing exactly the affective state of the potential recipient before the bad news is rendered makes it difficult for message producers to predict with any precision the recipient's affective state after the bad news is received (Tesser & Rosen, 1975). Of course, in this case the individual delivering the bad news knows that upon receiving it, the recipient very probably will experience negative affect, as the research reported on the MUM effect reveals; however, the open question for the message producer is just how much negative affect will be experienced by the recipient. Perhaps, a confident precommunication assessment of the recipient's affective state might provide some clues to answer this question, as the following conversational exchanges suggest:

Boss: How are you feeling today?
Employee: Fine.
Boss: Well, I'm sorry I have some bad news for you. Your job has been eliminated as of next month.

Perhaps, if the employee had responded "I'm feeling very badly today," the boss would have waited to deliver the bad news. If such relatively confident assessments are not possible, message producers may respond by shying away from delivering the bad news. Of course, individuals' answers to queries about their current affective states may not provide accurate information to message producers. Such stock responses as, "Oh, I'm fine" may frequently mask considerable emotional and physical discomfort, thus misleading message producers to predicate subsequent messages on inaccurate inferences. As noted in the case of goals and plans, affective states may also show considerable variation over the course of social interactions; consequently, the message producer's ability to track these state changes with varying degrees of certitude should impact message generation processes.

Uncertainty, Message Planning, and Message Plans

Having stipulated some potential sources of uncertainty with which message producers might have to deal, attention turns to how these sources may impact on message production processes themselves. Specifically, the relationships between uncertainty and the plans that guide message production are examined, as well as potential links between uncertainty and a variety of planning processes. Uncertainty emanating from one or more of the sources delineated above may impact message production processes at many different points and in many different ways; however, these effects are beyond the scope of the present presentation.

A commonplace assumption of theories of human action in general and discourse and speech production in particular is that action and discourse are guided by plans (e.g., Alterman, 1988; Brand, 1984; Bratman, 1987, 1990; Butterworth, 1980; Butterworth & Goldman-Eisler, 1979; Hjelmquist, 1991; Hjelmquist & Gidlund, 1984; Hobbs & Evans, 1980; Kreitler & Kreitler, 1987; Levelt, 1989; Miller, Galanter, & Pribram, 1960; Pea & Hawkins, 1987; Read & Miller, 1989; Sacerdoti, 1977; Srull & Wyer, 1986; Waldron, 1990; Waldron & Applegate, 1994; Wilensky, 1983). Plans are presumed to be hierarchically organized cognitive representations of goal-directed action sequences (Berger, 1995b), and there is considerable evidence to support their psychological reality (Abbott & Black, 1986; Black & Bower, 1979, 1980; Bower, Black, & Turner, 1979; Cahill & Mitchell, 1987; Lichtenstein & Brewer, 1980; Seifert, Robertson, & Black, 1985). Within the context of theories of human action, plans generally are conceived of as guides to action rather than energizers or motivators of action (Brand, 1984), although some action philosophers have argued for the potential utility of viewing plans as revocable commitments to future action (Bratman, 1987, 1990).

Some theorists (Hammond, 1989a, 1989b) have suggested that frequently used plans, or "canned plans" are stored in memory and can be instantiated and tailored to fit particular circumstances as goals arise. Since plans are presumed to play a pivotal role in guiding action generation and discourse production, when the sources of uncertainty outlined above come into play, the planning processes and plans subserving message production should be affected. What might these effects entail? In answering this question the potential effects of uncertainty on planning processes are considered. Then, how plans themselves might be influenced by uncertainty is explicated.

Effects on Planning. A number of theorists have proposed a distinction between top-down and bottom-up planning (Berger, 1995b; Hayes-Roth & Hayes-Roth, 1979; Sacerdoti, 1977). Bottom-up planning processes are data-driven. Planners use current perceptual inputs to devise new plans or to alter extant ones. Planning proceeds from concrete to abstract. By contrast, in the top-down planning mode, planners deduce progressively more specific actions from abstract plan elements. Given uncertainty arising from any of the sources identified previously, it is reasonable to postulate that under most conditions message producers would become more vigilant with respect to the target of their messages. Monitoring the message target more closely in order to try to reduce these uncertainties would be one course of action to follow. Being uncertain about the linguistic/knowledge status of one's target, their goals/plans, or their affective state should act to increase the data intake of the message producer. As a consequence, planning processes should be influenced in the direction suggested by the following proposition:

Proposition 1: *As uncertainty concerning the message target's linguistic/knowledge status, goals/plans, or affective state increases, planning should become increasingly data-driven or bottom-up.*

The implication of this proposition is that when uncertainties are assuaged, which they never are completely, individuals will plan from abstract levels downward toward concrete levels of plan hierarchies. Moreover, since the top-down/bottom-up distinction defines a continuum rather than two independent categories, much of the time both processes are being carried out simultaneously and the difference is one of emphasis.

Hayes-Roth and Hayes-Roth (1979) have argued that frequently human planning follows neither a deductive nor an inductive reasoning pattern. Instead, their observations of individuals planning to optimize the efficiency with which a person might accomplish a series of errands in a hypothetical small town led them to propose that planners frequently devise plans in an opportunistic manner. Rather than systematically deducing concrete actions from a set of more abstract act types, as a top-down planner would, or induce a set of abstract act types by observing concrete actions, planners may become aware of certain features of the environment that can be incorporated in their plans at various levels of abstraction in order for them to achieve their goals. Given one or more of the uncertainties with respect to a message target described earlier and the increased vigilance these uncertainty sources are likely to induce in the message producer, the following proposition concerning the degree to which planning is carried out opportunistically is warranted:

> Proposition 2: *As uncertainty concerning the message target's linguistic/knowledge status, goals/plans, or affective state increases, planning will become increasingly opportunistic.*

Again, the implication of this proposition is that message production at reduced levels of uncertainty about the message target should exhibit less evidence of opportunism.

Planning can be carried out at both conscious and nonconscious levels, and a number of theorists have suggested that when routine performance is disrupted, individuals become more mindful of the details of their actions (Langer, 1978, 1992; Vallacher & Wegner, 1985). Because, by definition, uncertainty is disruptive of performance and potential performance, it is reasonable to assume that uncertainty also affects the amount of conscious planning. The assumption of increased vigilance in response to increased uncertainty and the previous two propositions suggest the following proposition:

> Proposition 3: *As uncertainty concerning the message target's linguistic/knowledge status, goals/plans, or affective state increases, planning will become increasingly more conscious.*

As attentional resources are increasingly devoted to conscious planning processes, one would expect decrements in the degree to which action production in general and message production in particular can be monitored by the message producer. This decrease in monitoring should increase the frequency with which encoding disruptions appear in the verbal output of message producers preoccupied with planning activities. This relationship is expressed in the following corollary to Proposition 3:

> Corollary 1: *As uncertainty concerning the message target's linguistic/knowledge status, goals/plans, or affective state increases, increased conscious planning will produce increased rates of disruption in the production of communicative action.*

Here the term "communicative action" refers both to verbal and nonverbal productions. These disruptions might be manifested as vocalized and non-vocalized pauses in speech or false starts and lack of coordination between speech and gestures.

Effects on Plans. The questions addressed here concern how uncertainties with respect to preconditions, goals/plans, and affect influence attributes of plans themselves. An important plan attribute that has been the focus of considerable previous research is that of plan complexity (Berger, 1988a; Berger & Bell, 1988; Berger & diBattista, 1992; Kreitler & Kreitler, 1987; Waldron, 1990; Waldron & Applegate, 1994; Waldron, Caughlin, & Jackson, 1995). Plans can vary with respect to their complexity along at least two different dimensions: the number of distinct actions they encompass, and the degree to which they contain contingent actions (Berger, 1988a; Berger & Bell, 1988; Berger & diBattista, 1992). The first of these parameters has to do with the level of detail at which the plan is specified. Detailed plans contain more distinct actions than their less detailed counterparts; that is, the actions they contain are specified in greater detail. The contingency parameter indexes the degree to which the plan includes alternative courses of action that anticipate potential failure of specific actions contained in the plan. Detailed plans may or may not include numerous contingent actions, but increases in the level of plan detail and the number of contingencies included in a plan both serve to increase the plan's overall length. Furthermore, increases in one or both of these complexity parameters imply that the message producer is deploying more cognitive resources in the direction of message planning. With respect to the impact of uncertainty on the complexity of plans, it is necessary to consider each uncertainty source separately, since uncertainty emanating from different sources will have differential effects on the two plan parameters identified here.

Uncertainties surrounding the linguistic and/or knowledge capabilities of one's conversational partner are likely to deflect message producers away from primary and secondary instrumental and communicative goals with which they may have entered the interaction. Approaching a stranger to make a request only to find that the individual addressed does not speak one's language or possess the requisite knowledge to understand the request, forces message producers to redefine their initial goals and plans, if only temporarily, assuming, of course, that requesters choose to continue to purse their goals. Granting this assumption, the requester may try to assess the competence level of the requestee or focus on the goal of being understood before returning to the initial goals of the conversation. These diversions from the initial focus of the interaction should serve to deflect attention away from formulation of the message plans that were to be used to pursue the original goals. Consequently, the complexity of these initial plans should be undermined, as suggested in the following two propositions:

Proposition 4: *Increases in precondition uncertainty will lead to reductions in the level of detail of message plans designed to reach initial instrumental and communication goals.*

Proposition 5: *Increases in precondition uncertainty will lead to reductions in the*
number of contingent actions included in message plans designed to reach initial
instrumental and communication goals.

Of course, once message producers have obtained what they consider
to be reasonable assessments of the linguistic competence and knowledge
levels of their co-interlocutors, they may return to their original interaction
goals and message plans and elaborate them more fully. This elaborative
process might increase the complexity of plans. However, it is also possible
that the results of these competence assessments might induce producers
to alter significantly their prior goals and plans in the opposite direction.

Although the discussion of precondition uncertainty has focused on linguistic competence and knowledge, there are other preconditions to interaction that may influence both goals and plans. These preconditions may
involve attributes of the communication situation itself. Recently, I watched
a university provost squirm when he realized that two, instead of one, new
department chairs named "Berger" (although the second new chair was
actually named "Burger"), had been invited to the same lunch with him, as
part of his "get to know the new chairs" lunch series. The provost repeatedly
assured us that this was a "clerical error" (which it very likely was) and that
we would each have our "individual lunch" with him sometime later in the
academic year! Obviously, the simultaneous presence of two chairs from
different departments precluded the airing of certain issues specific to each
department. The provost was obviously well aware of this fact, as were we.
All of us had to alter or abandon certain goals and plans and formulate new
ones to deal with this unanticipated contingency. As a consequence, the
entire discussion focused on general, university-wide issues, and no depart-
ment-specific problems were broached.

For purposes of the present discussion, the effects of goal and plan
uncertainty on plan complexity must be considered separately since there
is reason to believe that these uncertainty sources are likely to affect message plan complexity in different ways. The effects of goal uncertainty are
considered first. Uncertainty with respect to the goals of one's interaction
partner should be especially discombobulating to message producers. As
noted previously, students of discourse understanding have argued strongly
that inferences concerning the goals and plans of individuals from whom
one is receiving messages play a vital role in the comprehension of those
messages (Green, 1989). Consequently, uncertainty about a conversation
partner's goals should undermine the ability of the message producers to
understand them.

Assuming that the message producers in question are seeking goals that
are predicated on but transcend the goal of understanding their partner's
discourse, being faced with the problem of understanding what one's inter-

action partner is seeking to achieve in the interaction should deflect attention away from these more regnant goals. Thus, assuming that message producers entered the interaction with relatively well articulated goals and message plans to achieve them, failure to understand the goals of the partner should undermine the complexity of the message producer's message plans for achieving these initial goals. These relationships are articulated in the following two propositions:

> Proposition 6: *Increases in goal uncertainty will lead to reductions in the level of detail of message plans designed to reach initial instrumental and communication goals.*

> Proposition 7: *Increases in goal uncertainty will lead to reductions in the number of contingent actions included in message plans designed to reach initial instrumental and communication goals.*

Again, using a variety of means, message producers may reduce their uncertainties about their co-interlocutors' goals (Berger, 1987; Berger & Bradac, 1982; Berger & Gudykunst, 1991). Depending on what message producers are able to find out about their co-interactants goals, they may elaborate, simplify, or completely abandon their initial message plans, and they may alter or abandon their initial goals.

Message producers may be quite certain of their co-interlocutors' goals but yet harbor considerable uncertainty about the plans their partners are using to pursue their goals. Given the postulate that plans are indexed in memory partially by the goals individuals are seeking to achieve (Hammond, 1989a, 1989b), certainty about one's own goals and the goals of one's interaction partner should activate a message plan for achieving one's goals at some level of abstraction. However, because of the uncertainties associated with the interaction partner's plan, message producers should have difficulties formulating plans with high levels of detail. Moreover, Bratman (1987, 1990) has argued that it is not rational to devise detailed plans when uncertainty is high. By so doing, one increases the chances of wasting energy if detailed plans, so developed, become obsolete when the plans of others become known. This line of reasoning suggests the following proposition:

> Proposition 8: *Increases in plan uncertainty will lead to reductions in the level of detail of message plans designed to reach initial instrumental and communication goals.*

Although it can be argued that detailed planning under conditions of high plan uncertainty has the appearance of being nonrational, this line of argument loses force when applied to the domain of contingent actions. Given that a plan has been instantiated because interactants' goals are clear, it seems perfectly reasonable that a message producer would devise message plans that contain contingencies to deal with potential actions that are part of the interaction plans of the producer's partner. Contingent actions are a potential hedge against the vagaries of the planned but the still unmanifested actions of one's partner. Consequently, in contrast to the previous proposition, Proposition 9 suggests:

> Proposition 9: *Increases in plan uncertainty will lead to increases in the number of contingent actions included in message plans designed to reach initial instrumental and communication goals.*

The divergent predictions offered by Propositions 8 and 9 and the findings of at least two studies (Berger & Bell, 1988; Berger & diBattista, 1992) suggest the wisdom of differentiating between plan detail and plan contingencies rather than conflating them into the broader construct of "plan complexity." In both of these studies, near zero correlations were obtained between measures of plan detail and plan contingencies, and, not surprisingly, the two parameters behaved quite differently with respect to a number of independent variables included in the studies.

Developing contingent plans online, as interactions unfold, is a potentially demanding cognitive activity. Communication contexts vary considerably with respect to the velocity with which goals and plans contained in message plans are acted out. Contexts in which there is considerable urgency surrounding the interaction may dampen or eliminate opportunities for message producers to incorporate contingencies into their message plans, even though they might wish to do so. Consequently, the relationship between plan uncertainty and the amount of contingent planning posited in Proposition 9 could be attenuated when individuals' interactions are hurried.

Uncertainty with regard to the affective state of one's cointeractant should also impact on the degree to which action plans are complex with respect to detail and the degree to which they contain contingent actions. The general problem high levels of affective state uncertainty present to message producers is deciding whether the target of strategic communicative efforts is in an emotional state that will lead to the achievement of focal goals; that is, is the target in a "receptive mood?" At this level of abstraction, the message producer's decision may be one of not initiating any goal-directed action at all. As a result, it would not seem reasonable for planners to devise highly detailed plans under conditions of elevated affective state uncertainty. Stated more formally:

> Proposition 10: *Increases in affective state uncertainty will lead to decreases in the amount of detail included in message plans designed to reach initial instrumental and communication goals.*

The rationale presented also suggests the following proposition regarding contingent planning:

> Proposition 11: *Increases in affective state uncertainty will lead to decreases in the number of contingent actions included in message plans designed to reach initial instrumental and communication goals.*

These two propositions cast the target's affective state in an enabling role with respect to other goals being pursued by the message producer. It is possible that in certain contexts, for example, offering comfort to a distressed other (Burleson, 1994), altering the affective state itself may become the focal goal. However, even in these cases, initial assessments of the target's affective state may be used to determine whether attempts will be undertaken to try to effect alterations in affect. The inability to glean confident assessments of the target's affective state may motivate message producers to abandon detailed and complex planning activity with respect to altering affect. Once a reasonably confident estimate of targets' emotional states has been achieved, however, more detailed planning may be undertaken.

HEDGING MESSAGE PLANS

The propositions just articulated concern the impact of various types of uncertainty on message planning and message plans. Although message producers may reduce their uncertainties about their co-interactants and be very adept at generating highly sophisticated message plans for achieving their goals, when it comes time to act on their plans, there always remains some residual measure of uncertainty with respect to the message target's states and the potential effectiveness and appropriateness of the actualized message plan. The question addressed here concerns devices message producers might employ to hedge against the downside risks of disseminating a particular message. One assumption underlying this discussion is that unanticipated positive outcomes do not need to be hedged against, but it is the potential unanticipated negative consequences that uncertain message producers must take into account. Clearly, if communication is as uncertain an enterprise as Reddy's (1979) toolmaker's paradigm suggests, there ought to be some fairly standard means message producers can use to minimize the downside risks associated with message dissemination.

One obvious way to attempt to reduce the uncertainties surrounding message production is to seek information about both one's co-interactants and the situation within which the interaction will be or is taking place. Considerable effort has already been expended to study the various strategies that individuals use to acquire information from others and the strategies that others may use to avoid revealing information about themselves (Berger, 1979, 1987, 1988b; Berger & Bradac, 1982; Berger & diBattista, 1992; Berger & Gudykunst, 1991; Berger & Kellermann, 1983, 1989, 1994; Kellermann & Berger, 1984).

This extensive literature is not reviewed here. However, as assiduously as these strategies might be deployed by message producers, the dynamic nature of social interaction and those engaged in it precludes perfect knowledge of co-interlocutors; therefore, hedging devices beyond information seeking must be invoked by message producers to minimize the considerable risks to their face, and in some cases to their limbs, that may be entailed by communicative miscalculations. It is to these devices that we now turn.

Hedging Devices

Framing. One way to avoid the potential perils of face loss, or worse, is to frame messages in such a way that their intent or goal can be denied or redefined after messages are disseminated, if denial or redefinition becomes necessary. Invoking this device might provoke utterances something like the following: "I didn't mean what you think I meant. In fact, I *really* meant this," or "I *really* meant the opposite." In the case of framing, in order for such an alternative interpretation of the message to be plausible however, the message producer must disseminate verbal or nonverbal cues with the message that set up the plausibility of such alternative interpretations. A situation in which such framing devices might be employed is that of asking someone for a date. In this case, the date-requester is faced with the problem of potential face loss if the party being asked out turns down the request. Several instances of employing humor as such a framing device to avoid potential embarrassment were encountered in a study that examined undergraduate students' date-request plans (Berger, 1988a). By delivering the date-request in a humorous way, date-requesters could claim that that they were "just kidding" if the target of the request turned them down. Of course, if the target responded affirmatively, the requester would have the option of treating the response seriously and continuing to move toward the goal. Criticism also may be delivered in the context of a humorous frame, if the message producer anticipates the likelihood that the criticism is likely to be excessively face threatening or hurtful to the target of the criticism, or if the message producer wishes to remain attractive to the target. Physical actions may also be framed in such a way that the intentions underlying them can be subject to multiple alternative attributions.

Ambiguity. Another device that may provide message producers with considerable maneuvering room after a message is disseminated is simply to deploy messages that are themselves at least somewhat ambiguous. After receiving such ambiguous messages, recipients are faced with the problem of assigning some kind of plausible interpretation to them. The very fact that there may be a multitude of such interpretations places the message producer in the position of being able to provide the interpretation that is most advantageous, if that becomes necessary. Again, message producers employing ambiguity are in the position of being able to assert that they *really* meant something other than the recipient's current interpretation.

Disseminating ambiguous messages also may provide the opportunity for the message producer to make critical assessments that aid in the reduction of the kinds of uncertainties discussed previously. Attempting to disambiguate equivocal messages requires more processing time than decoding and responding to relatively unequivocal messages. Consequently, ambiguous messages may be used by the message producer to "buy time" and increase information intake while recipients struggle to understand the message. Moreover, in the process of responding to ambiguous communications, recipients may divulge critical information verbally and leak highly diagnostic nonverbal action that reveals something about their goals, plans or affective states. This information may be used by message producers to hone more finely subsequent messages that will enable them to reach their goals.

Ambiguity may also be employed by message producers to avoid divulging information that might precipitate disagreement or conflict. If message producers are not certain about the attitudes or preferences of co-interactants, they may try to avoid revealing their own attitudes and preferences by deploying ambiguous messages in response to any queries from their interaction partners that might provide either direct or indirect information about such internal states. Although ambiguous messages may be effective in masking one's attitudes and preferences, there are some risks associated with their dissemination. The very fact that messages are ambiguous may cue message recipients that message producers are attempting to hide something, thus encouraging recipients to engage in second-guessing, and possibly ascertaining the intent underlying the message (Hewes & Graham, 1989).

Disclaiming. Whereas ambiguity and framing are relatively indirect ways of hedging against the downside risks of message dissemination, disclaiming is a relatively direct way of so doing. Message producers who harbor strong suspicions that the recipients of their messages may not agree with them or may somehow be offended by what it is they are about to say may explicitly acknowledge these possibilities before disseminating the critical message. Such disclaimers as, "I'm not sure how you feel about this, but I feel that . . . ," "You may not agree with me, but . . . ," "I don't mean to offend you, but . . . ," "I don't want to hurt you, but . . . ," or "I hope you don't think I'm being too critical of ____, but . . ." are formulaic utterances for anticipating the potential negative consequences of disseminating a specific message.

Unlike frames and ambiguity, disclaimers explicitly acknowledge the potential negative outcomes entailed by the recipient's interpretation of the message and they do not offer much in the way of deniability. Perhaps one assumption underlying their deployment is that they may act to offset, at least to some extent, any negative responses to the substance of the message. Here again, disclaimers themselves may prompt message recipients to inform message producers about their goals, plans, and affect, thus providing producers with potentially valuable information on which to predicate subsequent messages.

Retroactive Discounting. The disclaiming hedge just discussed is structured such that the message producers explicitly acknowledge their uncertainty about the target's attitudes and preferences before the assertion of one's own position or preference is made. It is also possible, however, for assertions to be made and discounted after the fact. In this context, the notion of discounting does not mean the denial of what has just been asserted, as in "I take that back;" rather, here discounting implies a way message producers may retroactively acknowledge their uncertainty about targets' attitudes and preferences. Such utterances as, "This is really nice music. What do you think?" or "I really like ____. I don't know how you feel though," indicate retroactive discounting.

As is the case with disclaiming, retroactive discounting allows message producers virtually no room for denial since they have asserted their position or preference. If these assertions express positions or preferences that disagree with those of the target, both disclaiming and discounting may provide an "excuse" for the dissemination of "disagreeable" messages; that is, the message producer was unaware of the position or preference of the message target. Whether such excuses are effective at blunting the potential negative consequences of disagreement most likely depends upon the level of negative affect generated by the disagreement.

Floor Control. If message producers entertain high uncertainty levels and they are involved in interactions with potentially significant consequences, they may attempt to minimize any downside risks associated with message dissemination by placing the message production onus on their co-interlocutors, at least temporarily. As is the case with ambiguity, this mechanism may enable message producers both to "buy time" and acquire additional information about their targets. Inducing message targets to talk about themselves initially may be a highly useful way of reducing uncertainties to levels that entail acceptable risks.

There are several ways in which the conversational onus can be shifted to one's partner. For example, one can assume the role of question-asker and place the target in the role of question-answerer (Berger & Kellermann, 1983, 1994; Mishler, 1975a, 1975b); however, in certain interaction contexts, for example, informal social situations, excessive interrogation may lead to reduced estimates of social appropriateness. Message producers can ask their partners to provide descriptions or explanations that are likely to be lengthy. For example, asking recently returned world travelers to describe their trips will very likely prompt lengthy responses; just as asking professors who are highly active researchers to provide details about their latest research project will frequently precipitate unwanted lectures. Lengthy responses may not result from asking a single question; however, an initial question followed by one or two probing questions may well do the trick. Of course, message producers may employ intensive question-asking and show interest in the various pursuits of their conversational partners for reasons other than hedging against the downside risks of message dissemination. Nonetheless, these means are available for message producers to employ for this purpose if necessary.

Deploying Direct and Indirect Hedges

The foregoing catalogue of hedging devices is far from complete; however, rather than attempting to provide an exhaustive enumeration of hedging devices, a task that itself might be close to impossible, we now consider some of the variables that prompt the deployment of these various hedging devices. In particular, as noted at several points in the discussion of these devices, some of them are quite direct (disclaiming and retroactive discounting), whereas others are considerably more indirect (floor control and framing). Since it is reasonable to postulate a continuum of directness underlying these devices, we now consider factors that propel message producers' choices among the devices arrayed along this hypothetical continuum. For the sake of this discussion, it will be assumed that message producers have a complete array of these options; however, in practice there is probably considerable individual difference variation in the number and variety of hedging devices available to individual message producers. Moreover, by dint of their occupation (e.g., politicians and university administrators), one would expect some individuals to be highly practiced in the use of some or many of these devices, while others might be aware of the devices but have little practice in their deployment.

Interaction Stakes. Interactions themselves vary with respect to what is "at stake" in them. In some encounters, message producers seek to achieve goals that are highly consequential to them, while in other situations the stakes are relatively low. If interaction outcomes are highly consequential, it is reasonable to suppose that message producers will do all they can to hedge against the downside risks associated with message dissemination. Deploying such direct devices as disclaiming and retroactive discounting is inherently more risky in terms of potential negative consequences than using more indirect means for hedging against uncertainty, since direct hedges expose message producers' attitudes and preferences; therefore:

> Proposition 12: *When interaction stakes are high, message producers will tend to deploy indirect hedges; whereas, lower interaction stakes will prompt deployment of more direct hedges.*

Within the present context, interaction stakes not only refer to such potential negative side-effects of interaction as embarrassment, they also refer to desired positive outcomes that might fail to materialize if goals are not achieved. Moreover, the concept of interaction stakes subsumes potential power differentials between interactants; that is, when message producers are faced with the task of interacting with another individual who has more power than they do, by definition, as that power differential grows, the stakes will become higher (Berger, 1994). Offending an individual with considerable power may carry serious negative consequences.

Finally, interaction stakes also include the likelihood of future interaction with the target individual. There is a considerable literature suggesting that anticipated future interaction with a target individual acts to alter the amount and type of information gathered about the target (Berger & Douglas, 1981; Berscheid, Graziano, Monson, & Dermer, 1976; Calabrese, 1975; Douglas, 1990; Harvey, Yarkin, Lightner, & Town, 1980; Kellermann & Reynolds, 1990), and knowing that one will interact in the future also acts to modify self-presentation in a positive direction (Kiesler, Kiesler, & Pallak, 1967). Thus, potential negative outcomes and the loss of positive outcomes of message dissemination, as well as power differentials and the likelihood of future interaction are all implicated within the domain of downside risk.

Interaction Urgency. For an array of possible reasons that cannot be enumerated here, message producers may wish to attain their desired goals as quickly as possible. Under other conditions, message producers may have relatively wide time windows within which to attain their goals. It is clear from the exposition of hedging devices that indirect hedges generally take more time to implement than their more direct counterparts. Such indirect devices as framing and message ambiguity imply considerable attention to message construction, and the use of floor control suggests careful and potentially effortful ongoing monitoring of the unfolding conversation. By contrast, disclaiming and retroactive discounting are more formulaic than framing or message ambiguity, and are therefore potentially less effortful to execute during ongoing interaction. Consequently,

Proposition 13: *When interaction urgency is high, message producers will tend to deploy direct hedges; whereas, less urgent interactions will encourage deployment of indirect hedges.*

When the effects of interaction stakes (Proposition 12) and urgency (Proposition 13) on directness are considered simultaneously, both stable and unstable outcomes are potentiated. Specifically, when interaction stakes are high and urgency is low, and when interaction stakes are low and urgency is high, hedging devices should be chosen respectively from the indirect and the direct regions of the indirect–direct continuum. While these are relatively straightforward and stable implications that follow from the confluence of Propositions 12 and 13, when interaction stakes and urgency are both high or both low, they create opposing forces that raise the complexity of the decision to be made. That is, given these latter two conditions, the message producer is simultaneously pulled in two different directions.

For the sake of making predictions about the degree to which hedging devices will be direct or indirect as a function of these two variables, there are at least two possible solutions. First, one might invoke a kind of "least squares" heuristic and argue the message producers will respond to the tensions provoked by these two combinations by choosing devices toward the middle of the direct–indirect continuum. A second approach would be to postulate that these two combinations give rise to a decision-making environment that is itself too unstable to yield precise predictions about choice. Under this approach, the message producer would employ cues that are local to the interaction to guide the ultimate choice of hedging devices in terms of their directness. Given the potential uniqueness of cues that might guide choice under these conditions, it is reasonable to assume that within these two combinations, greater variability in choice will be manifested. Given these two possibilities, it seems more reasonable to adopt the second approach in this case. Therefore, in aggregate terms the following proposition is warranted:

Proposition 14: *Given high interaction stakes and low urgency, indirect hedging devices will be preferred with low variability. Low interaction stakes and high urgency will encourage the deployment of direct devices with low variability. The combinations of high interaction stakes and high urgency, and low interaction stakes and low urgency will produce high levels of variability in the directness/ indirectness of hedging devices chosen.*

Certainly, dimensions in addition to direct–indirect can be invoked to account for choices among hedging devices; however, given the nature of the uncertainties considered in this chapter and the downside risks they entail for message producers, as well as the hedging devices message producers may employ to minimize these downside risks, the direct–indirect dimension must be among the more important ones.

CONCLUSION

If one takes seriously the idea that communication and social interaction processes are more akin to exercises in intelligence gathering and responding under uncertainty than a mutual "sharing" of ideas, opinions and the like, as several theorists have (e.g., Goffman, 1969; Reddy, 1979), the implications for the development of message-production theories and models are considerable. Typical cognitive theories and models of action and message production seek to describe and explain how intentions are realized in articulation (e.g., Levelt, 1989). Such theories and models usually postulate a series of processing stages that are responsible for transmuting thought into action and discourse. Generally, these theories and models feature the cognitive structures and processes responsible for these translations; however, these theories generally give short shrift to pervasive strategic problems message producers must face when they are engaged in social interactions with others.

Beyond the confines of individual cognitive structures and processes is the even more complex and messy world of social interaction. In this uncertain world, it is simply not good enough to generate the kinds of messages that one might produce while talking to oneself, to some fictitious audience, or while imagining a conversation between oneself and someone else. When communicating with others in the social world, one's words and actions have consequences, and, as we have seen, message producers cannot be certain that what they are about to say or do will necessarily forestall the most undesired of these consequences from becoming a reality. Moreover, given the dynamics of individuals and social interactions through time, message producers cannot be sure that the discourse and actions they deploy will bring about the end states they desire.

Because individuals producing messages in social contexts have had to face these uncertainties since humans became capable of social intercourse, it is a good bet that over the millennia, individual cognitive structures and processes as well as social conventions have adapted to meet these uncertain communicative exigencies. Consequently, it may not simply be a matter of loading the cognitive system with knowledge about the uncertainties attendant to message production and the hedging devices that might be used to deal with them. Such hedging devices as floor control and the ambiguation of both language and action may be preprogrammed into individual communicators to the point that they need not be learned, at least in a formal sense. If this is the case, then these devices cannot be relegated by cognitive theorists to the domain of "things that must be learned" by communicators; they must be formally integrated into message-production theories and models.

In order for cognitively oriented message-production theories and models to be of maximal use in accounting for message production during social interaction, the theories and models themselves must be "socialized." Explaining how individuals get from intentions to phonation is a beginning, but only a beginning. Because individuals are usually capable of producing a number of alternative messages to express the same concept or intention, theoretical descriptions of fundamental message-production processes need to be augmented by theoretical accounts of choice among competing alternative messages. Theories of message choice in the social interaction context must be "socialized" to be useful, since social factors are among those that enable message producers to choose among myriad message alternatives (McPhee, 1995). These choice accounts raise interesting questions about messages that are chosen for dissemination, as well as those messages that could have been articulated but were foregone by message producers. By necessity, these theories must deal directly with the potential problems created by the uncertainties that surround the dissemination of messages and the deployment of actions within the social interaction matrix. For in the world of social communication among humans, individuals are frequently called upon to act and produce discourse even when they cannot be certain of the consequences their actions and messages will produce. In much the same way that I, as a writer, cannot be certain how you, the reader, have understood and interpreted what it is I have written here.

REFERENCES

Abbott, V. A., & Black, J. B. (1986). Goal-related inferences in comprehension. In J. A. Galambos, R. P. Abelson, & J. B. Black (Eds.), Knowledge structures (pp. 123–142). Hillsdale, NJ: Lawrence Erlbaum Associates.

Alterman, R. (1988). Adaptive planning. Cognitive Science, 12, 393–421.

Berger, C. R. (1979). Beyond initial interaction: Uncertainty, understanding, and the development of interpersonal relationships. In H. Giles & R. St. Clair (Eds.), Language and social psychology (pp. 122–144). Oxford: Basil Blackwell.

Berger, C. R. (1987). Communicating under uncertainty. In M. E. Roloff & G. R. Miller (Eds.), Interpersonal processes: New directions in communication research (pp. 39–62). Newbury Park, CA: Sage.

Berger, C. R. (1988a). Planning, affect, and social action generation. In R. L. Donohew, H. Sypher, & E. T. Higgins (Eds.), Communication, social cognition and affect (pp. 93–116). Hillsdale, NJ: Lawrence Erlbaum Associates.

Berger, C. R. (1988b). Uncertainty and information exchange in developing relationships. In S. W. Duck (Ed.), *Handbook of personal relationships* (pp. 239–255). Chichester: Wiley.

Berger, C. R. (1994). Power, dominance, and social interaction. In M. L. Knapp & G. R. Miller (Eds.), *Handbook of interpersonal communication* (2nd ed., pp. 450–507). Newbury Park, CA: Sage.

Berger, C. R. (1995a). Inscrutable goals, uncertain plans, and the production of communicative action. In C. R. Berger & M. Burgoon (Eds.), *Communication and social influence processes* (pp. 1–28). East Lansing, MI: Michigan State University Press.

Berger, C. R. (1995b). A plan-based approach to strategic communication. In D. E. Hewes (Ed.), *The cognitive bases of interpersonal communication* (pp. 141–179). Hillsdale, NJ: Lawrence Erlbaum Associates.

Berger, C. R., & Bell, R. A. (1988). Plans and the initiation of social relationships. *Human Communication Research, 15,* 217–235.

Berger, C. R., & Bradac, J. J. (1982). *Language and social knowledge: Uncertainty in interpersonal relations.* London: Edward Arnold.

Berger, C. R., & diBattista, P. (1992). Information seeking and plan elaboration: What do you need to know to know what to do? *Communication Monographs, 59,* 368–387.

Berger, C. R., & Douglas, W. (1981). Studies in interpersonal epistemology III: Anticipated interaction, self-monitoring, and observational context selection. *Communication Monographs, 48,* 183–196.

Berger, C. R., & Gudykunst, W. B. (1991). Uncertainty and communication. In B. Dervin (Ed.), *Progress in communication sciences* (Vol. 10, pp. 21–66). Norwood, NJ: Ablex.

Berger, C. R., & Kellermann, K. A. (1983). To ask or not to ask: Is that a question? In R. N. Bostrom (Ed.), *Communication yearbook 7* (pp. 342–368). Newbury Park, CA: Sage.

Berger, C. R., & Kellermann, K. (1989). Personal opacity and social information gathering: Explorations in strategic communication. *Communication Research, 16,* 314–351.

Berger, C. R., & Kellermann, K. (1994). Acquiring social information. In J. A. Daly & J. M. Wiemann (Eds.), *Strategic interpersonal communication* (pp. 1–31). Hillsdale, NJ: Lawrence Erlbaum Associates.

Berscheid, E., Graziano, W., Monson, T., & Dermer, M. (1976). Outcome dependency: Attention, attribution, and attraction. *Journal of Personality and Social Psychology, 34,* 978–989.

Black, J. B., & Bower, G. H. (1979). Episodes as chunks in narrative memory. *Journal of Verbal Learning and Verbal Behavior, 18,* 309–318.

Black, J. B., & Bower, G. H. (1980). Story understanding as problem-solving. *Poetics, 9,* 223–250.

Bower, G. H., Black, J. B., & Turner, T. J. (1979). Scripts in memory for text. *Cognitive Psychology, 11,* 177–220.

Brand, M. (1984) *Intending and acting: Toward a naturalized theory of action.* Cambridge, MA: MIT Press.

Bratman, M. E. (1987). *Intentions, plans, and practical reason.* Cambridge, MA: Harvard University Press.

Bratman, M. E. (1990). What is intention? In P. R. Cohen, J. Morgan, & M. E. Pollack (Eds.), *Intentions in communication* (pp. 15–31). Cambridge, MA: MIT Press.

Burleson, B. R. (1994). Comforting messages: Features, functions, and outcomes. In J. A. Daly & J. M. Wiemann (Eds.), *Strategic interpersonal communication* (pp. 135–161). Hillsdale, NJ: Lawrence Erlbaum Associates.

Butterworth, B. (1980). Evidence from pauses in speech. In B. Butterworth (Ed.), *Language production: Volume 1. Speech and talk* (pp. 155–176). New York: Academic Press.

Butterworth, B., & Goldman-Eisler, F. (1979). Recent studies in cognitive rhythm. In A. W. Siegman & S. Feldstein (Eds.), *Of speech and time: Temporal speech patterns in interpersonal contexts* (pp. 211–224). Hillsdale, NJ: Lawrence Erlbaum Associates.

Cahill, A., & Mitchell, D. C. (1987). Plans and goals in story comprehension. In R. G. Reilly (Ed.), *Communication failure in dialogue and discourse* (pp. 257–268). New York: North-Holland.

Calabrese, R. J. (1975). *The effects of privacy and probability of future interaction on initial interaction patterns.* Unpublished dissertation, Department of Communication Studies, Northwestern University, Evanston, IL.

Douglas, W. (1990, November). *Uncertainty reduction during initial interaction: The effect of anticipated interaction.* Paper presented at the annual conference of the Speech Communication Association, Chicago, IL.

Goffman, E. (1969). *Strategic interaction.* Philadelphia, PA: University of Pennsylvania Press.

Green, G. M. (1989). *Pragmatics and natural language understanding.* Hillsdale, NJ: Lawrence Erlbaum Associates.

Hammond, K. J. (1989a). *Case-based planning: Viewing planning as a memory task.* New York: Academic Press.

Hammond, K. J. (1989b). CHEF. In C. K. Riesbeck & R. C. Schank (Eds.), *Inside case-based reasoning* (pp. 165–248). Hillsdale, NJ: Lawrence Erlbaum Associates.

Harvey, J. H., Yarkin, K. L., Lightner, J. M., & Town, J. P. (1980). Unsolicited interpretation and the recall of interpersonal events. *Journal of Personality and Social Psychology, 38,* 551–568.

Hayes-Roth, B., & Hayes-Roth, F. (1979). A cognitive model of planning. *Cognitive Science, 3,* 275–310.

Hewes, D. E., & Graham, M. L. (1989). Second-guessing theory: Review and extension. In J. A. Anderson (Ed.), *Communication yearbook 12* (pp. 213–248). Newbury Park, CA: Sage.

Hjelmquist, E. (1991). Planning and execution of discourse in conversation. *Communication and Cognition, 24,* 1–17.

Hjelmquist, E., & Gidlund, A. (1984). Planned ideas versus expressed ideas in conversation. *Journal of Pragmatics, 8,* 329–343.

Hobbs, J. R., & Evans, D. A. (1980). Conversation as planned behavior. *Cognitive Science, 4,* 349–377.

Kellermann, K. (1992). Communication: Inherently strategic and primarily automatic. *Communication Monographs, 59,* 288–300.

Kellermann, K. A., & Berger, C. R. (1984). Affect and the acquisition of social information: Sit back, relax, and tell me about yourself. In R. Bostrom (Ed.), *Communication yearbook 8* (pp. 412–445). Newbury Park, CA: Sage.

Kellermann, K., & Reynolds, R. (1990). When ignorance is bliss: The role of motivation to reduce uncertainty in uncertainty reduction theory. *Human Communication Research, 17,* 5–75.

Kiesler, C. A., Kiesler, S. B., & Pallak, M. S. (1967). The effects of commitment to future interaction on reactions to norm violators. *Journal of Personality, 35,* 585–599.

Kreitler, S., & Kreitler, H. (1987). Plans and planning: Their motivational and cognitive antecedents. In S. L. Friedman, E. K. Skolnick, & R. R. Cocking (Eds.), *Blueprints for thinking: The role of planning in cognitive development* (pp. 110–178). New York: Cambridge University Press.

Langer, E. (1978). Rethinking the role of thought in social interaction. In J. H. Harvey, W. J. Ickes, & R. F. Kidd (Eds.), *New directions in attribution research: Vol. 2* (pp. 35–58). Hillsdale, NJ: Lawrence Erlbaum Associates.

Langer, E. (1992). Interpersonal mindlessness and language. *Communication Monographs, 59,* 324–327.

Levelt, W. J. M. (1989). *Speaking: From intention to articulation.* Cambridge, MA: MIT Press.

Lichtenstein, E. H., & Brewer, W. F. (1980). Memory for goal directed events. *Cognitive Psychology, 12,* 412–445.

McPhee, R. D. (1995). Cognitive perspectives on communication: Interpretive and critical responses. In D. E. Hewes (Ed.), *The cognitive bases of interpersonal communication* (pp. 225–246). Hillsdale, NJ: Lawrence Erlbaum Associates.

Miller, G. A., Galanter, E., & Pribram, K. H. (1960). *Plans and the structure of behavior.* New York: Holt, Rinehart & Winston.

Mishler, E. G. (1975a). Studies in dialogue and discourse: II. Types of discourse initiated by and sustained through questioning. *Journal of Psycholinguistic Research, 4,* 99–121.

Mishler, E. G. (1975b). Studies in dialogue and discourse: An exponential law of successive questioning. *Language in Society, 4,* 31–51.

Pea, R. D., & Hawkins, J. (1987). Planning in a chore-scheduling task. In S. L. Friedman, E. K. Skolnick, & R. R. Cocking (Eds.), *Blueprints for thinking: The role of planning in cognitive development* (pp. 273–302). New York: Cambridge University Press.

Planalp, S., & Honeycutt, J. M. (1985). Events that increase uncertainty in personal relationships. *Human Communication Research, 11,* 593–604.

Planalp, S., Rutherford, D. K., & Honeycutt, J. M. (1988). Events that increase uncertainty in personal relationships: II. Replication and extension. *Human Communication Research, 14,* 516–547.

Read, S. J., & Miller, L. C. (1989). Inter-personalism: Toward a goal-based theory of persons in relationships. In L. A. Pervin (Ed.), *Goal concepts in personality and social psychology* (pp. 413–472). Hillsdale, NJ: Lawrence Erlbaum Associates.

Reddy, M. J. (1979). The conduit metaphor—A case of frame conflict in our language about language. In A. Ortony (Ed.), *Metaphor and thought* (pp. 284–324). London: Cambridge University Press.

Sacerdoti, E. (1977). *A structure for plans and behavior.* Amsterdam: Elsevier.

Seifert, C. M., Robertson, S. P., & Black, J. B. (1985). Types of inferences generated during reading. *Journal of Memory and Language, 24,* 405–422.

Srull, T. K., & Wyer, R. S. (1986). The role of chronic and temporary goals in social information processing. In R. Sorrentino & E. T. Higgins (Eds.), *Handbook of motivation and cognition* (pp. 503–549). New York: Guilford Press.

Tesser, A., & Rosen, S. (1975). The reluctance to transmit bad news. In L. Berkowitz (Ed.), *Advances in experimental social psychology* (Vol. 8, pp. 193–232). New York: Academic Press.

Vallacher, R. R., & Wegner, D. M. (1985). *A theory of action identification.* Hillsdale, NJ: Lawrence Erlbaum Associates.

Waldron, V. R. (1990). Constrained rationality: Situational influences on information acquisition plans and tactics. *Communication Monographs, 57,* 184–201.

Waldron, V. R., & Applegate, J. L. (1994). Interpersonal construct differentiation and conversational planning: An examination of two cognitive accounts for the production of competent verbal disagreement tactics. *Human Communication Research, 21,* 3–35.

Waldron, V. R., Caughlin, J., Jackson, D. (1995). Talking specifics: Facilitating effects of planning on AIDS talk in peer dyads. *Health Communication, 7,* 249–266.

Wilensky, R. (1983). *Planning and understanding: A computational approach to human reasoning.* Reading, MA: Addison-Wesley.

11

THE PRODUCTION OF SYMBOLIC OBJECTS AS COMPONENTS OF LARGER WHOLES

Robert E. Sanders
University at Albany, SUNY

THE OBJECTS THAT GET PRODUCED WHEN PEOPLE COMMUNICATE

The term "message" is not analytically neutral.[1] Though it lacks a strict technical meaning, both academic and popular uses of the term connote:

- a unit of communication that is complete and self-contained
- a unit whose communication value[2] is that it makes something known[3] (information, beliefs, feelings or wants, personal qualities) to those who are addressed

---

[1] I am indebted to Anita Pomerantz (especially Pomerantz, 1986) for planting the seed of doubt that led me to this conclusion. She expressed the view that, from her perspective as a conversation analyst, the term "message" in the Speech Communication literature seemed empirically vague and to be getting applied indiscriminately to ostensibly distinct phenomena. This led me at first to consider how the vagueness could be overcome—what a technical specification of objects that are messages would look like—and from attempting that to fully appreciate the analytic bias of the term itself.

[2] The "communication value" of a symbolic object that is produced and interpreted in the course of a particular communication event is what it contributes to the completion of that event either in terms of its content or social function. Although an object's communication value is generally tied to its interpretation, this is not always so. A symbolic object may have an interpretation but little or no communication value (e.g., a pun), or not have an interpretation but have a communication value anyway (e.g., "oops"), or have an interpretation entirely distinct

- a unit that makes known something that it was within the person who produced it to communicate about the matter at hand to those who were addressed
- a unit of communication that makes known what it does reliably, on the basis of rules of language and applicable social conventions

For reasons developed shortly, it is debatable whether objects of that kind exist at all, or at least whether people typically produce such objects when they communicate. To say they do is akin to saying that the moves a chess player makes are self-contained and have a fixed value, without reference to the game being played or when during the game they are made.

This is not to deny that people have things within them to make known, and that this is a prominent motive for producing symbolic objects.[4] But when that motive applies, more than that has to enter into producing symbolic objects if, as contended below, no particular thing can be made known necessarily just by producing a single symbolic object that expresses it, that is, a *message*. Hence, in raising this issue, I am not disputing the soundness of the questions that have been pursued in much of the research on message production, but given the complicating factors I've alluded to, some rethinking is warranted. This is addressed in the concluding discussion.

The issue here centers on the earlier base premise, whether the symbolic objects that people produce in communicating are complete, self-contained units that reliably make something known. From the analytic perspective developed here, they are not and cannot be *in principle*. The symbolic objects that people produce in communicating are invariably components of larger wholes (a discourse,[5] an interaction).[6] This has two practical con-

---

from its communication value (e.g., Searle's, 1969, example of an American soldier in World War II who recites a line of German poetry to his Italian captors so they will believe he is German).

[3]There is a restrictive versus a broad sense of "make something known," and the term "message" seems to involve the restrictive sense. Searle (1969) made the distinction with reference to the example noted above of the hypothetical American soldier in World War II who recited a line of German poetry so his Italian captors would believe he was German. The distinction is between what is made known by virtue of what an utterance directly and reliably expresses by virtue of its linguistic meaning (the restrictive sense of "make known") versus what else might be inferred based on the manner and circumstances of the utterance (the broad sense).

[4]The term "symbolic object" is used throughout to refer to any meaningful artifact produced for consumption by others, whether an utterance, a gesture, an item of clothing, etc. Besides those whose communication value is that they make something known, some portion (often a sizable portion) of the symbolic objects people produce have a quite different communication value—as social actions (Austin, 1962; Schegloff, 1995; Searle, 1969). These cannot be regarded as messages in the ordinary sense at all.

[5]An extended discourse, that is, a monologic linguistic structure, corresponds in many ways to an interaction in terms of the production and interpretation of component objects as parts

sequences. First, the communication value of those component objects, and what they additively communicate, is not determinate before the fact, and moreover it is fluid: It depends on how they are cohered with each other, that is, how their respective interpretations are adjusted against each other, to form the whole—something that is not only contingent but is based on discourse processing that is subject to revision. Second, a principal motivation for producing a particular symbolic object in any instance, maybe the primary one, is to have some effect on the larger whole that is evolving, for example, the course of the interaction (what it will include, how it will conclude), and usually only secondarily (if at all) to express what the person has within him or her to communicate about the matter at hand to those being addressed.

Empirical indications abound in naturalistic data that these considerations are operative in social interaction, sometimes dominant. An example is a conversation between Nurse Q and Nurse R, when Q asked R whether she would be interested in taking on a full-time, private-duty case, and R's immediate answer was "no," said boldly and unequivocally twice in successive turns (see Sanders, 1991, for more details and analysis). Even though that answer ostensibly expressed Nurse R's (cognitive) *message*—her disposition toward taking the job—it evidently did not communicate what she intended. After getting little response from Nurse Q to these initial answers, Nurse R went on to produce a series of progressively more elaborate excuses and justifications for why she did not want the job, each prompting a renewed request/proposal from Nurse Q how or why she could or should take on the job anyway. Only after this pattern repeated itself several times in the course of a relatively extended conversation about the matter did Nurse Q concede the point and the subject was dropped. This does not make sense if symbolic objects are produced to make some particular thing known, and they do this reliably (e.g., Nurse R's initial answer to the question, "no"). But the interaction does make sense if it is also a consideration, as suggested earlier, how the object(s) one produces might be interpreted, and what the larger whole might end up being. Nurse R might have oriented

---

of a larger whole. But from this point on the focus here will be entirely on interactions. There are important ways in which producing components of an interaction is a different communication problem from producing components of a discourse, akin to the difference between playing chess with another person and playing chess with oneself.

[6]Although the focus here is on the production of objects that are components of an interaction as the larger whole, an interaction can be analyzed in turn as an object that is a component of a still larger whole (e.g., a relationship), and participants can orient to and participate in interactions accordingly. In principle, any symbolic object (e.g., an extended discourse) can be analyzed as either the product of its components or as a component of a still larger whole. This echoes Pearce and Cronen's (1980) analysis of any given symbolic object as embedded in a nested hierarchy of "contexts," that is, as a component of progressively larger wholes, each embedded in the next.

to the possibility that her initial, flat "no" could have been understood as being unfriendly (to Nurse Q) or unprofessional. Nurse Q for her part might have oriented to the possibility that, if Nurse R's shift from a flat "no" to citing issues signified that R was ambivalent, then for Nurse Q to drop the matter could have been understood as indicating that Nurse Q did not really care about Nurse R's interests or the patient's enough to help Nurse R find solutions to the obstacles she cited. Further, for both women, though for different reasons, to have dropped the matter after Nurse R initially said "no" had the potential to bring the interaction to an unwanted personal or professional outcome.

The computational problem for persons producing a symbolic object at a given juncture, then—the pivotal consideration in what object to produce—cannot be primarily, if at all, to ensure that it expresses what the person has in him or her to communicate. (Sanders, 1996, showed that much of what Nurse Q and Nurse R told the other may have been deceptive, not their actual thoughts.) Equally important, perhaps, prior considerations would be (a) how the object one produces might be interpreted as part of the whole, for example, depending on how it would fulfill the presumption that one is participating "cooperatively" (in Grice's, 1975, sense), and (b) what the larger whole might end up being—what the interaction might include or how it might conclude—as a result of adding the particular object to the other objects that were or might yet be produced in that interaction.[7]

The claim I pursue here—that the *symbolic objects* people produce are components of larger wholes, whose production and interpretation is constrained accordingly—should not be confused with recent views that when people produce *messages*, they do not occur singly, and that people do not try to achieve goals through the production of a single message, for example, work by Berger (1987) and Waldron (1990). In their view, the inadequacy of single messages, and the need for planning and strategy, arises from the complexity of the demands of the task at hand, and the information-processing requirements of those involved. Their concern with planning and strategy thus differs from the one here in that it takes for granted the meaning and meaningfulness, the *informativeness*, of what is said or done. But consider that issues of meaningfulness are only moot under ideal conditions: Participants would have to have a common culture in the most comprehensive sense (including their language and "code"), and fully cooperate in the way Goffman (1959, 1967) indicates people must—but as Sanders (1995a) shows, sometimes do not—in order to achieve a sustained institutional reality.

---

[7]The reference here to "computational" aspects of producing a symbolic object, and references below to "strategic" aspects, do not necessarily suggest that it is a conscious, or self-conscious, process to produce a symbolic object. Miller, Galanter, and Pribram (1960), Chomsky (1965), Snyder (1974, 1979), Schank and Abelson (1977), Brown and Levinson (1978), and Heritage (1990–1991), among others, all make this point.

The communication value of symbolic objects is not determinate before the fact (Cronen, Pearce, & Xi, 1989–1990; Pearce & Cronen, 1980; Sanders, 1980, 1987; Schegloff, 1988, 1995). Yet the uncertainties inherent in producing and interpreting symbolic objects generally do not result in chaos; people usually succeed in understanding and coordinating with each other. My interest is in the systematic basis that must exist—and apply equally in interactions among strangers and intimates—to achieve the relative uniformity or reliability of interpretations that people do.

PRODUCING AND INTERPRETING OBJECTS AS COMPONENTS OF LARGER WHOLES

In previous work, I developed a candidate explanation for the relative uniformity or reliability of interpretations that people achieve; it comprises "principles of relevance" for sequentially producing and interpreting symbolic objects within a larger whole, based on the meaning relations among them (Sanders, 1987). These principles must be acquired early and be universal for even infants to begin orienting to and learning from the meaningfulness and meaning of what the adults and older children around them say and do. I want to revisit those principles here. They were formalized to capture the way that the sequential production and interpretation of symbolic objects, as components of interactions and other discursive forms, is constrained by their possible meaning relations with one or more other components of that larger whole. However, it has become apparent that the basis on which those principles were formalized was too narrow. As a result they are insensitive to details of some symbolic objects, and overlook other objects completely, that enter into the meaning relations among the components of interactions, and whose sequential production and interpretation is constrained accordingly.

O'Keefe and Lambert (1995) recently made summary statements about their own approach that serve as an apt preliminary here as well. Although O'Keefe and Lambert have a different view of the empirical realities and related technical matters from the one here (addressed later in closing), their statement about what an adequate computational device in this domain would have to capture applies directly to the Principles of Relevance I formalized, and even more so, the revision of them developed next:

> [A] theory must be offered to explain what allows people to reason through each moment's action by a fresh reasoning-through of that moment's situation . . . to explain the cognitive substrate that supports improvisation during situated activity. (p. 67)

From the standpoint of a theory of communication, one of the most critical ways in which input shapes focus [i.e., selection of what to communicate] is . . . through the way antecedent and projected contributions shape what is relevant to say at any particular juncture. (p. 75)

[W]e see focus as guided primarily by a model of the activity [in which speaker and hearer are engaged] and only secondarily, if at all, by a model of the specific addressee. (p. 75)

Principles of Relevance Applied to Interpretation

The Specific Interpretation of Utterances. Existing semantic and pragmatic theories have collectively identified at least three distinct kinds of meaning that uttered expressions of language have—their propositional content, their illocutionary force, and insofar as they breach a conversational maxim, what they conversationally implicate. Yet these theories have not addressed the interrelation among these types of meaning comprehensively. In particular, they fail to explain how it is that persons usually do not orient to or are even aware of this polyguity, but focus on and respond to just one meaning of one of these types in any instance. This led me (Sanders, 1980, 1987) to distinguish between the *possible* meanings of an utterance, based on linguistic and social rules for assigning meanings "timelessly," and its *specific interpretation*, which of those possible meanings it is warranted to focus on in a specific instance. But this presumes a principled basis for judging what possible meaning to focus on and respond to in the local moment.[8] Principles of Relevance were devised to capture this, such that a specific interpretation is the "most relevant" among an utterance's possible meanings, based on its sequential position in the unfolding interaction.[9]

Tying the specific interpretation of an utterance to that one of its possible meanings that is "most relevant" resembles, but differs in a critical way from, the operation of Grice's (1975) "maxim of relation." His idea was that there is a standing presumption that any given utterance in an interaction

---

[8]However, this way of formulating the matter accepts the validity of the interpretation rules for each type of meaning, and considers that the inadequacy of such rules for capturing what utterances mean in the local moment is because a further set of interpretation principles is involved. The following analysis makes a case that this is is not necessarily at odds with the view, and some naturalistic data, that the interpretation of utterances is a joint achievement of the participants in the local moment and may be novel (Cronen et al., 1991–1992; Schegloff, 1996).

[9]This approach is in marked contrast to Sperber and Wilson's (1986) analysis of "relevance." Their analysis ties the relevance of a linguistic or nonverbal object to whether it has any consequences for the adequacy of the cognitive "assumptions" a person is applying in the local moment. This attention to the relevance of an object for an *individual's* information processing is a wholly distinct matter from the concern here, the relevance of an object for *collectively* carrying on the present interaction coherently and achieving a resolution. Obviously, these are not mutually exclusive.

is relevant, and that it will be interpreted in such a way as to bear out this presumption, resulting either in attention to its propositional content if it is relevant, or the inference of some other, implicated proposition. However, Grice only concerned himself with two types of utterance meaning, propositional content and conversational implicature, and did not take illocutionary force (speech acts) into account as well. To do so requires a different analytic approach entirely.

If an utterance can be relevant at a given juncture with reference to any of three types of meaning, not two, then its specific interpretation at that juncture depends on something more complex than the default logic Grice employed (i.e., focus on propositional content if it is "cooperative," otherwise a conversational implicature). Rather, there must be a separate basis for assessing the relevance of each type of meaning (of an utterance's illocutionary force, and any conversational implicatures, as well as its propositional content), and for making a further assessment of which of those is "most relevant" at that juncture.

Accordingly, I initially formulated three main principles of relevance that apply respectively to the relevance of utterances in terms of each of three types of possible meaning (propositional content, illocutionary force, or implicature). Each principle specified features of meaning(s) of that type and designated features of the specific interpretations of other utterances in the same interaction (either antecedent utterances or subsequent ones) such that commonalities between them constituted relevance. But that was too weak. If it were just a matter of meaning relations between pairs of utterances alone, the utterance being interpreted could be relevant equally well to a number of distinct other utterances in the same interaction in terms of each of its alternative possible meanings, thus failing to warrant a focus on any one of its possible meanings in particular. But consider that as the number of utterances in an interaction grows, it will generally happen that one or more n-tuples of contiguous utterances will be relevant to each other on the basis of features of the same type of meaning. I termed this a "*ground of coherence*" (similar to what Reichman, 1985, termed a "context space"), for example, when their propositional content is about the same matter, or a series of reciprocal actions is produced such as questions and answers or cross-complaining. In that case, that one of an utterance's possible meanings can be weighted as "most relevant" whose meaning components have commonalties with features of the ground of coherence of the most extensive, most contiguous n-tuple of other utterances.

In a series of experiments to test principles of relevance formalized in this way (Sanders, 1987), when a sequence of several utterances was manipulated leading up to the same "target" utterance in a contrived interaction, the target utterance's specific interpretation shifted as predicted from its propositional content, to a speech act, to an implicature.

An additional basis on which utterances are relevant within interactions was also indicated by other analysts. Interactions can generally be analyzed as a progression from the initiation of an agenda that has a set of possible ways of being satisfied, toward one or another of those possible "satisfiers," or resolutions (Edmondson, 1981). Further, Schank (1977) observed that utterances in an interaction would be anomalous that did not advance the interaction toward a resolution (e.g., if they are tangential or redundant), and Tracy (1982, 1983) found that persons whose utterances do not move the interaction forward, but are relevant only in terms of local commonalities of meaning, are judged less competent. One can project at any point in an interaction possible sequences of future utterances that—based on the first set of principles, earlier—relevantly follow from the current utterance to arrive at a possible way of satisfying the current agenda. A possible meaning of a next utterance can then be said to be relevant if on that interpretation the utterance achieves "progress" toward a satisfier (i.e., reduces the minimal number of steps needed from that point on for it to become relevant to produce a satisfier of the current agenda).

Given two independent ways in which a possible meaning of an utterance can be relevant in the current interaction—(a) in terms of commonalities between that possible meaning and the ground of coherence among other utterances, and (b) in terms of incrementally advancing the interaction towards a possible satisfier of the current agenda—the great majority of utterances would tend to be relevant in both ways at once. The possible meaning involved would unequivocally be the "most relevant" one. However, these alternate ways in which utterances are relevant can serve as "checks and balances" on specific interpretations and the way the whole is being cohered. If the specific interpretation warranted on the basis of relevance to some ground of coherence does not move the interaction toward a resolution, there is reason to reconsider that specific interpretation and the interpretation of other objects. If the specific interpretation warranted on the basis of advancing the interaction toward a resolution is not relevant to some ground of coherence, there is reason to reconsider what the current agenda and its satisfiers are presumed to be.

Accordingly, principles of relevance were formalized as conditionals in a fuzzy logic that specify what specific interpretation of an utterance is warranted based on its interconnection with other interpreted objects in the interaction. Formalized in that way, such judgments are probabilistic, and subject to being changed over time. An individual could change the specific interpretation of the same utterance from $Time_1$ to $Time_2$ after new utterances are added to the interaction. It depends on whether new utterances make possible a new ground of coherence, or make apparent that the interaction was on a different course than had been projected. This could also happen after an interaction has ended: A different, more parsimonious way of interrelatedly interpreting some or all of its component utterances may become evident in retrospect. This contrasts with interpretation rules in most theories that apply "timelessly," with a constant result.

The Specific Interpretation of Nonverbal Displays. It was straightforward to formalize principles for the specific interpretation of nonverbal displays along the same lines as for utterances. Nonverbal displays generally have several possible conventional meanings, akin to the possible meanings that utterances have. These meanings tend to involve either: (a) an interior condition they are presumed to externalize (laughter, weeping, blushing, vocal qualities, posture, and bodily attitude, etc.); (b) the designated functions of institutionally defined gestures (genuflection, military salute, raised hand in class); (c) conditions or relationships whose existence or imminence is mimed (pillowing head on upraised hands to mime that sleeping exists or is wanted, or, following McNeill, 1985, and McNeill, Cassell, & McCullough, 1994, using the hands to trace movements or display spatial arrangements about matters being concurrently described in talk); or (d) encoded propositions (making a circle of forefinger and thumb to express "okay," various gestures that "curse" the observer). A nonverbal display is relevant as a component of a larger whole, an interaction, if for any of its possible meanings there are other components of the interaction that are proximate causes of relevant interior conditions, or applicable institutional frames, task requirements, and the like. These proximate causes, frames, requirements, generally occur in the references made in the propositional content or implicatures of concurrent talk, or among the conditions that are constitutive of a speech act (e.g., whether an utterance counts as a tease or an insult depends in part on the speaker's affect, so that a concurrent nonverbal display is relevant if at least one of its possible, conventional meanings expresses an affect that disambiguates the speech act it accompanies).

Principles of Relevance Applied to Producing Symbolic Objects: Neo-Rhetorical Participation in Interactions

As noted, the principles of relevance apply as much to the production of symbolic objects as their interpretation. By definition, the first imperative in communication is to produce objects that have the best chance of being understood and responded to as the person intends or wants, or at minimum not in an unwanted way. At any juncture, this can only be achieved by a subset of the symbolic objects a person could produce, and cannot be predicated solely, or even primarily, on what one personally is disposed to express and has a means of expressing, based on salient thoughts and feelings, social learning, and the like. This is because the way an object is *interpreted* depends on whether and how it is judged to *be* relevant; how it is *responded to* depends in addition on what that object, as interpreted, is judged to *make* relevant (alone or with other objects). Hence, in producing symbolic objects, persons generally must be constrained by what is relevant at that juncture, and what the object produced, styled in one way or another, will make relevant in turn (Sanders, 1984, 1985, 1987). The production (and fashioning) of any symbolic object is thus a potentially complex, potentially strategic matter. (Of course, in everyday life, producing symbolic objects is not usually as difficult as this makes it seem, but that is not counterfactual: An indeterminately large proportion of social interactions comprise routinized procedures that prescript how to understand and respond to component symbolic objects.)

When interactions are not routinized, the potential *complexity* in producing symbolic objects is that it is contingent what object to produce at a given juncture to warrant a desired specific interpretation, for example, express what one intends, or conversely, what specific interpretation in the interactional moment at hand might be warranted by an object one is disposed to produce. There is thus a standing potential for a conflict at any juncture between what one is personally motivated to say or do, and either or both (a) how that would be interpreted (if it were relevant and interpretable at all), and (b) what that would make relevant in the remaining interaction. For those whose priority is for the interaction to continue, to avoid breakdown—that is, for most people, most of the time—preference would be given to producing only objects that are relevant and thus interpretable, and within that set, those that would be interpreted in at least a not-undesired way.

Of course, persons from time to time (some persons more than others) may be disposed to produce objects that express some particular thought or feeling, or be unable to avoid it, despite a potential for its having an unwanted interpretation or unwanted effect on the course of the interaction. A conflict between one's disposition to produce an object and the specific interpretation it might receive could be mitigated or avoided, however, if the person produced symbolic objects beforehand, or subsequently, that made the object relevant in a way that offset an unwanted interpretation or interactional consequence.

There is also a *strategic* aspect in producing symbolic objects that arises when the person has a preference about, or an agenda that depends on, how the other(s) respond, and/or toward what resolution the interaction progresses, or what is included in or excluded from the interaction. In that case, within the limitations of what can be relevantly said or done at that juncture, a person would generally produce utterances and nonverbal displays that he or she projects would make wanted responses relevant or unwanted ones irrelevant, and moreover make the specific interpretation of wanted responses desirable (from the respondents' point of view) or of

unwanted ones undesirable. Principles of Relevance are candidate representations of the cognitive resources, the principled basis, for making such
projections. I have recently termed it *neo-rhetorical participation in interactions* to fashion one's turns anticipatorily, so as to constrain how others
respond and what course the interaction takes.

EMPIRICAL INADEQUACIES AND SOLUTIONS

For purposes of simplicity, the abbreviation "PrinRel$_0$," will be used hereafter
to refer to the original way Principles of Relevance were formalized, as
summarized earlier. As was noted, PrinRel$_0$ were formalized on the basis of
what now seems to be an overly narrow analysis of what constitutes a
symbolic object, and of the possible meanings that symbolic objects have,
with reference to which they are cohered to form a larger whole. As a result,
PrinRel$_0$ are not uniformly sensitive to symbolic objects that are consequential in interactions. In addition, they artificially restrict specific interpretations to the set of possible, conventional meanings of symbolic objects,
overlooking the possibility that objects may warrant specific interpretations
that are novel (but grounded) in the local moment. Thus, in general PrinRel$_0$
do not adequately capture the principled basis on which symbolic objects
produced in the course of an interaction are relevant, anticipatory of their
interactional consequences, and interpretable accordingly.

An instance in which the limitations of PrinRel$_0$ are apparent, and that
provides an empirical basis for reconsidering the possible meanings that
objects have and revising PrinRel$_0$ accordingly, involves an interaction between two 6 year old girls, Lorraine (6;11) and Rashia (6;7).[10] The interaction

---

[10]The reliance on children's interactions is particularly helpful here because they typically
involve engagement in both talk and physical activity at the same time, unlike most recordings
of adult interaction that have been published, a good portion of which are telephone
conversations. This provides an opportunity to examine the deployment of nonverbal as well
as linguistic objects, and analyze their interrelations. The further value of these data is that
they underscore how comprehensively Principles of Relevance in some form apply to the
symbolic objects people produce, and make plain that they are acquired early in a child's
communicative development. It should be emphasized in addition that these interactions do
not involve artificially simplified symbolic objects or interactions that bias the analysis, at least
in this instance. While it is true that adult interactions often involve more sustained talk on
topics and an orientation to making things known, the component symbolic objects that are
produced are no more self-contained "messages" than those that the children produce, as
countless analyses of talk-in-interaction consistently show (see Atkinson & Heritage, 1984; Drew
& Heritage, 1992; Jacoby & Ochs, 1995). Further, recent work on peer interactions among children
(Sanders & Freeman, 1995; also see Barnes & Vangelisti, 1995; and Sheldon, 1996) reveals an
unexpected degree of sensitivity among children as young as 5;0 years to constraints on what
they say or do, based on its consequentiality for the course of the interaction, as well as intricate
and adaptive adjustments to those constraints in the symbolic objects they produce.

was videotaped in a school setting as part of a study of children's communicative development (Sanders & Freeman, 1995). Each pair of children was recorded separately playing with a set of Lego system building blocks, after they were given the instruction that they should "build one thing, working together."

In an early segment of their interaction, Rashia produced three symbolic objects in succession that potentially constrained the course of the interaction away from collaboration, either by creating opportunities for inequities in participation (at least from Lorraine's perspective) or creating a basis for conflict. Lorraine produced symbolic objects in response that did not directly challenge Rashia, but seemed to ancitipate, and cancel or alter, the potential effect on the interaction of what Rashia said and did based on what she made relevant.[11]

However, $PrinRel_0$ cannot account for the specific interpretations that Lorraine evidently gave most of the objects that she responded to and produced, which either means that Lorraine was not producing objects anticipatorily, or that $PrinRel_0$ do not capture the principled basis she had for doing it. This question is resolved in the following three steps: first, an interpretive description is given of this segment of the interaction, focusing on the way Lorraine's turns at speaking seem to anticipate and correct for the interaction's possible course; second, evidence is given for regarding Lorraine's responses as adapted to the local moment and calculatedly anticipatory, not previously learned and applied by rote; third, a way of capturing the evident meanings of the objects is proposed, and corresponding revisions of $PrinRel_0$ rationalized.

Lorraine's and Rashia's Interaction

The following description of Lorraine's and Rashia's interaction is about the relevancies among the symbolic objects they produced, not what either child thought or intended in regard to what was taking place between them.

The First Object-Pair. During an initial exchange of proposals about what to build, Lorraine set down a green base on which to assemble things on her side of the table toward the back. Lorraine then suggested they make a house, with flowers, and Rashia agreed to this. However, as she did so, Rashia picked

---

[11]The analysis here focuses on Lorraine as having produced objects in response to Rashia, in the interests of seeking to achieve joint rather than individual effort. But of course, Rashia was producing objects in response to Lorraine, and may have been doing so anticipatorily also, but with a different agenda. A more balanced, comprehensive analysis of this interaction might thus give a somewhat different picture from the one here of the contributions of each of the girls, their effect on the interaction, and their relative competence. In fact there are grounds for analyzing Lorraine's responses as having been protective of her own control over their activity, with Rashia's as efforts to right the balance.

up the green base and repositioned it at the front of the table on her side, between the two of them (lines 20–21). After Rashia set the base down and thumped on it (as if to nail it down), Lorraine immediately pulled it out from under Rashia's hands (lines 23–26), holding it off the table at first, then repositioning it after Rashia protested (line 25) on her side toward the back, where it had been. At the same time, she self-narrated what she was doing.

17	Lorraine:	Well, ↑how ↓'bout just- a plain old- (0.2) ↑house?	
18	Rashia:	°Okay.°	
19	Lorraine:	(With) flowers.	
20	Rashia:	˙Okay. ⌐That'll be <u>easy.</u> ⌐	((˙R picks up the green base, sets
21	Lorraine:	└°m m m :: hm!° ┘	it down right next to her, and
22		(2.1) †	thumps twice on it; †L takes the
23	Lorraine:	And th<u>i</u>s (.) i:s (0.2)	green base from under R's hands,
24		aro⌐un:d ⌐ ‡ (0.2)	holds it off to the side; ‡after
25	Rashia:	└Hey:::┘	R's "Hey," L moves it to the
26		('<u>at</u>!) f'r now:. Okay.	back of the table on her side))

It is unclear why Lorraine moved to counter Rashia's repositioning the green base, since Rashia had positioned it as needs be to begin building their house. It may have been for self-interested reasons and not anticipation of the interactional consequences. But whatever her motive, there is good reason to consider that as Lorraine took the green base from Rashia, she was then oriented to the interactional consequences of what she herself then did (the nonverbal object she then produced), specifically whether it increased or decreased the chances that they would collaborate as they had been asked to do. This is apparent from considering Lorraine's options of response at that point. One option was to accept Rashia's repositioning, but that would make it relevant for Rashia to produce other nonverbal and linguistic objects that would be "controlling" as their activity progressed, jeopardizing collaboration. Another option for Lorraine was to reposition the base nearer to herself, but that would have been interpretable as a competitive and even aggressive response, and thus also would jeopardize collaboration by making it relevant for Rashia to retaliate. Instead of doing either, Lorraine made an incomplete response at first. She simply moved the base away from where Rashia put it and briefly held it in midair to her side. After Rashia voiced a protest (line 25: "Hey:::") Lorraine moved the base to the back of the table on her side where she had originally put it, thus not taking possession but suspending its active use, effectively removing a potential obstacle to their collaboration. At the same time, Lorraine self-narrated her motions (lines 23–26), and marked as temporary (line 26: "f'r now") the repositioning she ended up with, thus mitigating her interference with Rashia's positioning of the base, and the potential for conflict about it.

The Second Object-Pair. Despite Lorraine's mitigation of her having taken the green base, after she set the base down Rashia voiced a second protest, giving an instrumentally sound reason for objecting (line 30: "We need that."). This was an upgraded protest both by its being a reiteration, and by its being more elaborated, a "good reason" for objecting. Beside the practical need for the green base that Rashia correctly pointed out, what Lorraine then did about its positioning had potential interactional consequences: Rashia's having protested, and moreover repeated and upgraded her protest, made it relevant for Lorraine either to give in to Rashia's wishes, or to resist and risk conflict between them, either of which would jeopardize their working together as equals in the remaining interaction. Lorraine's response was to reverse herself and reposition the green base back in front of Rashia, but in a way that might offset interpreting that as giving-in.

```
30   Rashia:    We need that.
31              (0.5)
32              Lorraine: Yes. I know.
33              (0.5)                    ((L picks the green base back up))
34   Lorraine:  We need to be able to ↑reach it?
35   Rashia:    Yeah.                   ((R reaches for base; L evades her
36   Lorraine:  Put this down right here.    and puts it back where R had it))
```

Lorraine offset the potential for interpreting and responding to her self-reversal as simple compliance by making it relevant to her own cognitions rather than Rashia's protest. She repositioned the base in three steps that jointly had this effect. First, she responded to Rashia's second protest by agreeing ("Yes. I know."), even though her own prior action belied that, and *then* picking the base back up. Second, self-narrating again, she stated a rationale, an elaboration of Rashia's, for repositioning the green base before actually doing so (line 34: "We need to be able to ↑reach it?"). Third, when Rashia at that point reached to take the green base from her, Lorraine pulled the base up and over Rashia's hands in an exaggerated movement, and brought it down to where Rashia had previously set it, again self-narrating about where the base should go (line 37: "Put this down right here."), referring to the place she set it down in a way that made it seem a "new" place and not the place from where she had just taken it. The linguistic and nonverbal objects Lorraine produced in those three steps additively make the repositioning relevant to her own initiatives, responsive to Rashia but self-actuated rather than compliant.

The Third Object-Pair. Lorraine's repositioning the base back where Rashia had put it made it relevant for Rashia to assert control, and she promptly did so. She asserted (line 37) that *she* (first person singular) would now "make the house (on it)."

36   Lorraine: Put this down right here.= *((L put base in front of R))*
37   Rashia: =(And now) I'm going to make the house (on it).
38   (1.5)
39   Lorraine: Okay °then,° you make the house. (.) And I'll get the
40   flowers ready.

Lorraine's basic options in response to Rashia's assertion (line 37) were to accept it or to oppose it, but the former would functionally instantiate and make relevant continuing an inequality of participation, and the latter would make conflict relevant. Lorraine did not take either of those options (or more precisely, she took both). While she did agree to Rashia's plan, she did not do so completely and she did something more. She first marked her agreement as qualified ("Okay °then,°" rather than "Okay"); more importantly, she then stated a plan of her own that she conjoined with Rashia's, using vocal stress to mark the two plans as linked and parallel (lines 39–40: "you make the house. (.) And I'll get the flowers ready."). Because the two plans involve the two components of the project to which they originally agreed (to build a house, with flowers, both girls referring to these with definite articles that index their prior agreement), Lorraine's response formulates their respective activities as a division of labor on a common project, thereby supplanting/opposing the unilateralism of Rashia's plan.

Lorraine's Neo-Rhetorical Participation. For the purposes at hand, it would be a mistake to simply take for granted that Lorraine produced the objects she did anticipatorily. It should be considered whether Lorraine might instead have previously learned each of the specific object-pairs involved, so that her responses were not anticipatory but a local application of past experience (cf. Greene, 1984, 1995[12]). The three object-pairs involved are summarized in Fig. 11.1.

---

[12]It has been my understanding of Greene's action assembly theory that persons are considered to form and store a repertoire of previously acquired ways of producing actions (procedural records), so that one's action in the current moment is predicated on what one's past experience makes available for one to do, and how to do it, in response to current eliciting conditions. Greene (personal correspondence, 1996) takes issue with this. In analyzing actions in the current moment as "assembled" from a repertoire of atomic components, he takes the view that "it is the assembly of numerous behavioral features (at a variety of levels of abstraction) that gives rise to the fundamentally novel, creative character of actions" and that "various instantiations of the Principles of Relevance may well be reflected in the content of procedural records." While I do not disagree in the abstract, important particulars seem obdurate, especially the fact that every constituent detail of the "composition" of a given symbolic object is not equally important from one situation to the next, but it is not clear that

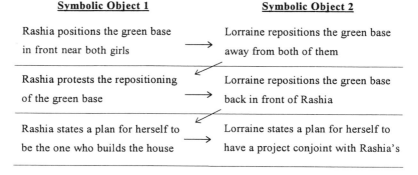

FIG. 11.1. Three object-pairs sequentially produced by Rashia and Lorraine.

With reference to the first object-pair, one could surmise plausibly that Lorraine learned, possibly from experience with adult interventions in children's conflicts, that when possession of a plaything is in dispute, to take the plaything out of contention entirely. The particular application of such learning in this instance, however, is complicated by the fact that the green base did not become a plaything whose possession was actively in dispute *until* Lorraine repositioned it. The "dispute" in question, then, can only have existed at that point cognitively, in Lorraine's interpretation of Rashia's positioning of the green base and/or the *consequences* she projected that would have.

With reference to the second object-pair, one can plausibly surmise that Lorraine had learned from her own direct experience to not resist upgraded protests such as Rashia produced, but to comply: thus, Lorraine returned the green base to Rashia after Rashia upgraded her protest. However, there are complications here too. Lorraine did not directly return the base when Rashia protested. Lorraine asserted that she already knew what Rashia had pointed out as the reason for objecting, but at the same time she picked up the base and held it. Lorraine then offered a task-related formulation of her own about the reason Rashia objected. Further, when Rashia reached for the base after Lorraine produced a rationale for returning it, Lorraine pulled it out of Rashia's reach and put it back herself, a maneuver that was superfluous if Lorraine were simply surrendering to Rashia's protest.

With reference to the third object-pair, it is difficult to surmise in any plausible way that Lorraine produced a learned response to the particular

---

action assembly theory could capture this. Further, Greene's comments seem focused on the object itself as novel or creative, whereas what I think makes an "assembled" symbolic object novel and creative is where it is *sequentially placed* in larger wholes, among what other component objects, and how details of its composition are adjusted accordingly. Still, Greene's view of the matter underscores that there is more of a complementary than a competing relationship between his work and mine, along the lines discussed in closing.

object Rashia produced, a stated intent to singly build the house. Hence, Lorraine would have had to be responding to the type of object Rashia produced. Let us characterize the object as a monopolization of a putatively shared activity, marked in this instance by Rashia's shift from the first person plural ("we") being used up to then, to the first person singular ("I"). But consider that the learned response to such an object would most likely be either (a) to protest or interfere, or (b) to withdraw from participation and turn to a distinct, preferably more desirable, alternative activity. Lorraine neither protested nor withdrew. She turned to the lesser component of the original project on which they (tacitly) agreed to collaborate, an option she would not typically have and thus not the response she most probably would learn.

Taking the details into account, it is implausible that any of the three object-pairs that were produced can have been learned previously, especially the third. And there is a further difficulty. Each of the three object-pairs promotes the same interactional result, which would be a striking coincidence if each of them involved separately learned ways of responding to particular symbolic objects. Each of the objects Rashia produced can be construed as seeming to Lorraine to potentially set the interaction on a course away from collaboration toward either conflict, or unequal or independent participation in building something with the Lego set. Each of Lorraine's responses countered in a consistent way by averting the potential for both of those interactional consequences, and promoting collaboration (however, in the second object-pair, priority had to be given to preventing conflict, since to avert conflict necessitated returning the green base to Rashia, thereby creating a new potential for unequal participation; but components of Lorraine's response reduced the potential for unequal participation by first, staging her response as self-actuated, thus not submissive, through verbalizing why the base should be returned, and second, by preventing Rashia from taking it from her).

If Lorraine's responses to the objects Rashia produced cannot be attributed to prior learning in any detail, or with any completeness, then it has to be considered that Lorraine produced her responses neo-rhetorically, on the basis of cognitive resources for projecting the interactional consequences of the objects that Rashia produced, and the interactional consequences of her own responses. This warrants pursuing the main concern here, the insensitivity of $PrinRel_0$ to the empirical particulars of these data.

Identifying and Repairing Analytic Deficiencies of $PrinRel_0$

For Lorraine to have produced her responses to Rashia anticipatorily, there has to be a principled basis by which she could project what would relevantly follow in the interaction both from the symbolic objects Rashia produced, and the responses Lorraine could optionally produce in turn. Specifically, Lorraine had to project (in some sense) what relevantly followed from each of the various objects that she and Rashia produced:

a. Rashia's positioning the green base in front of herself
b. Lorraine's repositioning the green base away from both versus in front of herself
c. Lorraine's marking as temporary ("f'r now") her respositioning the green base
d. Rashia's consecutive utterances "Hey:::" and "We need that."
e. Lorraine's statement of a reason to reposition the green base again ("We need to be able to ↑reach it?")
f. Lorraine's returning the green base to its original position in front of Rashia
g. Rashia's reaching to take the green base from Lorraine's hand
h. Lorraine's evasion of Rashia's reach to take the base from her
i. Rashia's utterance "I'm going to make the house (on it)."
j. Lorraine's utterance "Okay °then,° you make the house. (.) And I'll get the flowers ready."

However, $PrinRel_0$ can only project what follows relevantly from each of these symbolic objects in terms of the specific interpretation of each object. The problem is that of the 10 objects in that list, $PrinRel_0$ do not anticipate the evident meanings of 7 of them to which Rashia and Lorraine oriented. This involves the 5 nonverbal objects they produced (a, b, f, and g and h) and 2 of the 5 linguistic objects (e and j).[13]

---

[13]The three objects whose possible meanings, and thus specific interpretation, fall within the scope of $PrinRel_0$ are the utterances (c) "f'r now," (d) "We need that" following "Hey:::" and (i) "(And now) I'm going to make the house (on it)." The first, the object "for now," is predicated on a nonverbal object, repositioning the green base, and on the grounds that it breaches the quantity maxim it implicates that the repositioning was temporary (or cancels the implicature of the repositioning that it was permanent). This implicature arguably counts as the utterance's specific interpretation on the grounds that it coheres with the specific interpretation of Lorraine's repositioning of the green base as a suspension of the use of an item of property, rather than taking possession of it (and reciprocally the implicature warrants giving the repositioning that specific interpretation). Rashia's utterance, "We need that" counts as a protest on the basis of the constitutive rules of illocutionary acts. Those rules can be formulated provisionally as requiring that the speaker state a need or want and that the speaker believe the hearer has knowingly prevented its fulfillment. This possible meaning arguably counts as the utterance's specific interpretation on the grounds that it coheres with Rashia's immediately prior utterance of an idiomatically unambiguous protest ("Hey:::") and also Lorraine's having actively interfered with Rashia's want to use the green base. Note, however, that in both cases the possible meaning and specific interpretation depend on the meaning-

The Situated Meanings of Task-Related Nonverbal Objects. The non-verbal objects of interest that Rashia and Lorraine produced do not have conventional meanings before the fact at all, corresponding to the conventional meanings of various nonverbal displays. Although each of those non-verbal objects has an instrumental aspect—is an action as opposed to a motion—they and most other behaviors that persons produce are not conventional forms of expression. But as Lorraine's and Rashia's interaction indicates, it must be the case that the nonverbal objects one produces during an interaction that are instrumental for the business at hand are contingently interpretable, and thereby have consequences for the future course of the current interaction. The limitation of the way PrinRel$_0$ were formalized is that they are insensitive to this possibility; they only took into account nonverbal objects that are conventional forms of expression.

That there is an apparent option of taking at face value nonverbal objects that are produced as instrumental for undertaking the present task, or taking them as socially meaningful components of the present interaction, brings to mind the logic of Grice's (1975) Cooperative Principle. Let us posit that a nonverbal object produced in the course of interactively undertaking some task will be "cooperative" at face value if it is the most direct—simplest, most economical—way to satisfy the demands of the task. Any nonverbal object whose features are such that it deviates from being the most direct way to satisfy the demands of the task will *task*-implicate some thought, affect, disposition, or agenda that the person must have to have "deviated" in that particular way from what would directly satisfy task requirements. For example, when someone gets on a public bus, the task demand after paying his or her fare is for the person to take a place on the bus, with sitting down the preferred option. Sitting down in the first available seat would be the most direct way to fulfill that task demand. If that is what the newly boarded passenger does, that nonverbal object (taking that seat) is not meaningful except at face value as task-relevant. But if a newly boarded passenger passes up open seats, and either sits in a less available seat or stands, the nonverbal object(s) that were thus produced will task implicate that the person has certain thoughts, feelings, dispositions, or purposes. Thus, if one is seated on a bus, the seat next to one is empty, and a newly boarded

---

fulness of the positioning of the green base. The basis for the meaningfulness of such nonverbal objects has not been directly addressed and needs special attention, as in the remaining analysis. The third object, "(And now) I'm going to make the ho<u>u</u>se (on it.)", involves a "scalar implicature" (Gazdar, 1979; Levinson, 1983), where the use of a "weaker" or less inclusive term on a scale implicates *not* the stronger or more inclusive one. Hence, for Rashia to use the first person singular in announcing an intention to build the house does not logically exclude Lorraine, but it implicates exclusion. Lorraine's use of a concession marker in response ("Okay °then,°") coheres with that implicature, and based on PrinRel$_0$, warrants giving the utterance that specific interpretation.

passenger sits there, the passenger's taking that seat is a nonverbal object that would change in meaning, depending on whether (a) the seat taken were the only empty one on the bus, versus (b) there were no other passengers, and the new passenger passed by other empty seats before coming to the seat next to one and sitting right there.

In Lorraine's and Rashia's interaction, the positioning of the green base made up three of the nonverbal objects that Rashia and Lorraine produced that were each oriented to as meaningful. Taking these one at a time, first consider that in positioning the green base near her, Rashia put it in the position most directly responsive to the task demand—between the two girls, accessible by both—with reference to the requirement that they work together to build something. Yet Lorraine responded to that as problematic, thus meaningful. Now recall that in thus positioning the green base, Rashia unilaterally changed its position from where Lorraine placed it previously. Hence, Rashia's move could have been taken to task-implicate an agenda in opposition to Lorraine's about how they would pursue their activity, or about what the task demand was, not as simply instrumental to carrying on the task. The second repositioning, Lorraine's taking the base from the position in which Rashia put it, would thus also not be directly task-relevant, it would task-implicate an opposition to Rashia's move. Beyond that, what was task-implicated depended on where Lorraine repositioned the base: if not where Rashia had it, then a different agenda would be task-implicated if she put it down closer to herself, versus out of contention away from both of them. The third nonverbal object, the third respositioning of the green base, involved Lorraine's putting it back where Rashia had previously set it. This can no more be considered simply instrumental than when Rashia did it, even though again it was the best positioning for carrying on the task. It was not a direct response to the task demand, it was the third repositioning in their interaction and a self-reversal. Reversing herself, doing so in response to Rashia's protest, and restoring the base to the position Rashia favored, task-implicated Lorraine's acceptance of, or possibly submission to, Rashia's agenda.

It is in conjunction with this third repositioning of the base that two more nonverbal objects were produced whose meaningfulness has to be explained: Rashia's reaching to take the green base, and Lorraine's maneuver to evade her reach and set the base down herself. Let us identify a subtask that arose at that juncture, to put the base down where they could reach it (in Lorraine's words). The most direct way to have carried out this subtask was for the one who had the green base to put it down, and that was Lorraine. Hence, for Rashia to reach for the base introduced a means of carrying out the task which was less direct, and thus task-implicated that Rashia had an agenda, perhaps to take control. Conversely, once Rashia reached for the base, the most direct way to accomplish the subtask of putting it back would have been to let her take it. It was a less direct, more elaborate maneuver to evade Rashia's reach and then put it down. Hence, Lorraine's move task-implicated an opposition to giving Rashia control, or perhaps to surrendering it.

The Situated Meanings of Task-Related Linguistic Objects. In regard to the two linguistic objects of interest that Lorraine produced respectively before and after this third repositioning of the green base, the issue is that they seem to be meaningful in some way other than the possible meanings one could assign them before the fact in terms of their semantics, illocutionary force, and conversational implicature. First, Lorraine said, "We need to be able to ↑reach it?" to which Rashia answered "Yeah": yet even though this pair has the surface aspect of a question and answer, Lorraine's utterance seems to have prompted Rashia to reach for the green base, as if Lorraine had said, "Okay, you can have it back." But if we try to account for Rashia's response by characterizing Lorraine's utterance as an indirect speech act, an offer, along the lines of "Would you like to have it back?", it then does not follow that Lorraine would prevent Rashia from taking it. Second, when Rashia asserted "(And now) I'm going to make the house (on it)" after the green base had been returned, Lorraine agreed to that (but with a concession marker) and then added the utterance "you make the house. (.) And I'll get the flowers ready." On semantic grounds and in terms of illocutionary force, Lorraine's utterance has two parts, an elaborated agreement for Rashia to go ahead ("Okay °then,° you make the house") and a statement of her own intention ("I'll get the flowers ready). In those terms, the utterance also meets the conversational demand, and does not evidently implicate anything more. But where this utterance thus seems to underscore the separation of effort that Rashia initiated, this meaning is at odds with the way Rashia responded to it. She reintroduced use of the first person plural, in stating her intent to adjust the size of the house so that "we" (first person plural) "will have room >for the< ↑garden." (line 46).

Both the linguistic object Lorraine produced before returning the base, and the object that she produced after Rashia laid claim to building the house, thus seem to be meaningful on some other basis than their possible conventional meanings on linguistic/social grounds. This situation parallels the case of the nonverbal objects analyzed above, and a parallel solution seems warranted. Consider, then, that an utterance too can either be simply instrumental with reference to the requirements of the task at hand, a direct fulfillment of what the task requires in terms of one or another of its possible meanings, and if not, then producing that utterance *task*-implicates that the speaker has some further thought, feeling, disposition, or agenda. Care must be taken here: Such implicatures, produced with reference to the demands of the task at hand, resemble but are distinct from conversational implicatures, produced with reference to the demands of the conversation. Schegloff (1996) has examined a phenomenon that illustrates this. He noticed that at times a person can answer a question, or agree with a statement, by echoing the question or statement in their answer. In a radio interview of an author, Shreve, this phenomenon occurred three times in a row, marked in the transcript with arrows in answer to the interviewer's, Edwards', questions/prompts:

> Edwards: There:: lotsa different kindsa writers, (0.8)
>   you're:- a storyteller.
> Shreve: Yes:.
>   (.)
> → ⎧ Edwards: D'you:: (.) don' write fer- (.) English professors.=
>   ⎩ Shreve: = mhh No=I don' write fer English professors. ·hh
>   I don' think I have an enormous following amongst
>   English professors?nhhh
> → ⎧ Edwards: ·hhh You write fer readers.
>   ⎩ Shreve: ·hh I really write fer readers. 'n I think
>   ((*skip 3 lines of transcript*))
>   I grew up with stories, (.) both- in my own house,
>   and stories in my ^head.
> → ⎧ Edwards: ·hhh But there's more here than a ya:rn.
>   ⎩ Shreve: ·hh There's more here than a ya:rn:, an:d I . . .

In terms of the conversational demand that Edwards' questions or question/prompts created, Shreve's responses met it, albeit inefficiently (there is no breach of the quantity maxim here because Shreve's utterances do not provide more information than is called for, just more words). Accordingly, there is no conversational implicature in these responses. But in terms of the instrumental requirements of the task, Shreve's answers are not the most direct ways to fulfill it—the simplest and most economical. Given that these utterances are confirmatory, but in an unnecessarily elaborated form for the task at hand, they can be regarded as task-implicating a confirmation of something in addition to the actual question. Based on the aggregate of cases he examined, Schegloff found that these "repeats" come after the other person has formulated something that the speaker previously implied or alluded to, so that in Schegloff's view, the "repeat" of that formulation confirms both that there had been an allusion and that the other person had correctly formulated it.

We can now consider the evident interpretations of the two linguistic objects that Lorraine produced that are of interest here. The first is her rationale for the third respositioning of the base, "We need to be able to ↑reach it?" As noted earlier, Lorraine displayed an orientation to this utterance that rules out that it was a question or an indirect speech act. It also has to be ruled out that it involves a conversational implicature: Although the utterance is largely redundant, it does not violate the quantity maxim or any other. But we can consider that in terms of the task demand, the redundancy of the utterance is task-implicative. Rashia had asserted that they "need" the base, and Lorraine had asserted "I kn<u>ow</u>." The most direct response to the task demand at that point would have been to reposition the base or give it to Rashia. To instead formulate an elaborated version of the reason they needed it before actually repositioning the base thus task-implicated something further about repositioning the base, that is, that Lorraine was doing it based on her own thinking, not Rashia's. This implicature coheres, of course, with the implicatures that were inferred earlier from the nonverbal objects that followed (Lorraine's evasion of Rashia's reaching for the base and setting it down herself).

The second linguistic object of interest is Lorraine's response when Rashia stated her intention to personally build the house: "Okay °then,° y<u>ou</u> make the h<u>ouse.</u> (.) And <u>I</u>'ll get the fl<u>owers</u> ready." On the face of it, the utterance seems to state an elaborated agreement with Rashia's stated intention that she (singly) would make the house, and to conjoin that with Lorraine's intent that she (singly) would pursue another part of the task. But where those utterances seem to cohere semantically as references to the pursuit of separate activities, it is at odds with this that Rashia reintroduced the use of the plural pronoun "we" in her response. Consider, then, that the most direct way to have oriented to a division of labor *as* a separation of their joint activity into two would have been to simply agree to Rashia's plan and append her own ("Okay °then°, . . . <u>I</u>'ll get the fl<u>owers</u> ready."). The more elaborated utterance that Lorraine produced, however, enabled her to phonologically mark her own plan as a parallel to Rashia's, thus task-implicating that her agenda was for the two of them to be undertaking a coordinated effort on a single project. Rashia's reintroduction of the plural pronoun "we" in her response coheres with this.

A Revision of PrinRel$_o$

The foregoing analysis suggests that the limitation of PrinRel$_o$ was their insensitivity to the fact that people typically interact to engage in a task (or more broadly, an activity), where the objects they produce are meaningful and relevant to each other as components of that task, not just of the interaction. PrinRel$_o$ were formalized on the assumption that interactions are strings that are only constrained locally, first by what is sequentially relevant at each next juncture of an interaction, and secondly, the personal agenda(s) of one or more participants and their associated interest in achieving or avoiding certain resolutions. By taking into account that symbolic objects, and the interactions that comprise them, are produced in the course of engaging in a task or activity, $PrinRel_0$ can be adjusted to capture details that would otherwise be missed, such as the interactional importance of the nonverbal objects Rashia and Lorraine produced, and their connection to their talk.

The conceptual soundness of this revision was underscored recently by Levinson (1992), citing Wittgenstein's general proposition that how language is used and understood depends on the activity in which people are engaged:

> The intuitions that underlay Wittgenstein's emphasis on the embedding of language within human activities have not been accounted for in any modern theory of how language is used and understood. The purpose [in Levinson's essay] is to document from empirical materials that Wittgenstein's intuitions have a basis in fact, and moreover that his failure to make the distinction between speech acts and speech activities was not just an oversight—the two are interconnected in such fundamental ways that only a thorough-going pragmatic theory will be adequate to describe both phenomena. (p. 67)

Moerman (1990–1991), along the same lines, went further. He questioned giving talk *a priori* analytic primacy in the study of social interaction, on the grounds that its centrality depends on the activity in which the people involved are taking part (see also Sperber & Wilson, 1986, for a theoretical formulation that leads in the same direction). In summarizing a videotaped interaction between women in a Tai-Lue village as they prepared "sweets" to present in the village temple for the Lue New Year, he raised the issue as follows:

> All the socially significant village generations of women . . . are engaged in a distinctively and emblematically female activity, in doing important "woman's work," and in showing and teaching how the work should be done. This is their principal activity. They talk while doing it. How is their talk set into the social organization of making [sweets]? How important is their talk to what they are principally doing? (p. 181)

> We have yet to explore how collective, *ensemble*, activities are socially organized, and what role talk plays in that organization. (p. 182)

The analysis of the specifics of Lorraine's and Rashia's interaction obviously are consonant with Levinson's and Moerman's remarks. To capture what that analysis revealed, the basic logic of $PrinRel_0$ can be retained: The specific interpretation of a symbolic object is warranted as that one of its possible meanings that is relevant to (a) the most extensive, most contiguous ground of coherence among other objects in the interaction, and (b) a "next object" along a sequential progression toward a possible "satisfier" of the agenda at hand. But $PrinRel_0$ have to be revised to capture how the specific interpretation of the nonverbal as well as linguistic objects individuals produce depends not only on their interconnection with each other in the interaction, but their connection to the activity in which participants are engaged. This revision yields a candidate theory of the way language (and other forms of expression) is embedded in human activity, $PrinRel_r$.

First, it is obviously necessary to posit that $PrinRel_r$ do not just range over the propositional content, illocutionary force, and conversational implicatures of utterances, and the conventional meanings of nonverbal displays. They also range over another type of meaning that both nonverbal and linguistic objects can have: a task-based (not conversation-based) implicature of a thought, feeling, disposition, or agenda that results when the object in question is not the most direct response to the present demand of the task at hand. Thus, for example, of the possible meanings of Lorraine's utterance, "Okay °then,° you make the house. (.) And I'll get the flowers ready.", that Rashia oriented to, and produced a response relevant to, the relevant one was task-implicated and would not otherwise have been possible—that Lorraine's agenda was for the two of them to engage in a coordinated effort on a single project. The "logic" of this additional type of implicature, and the calculability of what is implicated by particular breaches of the task demand, obviously need attention that they have not gotten here. But at this point, there is no reason to think that an additional Principle of Relevance needs to be devised to apply to task implicatures, in addition to the original Principles that applied to conversational implicatures.[14]

---

[14]As noted earlier, the formalisms that expressed $PrinRel_0$ were in the general form of implications in a fuzzy logic, paraphrased as "To the extent that there are grounds for believing that Γ is true, it is warranted to that extent to judge that Σ is true," that are formally expressed as $\Gamma \Rightarrow \Sigma$. The basic principle that warrants focusing on a conversational implicature was expressed as follows:

$$(\text{Imp}_{ue} \cdot ((\alpha)(\delta)(SS_s)) \cdot (SS_s \approx SS{:}\text{Imp}_{ue})) \Rightarrow (\alpha/\delta)(SI_{ue} = \text{Imp}_{ue})$$

where Imp_{ue} is the conversational implicature of the uttered expression in question; SS_s is a subjective state of the speaker that one or more objects in the interaction disclose, cause, or result from; α is a quantifier indexing the number of objects in the interaction that express or assume SS_s; δ is a quantifier indexing the "distance" between the utterance and the nearest object that expresses or presupposes SS_s; $SS{:}Imp$ is the subjective state (the thought, feeling, disposition, or agenda) on which the implicature is predicated; SI is a specific interpretation; and α/δ is a quantifier based on the ratio of the number and distance of relevant objects from UE that expresses the strength of the warrant for focusing on the implicature as the utterance's specific interpretation.

Pending formal analysis of task implicatures, it seems the Principle of Relevance above could apply to them just as well as to conversational implicatures. On the other hand, the formalisms that represented warrants for the specific interpretation of nonverbal objects only apply to objects that in one way or another have a "signal value" before the fact, and this excludes

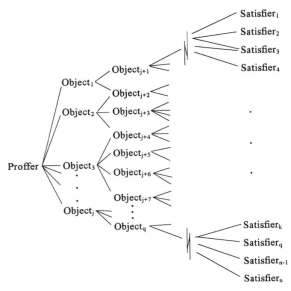

FIG. 11.2. Pathways from proffer to all relevant possible satisfiers based on PrinRel$_0$.

Second, PrinRel$_0$ assumed that the possible satisfiers of the agenda being pursued in an interaction were indefinitely large in number, as follows. Given any symbolic object that "proffers" an agenda, a set of relevant possible responses to the proffer directly follows, for each of which a further set of relevant responses follows, and so on, giving rise to a branching set of pathways each of which ends at a relevant possible satisfier, as in Fig. 11.2. Note that this makes the range of satisifiers to which the initiating proffer could relevantly lead open and indefinite. However, it has since become obvious to me that such a formulation fails to capture a key aspect of most interactions. In many interactions only a few possible resolutions are being sought. Participants generally orient to interactions as *not* being open-ended as to their resolution (except for special genres such as "small talk"), and thus they are attentive, with varying degrees of vigilance, to what gets made relevant by each turn. This is the case whenever at least one participant has personal wants about the interaction's resolution, or most typically and of special interest here, when the participants are engaged in some activity in which only a few particular resolutions are normative within the immediate institutional setting. A prototype of the latter is a service encounter. Of course,

---

objects like Lorraine's and Rashia's positioning of the green base whose meaning is predicated entirely on a task implicature. At least one additional formalism would be needed to express the warrant for focusing on such meanings of nonverbal objects, and further revisions and additions are conceivable in the details of others of these principles.

this restrictiveness on interactions when participants are engaged in an activity is fragile. A proffer such as a clerk's *Can I help you?* could relevantly lead to any of a wide range of satisfiers, as in Fig. 11.2, beyond what is normative for that activity. An activity, or participants' wants as to the resolution, are thus only restrictive on the way turns are fashioned to the extent that participants cooperatively and separately opt to uphold them.

The analytic gains from taking into account the task or activity people are engaged in when they interact—and the task implicatures of nonverbal and linguistic objects that this reveals—are summarized in terms of the following comparisons between $PrinRel_o$ and $PrinRel_r$:

- $PrinRel_o$ reflected that interactions generally arise from and are organized around participants' agendas, but those agendas and possible resolutions were treated as a product of each participants' personal interests, without giving due attention to how extensively such agendas and resolutions are products of a conventional (usually institutional) "activity" in which participants are engaged (Goffman, 1959; Cushman & Whiting, 1972; Moerman, 1990–1991; Levinson, 1992). By taking into account that linguistic and nonverbal objects may have task implicatures within a defined activity, $PrinRel_r$ capture that such objects may be relevant, and thus interpretable, not just to each other or the interaction, but also (most basically) to what the current task/activity itself makes available regarding what to do, how to do it, and the small number of possible ways that activity could be concluded.

- In regard to the production and specific interpretation of nonverbal objects, $PrinRel_o$ apply to just objects that are conventional forms of expression. By taking into account the task implicatures of nonverbal objects, $PrinRel_r$ range over a far more extensive set of nonverbal objects, now including ones with instrumental as well as conventionally expressive functions. This would take into account even the kinds of nonverbal objects that Pomerantz (1984) observed when dispreferred responses are produced (vocalized pauses, hedges, etc.). Further, where $PrinRel_o$ generally formulate the relevance, and interpretability, of nonverbal objects in terms of the specific interpretation of linguistic objects that precede or accompany them, $PrinRel_r$ are sensitive to the possibility that a nonverbal object can also be relevant in its own right to the activity in which participants are engaged.

- $PrinRel_o$ identify the specific interpretation of an object as one of its possible meanings "before the fact," based on applicable interpretation rules and social conventions. However, this fails to capture the potential for linguistic objects to have specific interpretations that are novel, not among their possible meanings before the fact, and fails to capture that nonverbal objects that do not have a conventional meaning at all before the fact may warrant specific interpretations. The potential for such objects to have task implicatures (in addition to the conversational implicatures of utterances) captures any novel meanings they have in the local moment whose relevance and interactional consequences are then captured by $PrinRel_r$.

CONCLUDING DISCUSSION

There are fundamental differences between the approach taken here and much of the work on message production, but there are also commonalities in terms of goals and questions. I want to stress the commonalities, taking up the differences along the way. Because of the variety of research and theory on message production, and its complexity, it would be unwieldy to try pursuing these matters comprehensively. I focus instead on two specific programs that are at the forefront of work in this area and that I consider representative, one John Greene's, the other Barbara O'Keefe's.

It is important to recognize that the work on PrinRel, presented earlier, and those two research programs, each pursue what is essentially the same question about essentially the same phenomenon. When individuals produce symbolic objects, they functionally "select" from among an indefinitely large set of things that can be expressed or done, to produce just what would be functional and responsive regarding the "demands" of the local moment. The question is how this works, what the cognitive resources or processes might be, considering the variety and complexity of the demands in the current moment to which individuals respond, and the relative speed with which they produce symbolic objects to do so (relative to the difference between producing a turn at speaking in a conversation, and producing an object on the scale of the present essay).

In these terms, there are commonalities and differences between the three programs about which dialogue is possible and potentially fruitful. Greene (1984, 1995) has conceptualized the cognitive resources involved as a repertoire of primitive behavioral units that persons can assemble and reassemble into "actions" (whether that consists of production of a message or other physical behaviors) in response to the physical or social demands of the current moment. Rather than attempt to model how "demand" is identified in any instance, and what makes the objects persons produce more or less functionally adequate in response, Greene has chosen to investigate what situational variables complicate or facilitate the process of assembling responses through experimentation in which situational demands are manipulated, and response latencies measured. In these terms PrinRel, could be regarded as complementary, a model of the computational device by which the demands (i.e., interactional constraints) of the current moment are identified, and the functional adequacy of alternative possible responses assessed.

O'Keefe (1988; O'Keefe & Lambert, 1995) has conceived the demands of the local moment, and thus the objects that get produced, differently from the way that either Greene or I have. She does not view the demand in the local moment as being for the person to *do* something, but for the person to *tell* others something (i.e., select from a repertoire of "beliefs" just what belief to express "now"). But unlike Greene, her concern, more akin to the approach here, has been to model the basis for identifying the demands of the local moment, and assessing the functional adequacy of alternative possible ways of responding to it. While this led O'Keefe and Lambert (1995) to state what an adequate model has to capture in terms highly compatible with $PrinRel_r$ (see their quoted remarks prefatory to the summary of $PrinRel_o$), it also led them in a direction opposed to the approach here, and possibly Greene's action assembly theory as well. They state that their "model assumes a connectionist (parallel distributed processing) architecture" (p. 68). Such an architecture can only apply when output consists of a finite set of strings of primitive units, and the primitive units that are input are also finite in number. An example on which much research has been done is for the set of speech sounds or alphabetic characters of a language to be input, with output the set of strings of those units that constitute the (uninterpreted) lexicon of that language. O'Keefe and Lambert may have been led to this by their findings that a finite corpus of beliefs tended to be used and reused in different "messages" that their respondents produced. However, viewing matters in this way is radical, considering its *a priori* commitment to the finiteness of output strings that is directly at odds with $PrinRel_r$ and dubious from the perspective of action assembly theory. It leaves unresolved how, if at all, the demand in the local moment can be formalized to constitute input units such that the output is *not* just any of the indefinitely many symbolic objects that *could* be "assembled," but one of the (relatively) few that would be functionally responsive to that demand. Perhaps more importantly, this overlooks that even if observation showed that persons do produce a relatively few symbolic objects as output with reference to some input condition, any such "output" is often oriented to by self and by other not only in terms of what object it was that did get produced, but also what other objects *could have been* produced at that juncture and were not.[15]

But whereas the matters we respectively have in common are noteworthy, and the foregoing issues worth debating, there are some fundamental differences that need to be considered. They are most visible from the contrast in the *data* we respectively examine: One does not find in Greene's or O'Keefe's work direct attention to the empirical particulars of naturalistic interaction, but (perhaps as a result) one does find the view that people

---

[15]Inferences about others and their current inner thoughts and feelings, whether with reference to attribution theory or some other model, depend on contrasting what occurred with what else might have occurred, and rationalizing the tacit "choice" the person is thereby perceived to have made (Sanders, 1987, 1995b). The analysis of the conversation between two nurses discussed above (Sanders, 1991) makes a case that their respective abilities to detect when strategies to achieve their ends had failed, and to construct new ones that avoided the same pitfall, depends on such covert "contrasts."

produce symbolic objects that are self-contained and complete. Obviously, for the questions they ask, in the experimental protocols they employ, both had good reason to have proceeded as they did. However, the approach taken here, and the data examined, raise the question whether the experimentation they have each relied on has been flawed as a result. I pursue the matter here by taking the empirical realities in naturalistic occurrences as something to which all our work ultimately has to be accountable, although this itself might be a subject of debate.

Both Greene and O'Keefe have employed an experimental protocol where respondents are presented with a written description of a hypothetical "demand" in the local moment, and asked to respond to it by producing a single object, a "message." However, the data above suggest that the subjective and empirical reality persons face in producing symbolic objects is different from this in ways that probably matter. "Demand" in the local moment may not be subjectively experienced as a goal (which is the way it has been presented to respondents in much experimentation) but an incrementally developed set of constraints, for which *the respondent* would technically be as responsible as the addressed (though persons' attributions of responsibility to themselves and others vary). And the "response" would not typically be produced as a complete or solitary attempt, at a single opportunity, to satisfy the demand in the local moment, but as one of a series of past and future efforts to incrementally change or protect existing constraints on the future course of the interaction. Adjustments of the experimental protocols employed to produce eliciting conditions that have those characteristics seem feasible without requiring changes in the questions asked or measures and analyses used. It would be a matter of presenting respondents with a goal or interactional problem prior to their participation in a controlled interaction—controlled for example by "scripting" their interlocutor's turns and situating the interaction in a computer-mediated print channel in real time—then analyzing one or more of the objects, response latencies, and the like that occur at particular interactional turns.

While possibly fruitful issues arise from comparing the approach here with programs of research on message production, PrinRel, and associated analyses make a contribution in their own right. PrinRel, bridge work being done in two camps. In language pragmatics and conversation analysis extensive gains are being made in bringing to light the empirical particulars, and intricacy of design, both of utterances (e.g., Drew & Heritage, 1992; Schegloff, 1995, 1996) and nonverbal objects (e.g., Kendon, 1994). At the same time, considerable attention is being given to the computational basis for producing linguistic objects, though not nonverbal ones (e.g., Greene, 1984, 1995; O'Keefe & Lambert, 1995; Rumelhart et al., 1986). However, these have generally not been intersecting efforts, and in many ways are at odds. From the perspective of the former, efforts by the latter have been insensitive to the empirical particulars of what people actually say and do, and the formal properties of the objects involved. From the perspective of the latter, work on the empirical particulars has not addressed the computational issues. Instead, for the most part, analysts who examine the empirical particulars tend to account for them more or less directly as a matter of social convention, and in doing so fail to capture the planning, adaptation, and improvisation that O'Keefe and Lambert (1995) in particular stress, and that Lorraine (if not Rashia) exhibited.

In sum, PrinRel$_r$ represent a computational device that ranges over sequences of symbolic objects that have been associated as components of some larger whole (possibly by virtue of having been produced by a single group of participants interconnected by some channel of communication, or produced within the boundaries of a particular activity or institution). At any juncture, the addition of new symbolic objects to such sequences is constrained by how they would be interpreted and what consequences they have for the course of the future interaction. The power of PrinRel$_r$ is that they are sensitive to the empirical particulars of both the linguistic and nonverbal objects that people produce, and at the same time capture the principled basis for both conventionality in producing such objects, and novelty or adaptation, as well as the fluidity of their specific interpretation and the complexities of interaction that this creates.

REFERENCES

Atkinson, J. M., & Heritage, J. (Eds.). (1984). *Structures of social action: Studies in conversation analysis.* Cambridge, England: Cambridge University Press.

Austin, J. (1962). *How to do things with words.* New York: Oxford University Press.

Barnes, M. K., & Vangelisti, A. L. (1995). Speaking in a double-voice: Role-making as influence in preschoolers' fantasy play situations. *Research on Language and Social Interaction, 28,* 351–389.

Berger, C. R. (1987). Planning and scheming: Strategies for initiating relationships. In R. Burnett, P. McGhee, & D. Clarke (Eds.), *Accounting for relationships: Social representations of interpersonal links* (pp. 158–174). London: Methuen.

Brown, P., & Levinson, S. L. (1978). Universals in language usage: Politeness phenomena. In E. N. Goody (Ed.), *Questions and politeness: Strategies in social interaction* (pp. 56–289). Cambridge, England: Cambridge University Press.

Chomsky, N. (1965). *Aspects of the theory of syntax.* Cambridge, MA: MIT Press.

Cronen, V. E., Pearce, W. B., & Xi, C. (1989–1990). The meaning of "meaning" in the CMM analysis of communication: A comparison of two traditions. *Research on Language and Social Interaction, 23,* 1–40.

Cushman, D. P., & Whiting, G. (1972). An approach to communication theory: Toward consensus on rules. *Journal of Communication, 22,* 219–238.

Drew, P., & Heritage, J. (Eds.). (1992). *Talk at work: Interaction in institutional settings.* Cambridge, England: Cambridge University Press.

Edmondson, W. (1981). *Spoken discourse: A model for analysis.* London: Longman.

Gazdar, G. (1979). *Pragmatics: Implicature, presupposition, and logical form.* New York: Academic Press.

Goffman, E. (1959). *The presentation of self in everyday life.* Garden City, NY: Doubleday.

Goffman, E. (1967). *Interaction ritual: Essays on face-to-face behavior.* New York: Anchor Books.

Greene, J. O. (1984). A cognitive approach to human communication: An action assembly theory. *Communication Monographs, 51,* 289–306.

Greene, J. O. (1995). Production of messages in pursuit of multiple social goals: Action assembly theory contributions to the study of cognitive encoding processes. In B. R. Burleson (Ed.), *Communication yearbook 18* (pp. 26–53). Thousand Oaks, CA: Sage.

Grice, H. P. (1975). Logic and conversation. In P. Cole & J. L. Morgan (Eds.), *Syntax and semantics 3: Speech acts* (pp. 41–58). New York: Academic Press.

Heritage, J. (1990–1991). Intention, meaning, and strategy: Observations on constraints on interaction analysis. *Research on Language and Social Interaction, 24* (Special Section, *Ethnography and conversation analysis,* Robert Hopper, Ed.), 311–332.

Jacoby, S., & Ochs, E. (Eds.). (1995). *Co-Construction* (Special Issue: *Research on Language and Social Interaction, 28*). Mahwah, NJ: Lawrence Erlbaum Associates.

Kendon, A. (Ed.). (1994). *Gesture and understanding in social interaction* (Special Issue: *Research on Language and Social Interaction, 27*). Hillsdale, NJ: Lawrence Erlbaum Associates.

Levinson, S. C. (1983). *Pragmatics.* Cambridge, England: Cambridge University Press.

Levinson, S. C. (1992). Activity types and language. In P. Drew & J. Heritage (Eds.), *Talk at work: Interaction in institutional settings* (pp. 66–100). Cambridge, England: Cambridge University Press.

McNeill, D. (1985). So you think gestures are nonverbal? *Psychological Review, 92,* 350–371.

McNeill, D., Cassell, J., & McCullough, K. -E. (1994). Communicative effects of mismatched gestures. *Research on Language and Social Interaction, 27* (Special Issue, *Gesture and understanding in social interaction,* A. Kendon, Ed.), 223–237.

Miller, G. A., Galanter, E., & Pribram, K. H. (1960). *Plans and the structure of behavior.* New York: Holt, Rinehart & Winston.

Moerman, M. (1990–1991). Exploring talk and interaction. *Research on Language and Social Interaction, 24* (Special Section, *Ethnography and conversation analysis,* Robert Hopper, Ed.), 173–187.

O'Keefe, B. (1988). The logic of message design: Individual differences in reasoning about communication. *Communication Monographs, 55,* 80–103.

O'Keefe, B. J., & Lambert , B. L. (1995). Managing the flow of ideas: A local management approach to message design. In B. R. Burleson (Ed.), *Communication yearbook 18* (pp. 54–82). Thousand Oaks, CA: Sage.

Pearce, W. B., & Cronen, V. E. (1980). *Communication, action, and meaning: The creation of social realities.* New York: Praeger.

Pomerantz, A. (1984). Agreeing and disagreeing with assessments: Some features of preferred/dispreferred turn shapes. In J. M. Atkinson & J. Heritage (Eds.), *Structures of social action* (pp. 57–101). Cambridge, England: Cambridge University Press.

Pomerantz, A. (1986). *The case study approach in the conversation analytic tradition.* Paper presented at the International Conference on Talk and Social Structure, University of California, Santa Barbara.

Reichman, R. (1985). *Getting computers to talk like you and me: Discourse content, focus, and semantics (an ATN model).* Cambridge, MA: MIT Press.

Rumelhart, D. E., & Group, t. P. R. (Eds.). (1986). *Parallel distributed processing: Explorations in the micro-structure of cognitions: Vol. 1. Foundations.* Cambridge, MA: MIT Press.

Sanders, R. E. (1980). Principles of relevance: A theory of the relationship between language and communication. *Communication and Cognition, 13,* 77–95.

Sanders, R. E. (1984). Style, meaning and message effects. *Communication Monographs, 51,* 154–167.

Sanders, R. E. (1985). The interpretation of nonverbals. *Semiotica, 55,* 195–216.

Sanders, R. E. (1987). *Cognitive foundations of calculated speech: Controlling understandings in conversation and persuasion.* Albany, NY: SUNY Press.

Sanders, R. E. (1991). The two-way relationship between talk in social interaction and actors' goals and plans. In K. Tracy (Ed.), *Understanding face-to-face interaction: Issues linking goals and discourse* (pp. 167–188). Hillsdale, NJ: Lawrence Erlbaum Associates.

Sanders, R. E. (1995a). A neo-rhetorical perspective: The enactment of role-identities as interactive and strategic. In S. J. Sigman (Ed.), *The consequentiality of communication* (pp. 67–120). Hillsdale, NJ: Lawrence Erlbaum Associates.

Sanders, R. E. (1995b). The sequential inferential theories of Sanders and Gottman. In D. P. Cushman & B. Kovacic (Eds.), *Watershed research traditions in human communication theory.* Albany, NY: SUNY Press.

Sanders, R. E. (1996). *Communicating deceptively: The manufacture of counterfeit grounds for action.* Paper presented at the annual convention of the International Communication Association, Chicago.

Sanders, R. E., & Freeman, K. (1995). *Children's neo-rhetorical participation in peer interactions.* Paper presented at the Children and Social Competence: An Interdisciplinary Conference, University of Surrey, England.

Schank, R. (1977). Rules and topics in conversation. *Cognitive Science, 1,* 421–441.

Schank, R. C., & Abelson, R. P. (1977). *Scripts, plans, goals, and understanding: An inquiry into human knowledge structures.* Hillsdale, NJ: Lawrence Erlbaum Associates.

Schegloff, E. A. (1988). Presequences and indirection: Applying speech act theory to ordinary conversation. *Journal of Pragmatics, 12,* 55–62.

Schegloff, E. A. (1995). Discourse as an interactional achievement III: The omnirelevance of action. *Research on Language and Social Interaction, 28* (Special Issue, *Co-Construction,* S. Jacoby & E. Ochs, Eds.), 185–211.

Schegloff, E. (1996). Confirming allusions: Toward an empirical account of action. *American Journal of Sociology, 102,* 161–216.

Searle, J. R. (1969). *Speech acts: An essay in the philosophy of language.* Cambridge, England: Cambridge University Press.

Sheldon, A. (1996). You can be the baby brother but you aren't born yet: Preschool girls' negotiation for power and access in pretend play. *Research on language and Social Interaction, 29* (Special issue, *Constituting gender through talk in childhood: Conversations in parent-child, peer, and sibling relationships,* A. Sheldon, Ed.), 57–80.

Snyder, M. (1974). Self-monitoring of expressive behavior. *Journal of Personality and Social Psychology, 30,* 526–537.

Snyder, M. (1979). Self-monitoring processes. In L. Berkowitz (Ed.), *Advances in experimental social psychology* (Vol. 12, pp. 85–128). New York: Academic Press.

Sperber, D., & Wilson, D. (1986). *Relevance: Communication and cognition.* Oxford, England: Blackwell.

Tracy, K. (1982). On getting the point: Distinguishing "issues" from "events," an aspect of conversational coherence. In M. Burgoon (Ed.), *Communication yearbook 5* (pp. 279–301). New Brunswick, NJ: Transaction Press.

Tracy, K. (1983). The issue-event distinction: A rule of conversation and its scope condition. *Human Communication Research, 9,* 320–334.

Waldron, V. R. (1990). Constrained rationality: Situational influences on information acquisition plans and tactics. *Communication Monographs, 57,* 184–201.

12

RESEARCHING NONVERBAL MESSAGE PRODUCTION: A VIEW FROM INTERACTION ADAPTATION THEORY

Judee K. Burgoon
University of Arizona

Cindy H. White
University of Colorado

In 1995, Waldron, reflecting on rising disenchantment with the "psychologization" of communication and its overemphasis on the nonsocial, posed the question, "Is the 'Golden Age of Cognition' losing its lustre?" His essay lucidly captured a view we share. It is one we have articulated elsewhere in the rationales for two recently advanced communication theories: Interaction Adaptation Theory (Burgoon, Stern, & Dillman, 1995; White, 1996) and Interpersonal Deception Theory (Buller & Burgoon, 1996; Buller, Burgoon, White, & Ebesu, 1994; Burgoon & Buller, 1996). Like Waldron, we believe that the crown of cognition is becoming increasingly tarnished and that its faddish reign should and will give way to a more comprehensive approach to human message behavior. Because we also believe that communication theorists will eventually "come home," doing what they do best by centering on truly communicative phenomena and leaving psychologists to predict and explain intrapsychic activity, we wish to advocate a research agenda that propels interpersonal communication work on nonverbal and verbal encoding in that direction. It is an agenda guided by Interaction Adaptation Theory (IAT).

In preview, IAT does not eschew reference to cognitions but places them within the broader context of a set of affective and conative factors that predispose communicators to produce certain kinds of messages. Further, the cognitive factors that are featured in IAT are a select group which are linked directly to communication behavior. IAT also acknowledges that message behavior varies in degree of intentionality, planning, and automaticity, so that deliberative cognitive planning and effort are "demoted" from the position of prominence they have held of late. Most importantly, perhaps, IAT, as an interpersonal and interactional theory, looks to cointeractants' *behaviors* as major influences on a given communicator's messages. In other words, once an interaction commences, the communication patterns of an interaction partner may gain prepotency over one's own cognitions and affect as determinants of communication behavior. Recognition that one communicator's message production is highly susceptible to the influence of another's communication, often in unconscious ways, warrants a paradigm shift toward much greater research emphasis on: (a) relationships rather than individuals, (b) interdependent rather than independent action, (c) overt rather than covert processes, (d) complexes of meaningful behaviors rather than single message elements, and (e) dynamic patterns and sequences of behavioral adaptation rather than initial, static, or stable displays. Such a paradigm shift would highlight a somewhat different view of communication and symbolic signaling than, we believe, is currently promulgated in much message-production research.

FORMS OF ADAPTATION

At heart, IAT is a theory of mutual influence in interaction. It seeks to explain how communicators adjust and adapt to one another. Before proceeding, we need to clarify what kinds of encoding patterns are within the scope of IAT. Although we are emphasizing nonverbal cues in this chapter, IAT actually encompasses a broad range of both nonverbal and linguistic cues that have the potential to be adapted to those of other interlocutors.

The concept of adaptation (also referred to as *accommodation*) appears under many guises. We follow Burgoon, Stern, and Dillman (1995) in our definitions. At the most basic level, an actor's communicative behaviors may be described as *matching* another's, in which case the behaviors of interest are highly similar between the two individuals, perhaps even identical. When matching takes the form of identical, static, or slowly changing visual cues such as postures or body lean, the pattern may also be called *mirroring*. The opposite of matching is *complementarity*, in which one actor's behavior is in some way dissimilar to or opposite the other's. Matching and complementarity do not imply that one person's behavior is caused by or contingent upon the other. Rather, these terms are merely descriptive of the manifest behavior patterns. (Mirroring, however, may be viewed as a contingent response because of the improbability of two or more people exhibiting identical body positions by chance alone.) Matching, mirroring, and complementarity, like the other patterns to be described next, are applicable to dyadic or group-level as well as individual message production. That is, a dyad or subset of a group may be said to show matching pause lengths, linguistic formality, and so forth, or complementary amounts of gesturing and floor-holding.

When message behaviors take the form of adjustments over time and in response to other social actors, additional terms come into play. If one person's behavior is directed toward *and* contingent upon another's, then the behavior may be characterized individually or dyadically as *reciprocity,* which is a response "in a similar direction, to a partner's behaviors with behaviors of comparable functional value," or as *compensation,* in which "one responds with behaviors of comparable functional value but in the opposite direction" (Burgoon, Stern, et al., 1995, p. 129). If one person increases involvement, for example, and the other follows suit, then reciprocity is taking place. If, instead, the response to increased intimacy is one of decreased intimacy, then compensation is occurring. The shift toward greater similarity is often described as *convergence* and the shift away from a partner's style, toward greater dissimilarity, as *divergence.* When reciprocity also entails a rhythmic component and a temporal coordination and meshing of behavior patterns, it is called *interactional synchrony.*[1]

Finally, actors may adhere to their own communication style rather than adjusting to another. Such consistency or lack of adaptation to another is variously described as *nonaccommodation, nonadaptation,* or *maintenance.* We use all three of these terms synonymously.

PRESUPPOSITIONS OF INTERACTION ADAPTATION THEORY

IAT by its very nature is oriented to interdependencies in relationships and communication. In line with the views of many ethologists, anthropologists, and sociolinguists, IAT presupposes that an essential property of communication is that interactants bring to it an assumed common ground that is derived from a shared signal/symbol system and shared experiences as members of the human species. This is coupled with an assumptive or apparent mutuality of orientation that is manifested through coordinated and cooperative interaction (see, e.g., Graumann, 1995; Krauss, Fussell, & Chen, 1995; Mead, 1934). As expressed by Gumperz (1995), "It is generally agreed that conversation is by its very nature a cooperative endeavour, requiring coordination of signaling strategies at a number of levels" (p. 101). Echoing the same sentiments is Rommetveit (1974), who asserts that achieving understanding at even the simplest levels of communication requires

---

[1]This distinguishes it from self-synchrony, in which the individual behaviors are synchronized to their own verbal-vocal stream.

participants' mutual commitment to "a temporarily shared social world" (p. 29).

Consequently, all message production, and especially that in interpersonal conversation, implicitly begins with an alignment toward the message recipient and a predisposition to calibrate one's messages to the characteristics of the target (as well as the topic, occasion, and setting). Put differently, adaptation is an intrinsic feature of all communication, and, as such, carries with it the implication that to fully understand message production requires knowing the extent to which message content and form are influenced by, and jointly constructed with, cointeractants.

Here is where IAT opens a potentially enlightening window on message production. Building on the presumptions that adaptation is the bedrock upon which interaction is founded, and that nonverbal and verbal communication patterns manifest this adaptation, IAT attempts to predict and explain the conditions under which these accommodative patterns will be facilitated or inhibited, potentiated or disrupted. Key elements in its predictive and explanatory calculus are three classes of factors that individuals bring with them to communicative episodes: *requirements,* which reflect basic human needs; *expectations,* which are largely socially defined; and *desires,* which are primarily related to personal preferences, goals, and plans. While individual requirements, expectations, and desires doubtless are necessary factors in accounting for an actor's own nonverbal and verbal encoding patterns, IAT postulates that they are insufficient to provide a full accounting for behavior produced in interaction. An equally, if not more, significant function performed by the required, expected, and desired elements is that they coalesce to set the stage for initially similar and synchronous (or dissimilar and uncoordinated) interaction and to predict when and how behavioral changes by one party instigate changes by another to produce conjoint interaction patterns such as reciprocity or compensation. Consequently, message production will be poorly understood unless seen as governed in substantial ways by cointeractants' communicative practices and as embedded within interdependent action patterns.

THEORETICAL UNDERPINNINGS AND ASSUMPTIONS OF IAT

Historically speaking, IAT is the progeny of several generations of interpersonal adaptation theories. The many branches of its family tree include biological perspectives on motor mimicry and interactional synchrony (e.g., Bernieri & Rosenthal, 1991; Chapple, 1982); biopsychological models such as affiliative conflict theory (Argyle & Dean, 1965), the arousal-labeling model (Patterson, 1976), and discrepancy-arousal theory (Cappella & Greene, 1982), which feature arousal and affect; sociological perspectives such as the norm of reciprocity (Gouldner, 1960), the dyadic effect (Jourard, 1959), and communication accommodation theory (Giles, Coupland, & Coupland, 1991), which emphasize cultural and group influences on interaction behavior; and more cognitive and communication-oriented perspectives such as the sequential-functional model (Patterson, 1983), expectancy violations theory (Burgoon, 1978), cognitive valence theory (Andersen, 1992), and the revised motor mimicry model (Bavelas, Black, Lemery, & Mullett, 1986) which thrust communication processes center stage.

Drawing upon this rich heritage and a wealth of empirical investigations, several of which were designed to test alternative theories, Burgoon, Stern, et al. (1995) derived several principles that are foundational to IAT's propositions. We summarize and elaborate eight of them here because of their potential relevance in explaining not only dyadic interaction patterns but also individual nonverbal and verbal message production.

Biologically Based Predispositions

1. Humans may be innately predisposed to adapt interaction patterns to one another. The apparently inherent inclination toward coordinating, synchronizing, and meshing interaction patterns may be due to biological benefits related to survival, information processing, and intraspecies communication, or perhaps to felicitous evolutionary effects of adaptation on social organization (see, e.g., Kemper, 1984). To the extent that interactional adaptation is an evolutionary adaptive response, it implies that a tacit universal objective in most, if not all, message production is selecting nonverbal and verbal elements that enable coordinated activity. Such an objective need not operate at a highly conscious or deliberate level to be an omnipresent component of any intention to communicate with another.

Considerable evidence points to invisible biological forces at work that cause people to mesh activity, entrain to each other's rhythm, and experience emotional contagion (see Burgoon, Stern, et al., 1995; Cappella, 1991; Hatfield, Cacioppo, & Rapson, 1994). That is, during interaction, people are drawn under the other's "spell" and come to exhibit similar communication patterns. Exceptions include compensation to ensure physical safety or comfort (as in increasing conversational distance from an approaching stranger) and to minimize stress or fatigue (as in averting gaze to reduce sensory stimulation during execution of a complex task). All of these processes can be conceived as embodying an often instantaneous and largely unconscious form of orientation between individuals.

From a message-production standpoint, the predominance of synchronized and behaviorally similar communication patterns means that a cointeractant's style may exert appreciable influence on any individual's message production. For example, speech tempo, rhythmicity, loudness, pause patterns, and fluency, rather than being independent and exclusive reflections of a communicator's own plans and meanings, may be responses designed in part to attune to a cointeractant's speech patterns (see Gallois, Giles, Jones, Cargile, & Ota, 1995). Other behaviors, such as avoiding gaze, shifting to an indirect body orientation, or keeping utterances very brief, rather than being mere indicators of excessive cognitive load, may be compensatory reactions to perceived physical or psychological threats from cointeractants.

Moreover, the semiautomaticity of much adaptation should facilitate efficient interaction. For instance, eye contact is important in achieving efficient turn-taking in conversation, but the role of eye contact in managing conversation often goes unnoticed by participants unless gaze norms are violated. It is precisely the automaticity of many behaviors that sometimes makes cross-cultural interactions seem awkward and difficult (Kempton, 1980). Different norms or expectations for the use of behaviors such as eye contact may bring a typically automatic behavior into conscious awareness and thus tax an individual's communication ability. Furthermore, semiautomatic behavior such as nodding in time with speech may assist interactants in timing their vocalizations so as to avoid overly long pauses or interruptions (Bernieri & Rosenthal, 1991). Thus, these types of accommodation may be essential to interaction and may enhance understanding even though they are doubtless a form of adaptation of which interlocutors are largely unaware.

2. *The competing push and pull of approach and avoidance drives leads to a mix of patterns within and between individuals.* Ploog (1995), noting that communication has a long evolutionary history of at least 150 million years and has evolved from very simple forms to more elaborate ones, speculates that,

> . . . in the beginning, the most basic modes of social behavior were nothing but approach and avoidance among members of the species. The outcome of such encounters was always unpredictable and depended upon each partner's actions and reactions. . . . Because communication between partners was advantageous, social signals evolved—as the theory goes—to permit more flexibility in encounters and a greater degree of information about the outcome. (p. 27)

On this view, at the very root of social signals were approach and avoidance forces that presumably still underwrite the more variable and specialized interaction patterns that have evolved.

Not surprisingly, the role of agonistic approach and avoidance drives in interaction has been the focus of considerable research. Despite the emergence of several competing theoretical frameworks (e.g., Argyle & Dean,

1965; Cappella & Greene, 1982; Patterson, 1976), the theories share a common recognition that arousal and affective reactions based in biological drive states can profoundly influence dyadic interaction patterns. Recent dialectical theorists (e.g., Altman, Vinsel, & Brown, 1981; Baxter, 1988) similarly aver the importance of approach and avoidance forces on message production in their assumption that oppositional tensions between centripetal and centrifugal (connection and autonomy) forces characterize all social interaction.

From a message-production standpoint, dialectical tensions between approach and avoidance and other competing drives suggest that the messages produced in interaction reflect, to some extent, the different need states that are paramount at different times in the interaction. As interaction progresses, the satiation of one need may lead to the emergence of the opposing need, with resultant fluctuations in each person's approach and avoidance behavior and consequent variability in whether the dyadic pattern appears to be matching or complementary. To illustrate, Cindy may start a conversation conveying high levels of immediacy and involvement in response to her own approach needs. But as the interaction progresses, those needs and her energy may wane, leading her to reduce immediacy and involvement in order to allow some respite and to satisfy waxing avoidance needs.

To the extent that both people are responding to the same approach and avoidance forces, their needs and gratifications may rise and fall in tandem, producing a consistent matching pattern. But to the extent that their approach and avoidance drives follow different trajectories and are out of sync with one another, a variety of patterns may surface. The degree of urgency of the needs additionally may impinge on each person's ability or motivation to accommodate to another's communication style.

An important implication of the oscillation between need states is that we should expect dynamic and cyclic patterns, both within and between individuals, rather than constancy in message production. As a verbal parallel, research by VanLear (1991) found self-disclosure in developing relationships to be cyclical, with alternating periods of openness and closedness emerging within single conversations and across multiple conversations; he also found that congruence between partners cycles emerged frequently.

Further, individual variability in arousal and affective states are not the only reasons varied patterns may arise within the same interaction. If we assume, for example, that many of the functions served by communication, such as the presentation of a unique identity and enactment of situated roles, are produced by both coordinating and differentiating behavior, then it seems likely that both reciprocity and compensation will appear between communicators as they enact patterns that fulfill these functions. In fact, it is intriguing to speculate on whether an underlying dialectical opposition between needs for similarity and needs for dissimilarity might in itself create a cycling between reciprocity and compensation in interactions.

The theoretical import of these conclusions is that communication theories must specify which needs are most likely to be operative under what conditions and how these need states articulate with an actor's choices among alternative message features. Will, for instance, requests, directives, and replies be overlaid with subtle nonverbal and verbal indications of an actor's current receptivity or nonreceptivity to another's approach, indications that may even modify or attenuate a message's propositional content or interpretation? Might indirect speech acts function not so much to protect another's positive face as to stave off overly intimate physical or symbolic approach and in so doing, secure one's own negative face? Might the rapidity or tardiness in responding to a computer-mediated message be read not so much as a status marker or indication that one is very busy but rather as a metasignal that the responder prefers privacy and solitude over social interaction? Dillard, Solomon, and Samp's (1996) contention that depending on the circumstances, social actors will tilt toward one interpretation of conflicting relational messages over another adumbrates our urging that research specify what conditions elicit what need states and accompanying social signals.

The methodological import of these conclusions is that approaches to measuring and/or manipulating need states must be developed if research is to reveal how message content and style are influenced by such needs. They may also necessitate more qualitatively precise distinctions in operationalizing nonverbal coding schemes. Measures of gaze frequency and duration may be insufficient, for instance, if an intense gaze coupled with smiling signifies a desire for affiliation, while an intense gaze coupled with a neutral or tense mouth is intended to ward off approach.

Social Predispositions

3. *Social norms create pressure toward reciprocity and matching.* A prerequisite to social organization and community is cooperative and coordinated social behavior. Communication, as one of the major cultural forms for social organization, will necessarily reflect these qualities. Social norms develop as a means for preserving order, thereby making interaction possible. Behavior during interaction is thus responsive to social as well as physiological and psychological needs.

As a result of the need to coordinate activity, norms for action may emerge which make behavior more predictable. Possibly the most fundamental norm organizing social behavior is the norm of reciprocity (Gouldner, 1960). The value of such a norm in producing predictability is readily apparent since reciprocity sets up a system where individuals are both aware of and, at some level, able to control the nature of the exchange. The role of the norm of reciprocity in interaction has been explored extensively in the research on self-disclosure (see Derlega, Metts, Petronio, & Margulis, 1993). If, for example, Judee discloses her private feelings on a sensitive subject, Cindy is likely to do the same. Such socially normative reciprocity is not confined to verbal behavior. If Judee attempts to reduce embarrassment and "intrusiveness" by reducing eye contact, Cindy is likely to reciprocate. Gift-giving and favor-doing typically follow the same reciprocal pattern. Across a large body of literature, the evidence documents that many social norms produce pressure toward reciprocity (Derlega et al., 1993; Roloff, 1987).

From this it follows that during normal, polite conversation, conversants are expected to adopt similar nonverbal and verbal interaction styles, except where social roles or task requirements dictate asymmetries. For example, the interviewer–interviewee context typically entails interviewers making brief utterances followed by interviewees giving lengthy ones. Supervisors are expected to be dominant; subordinates, deferent. But apart from these role-bound complementary patterns is a tacit objective underlying much message production that the creation of messages conform to social requirements and mirror the communication of other social actors.

Communicative Forces

4. *Interactants may make strategic use of both reciprocal and compensatory patterns.* Not all communication is strategic (i.e., volitional and deliberate), but because nonverbal and verbal behaviors can be managed to elicit desired responses from others, interactants may intentionally employ reciprocal or compensatory, convergent or divergent, patterns. For example, Judee may compensate for Cindy's seriousness by joking and laughing, in hopes of cajoling her into lightening the mood. The strategy is one of adopting the desired style as a model to which the other may entrain.

This principle connects the interaction adaptation literature to the broader body of research on strategic message production in that some (but certainly not all) communication will reflect deliberate attempts to influence another's communication through the force of one's own communication style. The theoretical importance of this connection is that is highlights the fact that one goal of message production is the elicitation of similar (or complementary) interaction patterns from coparticipants. Additionally, it poses the intriguing issue of what circumstances actually evoke intentional compensatory behavior patterns, especially in light of the numerous countervailing biological and social pressures toward reciprocity and matching.

The prospect of some communication being planned to draw forth a similar style from another of course may appear to raise the vexing problem of distinguishing that which is strategic from that which is not. In our opinion, some of both are present. This introduces the next principle.

5. *Messages are manifested as functional complexes of nonverbal and verbal cues.* Because we share with Bavelas (1994), Krauss et al. (1995), McNeill (1992; McNeill, Cassell, & McCullough, 1994), and others the view that many nonverbal behaviors (e.g., gestural activity) are part of a larger semantic or syntactic "plan," we believe that strategic activity will often be evident as part of functional complexes of behavior. By "functional complexes," we mean homeomorphic classes of behaviors that are equivalent in the communicative role they fulfill (Burgoon, Stern, et al., 1995). At a molar level, a large number of nonverbal and verbal cues can be substituted or complement one another to express relational messages of involvement, affection, similarity, or dominance. At a more microscopic level, some individual speech acts or nonverbal behaviors may fill the same conversational "slot" (see Schegloff, 1993; Tiersma, 1993) while others serve distinctly different functions. For example, backchannel head nods function to continue a speaker's turn, whereas backchannel utterances such as "huh?" disrupt a speaker's turn by signaling misunderstanding.

Two implications for message-production research are, one, the need for research to identify what verbal and nonverbal behaviors form meaningful or functional complexes that might reflect strategic activity, and two, more discernment of those cues that are not part of the message itself but rather a byproduct of message production or some other internal state. Hesitancies when equivocating would be an example of the former, adaptor behaviors during deception, an example of the latter. The current controversies regarding whether nonverbal cues are social and/or symbolic (see, e.g., Buck, 1995a, 1995b; Fridlund, 1994, 1995; Kendon, 1994; Krauss et al., 1995; McNeill, 1992; Rimé & Schiaratura, 1991) underscore the importance of determining what functions particular assemblages of nonverbal cues serve and what cues which occur within particular interactions are merely coincidental but unrelated accompaniments.

A third implication is that many predictions regarding interaction patterns may be more accurate when pitched at a gestalt, functional level than at a microbehavior level. Highly localized within-utterance analysis may miss the import of the larger discursive pattern and/or detect "noise" rather than meaningful activity. It is for this reason that we have urged, and continue to urge, viewing interpersonal message production multivariately and multifunctionally (see Burgoon & Baesler, 1991, for a discussion of matching size of measurement units to the phenomenological experience of interactants).

6. *Degree of adaptation will be constrained by: (a) individual consistency in communication style, (b) poor monitoring of self and/or partner, and (c) inability to adjust performance due to skill deficiencies or external constraints.* Despite

the strong biological, psychological, social, and communicative predispositions toward adaptation, nonadaptation will occur with some frequency.
This portion of the total variability in message production may reflect
unique goals, plans, and abilities separate from other cointeractants.

7. *Biological, psychological, and social forces combine to set up boundaries
within which most interaction patterns will oscillate, primarily producing patterns
of matching, synchrony, and reciprocity.* "Behavioral changes outside these
boundaries will often be met with nonaccommodation, as a means of retard-
ing movement away from the normative range, or with compensation to
return interaction to its previous style" (Burgoon, Stern, et al., 1995, p. 264).
The thesis here is that pressures will be brought to bear to retard radical
change and to keep communication patterns within a zone of acceptability.
Large departures from expected patterns will be met with resistance, "putting on the breaks," as it were, to prevent interactions from hurtling out of
control and to "smooth out" over-time trajectories. That is, they will function
as negative feedback loops that keep the dyadic system "on course."

In the larger context of message production, the implication is that some
features of messages, verbal and nonverbal, will be directed toward maintaining relatively stable patterns that operate within a particular range of
acceptable and preferred behavior and toward assuring that changes from
one state to another are gradual rather than abrupt. Some compensatory
reactions or apparently nonadaptive responses may be deliberately designed to retard change, to secure predictability in the face of possible
chaos. Under such circumstances, such message features would reflect, not
individual imperviousness to partner behavior, but rather a highly contingent and directed response. We should therefore not be misled into assuming that persistence of one person's behavior in the face of another's behavioral change is evidence of nonadaptation. It may instead be serving an
anchoring function whereby it sets what at least one interactant views as
the appropriate central tendency around which another interactant is temporarily diverging. For example, refusal to participate in another's flight into
fantasy-chaining may be intended to keep a discussion grounded in reality
rather than signifying an inability to maneuver through imaginal space. Or,
maintaining an affectively neutral demeanor amidst another's emotional
seesawing may reflect, not a lack of empathy, but a controlled effort to
restore the other to equanimity.

8. *Many variables may moderate the predicted patterns.* Because patterns of
interaction reflect the orientation of communicators to one another, the
nature of interaction may be moderated by a number of factors, some of which
are individual variables and others of which are relational. Factors such as
gender, ethnicity, age, relational familiarity, status asymmetries, culture, and
environmental constraints may alter the shape and amplitude of observed
patterns. For instance, because of gender socialization, women may be more

accommodating in cross-gender than in same-gender interactions. Likewise, features of the relationship between communicators, such as intimacy level or status, may impact adaptation. Workers may choose not to reciprocate a nasty remark by a supervisor even when offended because the role relationship constrains the types of behavior that are appropriate in asymmetrical relationships. Cultural differences in communication practices and expectations may also militate against particular forms of adaptations. The individual and relational factors should, to some extent, be reflected in the requirements, expectations, and desires individuals bring to an interaction. Although discussion of moderating factors is beyond the scope of this chapter, it should be kept in mind that IAT's propositions are not intended to ignore the substantial impact they may wield.

Although these foregoing empirically and theoretically grounded conclusions were originally articulated to establish the context for the specific propositions of IAT, we proffer them here as general principles that may govern message production in a variety of interpersonal circumstances. Their applicability is further explicated and elaborated in the sections that follow.

KEY CONCEPTS IN IAT: INDIVIDUAL FACTORS WITH A DECIDEDLY COMMUNICATION LOOK

IAT assumes that behavior in interaction is influenced by both personal and social factors and seeks to articulate how patterns of behavior are responsive to these. As previewed earlier, three classes of factors that are primary to the theory are requirements, expectancies, and desires (RED). The R (required) factors include physical and psychological needs that must be satisfied. The E (expected) factors include social norms that are salient for a given communication situation or function, plus idiosyncratic expectations based on the history of the relationship. The D (desired) factors include personal preferences, goals, and plans.

Each person's RED elements combine to form a derivative behavioral predisposition, labeled in the theory as the Interaction Position (IP). "The IP represents a net assessment of what is needed, anticipated, and preferred as the dyadic pattern in a situation" (Burgoon, Stern, et al., 1995, p. 266). The IP is a hypothetical construct from which to project the types of behavior an individual will display and the likely responses to the behavior of cointeractants. Specifically, the IP reflects the physiological, social and personal elements that facilitate and constrain the production of particular type of messages. For example, an individual who is anxious (R), expects that the interaction situation is a formal one (E), and prefers interaction that impersonal is likely to produce messages that indicate avoidance and social distance. The RED elements also provide a way to predict patterns of inter-action between individuals because they govern the valences attached to particular behaviors; for instance, the individual just described is likely to view messages which convey distance and formality positively and mes-sages that convey inclusion and personalness negatively. Observed verbal and nonverbal messages are predicted by examining the relationship be-tween one individual's IP and a coparticipant's actual behavior during the interaction (A), factoring in the respective valences of the IP and A.

The RED elements, which might be labeled as cognitive and affective components in other frameworks, are intended to capture the constellation of factors that are temporally most proximal to, and therefore most likely to exert influence on, actual message behavior. They do not exhaust all possible individual differences. Rather, they focus on those that are most relevant to communication and that provide the basis for linking internal individual events to externally manifested dyadic behavior. In this respect, the featured RED elements can be said to have a "decidedly communication look" because they are a select group that have clear implications for the types of messages communicators can and will produce in interaction. In short, they predispose communicators to produce certain types of messages.

Although we elaborate on each of these elements separately, it is impor-tant to stress that we view them as nonorthogonal and often interdependent. As illustration, if someone has gone without food or water for several days, sustenance is an urgent necessity; it falls into the required (R) category. However, once a person's hunger or thirst has been satiated, the person may still wish for more. Ordering dessert in a restaurant after a full meal better qualifies as a desired (D) response in that it is less urgent, more volitional, and more preference-based. Even if a person doesn't feel like a dessert but everyone else in a dinner party is ordering one, the person may do so to conform to what is expected (E). Turning to a communication example, gaze aversion to relieve stress may be a necessity (R) when a prisoner is undergoing a grueling interrogation, it may be expected (E) when the prisoner is showing subservience to a military officer, or it may be preferred (D) when the prisoner wishes to minimize conversation with a guard. Thus, the same behavior may vary across circumstances in the extent to which it reflects R, E, or D elements.

Furthermore, the extent to which behavior reflects a requirement, expec-tation or desire may change across the interaction. For instance, an individual who is anxious about taking a test (an R factor) may seek out others to talk with before the exam in order reduce anxiety. If interaction has the anticipated effect and anxiety subsides somewhat, then continued engagement in the conversation may be related primarily to social norms which dictate that continuing the conversation is the polite thing to do (E factors) or to the conversation's topics themselves sparking a desire (D) for further interaction.

Moreover, just as emotions can be viewed as cognitive and cognitions as emotional (see Buck, 1988), so, too, are requirements, expectancies, and desires, interlaced. For example, the desire to avoid blame for a serious mistake may cause actors to become highly aroused as they try to explain their behavior, which in turn may necessitate modifications in their account-making as they attempt to keep the internal arousal in check while still trying to conform to expectations for how plausible accounts should be performed. In sum, R, E, and D elements are themselves an interdependent system. Each may recruit facets of and/or feed back into another.

Often, the R, E, and D will be congruent with one another and lead to the same IP (interaction position), making it immaterial which of the three classes of factors is at stake. However, when the needs, expectations, and preferences are at odds with one another, it becomes important to distinguish among them and to predict which factor(s) will predominate. In IAT, analogously to Maslow's hierarchy of needs, the components of the IP are postulated to be hierarchical. Requirements are related to basic needs such as comfort and safety and are assumed to predominate until satisfied. When basic needs are met, expectancies and desires respectively are thought to become ascendant, with expectancies most likely to predominate in initial interactions, role-bound interactions, and interactions with strangers. In what follows, we consider what is subsumed under each of these factors, how they relate to one another, and how they are likely to influence the kinds of verbal and nonverbal patterns that communicators produce.

Requirements

Within the IAT framework, requirements were originally conceptualized as physical, emotional, and psychological needs that are essential to the well-being of the individual. That is, R elements were intended to reflect basic human drives such as sustenance, safety, comfort, and affiliation, underlying emotional states or moods such as happiness, and physiological states such as fatigue. Our discussion so far suggests that R elements might be construed more broadly to include social adaptation, or responsiveness to conspecifics, as a further requirement for efficacious individual survival and functioning. We elaborate this idea more fully momentarily. In any case, it should be apparent that R elements are strongly influenced by biological factors and form the foundation for interaction behavior.

As framed by IAT, these requirements differ from the types of situational or communication requirements identified by researchers who focus on cognition or message design (e.g., O'Keefe, 1992; Waldron & Cegala, 1992). Communication or situational requirements are typically seen as demands imposed by the communication episode. In some respects, these depart from the IAT definition of requirements because they focus primarily on characteristics of the situation rather than interactants' needs or drives. And, insofar as they include communication functions associated with a particular situation and the expectations or goals that those functions entail, situational requirements can be subsumed under expectations, discussed below.

Nevertheless, certain types of demands are captured to some extent in the IAT definition of requirements because situational demands are clearly related to needs that must be met, such as keeping cognitive taxation to a manageable level, opting for physical or psychological comfort, and reducing uncertainty so that one can anticipate a partner's future moves (Waldron, 1995). Moreover, if we take as a precondition of all communication the need for participants to be responsive to social stimuli and to orient to one another, then intrinsic to all communication situations is the "requirement" of some minimum level of adaptation. Graumann (1995), for example, points out that "social" by its very nature refers to the Wundtian concept of "die Wechselwirkung der Individuen," or an actual mutual other-orientation that yields reciprocal interaction. Foppa (1995) also argues that mutual understanding is not only a prerequisite for any human communication but also the goal. While we might dispute the latter claim that understanding is always the goal (deception being an obvious exception), the former claim bolsters our contention that communication is conditioned on orientation toward and responsiveness to others, making some degree of adaptation a necessary but not sufficient condition for human communication to be accomplished. It is the default "setting," if you will. Hence, at this most fundamental level, requirements may be seen to exert influence in all interactions.

Although a comprehensive analysis of the full complement of potential requirements present in interaction would exceed our page limitations, it is worthwhile to consider two additional intertwined requirements—one of which has been central in past research and the other which is receiving growing attention among communication scholars. The first requirement, arousal management, has been the object of much previous research. In general, research indicates that communication situations that include unexpected behavior by an interaction partner produce arousal (e.g., Le Poire & Burgoon, 1994), and high levels of arousal may interfere with message production (deTurck & Miller, 1985). In addition to dictating specific behavioral profiles that are manifestations of arousal intensity and arousal valence (see Burgoon, Kelley, Newton, & Keeley-Dyreson, 1989, for specific examples), arousal can have inhibitory or facilitative effects on other behavioral displays (Zajonc, 1980). For instance, an individual who is anxious and fatigued may attempt to reduce stimulation, which could result in an avoidant pattern of interaction.

The second requirement, affect management (Patterson, 1987), refers to the important communication function of regulating the experience and expression of emotions and affective states. Numerous researchers have declared emotions and mood states as important, but neglected, elements in communication situations (Planalp, 1993; Waldron, 1995). Here again, their importance in communication situations lies partly in the specific behavioral displays they generate and partly in their potential to influence cognitive processing in the interaction, with consequent impact on communicators' ability to produce particular types of messages. Although the research is varied and complex, there is clear evidence that mood influences the information individuals are able to retrieve and the ways in which individuals assess perceptions. The research suggests, for example, that memory and perception are typically mood congruent (Morris, 1992). Mood therefore facilitates access to some types of information and inhibits access to other types, which in turn is likely to influence the nature and content of messages produced in interaction.

As noted in the overview of IAT's theoretical underpinnings, biological pressures in interaction appear to lead to semiautomatic matching, reciprocity, and synchrony, with compensatory responses likely only under conditions of threat, discomfort, disequilibrium, or strategic modeling. Requirements therefore often operate below the level of conscious awareness and may not be wholly communicative in nature; however, even when not communicative, they may bias communication episodes by making particular responses more or less likely. Seen in the larger context of message production, R elements may govern a person's general responsiveness to another's influence. They may be likened to a window shade that opens or closes to let in light or block it out. Importantly, the degree to which R elements are satisfied may determine the extent to which meaningful communication is possible.

Expectations

The second class of factors, expectations, concerns communication patterns anticipated by interactants. Burgoon, Buller, and Woodall (1996) and Burgoon and Walther (1990) further subdivide expectations into those related to communicators, to relationships, and to communication contexts. Those related to communicators concern such individual difference variables as age, sex, ethnicity, socioeconomic status, birthplace, and personality. Those related to relationships concern such relationally defined factors as liking, familiarity, and equality or inequality. Those related to contexts concern the situational norms and/or communication functions that are expected to be accomplished, the behavioral routines typically enacted to achieve them, and any constraints on behavior imposed by the setting. Thus, the concept of communication goals is partially captured under the rubric of expectations.

Expectations can be generic—reflecting culture-level or group-level norms for an encounter—or individuated—tied to the knowledge about a cointeractant's specific communication style. Such individuated knowledge might come from direct observation, from secondhand information about the other's reputed communication practices, or from a history of actual interactions with the other. Where actors have individuating information about one another, their expectations should be a function of both generic and particular anticipations.

Consider, for example, a task-oriented meeting. The basic communication goals or functions that are likely to be operative include, for senders, creating understanding through the production of comprehensible messages (see Burgoon, Buller, Guerrero, Afifi, & Feldman, 1996; McCornack, 1992); projecting a desired identity and credible image; keeping the discussion running smoothly and on track; maintaining harmonious interpersonal relations; and possibly persuading others. These are prototypical communication functions for work-related interactions. (To the extent that the sender's personal goals depart from these—to include, say, a preference to be strategically ambiguous or deceptive—they are better viewed as part of the D category, which picks up idiosyncratic preferences.) The expected behaviors associated with these communication functions might include verbal content that is task-relevant; use of language that is standard, noncolloquial, professional, polite, and possibly formal; nonverbal behaviors that signify one's status and that express pleasantness, involvement, and respect for the other; and turn-taking patterns that facilitate a coordinated, synchronized flow of conversation. All participants might rightly expect these same general behavior patterns from one another. Thus, the IP would project essentially the same behavioral profile for everyone—when expectancies are the predominating influence. Of course, known status, expertise, or power differences might lead to differential expectations in accord with differential role requirements in asymmetrical relationships. So, for example, leaders might be expected to exhibit more vocal assertiveness and dynamism and followers to exhibit more vocal meekness. Leaders might sit at the head of a table and feel free to put their feet up on it, whereas followers, seated facing the leader, might be expected to maintain a "proper" upright, attentive posture.

It should be evident that innumerable mundane examples could be generated in which the generic behavioral expectations are fairly obvious and well-known to members of a given society, organization, or group. Presumably, such expectations represent schemata and scripts for how communication practices accomplish typical communication functions. That is, they are distillations of the kinds of communication that have typically succeeded in achieving such goals as understanding, identity and image management, conversation management, relationship management, affect management, and social influence. Their efficacy has resulted in their becoming normative.

However, not all expectations are immediately obvious, and projecting from anecdotal evidence can be risky business. Consequently, we believe one important direction for research on message production is determining the cultural, situational, and relational expectancies governing behavior. Waldron (1995) makes a similar plea when he advocates a requirement-centered approach to communication research, one which grounds work "in a communication-theory based analysis of the requirements of social situations and . . . the cognitive operations inferred from the requirements" (p. 181). Although Waldron uses the term "requirements" to reference what we are calling expectations, the idea is similar: We need to know what expectations people bring to different kinds of communication encounters. Theory provides important guidance but must be supplemented with empirical evidence. Just as Burgoon and Le Poire (1993), Honeycutt (1989), and others have established that the expectation for interactions among strangers is to be polite, pleasant, and moderately involved; and just as Guerrero (1997) determined that immediacy norms derived from stranger interactions are inapplicable to interactions among romantic couples; so, too, should other investigations ascertain what constitutes normative communication in different kinds of communication episodes.

Still, it seems fairly safe to predict that people commonly enter conversation with expectations for cointeractants to abide by cultural mores for cooperative, civil, and polite discourse (see Grice, 1989); to display pleasantness, moderately high involvement and attentiveness, and moderate composure; to maintain emotional self-control; to preserve each other's face; and to avoid domineering or threatening behaviors. Such general expectations should be supplemented or moderated by any particularized expectations derived from relational familiarity and prior interaction history.

These expectations should guide the planning and production of nonverbal (and verbal) messages at the outset of interactions. In other words, message production should partially reflect these expectations. Viewed from a systems perspective, these expectations should translate into the system's start values for interaction. They should predominate when requirements have been satisfied or are noncompelling. Social-level expectations should recede in importance as (a) interactions progress and/or (b) relationships become more familiar and idiosyncratic in their interaction patterns, under which circumstances expectancies should become relationship-specific. However, as we shall see, unless the start values for all participants are the same and stable interaction ensues, subsequent behavioral changes by participants may exert far more influence than preinteraction expectations, overriding any predictions derivable from those expectations.

So far, we have used the concept of expectation to signify that which is the modal, average, or central tendency. This is a view of expectations as "predictive" (see Staines & Libby, 1986). However, expectations may also be "prescriptive." They may specify what is ideal or preferred. Practices that are normative typically become what is also socially prescribed or preferred. In that sense, expectations about what is appropriate or acceptable are not devoid of valence connotations. They carry with them evaluative loadings, loadings which may also color individual-level preferences. However, because preferences often arise separate from expectancies, preferences are treated as part of the desire (D) factor in IAT. The point to be made here is that valences associated with expectations may have some carry-over effect to the D factors.

Desires

Desires reflect the personal preferences and goals of individual communicators. It may be useful to consider each of these separately, beginning with personal preferences. Personality and own communication abilities lead communicators to prefer certain styles of interaction for themselves and others. For instance, extroverts seem to prefer more eye contact in interaction (Simpson, Gangestad, & Biek, 1993). These preferences are most likely to be influential when the interaction occurs between individuals who know one another and in situations where there are few social rules or constraints. As illustration, Guerrero and Burgoon (1996), examining the impact of attachment style on communication between dating partners, found that responses to a change in partner involvement differed with attachment style. Individuals who were preoccupied in their attachment style, and thus felt the relationship was fragile and feared abandonment were more likely to attempt to offset decreases in partner involvement by increasing their own involvement than were those who had secure or dismissive avoidant attachment styles. The preoccupieds' attachment style led them to seek a more engaging interaction pattern, even in casual conversation in a research setting. Temperment and personality-based preferences may therefore lead to behavioral predilections.

Alternately, desires may reflect situation-specific goals related to achieving an individual's own communication outcomes. One basic assumption of IAT is that communicators deliberately may attempt to manage their behavior in interaction so as to impress or influence another. These objectives may override or temper instinctive, but inappropriate, responses, and they are key in determining the types of behaviors communicators are likely to want to enact.

Because situation-specific goals are likely to operate at a more conscious level and to take into consideration social norms, situation-specific goals have the potential to influence requirements, to determine how expectations will be valenced, and to aid in the retrieval and enactment of behavior necessary to create a particular message. Consider, for example, a situation where one person wishes to deceive another. The desire to deceive may create anxiety about getting caught, thereby influencing requirements. The deceiver may expect that a partner will be very attentive and involved in the interaction, behaviors which would be negatively valenced in this situation because they make discovery of the deception more likely. Moreover, the goal of deception will assist the deceiver in determining how to mask certain behaviors and how to highlight other behaviors.

As with requirements, goals need not predict particular behaviors but should set up parameters within which certain behavioral options are more or less likely. If an individual has as a goal, say, "making a good impression on a prospective employer," smiling and being kinesically expressive might be displayed because part of the goal is to convey that one is socially rewarding and sociable. (Note that in this example, the individual goal, which is a D factor, coincides with the social norm, which is an E factor, for favorable self-presentation.) But an individual wanting to "make a good impression" on a new friend who is upset or anxious might opt to be kinesically still rather than animated, to display concerned facial expressions, and sit nearby so as to emphasize being empathic and interpersonally accommodating. These are not conflicting display options but reflect different emphases and substitutable communicative options as part of the overarching "make a good impression" goal. Even so, some cues such as a sympathetic smile might be common in both cases.

From a message-production standpoint, this means that goals may provide the algorithm which assists communicators in packaging behavior in order to create the desired impression. A good illustration is a study by Palmer and Simmons (1995). When individuals were instructed to convey a relational message of liking or disliking, they did so by enacting a rather consistent behavioral profile, which included some conscious alterations of behavior and some more automatic, accompanying adjustments. This occurred even though communicators were often unable to identify the specific behavioral cues that they enacted to create the impression.

Although considerable research has explored the relationship between goals and communication, most research on this issue has focused on the verbal strategies employed in interaction (Dillard, 1990; Waldron, Cegala, Sharkey, & Teboul, 1990; Wilson, 1990). In cases where nonverbal behavior has been examined, it has typically been treated as evidence of cognitive functioning (Berger & diBattista, 1993; Berger, Karol, & Jordan, 1989). By assuming that patterns of interaction are communicative, IAT focuses on functional complexes of behavior that have message value within the interaction. It shifts analysis from single behaviors or strategies to the exploration of meaningful constellations of behavior. "If messages are understood as collections of interrelated verbal and/or nonverbal behavior that form meaningful gestalts . . . , then functional equivalents become all those behaviors and tactics that fit a larger message class, strategy, or function" (Burgoon, Stern, et al., 1995, p. 126).

In terms of message production, this again reinforces the need to allocate greater research energy toward linking goals and plans with actual performance. It also reinforces the need to tease out which nonverbal and verbal message features have semantic, syntactic, or pragmatic import and which are merely overt indicators of cognitive effort. The lack of deterministic relationships and one-to-one correspondences between cognitions (plans, expectations, goals, and the like) and behavior makes for a much more challenging task methodologically and analytically. It requires substantial inference-making that will inevitably be fraught with error. But it is bound to be much more faithful to the multifunctional, polysemous, and equifinal nature of communication.

In sum, goals seem likely to be particularly important in message production because they aid communicators in producing a total message which is goal appropriate and because they influence the type of interaction one individual will desire from, and try to instantiate with, the partner.

MOVING FROM THE INVISIBLE TO THE VISIBLE: INTERDEPENDENCIES IN BEHAVIOR

The Interaction Position

We have said that the IP is a summary term for the combined R, E, and D elements. As such, it acknowledges both the multiplicity of exogenous factors that can influence overt communication behavior and the different levels at which responses to behavior are determined. Sidestepping the issue of *how* the various R, E, and D elements are all weighted to arrive at a single quotient, the IP becomes the basis for projecting self or other behavior by taking into account each individual's R, E, and D factors. In this respect, IAT does not devalue cognitive or other preinteraction factors but zeroes in on those with greatest behavioral prepotency.

Consider a dyadic interaction between Judee and Cindy as they come together to work on this chapter. Judee may expect and prefer to have a productive but pleasant interchange; if she is not hungry, tired, achy, or irritable (i.e., does not have pressing physiological or psychological needs to attend to), the E and D factors should weigh most heavily in her IP, which would include a behavioral pattern of task-focused content, moderately formal language, intermediate arousal (neither too relaxed nor too tense), moderately high involvement, and pleasantness. Her projected IP for Cindy would be the same. Hence, each person's initial behavior should partly manifest their own IP and projected other IP. But it will also reflect other factors, including one's own social skills and behavioral repertoire, which may or may not enable actors to put expectancies and preferences into practice; external and environmental factors that may place constraints on behavior; and the observed behavior of other actors. Stated formally,

$A_{B1} = f(A_{IP}, A_{ss}, A_{B0}, B_{B1}, E)$ where

A_{B1} = Judee's present behavior,

A_{IP} = Judee's IP,

A_{ss} = Judee's social skills and behavioral repertoire

A_{B0} = Judee's previous behavior, in this interaction or previous situations

B_{B1} = Cindy's present behavior

E = environmental factors that are currently impinging on behavior

Put differently, Judee's behavior will partly reflect her own consistent style and her own communication abilities. It will partly be responsive to the immediate setting and environmental contingencies. And it will partly reflect the IP. But it will also be conditioned, often immediately, on Cindy's actual behavior, denoted as A in IAT theory. That is, only a small portion of the total variance accounted for in observable message behavior may be independently assigned to elements associated with a given actor. Far more of the variance may be accounted for by the redundancies between individual patterns of behavior that are present in interaction and by the contingent, conjointly determined interactions patterns that emerge between partners. This leads us to further consideration of partner behavior.

The Impact of Partner Behavior

We have already alluded to the fact that individual factors in place preinteractionally may pale in comparison to interactional ones in governing the kinds of messages interactants produce. Our conclusion is based on abundant evidence that alter's interaction behavior carries more weight in influencing an actor's own communication than the actor's prior expectancies, personality, evaluations of alter's rewardingness, attachment style, relational satisfaction, and so forth (e.g., Afifi & Burgoon, 1996; Burgoon, Buller, Afifi, White, & Buslig, 1996; Burgoon, Ebesu, White, Kikuchi, Alvaro, & Koch, in press; Burgoon, Le Poire, & Rosenthal, 1995; Guerrero & Burgoon, 1996; Manusov, 1995; Siegman & Reynolds, 1982; White, 1996). For example, Manusov (1995) found that both satisfied and dissatisfied couples were likely to reciprocate one another's reductions in involvement or activity and to reciprocate increased positive affect, although satisfied couples displayed more positive responses than did dissatisfied couples. Burgoon, Le Poire, and Rosenthal (1995) and Siegman and Reynolds (1982) found that even though preinteraction expectancies and evaluations influenced postinteraction judgments, behavior *during* interaction was far more affected by the partner's concurrent interaction behavior than by their own prior cognitions and evaluations. It is not that preinteraction factors are irrelevant but rather that another's immediately present communication patterns are the most proximal antecedents of own communication and hence more salient than temporally antecedent factors.

The research implications for message production are quite provocative. Much of what we witness during actual interaction may not be the result of acting out internal cognitive and affective events such as arousal, mood states, planning, or cognitive effort but rather the result of adapting interaction styles to that of other interactants to produce a coordinated, synchronized, reciprocal interaction or one that maximizes physical and psychological ease.

The Relationship of the IP to A

Within IAT, the main predictions for whether convergent and reciprocal or divergent and compensatory patterns should materialize hinge on the juxtaposition of the IP relative to partner's A (actual behavior). Put simply, if A is more positively valenced than IP, a positive violation of expectations exists and should prompt convergence toward A, resulting in a reciprocal interaction pattern. If A is more negatively valenced than IP, then a person will either compensate or resist alter's pattern by maintaining one's own communication style. Concretely, this means that if (a) Judee needs, expects, and desires that her husband Michael show some affection, (b) close proximity and affectionate touch are positively valenced forms of affectionate display, and (c) Michael sidles up to her to give her a hug, then (d) Judee should also move closer and reciprocate the hug. If instead, (c) Michael moves farther away, precluding touch, then (d) Judee is predicted to at least maintain the same distance, rather than also becoming more distant, or to compensate by moving closer and initiating touch (if the felt needs and desires are strong enough and expectancies do not mitigate against doing so).

Conversely, if (a) Judee needs, expects, and desires greater distance from Michael than usual, then (b) a large interaction distance becomes more positively valenced than close proximity and affectionate touch. Now if (c) Michael moves close and touches Judee, (d) Judee should compensate by rejecting the touch and moving farther away. If instead (c) Michael adopts a distant position, then (d) Judee should reciprocate that because Michael's actual behavior is more positively valenced than the IP.

To offer further examples, suppose Cindy likes gregarious, friendly people and expects John to be moderately so. If John is even more so than anticipated, Cindy should converge toward and reciprocate John's warmth and friendliness. Or if Cindy expects Judee to engage in a lively, fast-paced discussion and Judee is instead lethargic, Cindy may resist Judee's sluggishness by maintaining her own rapid speech tempo or may offset it by speeding up her own rate of speech. The result should be a dyadically divergent or compensatory pattern. The demand–withdraw pattern seen in marital conflict might be explained similarly as due to a large discrepancy between the wife's demand for engagement (A, actual behavior, within the IAT framework) and the husband's desire for nonengagement (IP), resulting in a compensatory pattern of withdrawal.

Note that the behavioral patterns can be described at the individual or dyad level. If Person X converges toward Person Y and Y converges toward X, the end result should be a reciprocal dyadic interaction style. If X converges toward Y but Y diverges, a compensatory dyadic pattern will have been established.

We have already presaged some of the larger message-production implications of these predictions earlier when we observed that many message features, while ostensibly geared toward other objectives, may have as a superordinate or metaobjective keeping the interaction within a zone of acceptable behavior, a goal that works to maintain interactional stability. Insofar as conversations appear to be nonrandom and temporal changes appear to be smooth rather than erratic, such patterned activity may be taken as corroborating evidence of a proclivity toward resisting abrupt deviations. Like an automobile's cruise control, by relieving participants of the necessity of keeping the conversation "managed," it may enable them to direct more of their attentional energies toward meaningful dialogue.

In other cases, IAT accounts for interactions heading in certain directions—specifically, toward more positively valenced behavior—by making behavioral valence a prominent guiding criterion for interaction. When interactants converge on a shared, preferred communication pattern, they meld into one well-oiled, sleek machine that can readily accelerate along the pathways toward intimacy, empathic understanding, and other desired objectives. In other words, adapting to another's communication style can transform separate actors into a single and well-calibrated entity that is better equipped to progress toward preferred ends.

This is not to imply that interactions only move toward positively valenced objectives and always resist pulls in undesirable directions. The frequent tailspins into which acrimonious interactions fall is compelling evidence to the contrary. Clearly, the hostility and aggression spirals so common during conflict better testify to the powerful impact of entrainment and emotional contagion principles in explaining behavior under emotionally charged situations. But short of emotionally volatile circumstances, where reflexive fight and flight instincts may surface, IAT predicts that the facilitative nature of reciprocal interaction will propel interactions more rapidly toward desired states than undesired ones and that interactants' own communication style will serve as an impedance to moves in undesired directions.

More fundamentally, IAT's premise that valences cannot be ignored argues for more research directed toward discovering the meanings and evaluations attached to those nonverbal and verbal elements that form the corpus of our communication system.

INTERACTION PATTERNS: FROM THE STATIC TO THE DYNAMIC

So far we have identified how factors brought to the interaction—requirements, expectancies, and desires—influence initial behavioral patterns. However, IAT, as a dynamic theory, must account for adjustments over time, and its emphasis on the dynamic nature of interaction is perhaps its most important contribution to understanding message production.

At any point in time, not just at the outset, one person's communication and adjustments will be a function of the factors identified earlier. Placed in a path-analytic framework that recognizes temporal ordering, the model looks something like this:

$$A_{SS} \to \quad A_{B0} \searrow$$
$$\nearrow$$
$$E \quad A_{IP0} \to A_{B1}$$
$$\searrow$$
$$B_{SS} \to \quad B_{B0} \nearrow$$

where A_{SS} and B_{SS} represent each person's social skills and behavioral repertoire,

E represents other exogenous influences including environmental constraints,

A_{B0} and B_{B0} represent Person A's and B's actual behaviors at $t\text{-}1$,

A_{IP0} represents A's IP at $t\text{-}1$, and

A_{B1} represents A's actual behavior at t.

In words, social actors' communicative behavior will partly reflect some consistency in communication style (i.e., maintenance) that is due to their own skills and behavioral repertoire, external influences and constraints, and forces toward stability in their own behavior. It will also reflect the IP but will now also come under the influence of another's actual behavior. Consequently, over time, Person A's and Person B's behavior will increasingly be drawn into the sphere of the other's influence.

Of course, common experience tells us that much of the time people maintain fairly stable interaction patterns. This is consistent with IAT. When actual behavior matches the IP, stable exchanges should ensue, and adjustments should only occur when E or IP changes. Importantly, IAT recognizes that various need states can be satiated, leading to "opposite" needs or preferences gaining greater sway and moving the IP in different directions.

To illustrate, a typically introverted person experiencing a lengthy period of solitude may feel the need for some affiliation and so seek out the company of others. But after awhile, that need will be fulfilled and the individual is likely to again seek separation from others. IAT is not designed to predict what will cause the IP to change but rather, how interaction patterns will respond to such changes. It underscores the principle that interactions are dynamic, often cyclical, and responsive to multiple influences.

It is also the case that thinking about the dynamic nature of communication forces us to switch from an analysis of variance mentality, in which our primary concern is mean differences, to a time series mentality, in which we are interested not only in intercepts (which capture initial mean differences) but also slopes and trajectories over time. In this respect, nearly all the previous work on interaction adaptation patterns has been overly simplistic in seeking single patterns. In reality, interaction patterns do not neatly fit into a reciprocity or compensation, matching or complementarity dichotomy.

For example, Burgoon, Le Poire, and Rosenthal (1995) found evidence of both mean-level changes in one person's involvement and pleasantness due to the influence of a confederate's involvement and pleasantness, and also differences in slopes and trajectories. Participants interacting with an uninvolved, unpleasant confederate showed a reciprocal decline in their own overall involvement (as captured by the mean) but also compensated over time for the partner's depressed interaction style. Participants interacting with an involved, pleasant confederate reciprocated the increase over time, although not to the same degree, and showed curvilinear over-time changes that paralleled those of the confederate. Thus, none of the changes could be characterized simply as reciprocity or compensation. Rather, a multifaceted description was needed to capture the full richness of the conjoint pattern—one that did not conform neatly to any single theory.

This, and similar findings in other investigations, point to the need to reconceptualize adaptation patterns in a more refined way that is multileveled and captures differences in both the level of behavior displayed (between-dyads) and the adjustments in behavior across time (within-subjects; see Burgoon, Stern, et al., 1995, for more detailed analysis of the conceptual and methodological implications for incorporating these refinements). Regardless of whether the specific predictions of IAT ultimately garner substantial or limited empirical support, the results to date expose previous conceptualizations as unduly simplistic in predicting and explaining interpersonal adaptation patterns.

INTERACTION ADAPTATION AND THE ROLE
OF MEANING

In this chapter, we have outlined a perspective on interaction adaptation which recognizes that message production is highly susceptible to the influence of another's communication, often in unconscious ways. One issue this perspective raises is the extent to which unconscious processes, which appear to have a basis in biological functioning, are meaningful and therefore communicative. It is important to note that the adjustment of interactants to one another may, in itself, come to be part of the social signaling system and thus take on symbolic meaning (Ploog, 1995). Some basic coordination may be necessary for communication to occur, but the form of the coordination may come to be meaningful, for instance, when reciprocity and synchrony are interpreted as indicators of rapport. This is important because the nonverbal and verbal communication patterns that manifest adaptation can be viewed not merely as a reflection of underlying individual processes but as a potentially rich repertoire for creating shared understanding.

Moreover, it is important to reiterate that we do not regard all adaptation as automatic or unconscious; clearly, some communication is strategic, some is conscious, and some is both strategic and conscious. We have highlighted automatic or unconscious forms of interaction in order to demonstrate the complexity of interaction and to broaden the discussion of message production. But, the total message includes verbal *and* nonverbal components, produced both strategically and nonstrategically. Both types of behavior may be used communicatively—even those behaviors that are managed automatically (Kellermann, 1992)—and therefore may be part of the repertoire for creating shared meaning. Communication accommodation theory's principle of attunement (Gallois et al., 1995) demonstrates this idea by postulating that some nonverbal behaviors are designed to adjust one person's communication style to another's abilities or limitations so as to maintain a smooth interaction. So, for instance, if an intergenerational conversation is bumping along awkwardly, speakers may adjust their tempo and language choices in an effort to make their messages more comprehensible. Kikuchi (1994) demonstrated this effect in an intercultural study. When people thought a cointeractant might not be understanding the language, they used more extensive backchanneling and "checking" behavior to determine if comprehension was occurring. In another investigation, Chen (cited in Krauss et al., 1995) found that when communicators perceived another was distorting or misunderstanding them, they suppressed backchannel cues. Thus, we would argue that patterns of interaction are eminently meaningful and are an important source of information for participants.

SUMMARY AND CONCLUSIONS

By articulating and highlighting the importance of adaptation in interaction, IAT (Burgoon, Stern, et al., 1995) provides a framework for understanding message production as a dynamic endeavor which reflects individual needs, expectations, and goals but which is strongly influenced by cointeractants' communicative actions. Our call for a deeper examination of interdependencies in message production might seem to some merely to be rewarmed sociolinguistics or little different than the call from conversational analysts to attend to context dependencies in the production and interpretation of discourse. It is true that our position partly resonates with theirs. However, the issue of adaptation goes beyond context to placing a significant locus of control over message production in the communication style of cointeractants. Moreover, our claim for the prevalence of reciprocity points to a systematic, predictable pattern that transcends situational and individual particularities. We have also attempted to specify a number of conditions under which reciprocal or compensatory patterns are likely to emerge, conditions that take account of situational and individual variability while still providing generalizations with broad applicability.

In the preceding pages, we have attempted to highlight some of the ways in which IAT offers implications for research on message production. By way of summary, we recommend that communication researchers consider the following conceptual and methodological issues as they work to develop models that are more responsive to the natural conditions of interaction.

First, it is important that researchers pay careful attention to the assumptions they bring to bear on the study of message production. We believe that message encoding in all but monologic, nonsocial contexts must be understood as the product of multiple causes, only one class of which includes the individual's own plans, cognitions, attitudes, affective states, and the like. Put differently, we must seriously entertain the extent to which message production is an interdependent activity. As a result, theory construction must begin to contemplate the ways in which cointeractants exert systematic influence on individual message production. For instance, are one person's lexical choices, argument constructions, persuasive strategies, conversational topic choices, or nonverbal patterns a product of what other social actors are doing during the same episode? Theorists who overlook the influence of cointeractants risk producing impoverished theories that are guilty of specification error and that fail to generalize to real communication situations.

Additionally, the language we use for describing message production may need to be modified and refined to make its conjoint or interdependent nature more explicit. Our common ways of talking about message production typically imply an active (not passive) individual whose messages reflect his or her independent goals, plans, abilities, and so forth. Because the language we use to describe human communication co-opts us into mindlessly embracing certain conceptions—something we believe is a common trap (Burgoon & Langer, 1995)—we need to be vigilant in examining the assumptions our descriptions implicate. For example, if major facets of message production are due to an unconscious mimicking of others' communication, we may need to temper the mental image of communicators as deliberate, choice-making, autonomous planners.

Further, if IAT's specific predictions continue to gain support and the accumulated evidence reinforces our current conclusions that much of communication reflects nearly inexorable pressures toward reciprocity, we may wish to reconsider how much one person's behavior is ascribed to their own intentions. Attribution theories may "overcognitize" what is essentially a fairly automatic, perhaps biologically driven adaptive process. We may wish to compile more evidence of the extent to which a wide range of message phenomena are subject to reciprocal patterns. And, we may be drawn to find deeper explanations of why communication so frequently reflects this particular form of adaptation.

These conceptual adjustments mean that operationally, theories must be tested within interactive contexts to assess whether intrapsychic factors retain their force in the face of social stimuli. Just as Interpersonal Deception Theory (Buller & Burgoon, 1996) was developed to demonstrate that deception findings derived from sterile, noninteractive contexts may be invalid when applied to interactive ones; and just as recent work on emotional expression (e.g., Carroll & Russell, 1996; Motley, 1993) has shown that the accuracy of judged emotions declines precipitously when placed within the context of ongoing conversation or incongruent contextual information; so, too, must theories of message production be submitted to the rigorous testing grounds of natural interaction to see whether relationships established under noninteractive circumstances evaporate or are transformed in the interactive world.

If understanding message production is viewed analogously to understanding interpersonal interaction patterns, which requires a variance components approach, then research must move to the next level of assessing the relative magnitudes of impact of actor versus partner versus relationship impacts on encoding. Kenny's (1994) social relations model offers one approach for decomposing variance in message behavior to these constituent components. IAT offers another paradigm for doing so. Regardless of method used, the key point to keep in sight is the necessity of measuring relative magnitudes of effect so that those factors accounting for the most variance in encoding attract the most research attention.

More generally, we must begin to think about patterns in less simplistic ways. So, for example, we can talk about one person's behavior having a net depressive or facilitative effect on another's performance while also considering temporal trends reflecting moment-to-moment contingent behavioral changes. Taken together, these recommendations should set us on the path toward a more interaction-focused approach to the study of communication.

In conclusion, we agree with Waldron (1995) that the past emphasis on cognitive explanations of communication behavior must give way to a more comprehensive approach to the study of interaction. We have outlined one such view, Interaction Adaptation Theory (Burgoon, Stern, et al., 1995), in an attempt to demonstrate how a more comprehensive view could frame our understanding of message production in interactive contexts. Specifically, we have argued that there is a need for further examination of the relationships between individual, interdependent actions, overt behavior processes which produce meaningful constellations of behavior, and dynamic patterns and sequences of behavioral adaptation. We believe that as communication researchers return to their roots—exploring communication processes and behavior—these will be fruitful areas of investigation that will provide a more complete understanding of message production as it occurs in ongoing conversation.

ACKNOWLEDGMENT

We are indebted to Amy Ebesu for her insightful comments and suggestions regarding this chapter.

REFERENCES

Afifi, W., & Burgoon, J. K. (1996, November). *Behavioral violations in interactions: The combined consequences of valence and change in uncertainty on interaction outcome*. Paper presented to the annual meeting of the Speech Communication Association, San Diego.

Altman, I., Vinsel, A., & Brown, B. B. (1981). Dialectic conceptions in social psychology: An application to social penetration and privacy regulation. In L. Berkowitz (Ed.), *Advances in experimental social psychology* (Vol. 14, pp. 108–160). New York: Academic Press.

Andersen, P. A. (1992, July). *Excessive intimacy: An account analysis of behaviors, cognitive schema, and relational outcomes*. Paper presented to the bi-annual conference of the International Society for the Study of Personal Relationships, Orono, ME.

Argyle, M., & Dean, J. (1965). Eye-contact, distance, and affiliation. *Sociometry, 28,* 289–304.

Bavelas, J. B. (1994). Gestures as part of speech: Methodological implications. *Research on Language and Social Interaction, 27,* 201–221.

Bavelas, J. B., Black, A., Lemery, C. R., & Mullett, J. (1986). "I *show* how you feel": Motor mimicry as a communicative act. *Journal of Personality and Social Psychology, 50,* 322–329.

Baxter, L. A. (1988). A dialectic perspective on communication strategies in relationship development. In S. Duck (Ed.), *Handbook of personal relationships: Theory, research and interventions* (pp. 257–288). Chichester, England: Wiley.

Berger, C. R., & diBattista, P. (1993). Communication failure and plan adaptation: If at first you don't succeed, say it louder and slower. *Communication Monographs, 60,* 220–238.

Berger, C. R., Karol, S. H., & Jordan, J. M. (1989). When a lot of knowledge is a dangerous thing: The debilitating effects of plan complexity on verbal fluency. *Human Communication Research, 16,* 91–119.

Bernieri, F. J., & Rosenthal, R. (1991). Interpersonal coordination: Behavioral matching and interactional synchrony. In R. S. Feldman & B. Rimé (Eds.), *Fundamentals of nonverbal behavior* (pp. 401–432). Cambridge, England: Cambridge University Press.

Buck, R. (1988). *Human motivation and emotion* (2nd ed.). New York: Wiley.

Buck, R. (1995a). Emotional and social factors in communication via facial expression: A rejoinder to Fridlund's reply. *Communication Theory, 5,* 398–401.

Buck, R. (1995b). Review of the book [*Human facial expression: An evolutionary view*]. *Communication Theory, 5,* 393–396.

Buller, D. B., & Burgoon, J. K. (1996). Interpersonal deception theory. *Communication Theory, 6,* 243–267.

Buller, D. B., Burgoon, J. K., White, C., & Ebesu, A. S. (1994). Interpersonal deception: VII. Behavioral profiles of falsification, concealment, and equivocation. *Journal of Language and Social Psychology, 13,* 366–395.

Burgoon, J. K. (1978). A communication model of personal space violations: Explication and an initial test. *Human Communication Research, 4,* 129–142.

Burgoon, J. K., & Baesler, E. J. (1991). Choosing between micro and macro nonverbal measurement: Application to selected vocalic and kinesic indices. *Journal of Nonverbal Behavior, 15,* 57–78.

Burgoon, J. K., & Buller, D. B. (1996). Reflections on the nature of theory building and the theoretical status of interpersonal deception theory. *Communication Theory, 6,* 311–328.

Burgoon, J. K., Buller, D. B., Afifi, W., White, C. H., & Buslig, A. L .S. (1996, May). *The role of immediacy in deceptive interpersonal interactions.* Paper presented at the annual meeting of the International Communication Association, Chicago.

Burgoon, J. K., Buller, D. B., Guerrero, L. K., Afifi, W., & Feldman, C. (1996). Interpersonal deception: XII. Information management dimensions underlying deceptive and truthful messages. *Communication Monographs, 63,* 50–69.

Burgoon, J. K., Buller, D. B., & Woodall, W. G. (1996). *Nonverbal communication: The unspoken dialogue.* New York: McGraw-Hill.

Burgoon, J. K., Ebesu, A. S., White, C. H., Kikuchi, T., Alvaro, E., & Koch, P. (in press). The many faces of interpersonal adaptation. In M. T. Palmer (Ed.), *Progress in communication sciences.* Norwood, NJ: Ablex.

Burgoon, J. K., Kelley, D. L., Newton, D. A., & Keeley-Dyreson, M. P. (1989). The nature of arousal and nonverbal indices. *Human Communication Research, 16,* 217–255.

Burgoon, J. K., & Langer, E. (1995). Language, fallacies, and mindlessness-mindfulness. In B. Burleson (Ed.), *Communication yearbook 18* (pp. 105–132). Newbury Park, CA: Sage.

Burgoon, J. K., & Le Poire, B. A. (1993). Effects of communication expectancies, actual communication, and expectancy disconfirmation on evaluations of communicators and their communication behavior. *Human Communication Research, 20,* 75–107.

Burgoon, J. K., Le Poire, B. A., & Rosenthal, R. (1995). Effects of preinteraction expectancies and target communication on perceiver reciprocity and compensation in dyadic interaction. *Journal of Experimental Social Psychology, 31,* 287–321.

Burgoon, J. K., Stern, L. A., & Dillman, L. (1995). *Interpersonal adaptation: Dyadic interaction patterns.* New York: Cambridge University Press.

Burgoon, J. K., & Walther, J. B. (1990). Nonverbal expectancies and the consequences of violations. *Human Communication Research, 17,* 232–265.

Cappella, J. N. (1991). The biological origins of automated patterns of human interaction. *Communication Theory, 1,* 4–35.

Cappella, J. N., & Greene, J. O. (1982). A discrepancy-arousal explanation of mutual influence in expressive behavior for adult and infant-adult interaction. *Communication Monographs, 49*, 89–114.

Carroll, J. M., & Russell, J. A. (1996). Do facial expressions signal emotions? Judging emotions from the face in context. *Journal of Personality and Social Psychology, 70*, 205–218.

Chapple, E. D. (1982). Movement and sound: The musical language of body rhythms in interaction. In M. Davis (Ed.), *Interaction rhythms: Periodicity in communicative behavior* (pp. 31–52). New York: Human Sciences.

Derlega, V. J., Metts, S., Petronio, S., & Margulis, S. T. (1993). *Self-disclosure.* Newbury Park, CA: Sage.

deTurck, M. A., & Miller, G. R. (1985). Deception and arousal: Isolating the behavioral correlates of deception. *Human Communication Research, 12*, 181–201.

Dillard, J. P. (1990). A goal-driven model of interpersonal influence. In J. P. Dillard (Ed.), *Seeking compliance: The production of interpersonal influence messages* (pp. 41–56). Scottsdale, AZ: Gorsuch Scarisbrick.

Dillard, J. P., Solomon, D. H., & Samp, J. A. (1996). Framing social reality: The relevance of relational judgments. *Communication Research, 23*, 703–723.

Foppa, K. (1995). On mutual understanding and agreement in dialogues. In I. Marková, C. Graumann, & K. Foppa (Eds.), *Mutualities in dialogue* (pp. 149–175). Cambridge, England: Cambridge University Press.

Fridlund, A. J. (1994). *Human facial expression: An evolutionary view.* San Diego, CA: Academic Press.

Fridlund, A. J. (1995). Reply to Buck's review of *Human facial expression: An evolutionary view. Communication Theory, 5*, 396–398.

Gallois, C., Giles, H., Jones, E., Cargile, A., & Ota, H. (1995). Accommodating intercultural encounters. In R. Wiseman (Ed.), *Theories of intercultural communication* (pp. 115–147). Newbury Park, CA: Sage.

Giles, H., Coupland, J., & Coupland, N. (Eds.). (1991). *Contexts of accommodation.* New York: Cambridge University Press.

Gouldner, A. W. (1960). The norm of reciprocity: A preliminary statement. *American Sociological Review, 25*, 161–179.

Graumann, C. F. (1995). Commonality, mutuality, reciprocity: A conceptual introduction. In I. Marková, C. Graumann, & K. Foppa (Eds.), *Mutualities in dialogue* (pp. 1–24). Cambridge, England: Cambridge University Press.

Grice, P. (1989). *Studies in the way of words.* Cambridge, MA: Harvard University Press.

Guerrero, L. (1997). Nonverbal involvement across interactions with same-sex friends, opposite-sex friends, and romantic partners: Consistency or change? *Journal of Social and Personal Relationships, 14*, 31–58.

Guerrero, L. K., & Burgoon, J. K. (1996). Attachment styles and reactions to nonverbal involvement change in romantic dyads: Patterns of reciprocity and compensation. *Human Communication Research, 22*, 335–370.

Gumperz, J. J. (1995). Mutual inferencing in conversation. In I. Marková, C. Graumann, & K. Foppa (Eds.), *Mutualities in dialogue* (pp. 101–123). Cambridge, England: Cambridge University Press.

Hatfield, E., Cacioppo, J. T., & Rapson, R. (1994). *Emotional contagion.* New York: Cambridge University Press.

Honeycutt, J. M. (1989). Effect of preinteraction expectancies on interaction involvement and behavioral responses in initial interaction. *Journal of Nonverbal Behavior, 13*, 25–36.

Jourard, S. M. (1959). Self-disclosure and other cathexis. *Journal of Abnormal Social Psychology, 59*, 428–431.

Kellermann, K. (1992). Communication: Inherently strategic and primarily automatic. *Communication Monographs, 59*, 288–300.

Kemper, T. D. (1984). Power, status, and emotions: A sociological contribution to a psychophysiological domain. In K. R. Scherer & P. Ekman (Eds.), *Approaches to emotion* (pp. 369–383). Hillsdale, NJ: Lawrence Erlbaum Associates.

Kempton, W. (1980). The rhythmic basis of interaction micro-synchrony. In M. R. Key (Ed.), *The relationship between verbal and nonverbal communication* (pp. 150–167). New York: Oxford University Press.

Kendon, A. (1994). Do gestures communicate? A review. *Research on Language and Social Interaction, 27*, 175–200.

Kenny, D. A. (1994). *Interpersonal perception: A social relations analysis.* New York: Guilford Press.

Kikuchi, T. (1994, July). *Effects of backchannel convergence on a speaker's speech rate and track-checking behavior.* Paper presented to the annual meeting of the International Communication Association, Sydney, Australia.

Krauss, R. M., Fussell, S. R., & Chen, Y. (1995). Coordination of perspective in dialogue: Intrapersonal and interpersonal processes. In I. Marková, C. Graumann, & K. Foppa (Eds.), *Mutualities in dialogue* (pp. 124–145). Cambridge, England: Cambridge University Press.

Le Poire, B. A., & Burgoon, J. K. (1994). Two contrasting explanations of involvement violations: Nonverbal expectancy theory versus discrepancy arousal theory. *Human Communication Research, 20*, 560–591.

Manusov, V. (1995). Reacting to changes in nonverbal behaviors: Relational satisfaction and adaptation patterns in romantic dyads. *Journal of Nonverbal Behavior, 21*, 456–477.

McCornack, S. A. (1992). Information manipulation theory. *Communication Monographs, 59*, 1–16.

McNeill, D. (1992). *Hand and mind: What gestures reveal about thought.* Chicago: University of Chicago Press.

McNeill, D., Cassell, J., & McCullough, K. (1994). Commuunicative effects of speech-mismatched gestures. *Research on Language and Social Interaction, 27*, 223–237.

Mead, G. H. (1934). *Mind, self, and society.* Chicago: University of Chicago Press.

Morris, W. N. (1992). A functional analysis of the role of mood in affective systems. In M. S. Clark (Ed.), *Emotion* (pp. 192–205). Newbury Park, CA: Sage.

Motley, M. T. (1993). Facial affect and verbal context in conversation. *Human Communication Research, 20*, 3–40.

O'Keefe, B. J. (1992). Developing and testing rational models of message design. *Human Communication Research, 18*, 637–649.

Palmer, M. L., & Simmons, K. B. (1995). Communicating intentions through nonverbal behaviors: Conscious and nonconscious encoding of liking. *Human Communication Research, 22*, 128–160.

Patterson, M. L. (1976). An arousal model of interpersonal intimacy. *Psychological Review, 83*, 235–245.

Patterson, M. L. (1983). *Nonverbal behavior: A functional perspective.* New York: Springer-Verlag.

Patterson, M. L. (1987). Presentational and affect-management functions of nonverbal involvement. *Journal of Nonverbal Behavior, 11*, 110–122.

Planalp, S. (1993). Communication, cognition, and emotion. *Communication Monographs, 60*, 3–9.

Ploog, D. W. (1995). Mutuality and dialogue in nonhuman primate communication. In I. Marková, C. Graumann, & K. Foppa (Eds.), *Mutualities in dialogue* (pp. 27–57). Cambridge, England: Cambridge University Press.

Rimé, B., & Schiaratura, L. (1991). Gesture and speech. In R. S. Feldman & B. Rimé (Eds.), *Fundamentals of nonverbal behavior* (pp. 239–281). Cambridge, England: Cambridge University Press.

Roloff, M. E. (1987). Communication and reciprocity within intimate relationships. In M. E. Roloff & G. R. Miller (Eds.), *Interpersonal processes: New directions in communication research* (pp. 11–38). Beverly Hills, CA: Sage.

Rommetveit, R. (1974). *On message structure: A framework for the study of language and communication.* New York: Wiley.

Schegloff, E. A. (1993). Reflections on quantification in the study of conversation. *Research on Language in Social Interaction, 26*, 99–128.

Siegman, A. W., & Reynolds, M. (1982). Interviewer-interviewee nonverbal communications: An interaction approach. In M. Davis (Ed.), *Interaction rhythms* (pp. 249–278). New York: Human Sciences Press.

Simpson, J. A., Gangestad, S. W., & Biek, M. (1993). Personality and nonverbal social behavior: An ethological perspective of relationship initiation. *Journal of Experimental Social Psychology, 29*, 434–461.

Staines, G. L., & Libby, P. L. (1986). Men and women in relationships. In T. L. Huston & R. D. Ashmore (Eds.), *The social psychology of female and male relations* (pp. 211–258). New York: Academic Press.

Tiersma, P. M. (1993). Nonverbal communication and the freedom of "speech." *Wisconsin Law Review, 6*, 1535–1589.

VanLear, C. A., Jr. (1991). Testing a cyclical model of communicative openness in relationship development: Two longitudinal studies. *Communication Monographs, 58*, 337–361.

Waldron, V. R. (1995). Is the "Golden Age of Cognition" losing its lustre? Toward a requirement-centered perspective. In B. R. Burleson (Ed.), *Communication yearbook 18* (pp. 180–197). Thousand Oaks, CA: Sage.

Waldron, V. R., & Cegala, D. J. (1992). Assessing conversational cognition: Levels of cognitive theory and associated methodological requirements. *Human Communication Research, 18*, 599–622.

Waldron, V. R., Cegala, D. J., Sharkey, W. F., & Teboul, B. (1990). Cognitive and tactical dimensions of goal management. *Journal of Language and Social Psychology, 9*, 101–118.

White, C. H. (1996). *Adaptation and communicative design: Patterns of interaction in deceptive and truthful interchanges.* Unpublished doctoral dissertation, University of Arizona.

Wilson, S. R. (1990). Development and test of a cognitive rules model of interaction goals. *Communication Monographs, 57*, 81–103.

Zajonc, R. B. (1980). Compresence. In P. B. Paulus (Ed.), *Psychology of group influence* (pp. 35–60). Hillsdale, NJ: Lawrence Erlbaum Associates.

FROM DNA TO MTV:
THE SPONTANEOUS COMMUNICATION
OF EMOTIONAL MESSAGES[1]

Ross Buck
University of Connecticut

This chapter defines formally spontaneous communication, outlines its characteristics, describes its relationship with symbolic communication, and discusses aspects of its influences upon human behavior. It was prepared in the context of a discussion of the adequacy of the traditional analytic–cognitive view of communication in general, and of message production in particular, initiated by John Greene. Specifically, Greene (personal communication, October, 1995) pointed out that "models of message production have tended to focus on intraindividual factors (i.e., cognitive structures and processes), with the assumption that the models are adequate for addressing the situated, social, inter-individual aspects of human interaction." He also noted that such models have given little attention to the physiological domain. Greene asked, among other things, whether these analytic-cognitive approaches are truly adequate in handling the social aspects of human communication, and whether physiologically based approaches have the potential to further understanding of communication processes in general, and message production in particular.

This chapter presents a physiologically based alternative or addition to traditional analytic-cognitive approaches, based on the notion of *spontane-*

---

[1]Portions of this paper were presented at "New directions for theories of verbal and nonverbal message productions, a panel discussion in honor of John O. Greene, 1994 Woolbert Award Recipient," at the annual meeting of the Speech Communication Association, San Antonio, TX. November 17–20, 1995.

ous emotional communication. This general view of the communication process was presented in its essential form in *The Communication of Emotion* (Buck, 1984). The central contention is that natural (human and animal) communication proceeds in two simultaneous streams: a symbolic stream that is learned and culturally patterned and a spontaneous stream that is a phylogenetically structured "conversation between limbic systems." The spontaneous stream is conceptualized in terms of a general Developmental-Interactionist, or Readout, theory of emotion (Buck, 1985, 1988a, 1994a).

The theory of spontaneous communication is meant to expand and enrich rather than to replace traditional analytic–cognitive approaches, and in fact the definition of *cognition* must itself be expanded to include holistic, synthetic, "syncretic cognition" associated with right hemisphere (RH) brain functioning (Chaudhuri & Buck, 1995a, 1995b; Tucker, 1981). It is true that the notion of spontaneous communication implies that there always must be something missing in models based on communication between artificial devices: no matter how "intelligent," artificial devices are incapable of spontaneous communication, the efforts of Data of *Star Trek, The Next Generation* to the contrary notwithstanding. Spontaneous communication has important implications for the understanding of such concepts as intuition, empathy, and rapport (Buck & Ginsburg, 1997), and of unintended influences of interpersonal expectations (Blanck, 1993; Rosenthal, 1967). Furthermore, the notion of spontaneous communication has important philosophical and epistemological implications. Specifically, spontaneous communication provides an answer to the "Problem of Other Minds" (Austin, 1959).

GENERAL CONCEPTUALIZATION

Spontaneous Communication: An Example from Paleobiology

Spontaneous communication is a direct, nonpropositional process involving biologically based sending and receiving mechanisms. The sender's display is a readout of phylogenetically structured motivational–emotional systems which, given attention, is "picked up" by the receiver who is prepared phylogenetically to "know" directly the meaning of the display and to respond appropriately.

Perhaps it is best to give a specific example, and to begin reasonably close to the beginning: the beginning of life on Earth via the DNA molecule. The cellular slime mold has a remarkable life cycle: it begins as a single celled amoeba that feeds on bacteria in rotting organic matter. When food runs low, individual organisms congregate and aggregate, coming together to form a multicelled slug that is able to move through the soil. When secure footing is encountered, the slug transforms into a "fruiting body": the individual ex-amoebae at the front of the slug are transformed into a cellulose stem and die, while those at the rear become encased in hard capsules and are released into the environment as spores, which given favorable conditions eventually wind up as single-celled individual amoebae (Davis, 1978).

The life cycle of the slime mold is notable for several reasons. First, it is an exceptionally ancient creature. It is neither animal, plant, nor fungus, belonging to the kingdom Protista which includes the Earth's earliest life forms. Second, the slime mold illustrates altruism, in a biological sense, in that the individuals in the front give up their reproductive possibilities, thereby enabling others to survive. Third, and most important for our present purposes, the slime mold demonstrates spontaneous communication in a concrete way when the individual single-celled organisms come together to form a whole multicelled creature. At the heart of this organization process are biologically based displays and preattunements that are relatively well documented. As food runs low, individual amoebae release a chemical pheromone into the environment. The pheromone in turn draws them together: the individuals follow the concentration gradient of the pheromone, and in so doing, aggregate. The pheromone in some cases is cyclic AMP, which is a significant "messenger substance" within and between human cells (Davis, 1978). The pheromone release is an example of a social signal or display, and the aggregative response shown by individual amoebae demonstrates that they are preattuned to the display: they "know" what to do when the display occurs as a kind of inherited knowledge. The display and preattunements are innate: that is, they are based upon genetic systems that have been structured and maintained over the course of evolution as phylogenetic adaptations.

Such a primordial biological capacity for communication based in the genes is a property of all creatures, from the simplest to the most complex forms (Buck & Ginsburg, 1991, 1995, 1997). The capacity for spontaneous communication is literally a fundamental property of protoplasm. Single-celled creatures cannot live indefinitely without exchanging genetic materials. To do this requires selective social communication in order to find their own kind, to identify mutually appropriate candidates for mating, and to engage in this fundamental affiliative act (Allee, 1931, 1938; Margulis, 1982). For example, Maier and Muller (1986) have described in detail how sexual pheromones released by algae regulate the sexual activity of others, resulting in the exchange and mixture of chromosomes.

The Readout Theory of Emotion

To provide a wider conceptual context for a detailed definition of spontaneous communication, it is useful to review the basic ideas and assumptions of the Developmental–Interactionist, or Readout, theory of emotion (Buck, 1984, 1985, 1988a, 1994a).

Special-Purpose and General-Purpose Processing Systems. Spontaneous communication involves biologically based *special-purpose processing systems (SPPSs)* structured over the course of evolution to serve specific functions. The pheromones and preattunements of slime molds are SPPSs. In more complex creatures, SPPSs interact with *general-purpose processing systems (GPPSs)* evolved to be shaped by the individual's experiences with reality, which are structured by individual experience involving conditioning, instrumental learning, and higher order cognitive processing over the course of ontogeny. SPPSs and GPPSs are seen to be two of the three general sorts of systems that control human behavior. The third kind of system is unique to human beings: It is *linguistic competence* that involves formal ways of processing information, including language, mathematics, symbolic logic, music, and dance notation (Buck, 1988a).

The basic relationship assumed between SPPSs and GPPSs/linguistic competence is illustrated in Fig. 13.1. The dimension presented on the X-axis mirrors the phylogenetic scale, with relatively simple creatures' behavior being mostly a matter of relatively simple reflexes, taxes, and tropisms (e.g., slime molds, ants, and bees) and creatures with significant analytic-cognitive capacities being at the other extreme. This progressive evolution of learning and cognitive abilities that confer increased behavioral plasticity has been termed *anagenesis* (Gottlieb, 1984). Thus, as more complex creatures have evolved, the interaction between SPPSs and GPPSs has increasingly favored the latter. The dimension presented on the X-axis of Fig. 13.1 arguably more accurately reflects the relationship between innate factors and learning than does the more usual categorical distinction between *emotion* and *cognition.* Also, other phenomena may be meaningfully placed on this dimension. For example, the developmental scale may be represented, with the mostly "hard-wired" infant at the left and the adult at the right; communication situations can be represented, with the "throes of passion" on the left and staid intellectual discourse on the right; relationships can be represented, with more intimate personal relationships toward the left and more formal social relationships to the right (Buck, 1984).

Defining Motivation, Emotion, and Cognition. It is a fundamental proposition of Readout theory that, to define any one of the terms *motivation, emotion,* and *cognition,* one must define all three, because none of these concepts exists independently of the others. Each of these concepts inherently involves the others: emotion has motivational and cognitive aspects; cognition has motivational and emotional aspects; and motivation has cognitive and emotional aspects.

Motivation is defined as potential for behavior built into a system of behavior control; *emotion* as the manifestation or *readout* of that potential when aroused by a challenging stimulus (see Fig. 13.2). Thus motivation and

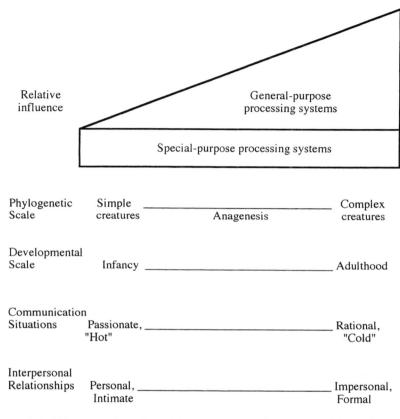

FIG. 13.1. Interaction of special-purpose processing systems (biogenetic factors) and general-purpose processing systems (learned factors). From Figure 1.1 in R. Buck (1984). *The Communication of Emotion.* New York: Guilford Press. Adapted with permission.

emotion are two sides of the same coin: a motivational–emotional system (Buck, 1985). The relationship of motivation and emotion is seen to be analogous to the relationship of energy and matter in physics. Energy is a potential that is never observed: a weight raised to a height, a coiled spring, or an explosive chemical possess potential energy, but this is not perceived as energy *per se.* Instead, we see the energy manifested in matter: in heat, light and/or force. Just so, we do not observe motivation: rather we observe in emotion the manifestation or readout of motivational potential. For example, the tendency of slime molds to aggregate is a readout of gene-based motivational potential that is aroused by a lowering of food levels, and although many theorists would perhaps not agree that slime molds possess emotion, in the present view their aggregative behavior is in fact seen to be an example of the operation of a motivational–emotional system.

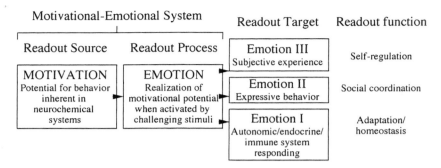

FIG 13.2. The readout model of motivational-emotional systems. From Figure 1 in R. Buck, C. Easton, & C. Goldman (1995). A developmental-interactionist theory of motivation, emotion, and cognition: Implications for understanding psychotherapy. *The Japanese Journal of Research on Emotion, 3*(1), 1–16. Adapted with permission.

The slime mold's behavior demonstrates that it possesses some degree of awareness of the state of affairs in the terrestrial environment regarding food and pheromones: this is one of the cognitive aspects of the operation of motivational-emotional systems. *Cognition* is defined as knowledge: of terrestrial events, of other creatures, of internal bodily processes (including, as we shall see, subjectively experienced feelings and desires). There are two sorts of knowledge: *knowledge-by-acquaintance* is raw, direct and immediate, involving the self-evident "presentational immediacy of experience" (Russell, 1912, p. 73); and analytic *knowledge-by-description* or knowledge ABOUT knowledge, that reflects the organism's experience via classical conditioning, instrumental learning, and/or information processing.

The complexity and reflexivity of knowledge expands greatly with anagenisis. We assume that the slime mold's awareness of food and pheromones is direct and immediate; but even simple creatures can demonstrate an elementary kind of knowledge-by-description. For example, the marine snail *Hermissenda crassicornis* innately responds to rotation by flexing its foot: It is thought that the foot flexion functions to anchor the snail during turbulence. If roation is paired with a light in a Pavlovian conditioning paradigm, the snail learns to flex its foot to the light (Alkon 1989). This demonstrates knowledge-by-description: The snail shows that it has learned something *about* the light: that it is associated with rotation. In more complex creatures consciousness—the awareness of being aware—emerged, and with human beings language developed, and with it a whole new level of behavior control affording sociolingistic construction, as we shall see.

There is evidence that different brain systems underlie functionally different levels of cognition. LeDoux (1994a) and Panksepp (1994) have distinguished "cortico-cognitive" processes based on the hippocampus and neocortex, as opposed to direct affective processing involving the amygdala.

Also, LeDoux (1994b) outlined two "central memory networks" that operate simultaneously and in parallel: explicit or declarative memory which involves the hippocampus, and implicit or emotional memory which involves the amygdala: these memory networks may not always agree, because they have different inputs.

Three Sorts of Readout. As noted, awareness of challenging stimuli in the terrestrial environment is one of the cognitive aspects of the operation of motivational–emotional systems; another is the awareness of the organism's state. Even in the simplest creatures, knowledge of food must be correlated with knowledge of the organism's need for food; and in complex creatures who possess conscious awareness of being aware, the bodily state is signaled by the subjective experience of feelings and desires (Buck, 1993a). As Fig. 13.2 illustrates, subjective experience is seen as being one of three sorts of emotional readout which serve three distinct functions: bodily homeostasis and adaptation via the autonomic, endocrine, and immune systems (*Emotion I*); social regulation via spontaneous communication involving expressive displays and preattunements to those displays (*Emotion II*); and self-regulation via subjectively experienced affects involving central neurochemical systems (*Emotion III*).

Accessibility, Emotional Education, and Emotional Competence. Another fundamental proposition of Readout theory is that the three readouts are differentially *accessible* to the individual and to others. Subjectively experienced Emotion III affect is accessible directly only to the self: others never know exactly how we feel. Expressive Emotion II displays are most accessible to others: we cannot see our faces or bodies, or hear our voices as others do. Finally, most Emotion I homeostatic-adaptive responses are normally not accessible either to self or others without special equipment.

This fact of differential accessibility makes learning about emotion—*emotional education*—fundamentally different from other sorts of social learning (Buck, 1983). One way of learning about one's feelings and desires is through *social biofeedback* (see Fig. 13.3): The child learns about subjective experience—labels, expectations, explanations, display rules—when others respond to the child's expressive behavior with labels, directions, and interpretations. Children use this feedback to learn to deal with their own subjectively experienced feelings and desires. Social biofeedback involves direct interpersonal emotional communication: It is necessary for children to display accurately their feelings to others, and for others to respond appropriately, for proper social biofeedback to occur. Another way to learn about one's subjective feelings and desires is through *modeling* and *imitation*, as when the child views and learns from the emotional expressions, explanations, and behaviors of others, including others presented via mass media (Buck,

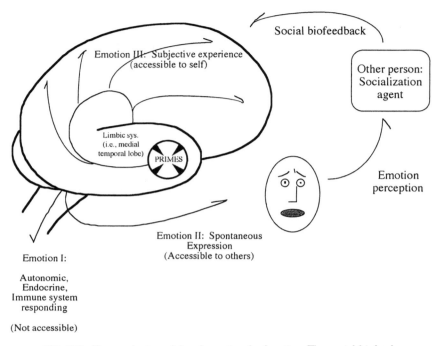

FIG. 13.3. The readout model and emotional education: The social biofeed-back process. From Figure 3 in R. Buck, C. Easton, & C. Goldman (1995). A developmental-interactionist theory of motivation, emotion, and cognition: Implications for understanding psychotherapy. *The Japanese Journal of Research on Emotions, 3*(1), 1–16. Reproduced with permission.

1988b). In these ways, the neurologically based, pancultural subjective experience of feelings and desires is linked with culturally variable linguistic labels, expectations, and rules. The result of successful or unsuccessful emotional education is a greater or lesser degree of *emotional competence*: the ability effectively to label and appropriately express one's feelings and desires (Buck, Goldman, Easton, & Norelli Smith, in press). More specifically, children must learn labels for feelings and desires and expectations about what is and is not appropriate to do when they occur—such learning is basic for the functioning of expression-management techniques and display rules (Ekman & Friesen, 1975).

The emotional education process in which the child learns about subjective experience, resulting in a greater or lesser degree of emotional competence, is based on emotional communication: both direct interpersonal communication in the case of social biofeedback, and mediated emotional communication in the case of modeling and imitation. The next part of this chapter reviews the conceptualization and definition of spontaneous emotional communication.

SPONTANEOUS VERSUS SYMBOLIC COMMUNICATION

Defining Communication

We should begin by defining exactly what we mean by "communication." Communication is often defined as involving a rule-governed *code* and specific encoding and decoding stages which involve information processing. Meaningful information is encoded by a sender into symbols, which are transmitted via a channel to a receiver, who decodes the symbols and thereby gains access to the meaningful information. The symbol system is held to be learned and culturally patterned, and the encoding and decoding processes are seen to be voluntary and intentional, but not necessarily actively conscious.

Linguistic Communication. The epitome of this sort of communication process is human linguistic communication, where sounds produced by the human vocal apparatus (phones) have through cultural evolution become elements of spoken language (phonemes). Phonemes are combined through linguistic rules to form symbols (morphemes) which have arbitrary and learned relationships with their referents. The morphemes are combined, again according to rules (grammar), into sentences. Many believe that the basic rules of grammar (deep structures) are biologically based (or perhaps they are ecologically based), but there is no question that the *content* of language is learned and culturally patterned. This basic linguistic structure is characteristic of language, and also mathematics, symbolic logic, computer programming, and musical and dance notation.

The "magic" of language is that a few dozen phonemes can be combined into a few hundred thousand morphemes that constitute the lexicon—the vocabulary or dictionary—of the language; and that the morphemes can in turn be organized into an infinite variety of sentences that can be decoded by anyone who has learned the lexicon and grammar of that language. This enables linguistic creatures to communicate about events that have never been, and could never be, directly experienced: the number of angels that fit on the head of a pin; the characteristics of a black hole. Nonlinguistic creatures—all creatures save human beings as far as we know—are forever constrained by their personal experience. Human beings can experience vicariously through language the thoughts and feelings even of those long dead, and it is this that arguably gives human beings an inherent dualistic quality.

From the time of the ancient Greeks, the processes governing human and animal behavior have been contrasted. As Cofer and Appley (1964) related, Plato and Aristotle granted animals "souls" capable of caring for basic bodily functions, but denied them "rational souls" which were the bases of human logic and reason. Thomas Acquinas analogously equipped human beings with "sensitive souls" which are shared with animals and "rational souls" unique to human beings. Descartes' mind–body dualism was similarly grounded on the distinction between animal behavior, which could be explained by mechanical forces, and human behavior which was partly mechanical but also affected by a nonmechanical "soul." Descartes' notion was ridiculed by Ryle (1949) as the "dogma of the ghost in the machine." But I submit that the notion of a ghost in a machine, an inherent dualism in human nature, is not so ridiculous after all: Linguistic competence allows human behavior to be influenced by ghosts, of a kind (Buck, 1988a).

Nonverbal Communication. Linguistic communication is doubtless the most powerful and flexible sort of communication that has evolved: it is the source of human civilization and is arguably the critical feature that distinguishes human and animal nature and social organization. Time may soon tell whether the human "rational soul" will also bring to an end the four billion year-old story of life on earth (Buck, 1988a). However, there has been a tendency to consider linguistic communication not only as the epitome of human communication, but as the only system of communication that counts in explaining human behavior. This tendency has been countered in recent years by the discovery of the importance of *nonverbal* communication in human behavior. However, the definition of nonverbal, and its relationship with linguistic communication, is often unclear. A influential definition by Weiner, DeVoe, Rubinow, and Geller (1972) contends that nonverbal communication also involves a rule-governed code, and that it differs from linguistic communication primarily in that its symbols are not verbal: they are facial expressions, gestures, postures, tones of voice, etc., which are used intentionally and strategically by the sender to "comment" on the words spoken. The nonverbal code is often described as analogic rather than digital, and more iconic than the verbal code. From this point of view, nonverbal communication must contain a code, and encoding and decoding processes, in order to qualify as "communication," otherwise the process should be named by a lesser term such as "influence."

An Alternative View. The insistence that communication must be voluntary and symbolic thus implies that any other process by which organisms influence one another is secondary, subordinate, inferior, and/or deficient; and of little interest in understanding human behavior. It is evident, however, that systems of influence that are clearly nonsymbolic and unlearned function to organize complex social systems in many species. We noted before the social psychology of the slime mold; other examples of such systems of influence are found in the social insects: ants, bees, and termites. E. O. Wilson

(1975) has defined communication as occurring whenever the behavior of one organism influences the behavior of another. More specifically: A's behavior X1 is defined as communicative if:

> The conditional probability that act X2 will be performed by individual B given that A performed X1 is not equal to the probability that B will perform X2 in the absence of X1. (p. 194)

This definition, being general and applicable to all species, is the definition of "communication" assumed in this chapter.

The communication process used by insects, let alone slime molds and algae, is obviously far removed from human linguistic communication, and many would argue that it is of little relevance in understanding human behavior. However, the central thesis of this chapter is that human behavior is significantly and indeed dramatically affected by a communication process whose structure is identical with the structure of the communication process in insects, slime molds, and algae, and is distinct from the process of intentional, symbolic communication. It is spontaneous communication: a direct, biologically based and entirely nonvoluntary system based on innate sending and receiving mechanisms. The state of the sender is displayed in such a way that it can be "picked up" and responded to directly by the receiver. The receiver is directly aware of the meaning of the display: It is inherited knowledge. Spontaneous communication sets the agenda of human behavior and interaction; it is at the essence of the "sensitive soul"; it organizes the domain of Gaia.

Defining Spontaneous and Symbolic Communication

The characteristics of spontaneous and symbolic communication are summarized in Fig. 13.4. As it indicates, *symbolic communication* is communication in its usual, verbal/linguistic sense: it is based on codes that must be learned by both sender and receiver; these codes involve *symbols* that bear an arbitrary relationship with the referent; it must be intentional at some level; its statements are propositions capable of logical analysis; it is based on left hemisphere (LH) processes (Buck, 1994b). *Spontaneous communication* in contrast is based on innate phylogenetically structured displays on the part of the sender and preattunements to those displays on the part of the receiver; the displays are *signs* of the referent, or externally accessible aspects of the referent; it is spontaneous or nonintentional; its statements are nonpropositional, because they cannot be false; and it is based on right hemisphere (RH) processes involving the expressive display of emotion (Emotion II). As we shall see, the spontaneous display is also inherently flexible: It can be influenced by conditioned suppression that inhibits the

CHARACTERISTICS	SPONTANEOUS COMMUNICATION	SYMBOLIC COMMUNICATION
Basis of signal system	Biologically-based Displays and Preattunements	Socially shared Learned, culturally patterned
Intentionality	Spontaneous Communication between limbic systems	Voluntary At some level
Elements	Signs Externally accessible aspects of referent	Symbols Arbitrary relationship with referent
Content	Nonpropositional Motivational/emotional states	Propositions Capable of logical analysis (Tests of truth/falsity)
Hemispheric processing	Right Hemisphere	Left Hemisphere

FIG. 13.4. Characteristics of spontaneous and symbolic communication. From Table 1.1 in R. Buck (1984). *The Communication of Emotion.* New York: Guilford Press. Adapted with permission.

display, and by learned display rules (associated with social emotions perhaps mediated by the LH) that can control spontaneous expression for tactical or strategic purposes, and even voluntarily activate displays virtually identical to spontaneous ones (voluntary expression initiation or emotive expression; see Arndt & Janney, 1991; Buck, 1984, 1994a, 1994b; Jurgens, 1979; Ploog, 1981). The following paragraphs discuss each of the distinctions between spontaneous and symbolic communication.

The Basis of the Communication Process. In any communication process there must be a basis of sharing between sender and receiver. Spontaneous communication is based on BIOLOGICALLY STRUCTURED SENDING AND RECEIVING MECHANISMS; these are genetically determined displays and preattunements to those displays which are innate (e.g., have evolved as phylogenetic adaptations). In contrast, symbolic communication is learned and culturally patterned. As noted, communication is seen to occur in two simultaneous streams: spontaneous communication is a direct stream of communication—literally a conversation between limbic systems—that occurs simultaneously and interactively with the symbolic stream of communication and serves functions of social coordination (Buck, 1984; 1988a; 1994a; 1994b).

In symbolic communication, this basis of the communication process is learned and culturally patterned: sender and receiver must posses the same code—the same lexicon and grammar in which information is represented.

These codes are learned during social development, and are associated with strong social motives and emotions that are often overlooked (Buck, 1994b). As Weiner et al. (1972) pointed out, these codes may be nonverbal as well as verbal: Specific sorts of gestures, expressions, and intonations may come to have specific meanings within a cultural context which, like the meanings of verbal language, are learned. This nonverbal language has been termed *body language*. Birdwhistell (1970) termed the study of such nonverbal codes *kinesics*, and in the linguistic–kinesic analogy explicitly compared its structure with the structure of language. More specifically, he suggested that the phones of language are analogous to kines, phonemes are analogous to kinemes, morphemes to kinemorphs, and sentences to complex kinemorphs. Thus kinemes are movements that have become specifiable elements of body language, and kinemorphs are combinations of such movements which have become symbols with arbitrary and learned relationships with their referents: a nonverbal lexicon. The kinemorphs are combined, according to a nonverbal grammar, into an infinite variety of complex kinemorphs that can be decoded by anyone who has learned the nonverbal lexicon and grammar.

This kind of learned body language undoubtedly exists, as has been demonstrated by observations of cultural differences in patterns of movement and gesture, and it is an important source of potential confusion in intercultural communication (as, for example, when persons of different cultures use space, touch, or gaze differently when interacting with one another). However, spontaneous communication is qualitatively distinct from this sort of body language. The foundation of spontaneous communication and the basis of sharing meaning between sender and receiver is not learned. It is biological, involving phylogenetically structured, universal sending and receiving mechanisms: expressive displays and perceptual preattunements.

Innate displays expressing motivational/emotional states are phylogenetic adaptations that evolve in a process of ritualization because of the social importance of that particular state (Eibl-Eibesfeldt, 1975). Threatening and submissive displays regulate aggression within the group functioning to avoid dangerous fights; courting displays regulate sexual behavior functioning to signal sexual readiness; parent and infant displays regulate behavior in the family group functioning to promote appropriate contact, etc. There is compelling evidence from widely different levels of the phylogenetic scale that sending and receiving tendencies are genetically based and coevolve in supporting spontaneous communication. We have already considered slime molds and algae; Bentley and Hoy (1974) demonstrated a specific genetic basis for the songs of crickets with one genetic system controlling the sending mechanism and another, overlapping one, encoding for the ability to receive. Also, different species of frogs and toads manifest different songs that are responded to preferentially by members of the same species, and hybrids manifest songs that are responded to preferentially by other hybrids (Bogert, 1961; Ryan, 1990). Another example concerns the coydog, which is a cross between a coyote and a beagle resulting in a remarkable dual personality of sorts. The defensive threat display of the coyote—a distinct U-shaped body posture, wide oral gape and sibilant hiss— is not shown by the beagle, but in the coydog the genetic potentials for the displays of both species are present. Some coydogs show coyote-like threat behavior from infancy; others show initial dog-like threat behavior that around puberty can be switched to that of the coyote by social stress mediated by an elevation in plasma cortisol (Ginsburg, 1986; Moon & Ginsburg, 1985).

Displays on the part of the sender must coevolve with preattunements to the displays on the part of the receiver. The receiver knows the meaning of the display as inherited knowledge; that is, the receiver is genetically preattuned to the display and knows the "meaning of the message" directly, so as long as the display is produced and the receiver attends, the receiver's knowledge is accurate in a sense, or veridical, by definition. The receiver's knowledge is not however accurate in a propositional sense: It is a vague, nonspecific, nebulous, and obscure direct awareness that is known by acquaintance (Buck & Ginsburg, 1997). We consider the nature of the receiver's knowledge later.

Elements of the Message. The elements making up the "message" of spontaneous communication are SIGNS, which are externally accessible aspects of the referent: externally accessible aspects of certain important motivational–emotional states. Examples include pheromones released by a slime mold, ant, or human being, and spontaneous facial expressions and gestures. More precisely, the elements of spontaneous communication are *indices that function as signs*. The term *sign* is meant in the sense of "dark clouds are a sign of rain." The darkness of the clouds is an aspect of the rain that is accessible to a perceiver at a distance. The relationship between the darkness and the clouds is not arbitrary, rather the darkness is an intrinsic property—an "index"—of the high moisture content of the clouds. Black (1962) defined sign in relation to index as follows:

> Any event of character A whose occurrence is invariably accompanied by another event of character B may be said to be an *index* of that event. Any index which is recognized as being such may be said to function as a sign. Thus, as contrasted with "index," the use of "sign" presupposes a triadic relations. (p. 292; italics in the original)

This definition of sign implies the classic components of a communication process: sender, receiver, and message (Shannon & Weaver, 1949). Thus, the index to be a sign must *inform a receiver*: it must constitute *information*. The sign constitutes a message, and the origin of the sign is a sender, even though no intent to communicate exists: the darkness of the clouds is an intrinsic aspect or index of the referent—the rain—that can potentially constitute a message that is informative to the receiver even though there is no intent on the part of the cloud to send such information.

These are ecological definitions of sign and information that relate to the old question of whether the tree falling in the forest made sound. The fall of the tree caused vibrations in the air that constituted an index of the event, but if unheard they did not constitute a sign; they did not constitute information. These definitions also relate to James J. Gibson's (1966) suggestion that the earth before life evolved was a physical reality but not an *environment*, because an environment is defined in terms of the organisms that inhabit it. Volcanoes have been exploding on Io, the moon of Jupiter, for eons; but until the image of their explosions was conveyed to Earth by the Voyager spacecraft the explosions did not inform any organism as far as we know, so they were indices but not signs that occurred in a physical reality but not in an environment. An uninhabited physical reality is not an environment in this ecological sense: there are events and indices of those events, but there are no signs and no information. In effect, the Voyager spacecraft brought the volcanoes of Io into the human environment.

Some would consider the notion of signs as *communication* to be nonsense. Dark clouds after all do not *intend* to communicate about rain, and the explosions on Io do not *intend* to communicate about volcanoes. Nevertheless, as noted, a sender, message, and receiver can be identified, and information is transferred, resulting in physical or behavioral changes: These satisfy Shannon and Weaver's classic requirements for communication. They do not, however, satisfy Wilson's (1975) definition (given earlier) since the acts of organisms are not involved. I am not suggesting that dark clouds or the volcanoes of Io are communicating spontaneously! Spontaneous communication involves displays, and all displays are signs and all signs are indexes, but it is not the case that indexes are necessarily signs or that signs are necessarily displays. *Displays* are defined as *ritualized behaviors that have evolved to function as indices/signs of motivational/emotional states*.

As noted, communication is often *defined in terms of codes*: an encoding process on the part of the sender, a coded message, and a decoding process on the part of the receiver. The sender must encode a message that is decoded by the receiver; otherwise it is not really communication but merely "influence" or some such. By definition codes do not involve signs, which are intrinsic indices of their referents; but rather they involve *symbols*, which have arbitrary relationships with their referents (Buck, 1984). Symbolic communication is communication in its usual sense of encoding and decoding, and the elements of symbolic communication are, naturally, symbols.

Intentionality of the Communication Process. From the foregoing it is clear that spontaneous communication is NOT INTENTIONAL; there is *no intent to communicate* on the part of the sender in spontaneous communication, rather the display is *spontaneous.* The signs comprising spontaneous messages are nonvoluntary readouts evolved with the function of displaying certain motivational/emotional states. The sign constitutes a message, and the origin of the sign is a sender, even though no intent to communicate exists. The darkness of the clouds is an intrinsic aspect or index of the referent—the rain—that can potentially constitute a message that is informative to the receiver even though there is no intent on the part of the cloud to send such information. In contrast, message production in symbolic communication is always voluntary and intentional at some level, although it does not necessarily involve conscious control: Body language may be overlearned and occur unconsciously.

Content of the Communication Process. The content of spontaneous communication is NONPROPOSITIONAL, because it cannot be false: Its content consists instead of motivational–emotional states. Because the display is a sign, or index, of the referent event, it cannot occur in the absence of the referent. Therefore, spontaneous communication by definition cannot be false. According to Russell (1903), a proposition is defined as a statement capable of logical analysis, and the simplest sort of logical analysis is the test for truth or falsity. Because spontaneous communication is by definition veridical, it is therefore nonpropositional. Symbolic communication, in contrast, is composed of propositions. However, we shall see that the sender can voluntarily produce a similar display for strategic purposes, producing a propositional message that uses spontaneous message elements that are voluntarily activated, initiated, or disinhibited.

Cerebral Lateralization and Communication

As noted, spontaneous communication appears to be particularly associated with the RH and symbolic communication with the LH, but the situation is more complicated than this, and the roles of the cerebral hemispheres in spontaneous and symbolic communication are incompletely understood.

The Left Hemisphere and Asymbolia. It does appear clear that the LH is associated with symbolic communication in both its sending and receiving aspects, at least in most right-handed persons. Damage to the posterior LH (Wernicke's area) tends to result in what has been termed *receptive aphasia*, where both verbal and nonverbal linguistic comprehension are affected, but expression tends to be spared. Damage to the anterior LH (Broca's area) in contrast tends to result in *expressive aphasia*, where comprehension may be intact, but abilities in verbal and nonverbal-linguistic production are affected. The deficits in symbolic communication abilities resulting from LH damage may be profound. Duffy and Liles (1979) suggested, following Finklnberg (1870), that since the deficits resulting from LH damage affect symbolic nonverbal as well as verbal behaviors (pantomime, sign language, finger spelling), that the condition be labeled *asymbolia* rather than aphasia.

The Right Hemisphere and Aspontania. It also appears clear that the RH is associated with the receiving aspect of spontaneous communication in most right-handed persons. Many studies, using both animal and human subjects and a variety of methods, have indicated RH involvement in the discrimination of emotional facial expressions and affective prosody in the voice (Etcoff, 1989).

The question of RH involvement in spontaneous expression is more complex. Studying brain-damaged patients' abilities to produce and recognize emotional intonation or prosody in the voice, Ross (1981) has suggested an analogy between the posterior–anterior control of symbolic receiving and sending processes in the LH and the RH: that posterior RH damage is associated with *receptive aprosodia* and anterior RH damage with *expressive aprosodia*. Patients with anterior RH damage show deficits in spontaneous facial–gestural sending accuracy compared with LH damaged and non-brain-damaged patients (Buck & Duffy, 1980; Borod, Koff, Perlman-Lorch, & Nichols, 1985). Following Duffy and Liles' (1979) example, we might suggest that the effects of RH damage be termed *aspontania*.

Hemispheric Control of Selfish versus Social Emotions. Studies of brain damage, albeit valuable, give an incomplete view of normal RH and LH functioning in communication. In the broader literature, two hypotheses can be distinguished: The *right hemisphere hypothesis* that the RH plays a special role in the regulation and display of all emotions, and the *valence hypothesis* that negative emotions and displays are right-lateralized and positive emotions and displays are left-lateralized (Ross, Homan, & Buck, 1994). Evidence supporting both hypotheses exists: Some of the strongest evidence for the valence hypothesis is the demonstration by Davidson and Fox (1982) of LH involvement in the smiling of infants and RH involvement in more negative emotional states. However, the fact that the medial forebrain bundle "reward system" is right-lateralized in the brains of human beings and other animals (Dennenberg, 1981, 1984; Oke, Keller, Medford, & Adams, 1978) seems contrary to the valence hypothesis.

An alternative view, consistent with the evidence for both hypotheses, is that the RH is particularly associated with "selfish emotions" that promote the survival of the individual, and the LH with "social emotions" that promote the survival of the species. The selfish–social distinction was suggested by MacLean (1969, 1990, 1993) in his analysis of the anatomy of emotions in the limbic system. He suggested that the amygdala/hippocampus in the temporal limbic region of the brain is associated with a neural network associated with the "selfish demands" of the preservation of oneself (and one's genes): feeding, fighting, fear, and copulation. In contrast there are two limbic system regions associated with emotions that support the survival of the species: parent–offspring behaviors, play, bonding, sociality, attachment, and, perhaps, love. These regions include the septal area and the mammilo-thalamic-cingulate system. The former is present in reptiles and is closely associated with the olfactory apparatus; the latter is virtually absent in reptiles and develops greatly during evolution, reaching its largest relative size in human beings. MacLean (1993) suggests that its elaboration during evolution may reflect the change from the olfactory to the visual control of behavior.

It is of interest that a recent study of brain metabolism in human beings found a majority in a sample of men to have higher relative resting brain metabolism in temporal limbic regions, while most women had higher relative brain metabolism in the middle and posterior cingulate gyrus (Gur et al., 1995). Does this mean that men tend to be relatively selfish and women relatively social? Even if it might, it should be noted that such differences in the brain activity of adults could be due to gender-role related social learning.

Gur et al. (1995) also reported relatively higher right-sided metabolism in the medial temporal regions, and relatively higher left-sided metabolism in the cingulate region. This is consistent with the notion that the RH may be associated with *selfish* emotions, both positive and negative in valence, and the LH with *social* emotions. Other evidence includes the observation by Buck and Duffy (1980) that, while most patient groups were most expressive to positive "familiar people" slides and least expressive to unpleasant slides, LH-damaged patients showed no such tendency. The LH-damaged patients did not seem to be following the proper "display rules," but rather perhaps displayed their spontaneous response directly. Another relevant study was reported by Ross et al. (1994) in which the emotional recollections of patients undergoing the Wada test, where the right hemisphere is temporarily inactivated, were observed. In a number of the patients, strong recollections of selfish emotions were lessened or replaced by recollections of social emotions; for example, a woman who has previously reported feeling "mad and angry" when she was teased as a child for having epilepsy, during the Wada test reported feeling "embarrassed" when the RH was inactivated. The selfish–social distinction can also explain the relative LH activation in infants associated with smiling observed by Davidson and Fox (1982): The smiles may have been communicative "social smiles" rather than spontaneous displays of pleasure. In addition, recent evidence that repressors (Aspendorf & Scherer, 1983) show relative tonic LH activation (Tomarken & Davidson, 1994) is consistent with this view.

The Inhibition and Control of the Spontaneous Display. I have emphasized that, although the spontaneous display is in itself an innate and reflexive SPPS—a ritualized readout of the state of motivational/emotional systems—it is at the same time "innately flexible" and open to influence from GPPSs of conditioning, instrumental learning, and higher order cognitive processing. This phenomenon is an example of the fact that, in a very real sense, in human beings free will is biologically determined.

The characteristics of inhibition and control are summarized in Fig. 13.5. *Inhibition* is unidirectional—always suppressive of the display (Buck, 1993b), while *control* involves the display rules or expression management techniques of Ekman and Friesen (1985). The latter include modulation (showing more or less emotion than experienced); qualification (adding a "nonfelt" display as a comment to a "felt" display); and falsification (showing a neutral expression when emotion is experienced, a display when no emotion is experienced, or an unfelt display to mask a felt emotion). Inhibition is classically conditioned or based upon temperament (with introverts being relatively inhibited and extroverts relatively uninhibited) and is associated with the behavioral activation and inhibition systems analyzed by Gray (1982). Control is instrumentally learned (goal-directed learning) and is en-

INHIBITION	CONTROL
Classically conditioned or based upon temperament.	Instrumentally learned display rules.
Involuntary.	Voluntary goal-directed.
Always <u>suppressive</u> of expression.	<u>Modulation:</u> increase or decrease felt emotion.
<u>**(The Suppression Hypothesis)**</u>	<u>Qualification:</u> add to felt emotion. <u>Falsification:</u> <u>Simulation</u> of unfelt emotion. <u>Neutralization</u> of felt emotion. <u>Masking</u> of felt by unfelt emotion.
Not sensitive to social context: affects expression while alone.	Sensitive to social context and cultural expectations
Associates with high sympathetic nervous system activity (and other physiological measures of stress/arousal?).	Not strongly related to peripheral physiological responding.
Associates with poor emotional education.	Associated with successful emotional education, emotional competence.

FIG. 13.5. Characteristics of inhibition and control.

hanced by the fact that the sender can voluntarily produce a display for strategic purposes. Jurgens (1979) and Ploog (1981, 1992) investigated the neural systems underlying what they term *voluntary expression initiation*. In rhesus monkeys, they found the voluntary control of innately organized displays to be associated with the supplemental motor cortex acting via the extrapyramidal motor system. Their data together with other considerations suggest that expressive displays are "hard wired" in brainstem systems and may be activated/disinhibited either by limbic system mechanisms (the spontaneous display) or voluntarily initiated (Buck, 1994b). Arndt and Janney (1991) have termed the former "emotional" communication and the latter "emotive" communication.

Inhibition is associated with limbic system processes, the lateralization of which is not well understood. Control is motivated by social emotions that may be associated with the LH (Buck, 1994b; Ross et al., 1994). With the argument that the spontaneous display is associated with the RH, the model in Fig. 13.6 is suggested. First, the spontaneous tendency to display in response to emotional stimuli is associated with RH processing. If the display has been related in the past with suppressive punishment ("Big boys don't cry!", "Young ladies do not hit!"), it will be inhibited. Such inhibition is in turn associated with increased stress-related autonomic-endocrine-immune system responding (the *suppression hypothesis*) and with deficits in emotional education, *alexithymia*—no words for mood (Nemiah & Sifneos, 1970), decreased emotional competence and, thereby, tendencies toward psychopathology (Buck et al., in press).

The question of the nature and implications of the suppression or control of emotional expression is a central unresolved issue in theories of psycho-

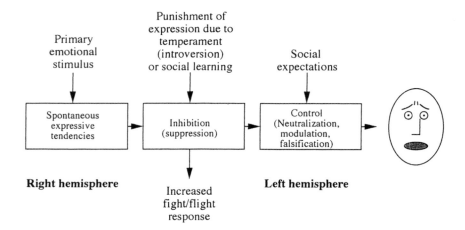

FIG. 13.6. A model of spontaneous emotional expression, inhibition, and control.

pathology and psychotherapy. Is it more psychologically healthy to express one's feelings openly, or to control and suppress certain socially undesirable tendencies? I suggest that suppression is *unhealthy* but control is *healthy:* that the effects of inhibition are typically negative with regard to mental and physical well-being and social functioning, while the effects of control are most likely positive. Control involves the instrumentally-learned and intentional management of the display to conform to social rules and expectations. It involves LH-mediated social emotions of attachment, affection, and bonding.

IMPLICATIONS AND CONCLUSIONS

Emotional and Social-Situational Regulation of Expression

A complex picture emerges from our consideration of spontaneous communication: It is a phenomenon which is genetically determined and biologically based, yet at the same time is intrinsically flexible and open to inhibition and control from environmental, situational, and, particularly, social factors. This complexity is perhaps the source of some confusion, as in debates in the literature over whether the management and regulation of facial expression is emotional or social (see discussions by Buck, 1991b; 1994; Buck, Losow, Murphy, & Costanzo, 1991b; Chovil, 1991; Chovil & Fridlund, 1991; Fridlund, 1991; Wagner & Smith, 1991). In my view it is clearly both, and in fact the tendency to see emotional and social factors as equivalent is arguably a category error, for all social factors are inherently emotional (Buck, 1991b).

The question remains about the extent to which spontaneous communication is really important in the control of human behavior, given the undoubted power of linguistic competence in human communication. This goes back to the issues initially raised by Greene at the outset of this chapter. My reply is that a consideration of spontaneous communication allows us to get a theoretical handle on phenomena that have resisted analysis by conventional "cold cognitive" theories. These include the profound, but from a cold-cognitive point of view rather peculiar, passion that human beings have for music, and the strange appeal of media, particularly television. Thus as we began this chapter with DNA, we end with MTV. From the primordial soup to the nuts, so to speak; or the slime to the ridiculous. Seriously, a consideration of the implications of global spontaneous emotional communication can shed considerable light on the nature of the "global village" (Buck, 1988b). Similarly, the changing nature of political charisma during the 20th century—from the great "radio voices" of leaders in the 1930s to the overwhelming importance of being telegenic today, can be understood in terms of what sorts of emotional cues are accessible over different media.

Empathy, Intuition, and Rapport

The Nature of the Receiver's Knowledge. The notion that the receiver is preattuned to the display means that spontaneous communication requires *no inference* on the part of the receiver—the receiver has *direct access* to the meaning of the message (i.e., of the display). The receiver knows directly certain "inner meanings" in senders—certain motivational/emotional states— because senders are constructed to "read out" directly such states in displays and receivers are constructed so that given attention they "pick up" directly that display and know directly its meaning. This knowledge is based on phylogenetic adaptation: It is conferred through inheritance via the genes (Ginsburg, 1976). The receiver's knowledge of the motivational/emotional states of the sender via spontaneous communication is as direct and biologi- cally based as one's knowledge of the feel of one's shoe on one's foot. This particular sort of immediate "raw" social knowledge-by-acquaintance on the receiver's part is arguably the epistemological basis of empathy, intuition, and rapport (Buck & Ginsburg, 1997). Arguably empathy, rapport, intuition, and related concepts are emergent properties of a primordial biological capacity for spontaneous communication that inheres in the genes. Such a capacity is the basis of the *communicative gene hypothesis* (Buck & Ginsburg, 1991, 1995).

Charisma and Deception. One of the most difficult aspects of sponta- neous communication to communicate in symbolic form (such as by the words on this page) is the fact that it is in itself *veridical*—true by definition since if the sign is there the referent must be present by definition—yet it might not be *accurate* in a propositional sense. The receiver is directly aware of the inner meaning signaled by an angry, or happy, display; but this aware- ness is not propositional knowledge as expressed by the statements "she is angry" or "he is happy." Instead it is a relatively vague "feeling" about the state of the other involving what some call "vibes," that may even be "unconscious"—unnoticed and unverbalizable—on the part of the receiver.

An example of unconscious reactions to displays involves audience re- sponses to the televised displays of political leaders. The notion of direct communication via media seems a contradiction in terms, but in fact there is plentiful evidence that direct spontaneous communication occurs via mass media (Buck, 1988b). A number of studies have used facial EMG to record minute tendencies to smile and frown that are not visible on the face or consciously noticed by the responder. McHugo and his colleagues used this technique to record the reactions of viewers to the videotaped smiles and frowns of Ronald Reagan and Walter Mondale during the 1984 Presidential election debates (McHugo, Lanzetta, Sullivan, Masters, & Englis, 1985). It was found that the expressions of Reagan, known as a charismatic "great communicator," elicited tendencies toward similar facial behavior in viewers: When Reagan smiled, the viewer tended to smile, when he frowned, the viewer tended to frown. Mondale's expressions did not have this effect, and the effect was not related to the self-reported political preferences of the viewers. Apparently Reagan's expressions had a direct impact on viewer, even hostile viewers, even via videotape (McHugo et al., 1985).

I suggest that, to be charismatic, politicians and other salespersons must effectively control their displays over the medium at hand, so that they are able to move the audience emotionally. The audience responds spontaneously via innate preattunements to a well-managed voluntarily initiated display just as they respond to an "authentic" display that is a readout of the sender's motivational/emotional state. The charismatic sender is able to "push the right buttons" of the audience, and in doing so gains enormous interpersonal power. Of course, the sender must be proficient in controlling the display, or the audience will see through the act and possibly respond with reactance, viewing the sender as "slick" and controlling rather than authentic.

This analysis implies that "empathic accuracy" in the propositional sense involves: (a) a direct pickup of the display responsible for the receiver's "raw" knowledge-by-acquaintance of the sender, and (b) a process of inference in the receiver that is responsible for the correct or incorrect interpretation of the sender's state given the receiver's direct and immediate knowledge (Buck & Ginsburg, 1997). The first, direct, process is spontaneous communication. It is affected by the clarity of the display on the part of the sender (sending accuracy) and the attention pattern on the part of the receiver; that is, the sender must display clearly and effectively the state in question and the receiver must attend to the display.

The Problem of Other Minds. This direct communication process suggests a solution to the philosophical problem which suggests that there is something puzzling about how we seem to know another person's "inner" meanings when we have access only to their behaviors (termed the Problem of Other Minds; Austin, 1959). At the end of *The Brown Book*, Wittgenstein (1965) noted that "when we communicate a feeling to someone, something which we can never know happens at the other end. All that we can receive from him is an expression" (p. 185). But we have seen that an expression is *all one needs* to know (by acquaintance) what happened at "the other end." Additional processes of inference are required to know *about* what happened.

SUMMARY

This chapter defined and compared *spontaneous* and *symbolic communication*. Symbolic communication is communication in its usual, analytic-cognitive, verbal-linguistic sense: It is based on codes that must be learned by both sender and receiver; these codes involve *symbols* that bear arbitrary relationships with their referents; it is intentional at some level; its statements are propositions capable of logical analysis; it is based on LH processes. In contrast, spontaneous communication is seen as biologically based, involving displays and preattunements that are innate, that is, which are phylogenetic adaptations involving direct, holistic, syncretic cognition (knowledge-by-acquaintance). Spontaneous communication involves phylogenetically structured displays on the part of the sender and preattunements to those displays on the part of the receiver; the displays are *signs* of the referent, or externally accessible aspects of the referent; it is spontaneous or nonintentional; its statements are nonpropositional, since they cannot be false; and it is based on RH processes involving the expressive communication of motivational-emotional states. Although the spontaneous display involves an innate system that functions reflexively, it is at the same time "innately flexible:" intrinsically open to inhibitory and controlling influences from social and situational factors. The display is influenced by learned display rules (perhaps associated with the LH) that manage it for strategic purposes (*voluntary expression initiation*). Spontaneous communication is a "conversation between limbic systems" that underlies intuition, empathy, and rapport; and solves the Problem of Other Minds.

ACKNOWLEDGMENT

Research reported in this chapter was supported by grants from NIMH (MH-40756), the EJLB Foundation, and the Harry Frank Guggenheim Foundation. Requests for reprints should be directed to Ross Buck, Communication Sciences U-85, University of Connecticut, Storrs, CT 06269-1085 USA.

REFERENCES

Alkon, D. L. (1989). Memory storage and neural systems. *Scientific American, 261*, 42–51.

Allee, W. C. (1931). *Animal aggregations: A study in general sociology.* Chicago: University of Chicago Press.

Allee, W. C. (1938). *Social life of animals.* New York: Norton.

Arndt, H., & Janney, R. W. (1991). Verbal, prosodic, and kinesic emotive contrasts in speech. *Journal of Pragmatics, 15*, 521–549.

Aspendorf, J. B., & Scherer, K. R. (1983). The discrepant repressor: Differentiation between high anxiety, low anxiety, and repression by autonomic-facial-verbal patterns of behavior. *Journal of Personality and Social Psychology, 45,* 1334–1346.

Austin, J. L. (1959). Other minds. In A. G. N. Flew (Ed.), *Logic and language.* Oxford: Basic Blackwell.

Bentley, D. R., & Hoy, R. R. (1974). The neurobiology of cricket song. *Scientific American, 231*(2), 34–44.

Birdwhistell, R. (1970). *Kinesics and context.* Philadelphia: University of Pennsylvania Press.

Black, M. (1962). Sign. In D. D. Runes (Ed.), *Dictionary of philosophy* (p. 292). Paterson, NJ: Little-field, Adams.

Blanck, P. (Ed.). (1993). *Interpersonal expectations: Theory, research, and applications.* Cambridge, England: Cambridge University Press.

Bogert, C. M. (1961). The influence of sound in the behavior of amphibians and reptiles. In W. E. Lanyon & W. N. Tavdga (Eds.), *Animal sounds and communication* (Pub. No. 7), Washington, DC: American Institute of Biological Sciences.

Borod, J. C., Koff, E., Perlman-Lorch, M., & Nicols, M. (1985). Channels of emotional expression in patients with unilateral brain damage. *Archives of Neurology, 42,* 345–348.

Buck, R. (1983). Emotional development and emotional education. In R. Plutchik & H. Kellerman (Eds.), *Emotion in early development* (pp. 259–292). New York: Academic Press.

Buck, R. (1984) *The communication of emotion.* New York: Guilford Press.

Buck, R. (1985) Prime theory: An integrated view of motivation and emotion. *Psychological Review, 92,* 389–413.

Buck, R. (1988a) *Human motivation and emotion* (2nd ed). New York: Wiley.

Buck, R. (1988b). Emotional education and mass media: A new view of the global village. In R. P. Hawkins, J. M. Weimann, & S. Pingree (Eds.), *Advancing communication science: Merging mass and interpersonal perspectives* (pp. 44–76). Beverly Hills, CA: Sage.

Buck, R. (1991a). Motivation, emotion, and cognition: A developmental-interactionist view. In K. T. Strongman (Ed.), *International review of studies of emotion* (Vol. 1, pp. 101–142). Chichester, Surrey: Wiley.

Buck, R. (1991b). Social factors in facial display and communication: A reply to Chovil and others. *Journal of Nonverbal Behavior, 15,* 155–162.

Buck, R. (1993a). What is this thing called subjective experience? Reflections on the neuropsychology of qualia. *Neuropsychology. 7,* 490–499.

Buck, R. (1993b). Emotional communication, emotional competence, and physical illness: A developmental-interactionist view. In H. Traue & J. Pennebaker (Eds.), *Emotional inhibition and health* (pp. 32–56). New York: Hogrefe Huber.

Buck, R. (1994a). Social and emotional functions in facial expression and communication: The readout hypothesis. *Biological Psychology, 38,* 95–115.

Buck, R. (1994b). The neuropsychology of communication: Spontaneous and symbolic aspects. *Journal of Pragmatics, 22,* 265–278.

Buck, R., & Duffy, R. J. (1980). Nonverbal communication of affect in brain-damaged patients. *Cortex, 16,* 351–362.

Buck, R., & Ginsburg, B. (1991). Emotional communication and altruism: The communicative gene hypothesis. In M. Clark (Ed.), *Altruism. Review of Personality and Social Psychology* (Vol. 12, pp. 149–175). Newbury Park, CA: Sage.

Buck, R., & Ginsburg, B. (1995, May–June). *Affects as voices of communicative genes: Implications for self regulation, social regulation, and bodily regulation.* Paper presented at the 25th meeting of the Behavior Genetics Association, Richmond, VA.

Buck, R., & Ginsburg, B. (1997). Communicative genes and the evolution of empathy. In W. Ickes (Ed.), *Empathic accuracy* (pp. 17–43). New York: Guilford.

Buck, R., Goldman, C. K., Easton, C. J., & Norelli Smith, N. (in press). Social learning and emotional education: Emotional expression and communication in behaviorally-disordered children and schizophrenic patients. In W. Flack & J. Laird (Eds.), *Nonverbal communication and psychopathology*. New York: Oxford University Press.

Buck, R., Losow, J., Murphy, M., & Costanzo, P. (1991). Social facilitation and inhibition of emotional expression and communication. *Journal of Personality and Social Psychology, 63,* 962–968.

Chaudhuri, A., & Buck, R. (1995a). Affect, reason, and persuasion: Advertising variables that predict affective and analytic-cognitive responses. *Human Communication Research. 21,* 422–441.

Chaudhuri, A., & Buck, R. (1995b). Media differences in rational and emotional responses to advertising. *Journal of Broadcasting and Electronic Media. 39,* 109–125.

Chovil, N. (1991). Social determinants of facial display. *Journal of Nonverbal Behavior, 15,* 141–154.

Chovil, N., & Fridlund, A. J. (1991). Why emotionality cannot equal sociality: Reply to Buck. *Journal of Nonverbal Behavior, 15,* 163–168.

Cofer, C. N., & Appley, M. H. (1964). *Motivation: Theory and research.* New York: Wiley.

Davidson, R. J., & Fox, N. A. (1982). Asymmetrical brain activity discriminates between positive and negative affective stimuli in human infants. *Science, 218,* 1235–1237.

Davis, F. (1978). *Eloquent animals.* New York: Coward, McCann, & Geoghegan.

Denenberg, V. H. (1981). Hemispheric laterality in animals and the effects of early experience. *The Behavioral and Brain Sciences, 4,* 1–19.

Denenberg, V. H. (1984). Behavioral asymmetry. In N. Geschwind & A. M. Galaburda (Eds.), *Cerebral dominance: The biological foundations* (pp. 114–133). Cambridge, MA: Harvard University Press.

Duffy, R. J., & Liles, B. Z. (1979). A translation of Finklnberg's (1870) lecture on aphasia as 'asymbolia' with commentary. *Journal of Speech and Hearing Disorders, 44,* 156–168.

Eibl-Eibesfeldt, I. (1975). Ethology: The biology of behavior (2nd ed.). New York: Holt, Rinehart & Winston.

Ekman, P., & Friesen, W. V. (1985). *Unmasking the face.* Englewood Cliffs, NJ: Prentice-Hall.

Etcoff, N. (1989). Recognition of emotions in patients with unilateral brain damage. In G. Gainotti & C. Caltagirone (Eds.), *Emotions and the dual brain.* Experimental Brain Research Series 18 (pp. 168–186). Berlin-Heidelberg: Springer-Verlag.

Finklnberg, F. (1870). Niederrheinische Gesellschaft, Sitzung vom 21. Marz 1870 in Bonn. *Erl. klin. Wschr. 7,* 449–450, 460–462.

Fridlund, A. J. (1991). Sociality of solitary smiling: Potentiation by an implicit audience. *Journal of Personality and Social Psychology, 60,* 229–240.

Gibson, J. J. (1966). *The senses considered as perceptual systems.* Boston: Houghton Mifflin.

Ginsburg, B. E. (1976). Evolution of communication patterns in animals. In M. E. Hahn & E. C. Simmel (Eds.), *Communicative behavior and evolution* (pp. 59–79). New York: Academic Press.

Ginsburg, B. E. (1986). Behavioral priming of gene expression. In C. Shagass, R. C. Josiassen, W. H. Bridger, K. J. Weiss, D. Stoff, & G. M. Simpson (Eds.), *Proceedings of the IVth World Congress of Biological Psychiatry.* New York: Elsevier.

Gottleib, G. (1984). Evolutionary trends and evolutionary origins: Relevance to theory in comparative psychology. *Psychological Review, 91,* 448–456.

Gray, J. A. (1982). Precis of *The neuropsychology of anxiety.* With commentaries. *The Behavioral and Brain Sciences. 5,* 469–534.

Gur, R. C., Mozley, L. H., Mozley, D. P., Resnick, S. M., Karp, J. S., Alavi, A., Arnold, S. E., & Gur, R. E. (1995). Sex differences in regional cerebral glucose metabolism during resting state. *Science, 267,* 528–531.

Jurgens, U. (1979). Neural control of vocalization in nonhuman primates. In H. L. Steklis & M. J. Raleigh (Eds.), *Neurobiology of social communication in primates* (pp. 11–44). New York: Academic Press.

LeDoux, J. E. (1994a). Cognitive-emotional interactions in the brain. In P. Ekman & R. J. Davidson (Eds.), The nature of emotion: Fundamental questions (pp. 216–223). New York: Oxford University Press.

LeDoux, J. E. (1994b). Memory versus emotional memory in the brain. In P. Ekman & R. J. Davidson (Eds.), The nature of emotion: Fundamental questions (pp. 311–312). New York: Oxford University Press.

MacLean, P. D. (1969). The hypothalamus and emotional behavior. In W. Haymaker, E. Anderson, & W. J. H. Nauta (Eds.), The hypothalamus. Springfield, IL: Charles C. Thomas.

MacLean, P. D. (1990). The triune brain in evolution: Role in paleocerebral functions. New York: Plenum Press.

MacLean, P. D. (1993). Cerebral evolution of emotion. In M. Lewis & J. Haviland (Eds.), Handbook of emotions (pp. 67–83). New York: Guilford Press.

Maier, I., & Muller, D. G. (1986). Sexual pheromones in algae. Biological Bulletin, 170, 145–176.

Margulis, L. (1982). Early life. Boston: Science Books International.

McHugo, G. J., Lanzetta, J. T., Sullivan, D. G., Masters, R. D., & Englis, B. G. (1985). Emotional reactions to a political leader's expressive displays. Journal of Personality and Social Psychology. 49, 1513–1529.

Moon, A., & Ginsburg, B.E. (1985, August). Genetic factors in the selective expression of species-typical behavior of coyote x beagle hybrids. Invited paper presented at the 19th International Ethological Conference, Toulouse, France

Nemiah, J. C., & Sifneos, P. E. (1970). Psychosomatic illness: Problem in communication. Psychotherapy and Psychosomatics, 18, 154–160.

Oke, A., Keller, R., Medford, I., & Adams, R. V. (1978). Lateralization of norepinepherine in the human thalamus. Science, 200, 1141–1413.

Panksepp, J. (1994). A proper distinction between cognitive and affective process is essential for neuroscientific progress. In P. Ekman & R. J. Davidson (Eds.), The nature of emotion: Fundamental questions (pp. 224–226). New York: Oxford University Press.

Ploog, D. (1981). Neurobiology of primate audio-vocal behavior. Brain Research Reviews, 3, 35–61.

Ploog, D. (1992). Neuroethological foundations of biological psychiatry. In H. M. Emrich & M. Weigand (Eds.), Integrative biological psychiatry (pp. 3–35). Berlin: Springer.

Rosenthal, R. (1967). Covert communication in the psychological experiment. Psychological Bulletin, 67, 356–367.

Ross, E. (1981). The aprosodias: Functional-anatomic organization of the affective components of language in the right hemisphere. Archives of Neurology, 38, 561–569.

Ross, E. D., Homan, R., & Buck, R. (1994). Differential hemispheric lateralization of primary and social emotions. Neuropsychiatry, Neuropsychology, and Behavioral Neurology, 7, 1–19.

Russell, B. (1903). The principles of mathematics. London: Allen & Unwin.

Russell, B. (1912). Problems of philosophy. New York: Simon and Schuster.

Ryan, M. J. (1990). Signals, species, and sexual selection. American Scientist, 78, 46–52.

Ryle, G. (1949). The concept of mind. New York: Barnes and Noble.

Shannon, C. E., & Weaver, W. (1949). The mathematical theory of communication. Urbana: University of Illinois Press.

Tomarken, A. J., & Davidson, R. J. (1994). Frontal brain activation in repressors and nonrepressors. Journal of Abnormal Psychology, 103, 339–349.

Tucker, D.M. (1981). Lateral brain function, emotion, and conceptualization. Psychological Bulletin, 89, 19–46.

Wagner, H., & Smith, J. (1991). Facial expression in the presence of friends and strangers. Journal of Nonverbal Behavior, 15, 201–214.

Weiner, M., DeVoe, S., Rubinow, S., & Geller, J. (1972). Nonverbal behavior and nonverbal communication. Psychological Review, 79, 185–214.

Wilson, E. O. (1975). Sociobiology: The new synthesis. Cambridge, MA: Belknap.

Wittgenstein, L. (1965). The blue and the brown books. New York: Philosophical Library.

AUTHOR INDEX

SUBJECT INDEX